IFIP Advances in Information and Communication Technology 366

T0181281

IFIP – The International Federation for Information Processing

IFIP was founded in 1960 under the auspices of UNESCO, following the First World Computer Congress held in Paris the previous year. An umbrella organization for societies working in information processing, IFIP's aim is two-fold: to support information processing within ist member countries and to encourage technology transfer to developing nations. As ist mission statement clearly states,

> *IFIP's mission is to be the leading, truly international, apolitical organization which encourages and assists in the development, exploitation and application of information technology for the bene t of all people.*

IFIP is a non-profitmaking organization, run almost solely by 2500 volunteers. It operates through a number of technical committees, which organize events and publications. IFIP's events range from an international congress to local seminars, but the most important are:

- The IFIP World Computer Congress, held every second year;
- Open conferences;
- Working conferences.

The flagship event is the IFIP World Computer Congress, at which both invited and contributed papers are presented. Contributed papers are rigorously refereed and the rejection rate is high.

As with the Congress, participation in the open conferences is open to all and papers may be invited or submitted. Again, submitted papers are stringently refereed.

The working conferences are structured differently. They are usually run by a working group and attendance is small and by invitation only. Their purpose is to create an atmosphere conducive to innovation and development. Refereeing is less rigorous and papers are subjected to extensive group discussion.

Publications arising from IFIP events vary. The papers presented at the IFIP World Computer Congress and at open conferences are published as conference proceedings, while the results of the working conferences are often published as collections of selected and edited papers.

Any national society whose primary activity is in information may apply to become a full member of IFIP, although full membership is restricted to one society per country. Full members are entitled to vote at the annual General Assembly, National societies preferring a less committed involvement may apply for associate or corresponding membership. Associate members enjoy the same benefits as full members, but without voting rights. Corresponding members are not represented in IFIP bodies. Affiliated membership is open to non-national societies, and individual and honorary membership schemes are also offered.

Markus Nüttgens   Andreas Gadatsch
Karlheinz Kautz   Ingrid Schirmer
Nadine Blinn (Eds.)

Governance and Sustainability in Information Systems

Managing the Transfer and Diffusion of IT

IFIP WG 8.6 International Working Conference
Hamburg, Germany, September 22-24, 2011
Proceedings

 Springer

Volume Editors

Markus Nüttgens
Nadine Blinn
Universität Hamburg, WISO Fakultät
22765 Hamburg, Germany
E-mail: {markus.nuettgens, nadine.blinn}@wiso.uni-hamburg.de

Andreas Gadatsch
Hochschule Bonn-Rhein-Sieg, Fachbereich Wirtschaftswissenschaften
53757 Sankt Augustin, Germany
E-mail: andreas.gadatsch@h-brs.de

Karlheinz Kautz
Copenhagen Business School, Department of Informatics
2000 Frederiksberg, Denmark
E-mail: karl.kautz@cbs.dk

Ingrid Schirmer
Universität Hamburg, MIN Fakultät
22527 Hamburg, Germany
E-mail: schirmer@informatik.uni-hamburg.de

ISSN 1868-4238   e-ISSN 1868-422X
ISBN 978-3-642-26952-3   ISBN 978-3-642-24148-2 (eBook)
DOI 10.1007/978-3-642-24148-2
Springer Heidelberg Dordrecht London New York

CR Subject Classification (1998): I.2, H.4, H.3, C.2, J.1, D.2

Typesetting: Camera-ready by author, data conversion by Scientific Publishing Services, Chennai, India

Printed on acid-free paper

Springer is part of Springer Science+Business Media (www.springer.com)

Welcome

This book constitutes the proceedings of the 2011 International Working Conference of the International Federation for Information Processing Working Group 8.6. The working conference entitled Governance and Sustainability in Information Systems - Managing the Transfer and Diffusion of IT – is focusing on subjects concerning sustainability and takes place in Europe's Green Capital 2011 – Hamburg, Germany.

In nowadays world, organizations act in globalized and competitive markets where information technology is the backbone of almost all distributed business processes. Therefore, products and services are increasingly affected by aspects of governance, risk and compliance in information systems. The information systems' point of view requires methods and procedures to achieve assurance in information systems. Being not compliant with legal requirements and internal or cross-organizational policies can cause highly negative impacts. Managing information systems needs to take into account these issues to achieve a sustainable use and adoption of information technology.

The 2011 International Working Conference of the International Federation for Information Processing Working Group 8.6 aims at promoting scientific and practical excellence on aspects of transfer and diffusion of information technology. In total, 47 submissions have been made to the conference. The reviews have been performed by a program committee consisting of 39 recognized researchers. This book contains 14 accepted full research papers and 16 research in progress and practice paper. The full research papers are divided into the clusters Governance (Part 1), Sustainability (Part 2), Design Themes (Part 3), Customer and User Integration (Part 4) and Future Subjects (Part 5).

The first part of research papers cover a wide scope of strategic an innovative aspects in IT-Governance. The paper written by *Arisa Shollo* "Using Business Intelligence in IT Governance Decision Making" paper discusses how BI can be used in a decision environment from a user's perspective validated by a case study . The article "Exposing Differences in Governance Approaches in Single and Multi Vendor Open Source Software Development" by *Mario Schaarschmidt, Matthias Bertram* and *Harald von Kortzfleisch* analyses open source software projects from different perspectives concerning government approaches. *Jan Pries-Heje* and *Ann-Dorte Fladkjær Nielsen* ("Innovative Project Idea Maturation: An important part of Governance") present an important proposal in order to support project manager by elicitation of innovative project ideas.

The papers of the track Sustainability comprehend aspects of sustainable partner selection within a supply-chain-management concept, governance teaching and barrier free usage of ICT. Partner selection within supply-chain-networks is an important success factor. *David Wittstruck* and *Frank Teuteberg*

("Towards a holistic Approach for Sustainable Partner Selection in the Electrics and Electronics Industry") develop an integrated multi-criteria decision model (MCDM) for partner selection. As sustainability requires the support of all company stakeholders, the paper of *Carl Stolze, Matthias Boehm, Novica Zarvic* and *Oliver Thomas* ("Towards Sustainable IT by Teaching Governance Practices for Inter-Organizational Dependencies") present an approach to support a networked teaching to unleash the full potential of IT as enabler for sustainability. *Daryoush Daniel Vaziri* ("Sustainability aspects of barrier-free information- and communication technology in the private sector") investigates the impact of barrier-free ICT on sustainability aspects and includes business economical, ecological and social perspectives.

Part 4 focuses on Customer and User Integration. "Design Themes" provides the reader with three research papers. *David Wastell* and *Sue White* ("Make kitsch the enemy: the "monstrous carbuncle" of the UK's vetting and barring scheme") analysed a major national IS initiative in the UK in order to show the influence of design principles on information systems. *Ranjan Vaidya, Michael Myers* and *Lesley Gardner* ("The design – reality gap: The impact of stakeholder strategies on IS implementation in developing countries") set a focus on developing countries and analyse the influence of stakeholder strategies to design and implementation of information systems. *Manuel Wiesche, Michael Schermann* and *Helmut Krcmar* ("Understanding the Role of Information Technology for Organizational Control Design: Risk Control as New Control") add a risk-based perspective for the body of knowledge on organizational control design.

The last chapter of full research papers comprises Future Subjects *Yogesh Dwivedi, Nripendra P. Rana, Hsin Chen* and *Michael Williams* ("A Meta-Analysis of the Unified Theory of Acceptance and Use of Technology (UTAUT)") analyse the literature of unified theory of acceptance. One important finding is that the majority of studies have ignored the structure of original theory. Web 2.0 applications increasingly used in companies to integrate their customers. The paper from *Ulrich Bretschneider* and *Jan Marco Leimeister* ("Getting customers' motives: Lean on motivation theory for designing virtual ideas communities") analyses the motives of the participants of the SAPiens ideas community which generates on a voluntary basis valuable ideas. *Björn Johansson* ("Diffusion of Open Source ERP systems development: How Users are Involved") explores how the requirement management process is organized in development of open source ERP systems and compares it with the procedure in developing proprietary ERP products.

We would like to acknowledge the contributions of the program committee, additional reviewers as well as Hamburg University and the organizing committee for their efforts.

July 2011

Karlheinz Kautz
Markus Nüttgens
Andreas Gadatsch

Organization

Conference Chairs

General Chair

Karlheinz Kautz   Copenhagen Business School

Program Co-chairs

Markus Nüttgens	Hamburg University
Andreas Gadatsch	Bonn-Rhine-Sieg University of Applied Sciences

Organizing Chairs

Markus Nüttgens	Hamburg University
Ingrid Schirmer	Hamburg University

HISDoC Chair

Tilo Böhmann   Hamburg University

Organizing Committee

Nadine Blinn	Hamburg University
Paul Drews	Hamburg University
Niels Müller-Wickop	Hamburg University
Martina Peris	Hamburg University
Martin Schultz	Hamburg University

Conference Sponsor

This conference was funded with the generous support of:

- The faculty of economics and social sciences (Hamburg University)
- The faculty of mathematics, computer science and natural sciences (Hamburg University)
- PricewaterhouseCoopers AG
- Board of trustees of degree programme "IT Management and Consulting - ITMC"

Program Committee

Michel Avital	University of Amsterdam
Richard Baskerville	Georgia State University
Deborah Bunker	The University of Sydney
Jan Damsgaard	Copenhagen Business School
Linda Dawson	Monash University
Rahul De	Indian Institute of Management
Brian Donnellan	National University of Ireland
Yogesh Dwivedi	Swansea University
Amany Elbanna	Loughborough University
Fernand Feltz	Public Research Centre G. Lippmann
Ulrich Frank	University of Duisburg-Essen
Nick Gehrke	NordAkademie
Helle Zinner Henriksen	Copenhagen Business School
Helmut Krcmar	Technische Universität München
Tor Larsen	Norwegian School of Management
Jan Marco Leimeister	University of Kassel
Gonzalo Leon	Ciudad University
Linda Levine	SEI, Carnegie Mellon University
Peter Loos	University of Saarland
Kalle Lyytinen	Case Western Reserve University
Lars Mathiassen	Georgia State University
Heinrich C. Mayr	Alpen-Adria-Universität Klagenfurt
Tom McMaster	Night Sky
Björn Niehaves	University of Münster
Peter Axel Nielsen	Aalborg University
Andreas Oberweis	Karlsruhe University
Jan Pries-Heje	Roskilde University
Norbert Ritter	Hamburg University
Christoph Rosenkranz	Goethe-University Frankfurt
Steve Sawyer	Syracuse University
Pål Sorgaard	Telenor Research and Innovation
Burton Swanson	University of California
Oliver Thomas	Osnabrück University
John Venable	Curtin University of Technology
Richard Vidgen	University of New South Wales
Harald v. Kortzfleisch	University of Koblenz-Landau
David Wastell	Nottingham University
Robert Winter	University of St. Gallen
Eleanor Wynn	Intel

Table of Contents

Part IV: Customer and User Integration

Part V: Future Subjects

Part VI: Research in Progress and Practice

Part I
Governance

Using Business Intelligence in IT Governance Decision Making

Arisa Shollo

Howitzvej 60, 2000 Frederiksberg, Denmark
Tel.: +45 27965833
as.inf@cbs.dk

Abstract. 'Business Intelligence' (BI) has been widely used to describe the process of gathering, analyzing and transforming large amounts of data into information useful for decision making. This paper examines BI from a decision-maker's perspective in an IT governance context through a case study of a large Scandinavian financial institution. The key findings indicate that BI is primarily used to inform structured operational decisions and as an instrument for dialogue in unstructured strategic decisions. Our study shows how 'hard facts' provided by BI are used as a foundation for opening a dialogue and as a supporting instrument to make arguments seem more convincing during decision-making discussions. We also found that standard performance reporting is used more for operational decision making, whereas predictive analytics are utilized primarily in strategic decision making. These results can assist managers looking to improve their operational and strategic decision-making processes by indicating the appropriate type of BI for each type of decision.

Keywords: Business Intelligence, decision making, case study, strategic decisions, predictive analytics.

1 Introduction

The importance of intelligence in decision making is recognized from ancient times (Tzu, 2006). People have developed processes, techniques and tools for collecting and analyzing intelligence to support decision making, especially during times of war (Kinsinger, 2007). Despite the considerable amount of research already conducted, decision making still remains one of the biggest challenges. The issues of decision making and computerized decisions have attracted the attention of academics and practitioners since the use of computers in organizational settings began. In the 1960s operations analysis was seen as the solution. Later, decision support was coupled to the use of computers, leading to decision support systems (DSS) (Sprague, 1980) and executive support systems (ESS) (Rockart & De Long, 1988). After data warehousing (Inmon, 2005; Kimball & Ross, 2002) and on-line analytical processing (OLAP) (Chaudhuri & Dayal, 1997; Gray et al., 1996) began to broaden the realm of decision support systems in the 1990s, many organizations realized the importance of business intelligence (BI) and sought to leverage it in their work (Golfarelli et al., 2004; Wixom & Watson, 2010).

M. Nüttgens et al. (Eds.): Governance and Sustainability in IS, IFIP AICT 366, pp. 3–15, 2011.
© IFIP International Federation for Information Processing 2011

The concept of BI has acquired wide recognition in the business world over the last two decades. Although the term 'business intelligence' has been in use since 1800, (Google Ngram Viewer, 2011), it was used in scientific context for the first time in an article by Hans Peter Luhn, an IBM researcher. In the article, Luhn (1958) described an "automatic method to provide current awareness services to scientists and engineers" who needed help to cope with the growth of the scientific and technical literature. However, it was only in the 1990s when Howard Dresner, (Dekkers et al., 2007), popularized the term BI, that it was widely adopted to convey the idea that the collected information in a business' IT systems could be exploited by the business itself to extract new insights. Today, the term is used to describe all decision support applications, processes and technologies (Shollo & Kautz, 2010; Wixom & Watson, 2010).

Over the last two decades, both industry and academia have been focusing on developing and adopting BI technologies to provide intelligence and insights to decision-makers. On one side, organizations have built data warehouses, acquired BI tools, supported acceptance by end users and applied the information to make business decisions. On the other side, academics have been refining the concept of BI along with its associated development processes and best practices. Many organizations have succeeded in transforming raw data into information, actionable insights or knowledge. According to Wixom and Watson (2010), BI has moved from being a peripheral contributor to being a prerequisite for organizational success. However, the outputs of BI - information, actionable insight or knowledge - do not by themselves guarantee its use by decision-makers.

In this paper, we examine how BI is used in decision making from a decision-maker's perspective. We conducted an extensive and in-depth literature review on the subject along with an empirical study in a financial organization to explore the use of BI in a decision-making environment. This study is part of a larger project in which we are investigating how we can use BI in IT governance and specifically in the IT project prioritization process.

The remainder of the paper is structured as follows. The next section presents previous work on the topic and describes the research gap. In section three we describe the methodology used to conduct the empirical study. Section four presents the results of the study and in section five we discuss the findings of the research and indicate future research directions.

2 Background

From a first look at the literature (Davenport & Prusak, 1998) one understands that BI is related to strategic management and performance management. Looking at BI from a decision-maker's perspective, we investigated the current state of BI in relation to strategic management, performance management and decision making. We conducted a literature review with a focus on how managers use BI, for what purposes and with what effects on performance and strategies in an organization. For an extensive review read Shollo & Kautz (2010).

The literature review revealed a gap in the research related to the role of decision making within BI. According to Arnott and Pervan (2008) and Yi-Ming and Liang-Cheng

(2007), most of the studies of BI have focused on design, development and application of BI tools, neglecting the use of information and knowledge. Thus, there is a substantial amount of literature on how to gather and store raw business-related data. This literature includes studies of structured and unstructured data as well as internal and external data. These studies are combined with literature on developing and employing required technologies, such as data warehouses and document warehouses (Baars & Kemper, 2008; Inmon, 2005; Kimball & Ross, 2002).

There are fewer studies the analysis and transformation of data into information and information into knowledge. The focus in these studies is on methods (Golfarelli et al., 2004; Yi-Ming & Liang-Cheng, 2007), techniques (Blumberg and Atre 2003; Baars & Kemper, 2008; Chung et al., 2005; Negash, 2004) and technologies, such as OLAP and data mining, that facilitate the transformation of raw data into information and knowledge. Despite the fact that there is a considerable body of literature on technology support, researchers have focused mainly on technology from a problem-centric perspective, overlooking the decision-maker's perspective.

The critical research gap, however, lies in the fact that there are almost no studies, with the exception of a few (Davenport, 2010), which address decision making based on business intelligence. We argue this represents an oxymoron: while there is a consensus among the authors of all reviewed articles that BI supports decision making, none of them couple the development or use of information with the decision-making process itself. The literature on BI thus does not cover how BI addresses the needs of the decision-making process. Moreover, no studies were found that focus on how the intelligence provided is used in decision making or what processes are in place to ensure the use of intelligence in the decision-making process. One reason for this could be that BI is not a well established field and "current research is largely focused on technology and getting the data right" (Arnott & Pervan, 2008), leading companies to focus only on those aspects when making decisions (Presthus et al., 2010; Davenport et al., 2001).

We agree with the contention of Martinsons (1994) and Davenport (2010) that it is not enough to analyze data, provide information and use knowledge. Organizations must look specifically into decision processes in order to deliver useful information to the decision-makers and for those decision-makers to act upon the information and knowledge obtained. Intelligence is only produced through action (making decisions). As Fuld (2003) states, "intelligence is an asset only if it is used". Unfortunately, in many cases, the produced information is not used, is unsuited for decision-making purposes or is ambiguous and interpreted differently across different contexts (Davenport, 2010).

The product of BI, among other properties, must match the decision-making environment in which it is used (Clark et al. 2007). However, recent studies suggest that many organizations do not fully understand the link between their BI and the decision-making environment they use it in (Clark et al., 2007; Hostmann et al., 2007; Davenport, 2010).

In the decision-making literature, decision-making environments have been classified according to decision types. A distinction is made between structured and unstructured decisions or, as introduced by Simon (1977), between programmed and nonprogrammed decisions. Simon stated: *"Decisions are programmed to the extent that they are repetitive and routine, to the extent that a definite procedure has been worked out for handling them so that they don't have to be treated from scratch each time they occur"* (p. 46). On the other hand, decisions are nonprogrammed *"to the extent that they are novel, unstructured and unusually consequential"* (Simon, 2007, p. 46). Programmed or structured decisions involve well-defined, measurable and compatible criteria, while nonprogrammed or unstructured decisions come under the heading of "problem solving" (Simon 1977, p. 64-65). Operational decisions tend to be structured, while strategic decisions tend to be unstructured (Simon 1977). Based on this distinction we will use the following analytic framework to conduct the research study as presented in Table 1.

Different decision types call for different methods of decision making and different information requirements (Gorry & Scot, 1971). Techniques used for operational decisions, for instance, are rarely used in strategic decisions. In this study we focus on the distinction between operational versus strategic decisions as it relates to the use and type of BI used.

Table 1. Analytical framework

Structured / Operational decisions	Unstructured / Strategic decisions
How is BI used in structured / operational decision making?	How is BI used in unstructured / strategic decision making?
What kind of BI is used in structured / operational decision making?	What kind of BI is used in unstructured / strategic decision making?

The purpose of this paper is to explore how decision-makers use BI in the context of different decision types based on the analytical framework illustrated in Table 1. In the next section, we describe the methodology used to investigate how decision-makers use BI as a product, in terms of information, insights and knowledge in decision making.

3   Research Design and Presentation of the Case Study

The empirical basis for this research was an in-depth case study exploring the role of BI in decision making. We conducted an exploratory case study to provide insights into the use of different types of BI in different decision-making environments. Case studies are particularly valuable for exploratory research where a thorough understanding of a phenomenon in its context is preferred (Benbasat, Goldstein, & Mead, 1987).

As an empirical setting we chose a financial institution in Scandinavia to explore how managers use BI in an organization with a strong tradition of using of hard data and financial models in forecasting activities.

3.1   Research Setting

The organization is an international financial institution with its headquarters in Scandinavia. The organization is recognized as a successful financial company with a high market share. The study was conducted in the IT unit, which is responsible for standardizing and automating processes, and developing IT systems to enhance the efficiency of the entire organization. The IT unit run by the chief information officer (CIO) and is composed of seven development areas managed by development directors. Each development area is further subdivided into departments headed by development managers. In total, there are 38 IT departments, employing 2200 employees.

3.2 Data Collection

We conducted eight interviews with key IT governance personnel in the case organization. Two additional interviews were conducted with external subject experts to triangulate the data. Background information about the company was also collected and served as complementary material to the interviews. The participants used BI in their everyday work and they were from different levels of the organization. The form of the interviews was semi-structured, with open-ended questions asked about the use of BI in decision makingAn interview guide was created before the interview that included questions such as:

- For what purposes do you use BI?
- Does the information in the reports support many decisions or does each report target a specific decision?
- How much do you believe BI influences your decisions?
- Do you base your decisions only on the numbers in the reports?
- Do you use other channels, methods, connections or tools to support your decisions?

Each interview was conducted at the interviewee's office and lasted an average of 60 minutes. Participants were informed that the interview was about the use of Business Intelligence in their decision-making activities, but were not shown the questions ahead of time. All the interviews were recorded with the consent of the interviewees. The interviews were carried out in English and were transcribed by the researcher afterwards. Table 2 presents the participants and their roles in the organization.

Table 2. Details of the interview participants

Participant	Role in the organization
Participant 1	Head of IT Management Support
Participant 2	Head of IT Credit Processes
Participant 3	Regional Manager
Participant 4	Business Analyst
Participant 5	Head of Forecasting Models
Participant 6	Business Analyst
Participant 7	IT Finance Business Analyst
Participant 8	Performance Management Specialist
Participant 9	External expert on Project Portfolio Management & BI
Participant 10	External expert on BI

The collected background material included organization charts, reports, spreadsheets, forms, PowerPoint presentations, memos, and meeting minutes. This documentation was collected in order to triangulate the data with the interviews.

3.3 Data Analysis

We carefully read through the transcripts of the interviews and the meetings as well as the official notes and the field notes to get a detailed picture of the empirical setting. While reading the interviews and meeting transcripts we were looking for indicators of how BI was used in decision-making processes. In order to investigate our research question, we employed constant comparative techniques (Strauss, & Corbin, 2008) in which we gathered and analyzed qualitative data in a systematic and iterative manner.

During data analysis we applied open coding inspired by grounded theory (Strauss & Corbin, 1998). Content analysis (Strauss & Corbin, 1998) was also employed to assess the collected material. In particular, we read the documents and transcripts to identify themes in the raw data across the different sources. The themes pursued included concepts such as "reports", "hard facts", "scorecard", "performance", "data" and "decision". We organized these first order codes into tables that illustrated a single theme across the various data sources, inspired by the in-vivo coding technique (Strauss, & Corbin, 2008). In the next step, we developed second order themes by using the four key questions of the framework to sort through the data. Those questions were: 1) How is BI used in unstructured strategic decisions? 2) How is BI used in structured operational decisions? 3) What type of BI is used in strategic decision making? 4) What type of BI is used in operational decision making? In the final step, through an iterative analysis of the data, "informing", "dialogue" and "convincing" and their relationship to "BI and decision making" emerged as transparently observable phenomena (Eisenhardt, 1989) in the data.

4   Results

In this section, we present how and in what forms BI is used in decision making in the following categories that emerged from the data analysis phase.

4.1 The Use of BI in Decision Making

Decision-makers use BI for different purposes in the decision-making process. We illustrate each purpose observed in our case in the next paragraphs, attaching representative quotes from the interview data.

Using BI to Inform Decisions
The interviewees reported that they use BI to directly inform their decisions. This is especially obvious when BI addresses specific or structured decisions, creating a tight linkage between intelligence and decisions. In this case, data are analyzed with a specific question in mind and the report adresses this specific question.

"So therefore, we need to … come up with some good reporting on how we can allocate our capital in the best manner. So, where do we actually target the customer groups which we want to target and on what kind of product areas do we actually

want to target in order to allocate our capital in the right way? So that's sort of the reporting we do, saying okay, we need this, we know that this customer group is very profitable and also have a potential long term relation with the company. So, we need to focus on this area and that's where we should allocate our capital and that would be a clear decision based on our reporting, saying okay, this is the target group that we need to focus on." (Participant 8)

"I think, what we learned was that the margins for instance regarding price need to be adapted to the new environment in the financial crisis. So that's something that came quite clear in the reporting that we did, meaning that each brand initiated various projects in order to sort of adopt the price level margins to current environment, so there you can see actually direct sort of decisions being based on the reporting." (Participant 6)

Using BI as an Instrument for Dialogue

When asked how BI influences their decisions, managers responded that they use the reports, scorecards and dashboards as an instrument for dialogue with other employees and departments in the organization and thus as the basis for further investigation.

"It is a dialogue tool, primarily because other factors are also in play, which are not captured by our scorecard. So, the scorecard is a foundation for measuring performance, no doubt about that, but other factors, I think we call them hygiene factors ... it could be other information that [the manager] is just extracting from the market, providing it to the management or all other things that are sort of intangible, that we cannot measure. So we don't believe that you can measure business purely by mathematical numbers and performance, you need to look it as a whole perspective that's why I mentioned it as a dialogue tool." (Participant 8)

"We use it both for ourselves correcting the accounts when it is wrong, but we also use this information to have a dialogue with the system owner..." (Participant 7)

"Well it creates a dialogue, it creates a conversation in the executive committee saying, do we actually have the right price focus on each sub-customer segment. And that creates a sort of decision-making process" (Participant 8)

BI is thus seen as a dialogue opener, allowing managers to engage in a discussion as they interpret the results and try to make sense of the numbers. According to the interviewees, there are other aspects not captured by BI. As indicated in the following quotes, BI is only part of the picture that initiates the dialogue. Tacit knowledge and experience also play a very important role in creating a full picture of the problem or issue discussed.

"I call the managers and ask them what do you do since you are doing so well and what is the problem since you are red in this area." (Participant 4)

"So, as I mentioned it, ... I think you need to have a dialogue. You need to have this human touch and you need to get a feeling also what's going on in the business. Also, lots of information is impossible for us to measure, so lots of information is coming, sort of, from discussions and that's also part of the decision-making process. So, I think, all the reporting that we do, all the ratios that we deliver, all the numbers are just a part of it and then the rest is based on your, I wouldn't say gut feeling, but your business knowledge and your conversations with the business, that is also a very important part of decision making." (Participant 8)

"When you see the results or the data you should use your common sense, so when you make a decision you should sort of respect your data and the story, you should investigate: does it make sense?" (Participant 2)

Using BI as a Convincing Argument

The interviewees use data as a powerful tool to convince top management about the significance of an issue and its impact. Having data to support your argument legitimizes decisions, particularly in front of other people. In the following quotes one can observe how data are used to convince others in making a certain decision and taking action.

Interviewee: No, [the data] is just the argument, but very often if you want to have something in a hurry, then you need the data because it is the only way that you can convince people that this is a serious problem. You have to be able to tell to people, well this is affecting 100,000 customers, this is affecting all brands and you always have to tell how serious is this issue." (Participant 2)

"...well, we have been looking into your data for the last month. We really have some deviations here, you need to solve it and there we have the material, you know, you can present it to them saying, okay you can see it here, these are the dated deviations throughout the last 30 days." (Participant 7)

4.2   Types of BI in Decision Making

The mainstream BI used by the interviews consisted largely of reports and spreadsheet analysis of past historical performance data. However, the interviewees reported that more advanced analytics such as what-if scenarios are often more useful in strategic decision making.

Standard Reporting of Past Performance

The interviewees stated that they use the information from reports in structure / operational decisions where the steps to solve the problem are well defined. We provide examples here of how one of the managers uses BI in operational decision making.

"As I said, we need to close the books ... so I needed to go down to transaction level actually to see if those transactions ended up correctly in the accounting system, so that was the main purpose..." (Participant 7)

"So, BI tools are used ... rather for investigations in connection with testing activities or tracing errors, alright? So I'm not using BI for making decisions if we need to man up by one FTE [full time employee] or see if I should get rid of one FTE and which one or whatever could be a part of my decision making as a department head, right?" (Participant 7)

Predictive Analytics

The use of what-if scenarios along with correlations between events and their implications can provide a sound foundation for decision making. This type of BI falls into predictive analytics and is particularly important for strategic decisions.

Predictive analytics are used to create a variety of what-if scenarios in order to predict future outcomes through forecasting and deep data analysis.

"At the end of the day, it is a business decision which projects you would like to support. So, you can never automate, but what makes sense is actually not to create the portfolio but when you need to make changes in the portfolio if you take the resources into scope, the bottlenecks, the limitations into scope, then you can use it for a kind of decision base. But it is really more to have a foundation for an enlightened decision ... you can never use it mechanically, it would never work. But you can say the consequence of doing this is X and the consequence of doing this is Y. But I think the effect is indirect." (Participant 9)

5 Discussion and Conclusion

The results presented in the previous section show how BI directly informs structured decisions. BI may also inform partially tactical and strategic decision making when it addresses the specific decision. However, when BI addresses a range of different decisions it is primarily used as an instrument for dialogue or as a convincing tool in tactical and strategic decision making.

BI extracted by standard reporting, including scorecards and dashboards, addresses a range of different decisions. This limits its use in tactical and strategic decision making because the information extracted does not address a specific decision but rather generates questions in an effort to illuminate multiple decisions. Organizations face a trade-off between providing BI for decision-specific support and providing BI for a variety of decisions. Decision-specific support requires considerable organizational effort and capital. At the same time, providing BI for a range of different decisions does not necessarily assure adequate support of the individual decisions. Davenport (2010), considering the above trade-off, suggests that companies should select the most important organizational decisions and create the appropriate BI support.

BI also appears as an instrument for dialogue in decision making. While the information or knowledge extracted does not address specific decisions, it can help managers to engage in dialogue to make sense of information and to investigate options. Decision-makers often need to tackle tactical and strategic decisions in which the decision criteria are not well defined or measurable. In this case, information or knowledge extracted is only part of the picture and managers need to engage in a dialogue in order to consider and discuss "the rest of the truth" that is not captured in reports. As the interviewees stated, the dialogues iniated by BI often bring up contextual and business knowledge as part of the discussion. Choo (1998) refers to this use of information as "enlightenment" in which "information is used to develop a context or to make sense of a situation."

BI is premised on the rational-scientific paradigm that there is an objective truth that can be measured. We found that BI is often positioned as "hard facts" and is used by decision-makers as an argument to support or justify their decisions and to convince others. However, using BI as a convincing argument could have some negative implications for organizations. For example, according to March (1995, pp.), "numbers presuppose a concept of what should be measured and a way of translating that concept into things that can be measured". He continues by positioning "...the pursuit of truth as a sham..." in which "decision-makers find it possible to "discover" a truth that happens to be consistent with their own interests." In this view, data provides knowledge, knowledge is power and, therefore, data is power. In organizations in which evidence is required to legitimize decisions, the power of hard facts increases, as does the likelihood that managers will "find" hard facts that confirm their beliefs. This behavior is similar to a decision-based evidence making approach (Tingling, & Brydon, 2010).

Our results show that information extracted from reports, scorecards and dashboards largely addresses and informs structured, operational decisions. This finding is consistent with the results of Isik et al. (2010) who found that data-oriented BI capabilities are more critical for operational decisions than for strategic decisions. As we move from structured to unstructured decisions, the use of BI in decision making changes from informing decisions to serving as an instrument for dialogue. The use of BI as a dialogue tool initiates conversations that, according to May (2009), have a positive impact on organizational performance because they stimulate learning.

The impact of using BI as a dialogue tool in decision making is indirect. Although it does not directly support or inform decisions, it creates a context in which decision-makers can interpret the information and discuss the problem. Predictive analytics, techniques that exploit patterns found in historical data to identify risks and opportunities, appear to be especially useful in this case. These techniques capture relationships among many factors and allow the development of different possible scenarios in decision making. With predictive analytics, the range of situations in which BI can be used expands considerably, especially in strategic decision-making. On the other hand, we observe that BI extracted by standard reporting, including scorecards and dashboards, is generally used in operational decision making. Their actual use in strategic decisions is limited because of their reactive nature.

The contribution of this paper is twofold. First, our findings illustrate the role of BI in strategic decision-making environments. These findings suggest that BI as a product – information, insight or knowledge – is used to foster dialogue or as a convincing instrument in strategic decision making, but appears to have a more direct impact in operational decision making because it informs specific decisions. Second, we have found that BI standard reporting capabilities that analyze past performance are useful for structured, operational decisions, while predictive analytics that focus on modeling to create competitive advantages are more useful in unstructured, strategic decision making.

This study has several implications for research and practice. From a research standpoint, our study explores the role of BI in decision making as an instrument for dialogue that engages managers in interpretation and knowledge externalization. This use of BI as an instrument for dialogue indicates new perspectives for IS researchers, suggesting that we address BI not as mere facts but as a sensemaking mechanism in decision making. From the point of view of practice, the study has implications for designing and developing BI decision support infrastructures. Organizations should consider the right type of BI according to the nature of the decision and should be aware of the degree to which evidence is required in legitimizing decisions in order to avoid evidence making by decision-makers. To provide adequate support for each type of decision-making environment, we need further studies of the relationship between the use of BI in both strategic and operational decision-making environments. We propose these as possible future research streams.

The purpose of this paper has been to explore the role of BI in decision making. We have reported findings from an empirical study in which managers from a large organization were interviewed in relation to their BI-use in decision making. We have argued that BI is used as a dialogue and convincing instrument in strategic decision making, and have introduced new theoretical insights into BI research.

Acknowledgments. The author wishes to express her gratitude to her supervisor, Professor Karlheinz Kautz and Associate Professor Ioanna Constantiou who offered invaluable assistance, support and guidance. Special thanks also to her friends and Ph.D. students Konstantinos Manikas and Maria Ie Pedersen for invaluable reviewing assistance.

References

Arnott, D., Pervan, G.: Eight Key Issues for the Decision Support Systems Discipline. Decision Support Systems 44(3), 657–672 (2008)

Blumberg, R., Atre, S.: The Problem with Unstructured Data. DM Review Magazine (2003)

Baars, H., Kemper, H.-G.: Management Support with Structured and Unstructured Data - an Integrated Business Intelligence Framework. Information Systems Management 25(2), 132–148 (2008)

Benbasat, I., Goldstein, D.K., Mead, M.: The case research strategy in studies of information systems. MIS Quarterly 11, 369–386 (1987)

Chaudhury, S., Dayal, U.: An Overview of Data Warehousing and OLAP Technology. ACM SIGMOD Record 26(1), 65–74 (1997)

Choo, W.C.: The Knowing Organisation: How Organisations Use Information to Construct Meaning, Create Knowledge, and Make Decisions. Oxford University Press, Oxford (1998)

Chung, W., Hsinchun, C., Nunamaker Jr., J.F.: A Visual Framework for Knowledge Discovery on the Web: An Empirical Study of Business Intelligence Exploration. Journal of Management Information Systems 21(4), 57–84 (2005)

Clark, T.D., Jones, M.C., Armstrong, C.: The Dynamic Structure of Management Support Systems: Theory Development, Research Focus and Direction. MIS Querterly 31(3), 579–615 (2007)

Davenport, T.H.: Competing on Analytics. Harvard Business Review 84(1), 98–107 (2006)

Davenport, T.H.: Bi and Organisational Decissions. International Journal of Business Intelligence Research 1(1), 1–12 (2010)

Davenport, T.H., Prusak, L.: Working Knowledge: How Do Organisations Manage What They Know. Harvard Business School Press, Boston (1998)

Dekkers, J.V., Johan, Batenburg, R.: Organising for Business Intelligence: A Framework for Aligning the Use and Development of Information. In: BLED 2007 (2007)

Dybå, T., Dingsøyr, T.: Empirical Studies of Agile Software Development: A Systematic Review. Information and Software Technology 50(9), 833–859 (2008)

Eisenhardt Strauss, A., Corbin, J.: Basics of qualitative research: Grounded theory procedures and techniques, 3rd edn. Sage Publictions, Newbury Park (2008)

Fowler, A.: The Role of Ai-Based Technology in Support of the Knowledge Management Value Activity Cycle. The Journal of Strategic Information Systems 9(2-3), 107–128 (2000)

Fuld, L.: Be Prepared. Harvard Business Review 81(11), 20–21 (2003)

Golfarelli, M., Stefano, R., Iuris, C.: Beyond Data Warehousing: What's Next in Business Intelligence? In: Proceedings of the 7th ACM international workshop on Data warehousing and OLAP. ACM, Washington, DC, USA (2004)

Google Ngram Viewer (2011), http://ngrams.googlelabs.com/

Gorry, G.A., Scott, M.M.S.: A Framework for Management Information Systems. Sloan Management Review 13(1), 55–72 (1971)

Gray J., Bosworth A., Layman A., Pirabesh H.: Data cube: a relational aggregation operator generalizing groupby, cross-tab, and sub-totals. Microsoft Technical Report (1996)

Hostmann, M., Reichert, P., Borsuk, M., Schweizer, S., Spörri, C., Tockner, K., Truffer, B.: Concepts of decision support for river rehabilitation. Environmental Modelling and Software 22, 188–201 (2007)

Inmon, W.H.: Building the Data Warehouse, 4th edn. Wiley, Indianapolis (2005)

Isik, O., Jones, M., Sidorova, A.: Business Intelligence Success: An Empirical Evaluation of the Role of BI Capabilities and the Decision Environment. In: Proceedings of the SIGDSS/TUN, Business Intelligence Congress II, Saint Louis, MI, USA (2010)

Kimball, R., Ross, M.: The Data Warehouse Toolkit, 2nd edn. John Wiley & Sons, Chichester (2002)

Kinsinger, P.C.: The Business Intelligence Challenge in the Context of Regional Risk. Thunderbird International Business Review 49(4), 535–541 (2007)

Luhn, H.P.: A Business Intelligence System. IBM Journal (1958)

March, G.J.: A Premier in Decision Making: How decisions happen, 1st edn. Free Press, New York (1995)

Martinsons, M.G.: A Strategic Vision for Managing Business Intelligence. Information Strategy: The Executive's Journal 10(3), 17 (1994)

May, T.: The New Know: Innovation Powered by Analytics. Wiley & Sons, New Jersey (2009)

Negash, S.: Business Intelligence. Communications of AIS 13, 177–195 (2004)

Presthus, W., Brevik, E.: E-business in entertainment: Insights from the use of Business Intelligence in the Norwegian music industry. In: Proceedings of AMCIS 2010, Paper 40 (2010)

Rockart, J., De Long, D.: Executive Support Systems. Dow Jones-Irwin, Homewood (1988)

Simon, H.A.: The New Science of Management Decision, 3rd revised edn., 1st edn. 1960. Prentice-Hall, Englewood Cliffs (1977)

Shariat, M., Hightower, J.R.: Conceptualizing Business Intelligence Architecture. Marketing Management Journal 17(2), 40–46 (2007)

Shollo A., Kautz K.: Towards an Understanding of Business Intelligence. In: Australasian Conference on Information Systems, Brisbane, Qeensland (2010)

Sprague, R.H.: A Framework for the Development of Decision Support Systems. MIS Quartely 4(4), 1–26 (1980)

Steiger, D.: Decision Support as Knowledge Creation: A Business Intelligence Design Theory. International Journal of Business Intelligence Research (IJBIR) 1(1), 29–47 (2010)

Strauss, A., Corbin, J.: Basics of qualitative research: Grounded theory procedures and techniques, 3rd edn. Sage Publictions, Newbury Park (2008)

Tzu, S.: The art of war. Filiquarian Publications, LLC (2006)

Tingling, P.M., Brydon, M.J.: Is Decision-based Evidence Making necessarily bad? MIT Sloan Management Review 51(4), 71–76 (2010)

Webster, J., Watson, R.T.: Analyzing the Past to Prepare for the Future: Writing a Literature Review. MIS Quarterly 26(2), 13–23 (2002)

Wixom, B., Watson, H.: The BI-Based Organisation. International Journal of Business Intelligence Research (IJBIR) 1(1), 13–28 (2010)

Yi-Ming, T., Liang-Cheng, C.: Dynamic Interactive Framework to Link Business Intelligence with Strategy. International Journal of Information Technology & Management 6(1), 2 (2007)

Exposing Differences of Governance Approaches in Single and Multi Vendor Open Source Software Development

Mario Schaarschmidt, Matthias Bertram, and Harald F.O. von Kortzfleisch

Universitätsstr. 1, 56070 Koblenz, Germany
Tel.: +49 (0) 261 287 2864, +49 (0) 261 287 2544, +49 (0) 261 287 2523
{mario.schaarschmidt,matthias.bertram,
harald.von.kortzfleisch}@uni-koblenz.de

Abstract. Research confirms that commercial OSS exists in many different ways according to its revenue model, type of license, development style, number of participating firms, number of participating volunteers or governance mode. In order to differentiate between an increasing variety of commercialization approaches, one may distinguish between projects with one dominating company, so called *single vendor projects* and those where more than one company is active, so called *multi vendor projects*. Furthermore, in order to structure different approaches, a project's history is equally of importance in terms of whether a project was initiated by a firm or a community. In this paper, we therefore analyze and compare single and multi vendor as well as *firm initiated* and *community initiated* OSS projects with regard to technical contribution of voluntary and paid project members. Based on a dataset build upon Eclipse projects we expose, that the number of paid members is significantly higher in firm initiated and multi vendor projects.

Keywords: Open Source Software, Single Vendor Projects, Multi Vendor Projects, Communities, Governance.

1 Introduction

The commercial production of open source software (OSS) has attracted a lot of attention in recent years (Dahlander and Magnusson 2005; Fosfuri et al. 2008). Success stories like Linux, MySQL or JBoss have proven that nowadays OSS has the quality and the customer acceptance to compete with its proprietary rivals. However, although the term open source suggests that software which claims to be OSS share a coherent body of attributes, at its core, the only connecting attributes are (1) delivery of the source code in a human readable form and (2) a license approved by the Open Source Initiative (OSI). Based on these two factors, many development styles or commercialization approaches are possible, which, although very different in terms of motivation and goals, are considered to be open source (Raymond 1999). For

M. Nüttgens et al. (Eds.): Governance and Sustainability in IS, IFIP AICT 366, pp. 16–28, 2011.

example, even Microsoft, a candidate for high quality proprietary software products has released open source licenses, such as Microsoft Reciprocal License (Ms-RL), which are consistent with OSI requirements.

Recent research confirms that commercial OSS exists in many different ways according to its revenue model, type of license, development style, number of participating firms, number of participating volunteers or governance mode (Bonaccorsi et al. 2006; Dahlander and Magnusson 2008; West 2003). Consequently, core business functions like community management, sales, marketing, product management, engineering and support differ among different commercialization strategies (Watson et al. 2008). For example, relevant revenue models range from dual licensing approaches, where a product is offered under two licenses, one OSS license and (at least) one proprietary license, to approaches where the revenue stream entirely is generated through the sale of complementary products or services (c.f. Alexy 2009; Fitzgerald 2008).

In order to differentiate between an increasing variety of commercialization approaches, one may distinguish between projects with one dominating company, so called *single vendor projects* and those where more than one company is active, so called *multi vendor projects*. Whereas single vendor approaches show similarities to proprietary software vendors' behavior (Riehle 2011), in cases of multiple firms active in a project, development is being processed like in R&D alliances or joint ventures (Schaarschmidt and Von Kortzfleisch 2009). In the latter case, usually a direct revenue stream is not intended. Instead, multiple firms combine their resources in order to build a platform and to promote standards with the aim to sell on top applications along with complementary products or services.

Furthermore, as shown by Dahlander (2007), in order to structure different approaches, a project's history is equally of importance in terms of whether a project was initiated by a firm or a community. However, despite the fact that there are differences among different approaches, yet, little is known about the differences in detail, e.g. in terms of governance or control. For example, what does it mean if a project is controlled by more than one firm? How does firm involvement or a project's history affect voluntary participation? In this paper, we therefore analyze and compare single and multi vendor OSS projects as well as firm initiated and community initiated ones with regard to technical contribution of voluntary and paid individual contributors. Based on a dataset build upon Eclipse projects we show, along with other results, that the number of paid contributors is significantly higher in firm initiated and multi vendor projects, reflecting a firm's wish to influence a project's trajectory.

2 Conceptual Background and Driving Phenomena

2.1 Commercial Open Source Software

OSS has come a long way. In the beginning, the majority of projects named OSS were initiated and driven by a handful of pioneers working for free, mostly due to fun in programming and problem solving or in order to build applications which were not available in a market (Bitzer et al. 2007; Shah 2006). Over the last decade, however, prices for proprietary licenses decreased resulting in an increased interest of adopting firms and commercial vendors in OSS. With the presence of firms in OSS projects, clear distinctions between proprietary and OSS products began to dissolve. Within the group of OSS projects Riehle (2009; 2011) distinguishes between community and commercial OSS. In his arguments, control and ownership structures are the critical indices in order to differentiate between these two types. While community OSS is controlled by a community of stakeholders (including multiple individual programmers and/or firms), commercial OSS is controlled by exactly one stakeholder with the purpose of commercially exploiting it. In addition, Dahlander (2007) focuses on a longitudinal perspective, including the history of a project as a means to categorize different approaches. By examining more than 60 successful open source projects in detail he formulated a 2x2 matrix indicating whether a project was started by a community or a firm or is driven by a community or firm, respectively.

Despite their ability to structure different types of OSS projects, both views share the limitation of incompleteness. While Riehle (2009) ignores the history of a project and (implicitly) assumes that control and ownership structures are stable and will not change over time, Dahlander (2007) subsumes both, single vendor and multi vendor projects under the same umbrella, namely, firm driven projects. To capture both limitations we propose a framework based on the distinction between the single and multi vendor projects (X-axis) and a project's initiation (Y-axis) (figure 1).

Table 1. A typology of commercialization approaches combining on Dahlander (2007) and Riehle (2009)

	Single vendor project	Multi vendor project
Firm initiated	Approach I	Approach II
Community initiated	Approach III	Approach IV

By looking at representative projects for each of the four approaches we find differences. Trolltech or MySQL are prominent examples for single vendor approaches and are characterized by the fact that one firm is the sole owner of the product they generate revenue from (Fitzgerald 2008; Watson et al. 2008). In cases of sole ownership of the entire code, dual licensing approaches are possible, meaning that a customer may chose between an OSS license without paying license fees and a more sophisticated version under a proprietary license the customer has to pay for. Although it is not entirely clear if these approaches are profitable – the most of these firms are not traded in a stock market and therefore do not have the obligation to publish their revenue figures – recent venture capital investment in OSS mirrors its potential (Schaarschmidt and Von Kortzfleisch 2010). According to a recent Gartner report, by 2012 more than 50% of all revenue generated from open source projects will come from projects under a single vendor's patronage (Riehle 2009). In contrast, in cases where many firms are active, like Linux or Apache, the code is not owned by a single firm which makes dual licensing approaches impossible. Moreover, those multi vendor projects usually aim to reducing costs for a product, each firm otherwise had to build alone and not to a direct revenue stream from license fees (in case of dual licensing) or complementary services.

Despite the presence of firms in the development of OSS, many projects rely on a heavy voluntary user and/or developer base. Even in single vendor approaches, where one might assume that marketing reasons are the predominant driver for offering OSS licenses, working with a community of users and developers is important for two reasons. Firstly, the risk of getting an evil reputation as a consequence of community mismanagement is too high. Secondly, and more importantly, these communities are valuable resources for OSS companies, as complementary assets in some cases and as will-be future employees in others (Dahlander and Wallin 2006). According to interviews with its CEO, JBoss, for example, recruits its future employees almost entirely out of the community of programmers. As a consequence, the extent of JBoss's contribution to their affiliated projects is between 60 and 95 % – although they do *not* own the code (Watson et al. 2008).

The presence or absence of a community of programmers external to a firm affects the way a project is managed. Depending on factors like type of license and business model, furthermore, the importance of a user and/or developer community varies for a firm active in an OSS project. Consequently, the importance and the extant of community management differ as well. In the following, we will formulate hypothesis to predict number of technical contributions as well as number of paid or unpaid individuals in single and multi vendor projects and, additionally, predict if the distribution of developers is dependent on a project's history.

2.2 Hypotheses Development

By considering number of firms participating in OSS projects, our framework implicitly puts emphasis on different governance modes. When talking about governance in the context of various theories of the firm, human resources a firm has to pay for to obtain differ from freely available resources in the following way. If someone is paid, generally speaking, in order to receive monetary compensation for the work which is pursued, he or she accepts certain responsibilities such as following a supervisor's authority. In contrast, at first glance, in cases of free contributors, those people are not legally bounded and therefore free to deicide to retire from a project at any time (Shah 2006). However, as several studies have revealed, giving signals to a future employee, status in a community of developers or fun in problem solving are motives for free programmers to stay with a project (Lerner and Tirole 2002; Bitzer and Geishecker 2010; Franck and Jungwirth 2003).

Firms applying a single vendor approach differ from firms active in a multi vendor project. As discussed in the section above, a community of voluntary developers is a valuable resource pool and complements a firm's own capabilities (De Laat 2007). In a similar vein, this holds true for firms cooperating with other firms in multi vendor projects. However, in order to complement own capabilities, the focal firm now gets access to other firm's resources. Furthermore, by sharing technical and financial risks with other firms, the importance of a developer community consisting of a high number of volunteers is decreasing.

An important part of a governance approach's composition is the role of leadership.[1] We therefore draw on the notion of leadership as a strong vehicle to obtain control (Jago 1982). Referring to our research objective we find formal and informal leadership structures such as those derived from following an archon and leadership structures as a consequence of contractual obligations. For example, based on interviews with Free/Libre Open Source Software development team members Scozzi and colleagues (Scozzi et al. 2008) suggested that leadership seems to be correlated with sustained contribution in these teams, pointing to a more informal leadership structure.

Drawing on different leadership types we therefore hypothesize, how the number of technical contributions, the number of committers, and the number of paid as well as voluntary project leaders differ between single and multi vendor projects. In this context committers are defined as programmers who are allowed to change parts of the projects source code.

Hypothesis 1:   *Multi vendor projects receive more technical contributions by firms than single vendor projects.*

Hypothesis 2:   *The number of paid committers is higher in multi vendor projects.*

Hypothesis 3:   *The number of voluntary project leaders is higher in single vendor projects.*

Hypothesis 4:   *The number of paid project leaders is higher in multi vendor projects.*

Dahlander (2007) further points to the importance of a project's history for different governance modes. The evolution of many OSS projects has shown that a founder's personality as well as his technical abilities influences the composition and activity of a community (O'Mahony 2007). Linux, one of the big success stories within the OSS movement, until now is dependent on Linus Torvalds, its founder. We therefore propose that a project initiated by a community of developers (or a sole influencing developer) differs from a project initiated by a firm. For instance, to avoid the impression of harnessing a community's work, firms entering a stable community initiated project are likely to limit their effort in managing and controlling a project's trajectory (West and O'Mahony 2008). Therefore, we assume community initiated projects to consist of less paid project leaders than their firm initiated counterparts. In addition, due to a founder's personality, community initiated projects might be more attractive for other voluntary programmers (Stewart and Gosain 2006). In contrast, projects initiated by one or more firms are most likely to be led by paid project leaders in order to align with a firm's goal.

Hypothesis 5:   *Community initiated projects receive more technical contributions by volunteers than firm initiated projects.*

Hypothesis 6:   *The number of paid committers is higher in firm initiated projects.*

Hypothesis 7:   *The number of voluntary project leaders is higher in community initiated projects.*

Hypothesis 8:   *The number of paid project leaders is higher in firm initiated projects.*

---

[1] We skip a discussion about transaction cost economics here and point to the seminal work of Oliver Williamson.

3   Methodology

3.1   Research Setting: The Case of the Eclipse Foundation

In a search for data reflecting our research question, namely to identify different governance approaches for multi and single vendor OSS projects, we found the Eclipse foundation a suitable case to study. Eclipse itself is a hybrid, not just being a project; it is also a foundation which hosts several other projects. The foundation is one of the most successful ones with more than 100 members beside Mozilla and Apache Foundation. Characteristic for Eclipse is that a number of governance mechanisms are publicly available like the process of becoming a contributor or the responsibilities of its members. Furthermore, in the case of Eclipse, governance rules ignore the size of a firm. Every strategic board member has only one vote even if they donate much more than the others. The foundation's website provides a lot of information concerning Eclipse projects like the name of every committer, his affiliation, the status of a project, and especially the commitments to a project.

Eclipse as both, software product and foundation has a fascinating history. Eclipse was a development environment originated inside the boundaries of IBM. The major competitors to the Eclipse development environment were Microsoft's Visual Studio and Sun's NetBeans. To gain momentum IBM open sourced its development although they were sharing a $ 40 million dollar investment with its competitors (Wagstrom 2009). However, other vendors were now able to build their products on top of Eclipse rather than using proprietary software from competitors. Although in general every individual is welcome, possible future committers have to run through a process where they have to prove their programming qualification. Additionally, voluntary contributors as well as participating firms have to agree to certain process rules and a project charter. Furthermore, it is worth noting that every project is based on the principle of meritocracy which means that the more you contribute, and the higher the quality of your contribution, the more you are allowed to do.

3.2   Research Approach

We took data from the Eclipse website both manually and using a web miner, and stored it in a relational database. The data served as a pool to identify a number of variables we discuss in the following.

Technical Contribution
OSS vendors often use software tools like the Concurrent Versioning System (CVS)[2], Subversion (SVN)[3] or Git[4] to organize their source code in a so called software repository. In simple terms the software repository can be described as a container keeping all technical information (source code, Texts, images, database scripts…) necessary to build a software product. Furthermore through dedicated check-in/out and versioning functionalities the software repository enables developers to keep

---

[2] http://www.cvshome.org/
[3] http://subversion.apache.org/
[4] http://git-scm.com/

track of contributions to a software repository. This becomes important throughout the development and build phase of a software project. During the development phase a developer need to constantly add new, change existing or delete obsolete source code from the software repository.

Each contribution to a software repository as described above is logged by the software repository. By that, researchers may not only analyze the source code at the actual point in time but also gather information about the contributions made to the source code over a whole period of time. However, a recorded commit ignores the size of an actual contribution (Arafat and Riehle 2009). Therefore, it is not possible to identify directly if a contributor changed a whole function or just a few lines. Despite this limitation, many commits signal firm or community activity and a party's interest in a project - regardless of the actual size of the commit. We therefore coded technical contribution as the natural log of a commit made by a committer either being a volunteer or employed by a firm. Only projects where at least one commit occurred in the observed period are considered (December 2006 till December 2008).

Number of Committers
We were able to isolate information about each programmer's affiliation as well as his role within a project (committers can be active in more than just on project). Only those who have received the status of a *committer* are allowed to change parts of the source code. As the right to change is important in order to influence a project's trajectory, we only considered programmers with committers status – ignoring other types of contributions like bug identification or change requests. Based on our dataset, we were further able to distinguish between those paid by a firm and those who contributed voluntarily.

Number of Project Leaders
In a similar vein, the number of project leaders was counted. Again, as the Eclipse website provides a clear affiliation of each programmer as well as his role, leaders with a firm affiliation are coded as paid leaders; programmers without any affiliation are coded as voluntary leaders.

Project Initiation
In order to identify if a project is initiated by a firm or a community, we checked for who submitted the first commit for the focal project. In few cases first commits came from developers affiliated with a firm and voluntary developers. We then distinguished based on the number of commits. For example, if a project was founded in August 2004 and received 500 commits by firms and 20 by volunteers in the first month, this project was coded to be a firm initiated project.

Project Vendor Type
With our dataset we were also able to count for the number of firms in projects. As the Eclipse foundation has a commercial focus, we were not able to find a single project without firm participation. Based on the number of firms, we coded single vendor projects those who received commits by only one entity. Consequently, in cases of two or more firms active in project this project was considered a multi vendor project.

3.3 Research Results

After checking for projects with little or no activity or one without any commits, we ended up having a list of 83 projects. Of these projects, 17 were single vendor projects, 66 multi vendor projects, 33 were community initiated, 50 were firm initiated. In order to illustrate commit different behavior in single and multi vendor projects we chose two representatives (figure 1).

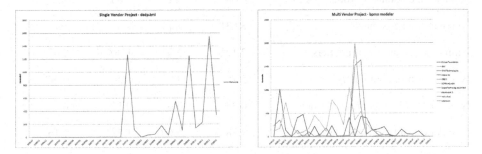

Fig. 1. A comparison between selected single (left) and multi (right) vendor projects

However, to test our hypotheses, we conducted an analysis of variance (ANOVA) to compare the mean values for each of our categorical variables. Specifically, we examined whether the mean values for the numbers of commits of firms, of volunteers, and number of paid project leaders in a project differ between different approaches. Although of high interest, we did not check for any combinations, such as community initiated single vendor projects. We abandoned this investigation due the impossibility to run statistical methods on small data sets. To run the ANOVA, we split the sample of projects into single vendor and multi vendor projects for a first analysis (table 1) and into firm initiated and community initiated for a second one (table 2).

Consistent with H1, the results show that multi vendor projects receive significantly more commits than single vendor projects. Furthermore, it is worth noting, that with regard to H2 the number of paid committers in multi vendor projects is nearly three times the number of committers in single vendor projects. As expected, the distribution of voluntary and paid project leaders among single and multi vendor projects reflects our hypotheses H3 and H4. However, it is worth noting that the overall number of voluntary project leaders is indeed very low (mean of 0.35 in single vendor, 0.12 in multi vendor projects). To further illustrate differences between single and multi vendor projects we calculated the ration of paid to all committers. Here we find multi vendor projects to have 87.54 % paid committers in contrast to 76.06 % in single vendor projects.

In a line with H5, community initiated projects receive significantly more commits by volunteers than their firm initiated counterparts. Interestingly, the number of commits by firms does not differ between community and firm initiated projects. We also find support for H6 in that the number of paid committers in firm initiated

Table 2. Means (M) and standard deviations (SD) after ANOVA on factor VENDORTYPE

	Single vendor project		Multi vendor project	
	M	SD	M	SD
Number of commits by firms	7.41[a]	n.c.	9.06[b]	n.c.
Number of commits by volunteers	4.08[a]	n.c.	5.05[a]	n.c.
Number of all commits	8.63[a]	n.c.	9.37[a]	n.c.
Number of voluntary committers	2.12[a]	3.57	1.80[a]	2.63
Number of paid committers	5.18[a]	2.90	14.83[b]	15.92
Number of voluntary project leaders	0.35[a]	0.61	0.12[c]	0.45
Number of paid project leaders	0.88[a]	0.60	1.58[b]	1.16
Ratio paid to all committers	76.06[a]	35.13	87.54[b]	17.14

Notes: Mean values reported, $N=82$. Within each row, means with a *different* superscript are significantly ($p < .05$ for b; $p < .1$ for c) different from each other. n.c.=not calculated by SPSS

Table 3. Means (M) and standard deviations (SD) after ANOVA on factor INITIATION

	Community initiated		Firm initiated	
	M	SD	M	SD
Number of commits by firms	8.10[a]	n.c.	8.95[a]	n.c.
Number of commits by volunteers	6.07[a]	n.c.	4.03[b]	n.c.
Number of all commits	9.26[a]	n.c.	9.11[a]	n.c.
Number of voluntary committers	2.36[a]	3.53	1.60[a]	2.26
Number of paid committers	8.45[a]	6.44	15.46[b]	17.77
Number of voluntary project leaders	0.21[a]	0.48	0.16[a]	0.51
Number of paid project leaders	1.33[a]	1.13	1.48[a]	1.09

Notes: Mean values reported, $N=83$. Within each row, means with the *same* superscript are not significantly ($p < .05$) different from each other. n.c.=not calculated by SPSS

projects is nearly twice the number of paid committers in community initiated ones. With regard to H7 and H8, namely the leadership structure in both types of projects, we do find figures reflecting our arguments; however, they are not significant. As we expected the number of paid project leaders to be significantly higher in firm initiated

Table 4. Overview on supported and not supported hypotheses

Hypothesis	Considered variable	Is significantly higher in	*Supported*
H1	Number of commits by firms	Multi vendor projects	Yes
H2	Number of paid committers	Multi vendor projects	Yes
H3	Number of voluntary project leaders	Single vendor projects	Yes
H4	Number of paid project leaders	Multi vendor projects	Yes
Hypothesis	Considered variable	Is significantly higher in	*Supported*
H5	Number of commits by volunteers	Community initiated	Yes
H6	Number of paid committers	Firm initiated	Yes
H7	Number of voluntary project leaders	Community initiated	No
H8	Number of paid project leaders	Firm initiated projects	No

Notes: A hypothesis is considered to be significantly supported if $p<.05$

projects, especially the comparatively high number of paid project leaders in community initiated projects was a surprise. Putting single and multi vendor projects together might be a threat in order to distinguish between community and firm initiated projects (see beginning of section *Research Results* for reasons to combine both approaches). Table 4 gives an overview on supported and not supported hypotheses.

4 Discussion and Conclusion

The aim of the paper was to find differences in governance approaches between single and multi vendor projects as well as between community and firm initiated ones. In our study we therefore focus on areas somewhat neglected by dominant OSS research streams. The objective of our research was a number of projects hosted under the umbrella of the Eclipse foundation. We treated leadership as a strong vehicle for firms to obtain control in an OSS projects. However, in a similar vein, having a high number of paid committers who have the right to change parts of the software code is equally an important instrument to perform control. We find support for six of our eight major hypotheses. Before discussing our results in the light of existing and future research, we have to point to a number of limitations.

Firstly, one important limitation is that we were not able to identify a measure for a project's size. Yet especially the size of a project, for instance, measurable in lines of code, determines the number of contributors and committers in a project. Secondly, as stated in the research results section, we were not able to run an ANOVA for each quadrant due to the limited size of our data set. In order to further distinguish approaches within the group of multi vendor projects, looking to a project's history (community vs. firm initiation) is an avenue for further research. Finally, we have to be careful in generalizing our results. Projects hosted by the Eclipse foundation inherently have a commercial focus, which means that conclusions from this research cannot be easily extrapolated to other OSS cases. Furthermore, the Eclipse foundation oftentimes acts as a platform for selling complementary products. For instance, Deutsche Post, a major German logistic company, has developed a service-oriented IT infrastructure over the last eight years. Service-oriented architectures (SOA) are a heavily discussed topic in IT settings due to the ability to create a flexible IT infrastructure. Recent developments at Deutsche Post made it necessary to offer the in-house solution, a SOA-framework, under the umbrella of the Eclipse Foundation as an openly available product named Swordfish; hoping for external contributions to the ongoing process of maintaining the software. However, although being a single vendor project, the product was never intended to be sold to third parties like in cases of dual licensing. Moreover, several firms use Swordfish as a basis for on-top products and solutions. The fact that the Swordfish project has failed to attract an active developer community external to the firm until now, points to challenge for single vendor, firm initiated projects to establish sustainable external contributions.

Drawing on our hypothesis we find different approaches to administrate commercial OSS projects from a firm's point of view which we will discuss in detail. Single vendor approaches are characterized by the fact that only one firm is active in an OSS project. The majority of these firms are startups or SMEs which need a community of developers to complement missing own resources. For them, having programmers external to the firm they do not have to pay for is crucial to compete with sustained rivals. In addition, when a firm wants to internalize resources, the developer community is a talent base they can directly recruit from. This, on the other hand, signals to voluntary programmers who then might spend their time for a project which they can benefit from in the long run.

In contrast, multi vendor projects are characterized by more than one firm. From a firm's point of view, as other firms also spend resources or pay developers to work in the project, the need to complement missing internal resources through volunteers decreases. Multi vendor projects therefore permit firms to complement resources not to be found internally with other firm's resources. These resources are usually skillful paid developers. Although they are still external to the focal firm, they are legally bounded to the project through contracts with external firms. However, as a downside, multi vendor projects inherent the problem of multiple firm interests which results in a high number of paid project leaders. As a consequence, these projects seem to be less attractive for voluntary programmers due to an increased firm presence.

Community initiated projects receive more commits by volunteers and consist of more voluntary project leaders than firm initiated projects. These findings mirror the assumption that individual programmers follow a founder or a group of founders, respectively. For firms entering such projects, in order to not disrupt established informal structures and norms they have to accept that too much influence, e.g. by sending too many paid programmers to work for the project, inherent the risk of a fork as a consequence of losing contact to community rules.

Firms initiating an OSS project have to put emphasis on the development of both, a user and a developer community. Depending on the type of software various strategies are possible. In cases of technology exploitation, where a firm opens an internally developed product it is important to know, if the firm wants to capture value itself or if it accepts to share value with others. In the latter case, the community of developers consists of programmers of other firms which also have an interest in the open project. In cases where a firm, e.g. a startup, offers a product under an OSS license, usually first efforts have to be made to establish a user community which then over time evolves to a community of voluntary developers.

As our study has shown, OSS projects differ among different dimensions and therefore require different management approaches. While sending paid programmers to established OSS communities can be useful in one case, this can be the wrong strategy in another. We therefore call for future research of differences in managing commercial OSS communities.

References

Alexy, O.: Free Revealing. How Firms Can Profit From Being Open. Gabler, Wiesbaden (2009)

Arafat, O., Riehle, D.: The Commit Size Distribution of Open Source Software. In: Proceedings of the 42nd Hawaiian International Conference on System Science (HICSS-42) (2009)

Bitzer, J., Schrettl, W., Schröder, P.J.H.: Intrinsic Motivation in Open Source Software Development. Journal of Comparative Economics 35, 160–169 (2007)

Bitzer, J., Geishecker, I.: Who Contributes Voluntarily to OSS? An Investigation Among German IT Employees. Research Policy 39, 165–172 (2010)

Bonaccorsi, A., Giannangeli, S., Rossi, C.: Entry Strategies Under Competing Standards: Hybrid Business Models in the Open Source Software Industry. Management Science 52(7), 1085–1098 (2006)

Dahlander, L.: Penguin in a New Suit: A Tale of How De Novo Entrants Emerged to Harness Free and Open Source Software Communities. Industrial and Corporate Change 16(5), 913–943 (2007)

Dahlander, L., Magnusson, M.G.: Relationships Between Open Source Software Companies and Communities: Observations From Nordic Firms. Research Policy 34(4), 481–493 (2005)

Dahlander, L., Magnusson, M.G.: How Do Make Firms Make Use of Open Source Communities? Long Range Planning 41, 629–649 (2008)

Dahlander, L., Wallin, M.: A Man on the Inside: Unlocking Communities as Complementary Assets. Research Policy 35, 1243–1259 (2006)

De Laat, P.B.: Governance of Open Source Software: State of the Art. Journal of Management and Governance 11(2), 165–177 (2007)

Fitzgerald, B.: The Transformation of Open Source Software. MIS Quarterly 30(3), 587–598 (2006)

Fosfuri, A., Giarratana, M., Luzzi, A.: The Penguin Has Entered the Building: The Commercialization of Open Source Software Products. Organization Science 19(2), 292–305 (2008)

Franck, E., Jungwirth, C.: Reconciling Rent-Seekers and Donators - The Governance Structure of Open Source. Journal of Management and Governance 7(4), 401–421 (2003)

Jago, A.G.: Leadership: Perspectives in Theory and Research. Management Science 28(3), 315–336 (1982)

Lerner, J., Tirole, J.: Some Simple Economics of Open Source. Journal of Industrial Economics 50(2), 197–234 (2002)

O'Mahony, S.: The Governance of Open Source Initiatives: What Does It Mean to Be Community Managed? Journal of Management and Governance 11(2), 139–150 (2007)

Raymond, E.S.: The Cathedral and the Bazaar (1999), http://www.catb.org/~esr/writings/cathedral-bazaar/ (last access: 10/21/2010)

Riehle, D.: The Commercial Open Source Business Model. In: Proceedings of the 15th American Conference on Information Systems (AMCIS), San Francisco, CA (August 6-8, 2009)

Riehle, D.: The Single Vendor Commercial Open Source Business Model. Information Systems and e-Business Management (2011) (forthcoming)

Schaarschmidt, M., Von Kortzfleisch, H.: Divide et Impera! The Role of Firms in Large Open Source Software Consortia. In: Proceedings of the 15th American Conference on Information Systems (AMCIS), San Francisco, CA (August 6-8, 2009)

Schaarschmidt, M., Von Kortzfleisch, H.: The Business of Venture Capital in Open Source Software. Working Paper, presented at 10th EURAM Conference, Rome, Italy (May 19-22, 2010)

Scozzi, B., Crowston, K., Eseryel, Y., Li, Q.: Shared Mental Models Among Open Source Software Developers. In: Proceedings of the 41st Hawaii International Conference on System Science, HICSS-41 (2008)

Shah, S.: Motivation, Governance, and the Viability of Hybrid Forms in Open Source Development. Management Science 52(7), 1000–1014 (2006)

Stewart, K.J., Gosain, S.: The Impact of Ideology on Effectiveness in Open Source Software Teams. MIS Quarterly 30(2), 291–314 (2006)

Wagstrom, P.A.: Vertical Interaction in Open Source Software Engineering Communities, PhD Thesis, Carnegie Mellon University, Pittsburgh, PA (2009)

Watson, R.T., Boudreau, M.-C., York, P.T., Greiner, M., Wynn, D.: The Business of Open Source. Communications of the ACM 51(4), 41–46 (2008)

West, J.: How Open is Open Enough? Melding Proprietary and Open Source Platform Strategies. Research Policy 32, 1259–1285 (2003)

West, J., O'Mahony, S.: The Role of Participation Architecture in Growing Sponsored Open Source Communities. Industry and Innovation 15(2), 145–168 (2008)

Innovative Project Idea Maturation: An Important Part of Governance

Jan Pries-Heje and Ann-Dorte Fladkjær Nielsen

Roskilde University, Universitetsvej 1, DK-4000 Roskilde &
Jyske Bank, Vestergade 8-16, DK-8600 Silkeborg
Tel.: +45 2347 4463, +45 8989 2765
janph@ruc.dk, afn@jyskebank.dk

Abstract. Project Governance includes the elicitation of ideas for projects, choosing the best ideas, initiating projects, assigning resources, and nurturing the projects to success. In the third largest bank in Denmark – Jyske Bank – IT project managers often became uncertain when they were assigned new projects; their descriptions were either to vague or broad or sometimes even both. There was a need for better project scoping and improved idea descriptions. In this paper we describe how we committed ourselves to solve this problem. Based on a literature study on innovation and using an existing creative space (room) called the "land of opportunity", we used a design science approach to formulate a new idea maturation concept. Here two years later, we have developed and evaluated our concept on several project ideas. The uncertain project managers are now very enthusiastic; they really feel that they have a much clearer scope and idea description as well as an early prototype of the idea. After four design iterations, the concept stabilized. In this paper we present the idea maturation concept and the organizational design science research process we have used.

Keywords: Governance, project idea, design science research, project management.

1 Introduction

Peter Weill & Jeanne Ross (2004) talk about five key IT decisions in IT governance: (1) IT principles decisions, (2) IT architecture decisions, (3) IT infrastructure decisions, (4) Business application needs, and (5) IT investment and prioritization decisions. As part of the last decision area project governance is a major part. Project Governance includes the elicitation of ideas for projects, choosing the best ideas, initiating projects, assigning resources, and nurturing the projects to success. Only then can the investment represented by the projects be ʾharvestedʾ.

Jyske Bank is Denmark's third largest bank, formed through a merger of smaller banks in 1967 and headquartered in Silkeborg. There is still a long way to the two largest banks in Denmark, so Jyske Bank is very conscious of differentiating themselves. "Make a Difference" is their mantra. On their homepage Jyske Bank presents themselves as the (social) climber in the banking industry who "always treads new

M. Nüttgens et al. (Eds.): Governance and Sustainability in IS, IFIP AICT 366, pp. 29–42, 2011.

paths." Innovation has, for many years, been an important parameter to differentiate Jyske Bank from others. In order to differentiate oneself and be innovative, one must constantly come up with new ideas. In Jyske Bank, the effort towards this has been very conscious. Among others, they have designed a large room on the ground floor in the Silkeborg headquarters, dubbed "the land of opportunity." The room is furnished as a fantasy world based on Norse mythology, with a large painting in one end of the room and a wide canvas in the other. Colours, soft shapes and flexible partitioning is part of the design. Even the coffee mugs and the cutlery are "different". The room's purpose is to promote the creative process, by bringing humans into other environments than those they are usually surrounded by in their work.

Many good ideas arise around Jyske Bank, but they are not always presented or described well enough. In autumn 2007 an interview survey among project leaders revealed that the individuals often felt that the project descriptions they were given were too vague and superficially described, so they felt uncertain about the projects they were responsible for. The survey led to the creation of a new project, with the definition that Jyske Bank did not need more ideas, but better descriptions of the ideas. Focus was thus the transformation from draft proposals to better project descriptions. We formulated the central question as thus: What does a concept for better project descriptions look like?

How is the remainder of the paper organized?
The remainder of the paper is structured as follows. First, we talk about the theoretical anchorage of the concept, both in innovation theory, and in situational theory. Then we briefly describe our approach as a mixture of action research and design science. Thereafter follows a long section where we describe the concept in detail. This is followed by a series of selected examples of the use of the concept. Finally, we summarize the points of the article and discuss further research.

2 Creativity and Innovation

"Creative" comes from the Latin *Creare*, which means to create. As a starting point, "Creative" is a positive word, (something everybody looks positively on). A usable definition of creativity is: "A systematic to break the habit of thinking". Innovation is the deployment of an idea or an approach that relates to a product, service, device, system, policy or program that is new to the organization deploying it (Damanpour & Gopalakrishnan, 2001). Coming up with new ideas is creative. To implement it is innovation - when it is experienced as new and creates something of value.

Edward de Bono (1968, 1969, and 1970) did research on how people think, be it innovative and/or creative. De Bono notes that all self-organizing systems form patterns - habits, we call it often. This means that one is forced to move across these patterns instead of just following them, if one wants to think thoughts that are different. De Bono calls this "Lateral Thinking".

If one is to think laterally - to the side - then it is necessary to put oneself in a situation that changes ones starting point and perception of how things link, to actually force one to think in a fundamentally different way.

Another source of inspiration is IDEO (Kelley & Littman 2001, Kelley 2005) that helps companies innovate. They create strategies for innovation and they design products, spaces, services and experiences. Key to their success as a design and innovation firm are the insights they derive from understanding people and their experiences, behaviours, perceptions and needs.

Donaldson (2001, p.5) defines contingency theory in the following way: "At the most abstract level, the contingency approach says that the effect of one variable on another depends on some third variable ..." The core of the situational theory, therefore, is that organizations that want to work optimally need to take account of the situation; it is the factors of the situation that determine what the best approach would be. Contingent models have, for example, been applied in vague and ambiguous situations, where the information available could be interpreted in many ways depending on perspective (Galegher & Kraut, 1994). Contingency factors have included leadership style (Hersey & Blanchard, 1969, 1981), communication support, process structuring and information processing (Zigurs & Buckland, 1998; Zigurs, Buckland, Connolly, & Wilson, 1999), as well as task complexity and whether the technology is appropriate for the task (Van de Ven & Drazin, 1985).

Contingency theory has been criticized for having an excessively static view of the relationship between structure and technology (Barley, 1990). Nevertheless, we found characteristic features in the situation, related to the idea maturation context, that we then used to develop a situation specific concept. Obviously we can not rule out that it is a very static picture we've seen, that would be are outstripped by the dynamics of reality; but it has simply not occurred here more than a year after we identified the main situation specific factors.

3 Research Method

Herbert A. Simon (1996) defined in the book "The Sciences of the Artificial", a science that focuses on design/construction of artefacts or human systems with the "desired" properties. Simon defined design science as the counterpart to the (natural) sciences that study given things (in nature or society) and how they work.

Hevner et al. (2004) presents a definition of Design Science Research (DSR) and outline three key processes. First there is iteration between building and evaluation. Second is the relevance-process, i.e. once the design has gone through a number of iterations in the middle, it turns back and is attempted to be used to meet the needs or solve the problem. Third, we find the research process ("rigor"), where the input from the existing research knowledge base is obtained, and it is reported what contributions to scientific knowledge the design allows. Whether the knowledge is in the form of theory, model, method, framework or something similar, it is the researchers job to take existing knowledge into account, and "stand on the shoulders of it" i.e. to build on the existing. Thus DSR relates to the needs and problems with focus on satisfying the needs or solving the problems. Design science is prescriptive, or perhaps even normative. Thereby, design science differs from analytically oriented sciences, where the objective is to understand and describe.

We decided to use DSR as our approach for designing and building a solution to the problem at hand in Jyske Bank, for testing it, learning from it and becoming wiser, built an improved concept, test it, learn from it and become wiser, etc. The main reasons for choosing DSR was the close engagement with practice, the iterative nature of DSR that ensures that learning can be captured and used. Further the 'scientific' cycle of DSR ensures that what is designed is done on a sound scientific state-of-the-art foundation.

The first version of the idea maturation concept was developed after studying the problem and its scope closely (relevance process). We interviewed around 10 project-managers in the organization and dived into the old project descriptions and business cases to get insight into the content and quality of it. It quickly became clear that many immature ideas were launched. This was documented in a presentation that spawned our work on creating a concept that could improve project descriptions.

It was with these inputs, as well as our own experience and the knowledge that the literature on innovation and creativity has given us (the research process) that the first version of the concept saw the light of day.

Alongside studying projects from their own organization, we read what others had written about for example innovation. The literature gave us an overview and inspired us to create a concept that could actually be used to improve and mature ideas.

We worked with the concept in four design iterations. Our first version of the concept was ready in June 2008. In each iteration, we have received feedback from users, and their comments for each step in the process gave rise to (many) adjustments.

In general we have chosen a naturalistic examination (Venable, 2006) in a real organization - Jyske Bank - with a perceived problem. The first evaluation trial took place in June 2008. This evaluation gave rise to many changes in the first version of the concept. The same happened after the second and third evaluation of the concept.

4 The Idea Maturation Concept

Finally in 2009 we ended up with the concept presented here with four steps:

- Step 1: A discussion of: How clear is your idea?
- Step 2: Determining what idea maturation process would be best suited for that specific business idea?
- Step 3: Arrange idea maturation workshop
- Step 4: Secure results of idea maturation process including relevant reviews

The purpose of step 1 - How clear is your idea? - is to uncover a focused phrase that describes the idea. Experience from Jyske Bank shows that it is often wasted work to pursue an idea if the wording is unclear. That is similar to having been through a phase with divergent thinking, but without closing and deciding, similar to the convergence phase (Jakobsen & Rebsdorf, 2003).

To be sure that the idea owner has the right starting point for further idea maturation, we have selected some questions from (inspired by Pries-Heje et al., 1999), which gives a clear indication of whether the idea is sharp (= clear wording of idea - convergent phase completed) or open (= unclear wording of idea - convergent phase *not* completed).

The questions we use in the concept to be answered by the idea owner is shown in Figure 1. It takes approximately an hour to give and receive answers to the questions in Figure 1. We note the idea owner's responses as they are obtained. There are 3 possible outcomes of Step 1:

1. The idea owner has a concrete answer to the questions (Figure 2) and is therefore ready for step 2 of the concept.
2. The idea owner has been unable to respond to one or more of the questions and should therefore continue working to concretize the idea before it the idea is pursued. (New meeting is planned)
3. Idea owner has found out that the idea is not sustainable enough and the work on the idea ends here.

The knowledge that is the result of questions and answers session can be used directly in various sections of the project description. As a result, the idea owner is no longer left standing with just a blank and empty description.

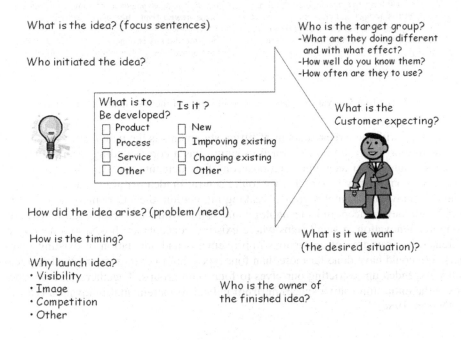

Fig. 1. Artefact from workshop used to give an overview of the questions in step 1 of the idea maturation concept

The purpose of Step 2 is to get a characterization of the idea, so that we can find the idea-process just sufficient enough to mature the idea. The idea-owner will be asked to decide which group of statements from Figure 2 best matches his idea.

TYPE 1	TYPE 3
• The idea may be vital for Jyske Bank • The idea may be a new business or 1/more business areas seen in a whole new light • The idea may be difficult to predict • The idea has not yet become a common awareness among all key stakeholders • We will read about it in the newspaper when this idea is realized • The idea may intervene with Jyske Bank's strategy	• The idea can be compared to anything we know (everyday situations) • The idea stems from an easily understandable, everyday need (something an advisor / client is missing in their everyday life) • Realization of the idea requires no new knowledge at Jyske Bank • The idea is already fully or partially on the market but not at Jyske Bank
TYPE 2	**TYPE 4**
• The idea requires that many different experts give their input before the project configuration can be written • The idea should be studied from many viewpoints • The idea has many interfaces • The idea will lead to more 50% renewal as seen from the target audience's point of view • The idea is an expression of something *need to have* compared to Jyske Bank's overall strategy	• The idea is based on something already known at Jyske Bank, but must be extended, renewed or corrected • The idea must be resolved by Jyske Bank's own specialists • The idea must fit into the existing set up • The idea is an expression of something *need to have* viewed from the target audience's point of view • The idea did not change significantly in the target group's way of thinking and acting

Fig. 2. The four innovation types included in step 2 of the idea maturation concept

The type with the largest amount of fitting statements is the type that forms the basis for further work on the idea. Each grouping has a corresponding idea maturation process, a number of techniques, proposition of participants, etc. The four types represent the contingency factors that we found central in idea maturation at Jyske Bank. Radical innovation connotes groundbreaking innovation: the surprisingly new, that in a radically new concept links technology and value from use. Incremental innovation connotes innovation in small steps where existing concepts are linked in a new way. Often, it is a question of continuous improvements and adaptation of existing products. We could have done far more than four types, but to ensure its practical applicability we ended up restricting ourselves to four main groups. Together, the four types cover the entire innovative spectrum, from radical to incremental innovation (Dewar & Dutton, 1986)

5   The Four Innovation Types in the Idea Maturation Concept

In Figure 3 we have shown the four innovation processes that are implicit in the four innovation types covered by our concept. The result of a workshop is always a prototype that visually describes the ideal solution or solution elements.

Radical innovation often has a very divergent and convergent phase. In Figure 3, the divergent part is illustrated as a lateral "V", which opens from left to right. Similarly, the convergent part is illustrated as an interim "V", which closes from left to right. The difficulty of an idea maturation workshop for radical innovation is that the uncertainty is very high. Some workshop participants won't be comfortable with very high uncertainty. It may also be that the participants at the workshop are okay with it, but it is as much about the organization's expectations: "Will we get some answers to our questions soon?" rather than just generate more questions. Therefore, it has to be a very 'strong' idea-owner to be responsible for an idea of this nature. Otherwise, you risk the process being closed too rapidly - it travels too fast from divergent to convergent - and then the result won't be radical innovation anyhow.

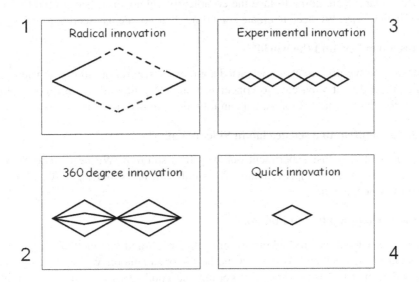

Fig. 3. How the process runs dependent on innovation type

360 degrees innovation, corresponding to drawing 2 in Figure 3, is special because each of the divergent and convergent phases needs to be able to handle several different opinions and angles. There might, for example be several target groups that have to be evaluated at the same time. Or it could be several sources of inspiration that are used in parallel. Idea maturation workshops of this nature are often more complex, and require more advanced techniques and external contributions. We spend from 1-2 days on workshops of this type.

Experimental innovation, equivalent to drawing 3 in Figure 3, has a lot of small and rapid divergent and convergent phases. This workshop is about developing some ideas and getting them translated into a prototype that can be assessed and improved. The improvements should in turn be incorporated in the prototype and evaluated, etc. This process is repeated until the user accepts the prototype. Often we use 1 day on the idea maturation workshop.

Quick innovation (drawing 4 in Figure 3) is a single small process, where we get through both a divergent and a convergent phase in a very short time span. We use simple techniques that are known to many in the organization. An idea maturation workshop of this type often takes 2-4 hours. To get the participants in a workshop to identify with the activities related to the situation-specific group, we decided to use metaphors. Something similar has been done with very good results in systems development (Kendall & Kendall, 1993 & 1994).

More specifically, in the workshop we have chosen to use a travel metaphor corresponding to the four types as follows:

Type 1 is 'The journey into space'

This means that we are going to face the completely unknown. It is essential to think in a totally new way. We need to create something that no one has seen before

Type 2 is a trip 'Around the world'

This means that we need to examine varied sources of inspiration, look elsewhere, try to work in a different way, etc., to conceive completely new ideas into the existing situation. We know what the job is, but can it be done in another way?

Type 3 is a 'fieldtrip to a science lab in Silicon Valley'

This means that we must experiment our way to a solution. We need to work with prototypes, assessments, improvements. We steal with arms and legs! We need not reinvent the wheel again.

Type 4 is a 'Shopping trip to London'

This means that what we are looking for are easy, small and fast methods to get a lot of ideas out in the open and then select the best – one or more. We're short on time, but we would like to spend some of it getting the good ideas out. Maybe a slightly more modern product will cover more needs. Often adds bits to something existing.

Travel metaphors have proven to work really well at giving participants a sense of how much innovation is required for idea maturation. Moreover, the travel metaphor gives inspiration to the staging of the workshop. We aim to adjust the staging to fit the idea. If we are to mature an idea that falls into group 4: 'Shopping trip to London' we aim to create a workshop environment with shops, for the right age group and market segment.

As part of the concept, step 2, we co-operate with the idea-owner to asses who should participate in the workshop. The purpose of step 3 - arranging the idea maturation workshop - is to get a group of well-chosen people to specify the idea and generate proposals for the first draft of the solution. The result of step 3 is a clear description of which solution proposals or solution elements to pass on to a development project - including a clear definition of what to include and what to exclude. Also step 3 results in a simple prototype that visualizes the product or process being generated by the idea.

Many different creativity increasing techniques can be found in the literature. We have tested many but have no final set of techniques to recommend. We can only say that it is contingent on the experience of the participants and the facilitator. We use the travel metaphor to plan the progression of the workshop. First we're going out and then were returning home - we must first open, then close the idea generating process - divergence and convergence.

The prototype developed at the workshop need not be a working functional prototype. It may be a simple drawing of a process, a sketch of a product or something similar. For the workshop we use "the land of opportunity". Figure 4 shows an example of the workshop setup from "a hike in the Alps"; the idea is to imagine being in a tent camp in the mountains.

Fig. 4. Tent camp in the Alps; a travel metaphor implemented in the "land of opportunity"

We have also found that things like appropriate catering, music and effects that the participants can touch and play with are important and help them live themselves into the fantasy.

At the beginning of a workshop we have found it to be a good idea to have an employee from the business area of the idea tells a little about how the new idea fits into the overall strategy of the company, the thoughts behind the idea, if the idea is part of a larger context etc. We have also had inspirational presentations from external specialists. If the purpose is, for example, to come up with ideas for the customer segment from 18 to 24 years, it might be appropriate to have a futurologist talk about current or upcoming trends for this segment.

Table 1. Four examples of projects and innovation types

No.	Project & Type	Result
1	Strategic concept for corporate customers & **360 degree innovation**	A strategic concept for corporate customers. Many bank products require that corporate customers can produce a strategic plan. However, many small and medium corporate customers do not have the ability to develop a proper strategic plan. Therefore Jyske Bank will offer to help with it expertise; a kind of add-on banking product offered to clients.
2	iVenture & **Radical innovation**	Financial guide to a Jyske Bank advisor when he is in dialogue with customers. For risk assessment of clients' securities composition.
3	Budget zone in online banking & **Quick innovation**	New feature included in online banking as an application for private customers.
4	Secure buy & **Experimental innovation**	A new banking product for securing corporate clients, when trading with foreign countries.

In Table 1 we have given four examples of using our idea maturation concept for four different types of innovation.

6 An Example of an Idea Maturation Workshop

To convey the core of how the idea maturation workshop is held, we give an example from one of our evaluation. In the example (no. 1 in Table 1) the problem to address was the fact that many SMEs are required to present a strategic plan to Jyske Bank to obtain a loan or another Baking product. However, this requirement can sometimes be difficult to meet for SMEs because they do not have the expertise in-house to develop a strategic plan. Thus the idea we started out from was that the bank could offer customers expertise to help them with their strategy process. This would create a win-win situation in that the companies would get assistance and the Bank would get insight into the company and thereby be able to offer customers the right banking products.

Our focus in this example is on process rather than outcome (the product that was matured). In this example, we will discuss an idea from group 2, so we needed to build an idea workshop with 360-degrees innovation - a trip around the world.

The day began at a check-in counter at the airport. Participants were each provided with a travel suitcase, a boarding pass, a bread roll in a paper bag and a newspaper. Then they were allowed to check in and go ahead with the workshop. This start-up was created so the participants could become aware that there would be something different going on - not the usual meeting, nor a normal meeting room.

In the room where the participants entered, we created four different "client countries", in the form of staging of 4 different types of businesses which participants would go to. For each country, participants were given the task to discover what the customer's thoughts about the product/service were. In the carpentry workshop, they literally sat amongst wooden boards, laths and machinery, and tried to imagine how a carpenter thought and felt about the particular subject.

The next process of the workshop was a presentation by an outside consultant. From what he told me and from the inputs the participants had gotten from their travels to different types of businesses, we produced the first draft of a prototype. A process, where the facilitator tried to assemble the many inputs into a drawing, they could all say yes to.

Thereafter, the first prototype had to be made marketable, so the next task was called "How do the advisers work with this model, so the customers experience Jyske Differences?" To get participants to think "differently", we chose to let them work in different cities. We made a scene setup with three different cities (Paris, London and New York). For this, we used images, sounds and props that characterized each of the big cities. Participants would then in turn go to the three cities and gather inspiration on how to market the product. With the combined associations they had created on their journeys, we developed the next version of a prototype. This prototype was then tested against the different types of customers; again in the form of a journey to the four "customer countries".

The above is an example where we constantly "force" the participants to see the problem from different angles. We tried to bring them into realistic environments and environments which could hopefully create very different connotations than the usual ones. We believe that both parts were successful. Also, it should be emphasized that this is only one example. For other idea workshops, we will probably create quite different destinations, tailored to the specific idea. As the example shows, the organization of the idea workshop is contingent on the chosen innovation type. The trip is never a "standard trip".

The outcome related to the idea that has come from steps 1, 2 and 3 needs to be secured and described in a project description. There are several target groups for the project description, which is extremely important to keep in mind when the writing process starts. The target groups are decision makers in the organizations and the upcoming projects and project teams. These two groups have widely varying needs. The decision makers require a project description that describes the project idea in a clear and concise manner with just enough information to enable them to make the decision of whether the project idea is to be realized or rejected.

It is in the interest of the future project -manager and group to have the project presented in such a way, that they are not forced to start from scratch, but can draw on the information that has already been studied and described in the project description.

When the project description has been written - with all the details of steps 1, 2 and 3 – it is ready to be enriched. The idea-owner can have two needs of enrichment - they may need, some people who can contribute knowledge directly to the project description, or they may need to have internal experts review the resolution, to make sure it is sound and in accordance to Jyske Bank's values and strategies.

7 Conclusion and Learning Points

We believe we have designed a successful idea maturation concept in four steps, which Jyske Bank has benefited considerably from. The largest benefit is when starting a project, as the project group gain a quicker start because the idea is better described and documented through an idea prototype. This means that the project group doesn't waste time getting acquainted with the task, but instead can 'dive' directly into its solution.

The process we designed ensures that you focus better and think the right thoughts before writing the project description. The contribution is the contingent grouping of business ideas, and the consistent use of the groups, as well as metaphors, to determine the actual idea maturation process.

One criticism that we have encountered is that all ideas "swell" with the use of the described concept. To counter this, we can only say that in practical use, the concept has proven not only to get ideas to "swell" up; it has also put ideas to death!

The main adjustments in the four design iterations are summarized in the following ten detailed learning points, structured by the four stages of the concept:

1. Questions should be good enough, to determine whether the idea is viable. The first time around, our questions (see Fig. 2) weren't broad enough and lacked focus on how the idea fit with the bank's overall strategy, the target group's expectations, etc.
2. Reduce contingent groups as much as possible to ensure clarity. We started with 6 contingency groupings with a corresponding travel metaphor, but it soon became apparent that it was too difficult to ask questions that accurately characterized the group; they overlapped to easily.
3. Metaphors may be a hindrance. We found that Innovation Types were easier to understand than the travel / journey metaphor. Innovation types proved to be more understandable for the idea owner. But the journey metaphor is still important to use, to bring about a framework and thereby the staging of the idea maturation workshop.
4. Design presentation style needs adaptation to targets group. We evaluated the production of the idea characteristics in three different ways. They were: (1) XY-axes with statements for given situation factors. (2) Groupings of statements to cross off. (3) A matrix of key statements, which together made a room. As described earlier participants preferred (2), so this is the approach we have presented here.
5. Transformation processes are hard! Generally participating in a creative process such as our idea maturation workshop requires something completely new for the vast majority of our employees. You have to overcome some resistance.
6. It is very important to have the right people must participate in the workshop. In the beginning, we were not focused enough on getting the right people invited to the workshops. After the first two pilot tests we realized the importance; and it made a (positive) difference to have them joining.
7. Very difficult to escape the everyday life and challenges. We have learned that our participants have difficulty getting away from their daily life in the organization. In the first pilot we were not sufficiently aware that the choice of travel metaphor had to be placed in the participants' consciousness several times during the workshop.

8. People are different. Some are better than others at associating, brainstorming and living themselves into a (travel / journey) metaphor. The concept needs to allow for this difference.
9. Some people are very solution-oriented. Some participants find it very hard to work for period of time in the open phase. They immediately start evaluating ideas and discard some ideas as unrealistic. Thus you need facilitation to "keep" people in the creative mode. In the concrete we have meet four distinct types of people:

  1. Those who just throw themselves into deep water and play along
  2. Those who can participate well in the creative thinking games, but have a strong need for a facilitator to manage the process
  3. Those who might feel as group two, but let's it depend on the rest of their group
  4. Those who think stuff like "creative processes" is a complete waste of time

  Groups 2 and 3 have in this case been by far the largest groups and roughly equal in size.
10. Continuous adjustment of the project description template has been needed. Thus we have not only designed a new process for idea maturation but also the artefact coming out of idea maturation.

Finally, we have written this paper in the hope that others can use or be guided by our concept. We have emphasised details to an extent where it should be possible to learn from our example. Further, we have given the details of our design science research method thereby giving the academic reader a better insight into our work and giving the opportunity of judging the quality.

References

Barley, S.R.: The Alignment of Technology and Structure Through Roles and Networks. Administrative Science Quarterly 35(1), 61–103 (1990)

Damanpour, F., Gopalakrishnan, S.: The dynamics of the adoption of product and process innovations in organizations. Journal of Management Studies 38, 45–65 (2001)

De Bono, E.: New think; the use of lateral thinking in the generation of new ideas. Basic Books, New York (1968)

De Bono, E.: The mechanism of mind. Simon & Schuster, New York (1969)

De Bono, E.: Lateral thinking - creativity step by step. Harper & Row, New York (1970)

Dewar, R.D., Dutton, J.E.: The adoption of radical and incremental innovations: an empirical analysis. Management Science 32(11), 1422–1433 (1986)

Donaldson, L.: The Contingency Theory of Organizations. Sage Publications, Thousand Oaks (2001)

Galegher, J., Kraut, R.E.: Computer-mediated communication for intellectual teamwork: An experiment in group writing. Information Systems Research 5(2), 110 (1994)

Hersey, P., Blanchard, K.H.: Life Cycle Theory Of Leadership. Training and Development Journal 23(5), 26–34 (1969)

Hersey, P., Blanchard, K.H.: So You Want to Know Your Leadership Style? Training and Development Journal 35(6), 34–54 (1981)

Hevner, A.R., March, S.T., Park, J., Ram, S.: Design Science In Information Systems Research. MIS Quarterly 28(1), 75–105 (2004)

Jakobsen, H.S., Rebsdorff, S.O.: Idéudvikling ved kreativ innovation. Gyldendal, Copenhagen (2003)

Kelley, T., Littman, J.: The Art of Innovation: Lessons in Creativity from IDEO, America's Leading Design Firm. Broadway Business (2001)

Kelley, T.: The ten faces of innovation. Currency/Doubleday, Random House (2005) ISBN 0-385-51207-4

Kendall, J.E., Kendall, K.E.: Metaphors and Methodologies: Living beyond the Systems Machine. MIS Quarterly 17(2), 149–171 (1993)

Kendall, J.E., Kendall, K.E.: Metaphors and their meaning for information systems development. European Journal of Information Systems 3(1), 37 (1994)

Pries-Heje, J., Tryde, S., Nielsen, A.-D.F.: Lær at implementere: Software procesforbedring der virker i praksis. Økonomistyring & Informatik 15(1) (1999)

Simon, H.A.: The Science of the Artificial, 3rd edn. MIT Press, Cambridge (1996)

Susman, G.I., Evered, R.D.: An Assessment of the Scientific Merits of Action Research. Administrative Science Quarterly 23(4), 582–603 (1978)

Weill, P., Ross, J.: IT Governance: How Top Performers Manage IT Decision Rights for Superior Results, 1st edn. Harvard Business Press, Boston (2004)

Van de Ven, A.H., Drazin, R.: The Concept of Fit in Contingency Theory. Research in Organizational Behaviour 7, 333–365 (1985)

Venable, J.: A Framework for Design Science Research Activities. In: Proceedings of the 2006 Information Resource Management Association Conference, Washington, DC, USA, pp. 184–187 (2006)

Zigurs, I., Buckland, B.: A Theory of Task/Technology Fit and Group Support System Effectiveness. MIS Quarterly 22(3), 313–334 (1998)

Zigurs, I., Buckland, B., Connolly, J.R., Wilson, E.V.: A test of Task/Technology Fit Theory for Group Support Systems. Database 30(3/4), 34–50 (1999)

Part II
Sustainability

Part II

Sustainability

Towards a Holistic Approach for Sustainable Partner Selection in the Electrics and Electronics Industry

David Wittstruck and Frank Teuteberg

Institute of Information Management and Corporate Governance,
Research Group in Accounting and Information Systems,
University of Osnabrueck, Katharinenstraße 1, 49069 Osnabrueck, Germany
Tel.: + 49 541 969-4523, + 49 541 969-4961
{david.wittstruck, frank.teuteberg}@uni-osnabrueck.de

Abstract. In recent years numerous publications in the field of Supply Chain Management have dealt with partner selection methods. So far, research has failed to offer a holistic approach for the selection of recycling partners that accounts for financial, social and environmental factors. In view of this fact, our ,;that supports recycling partner selection in the electrics and electronics industry. Based on a systematic literature review we identify limitations of existing approaches and design an integrated Fuzzy-AHP-TOPSIS model. In addition, relevant criteria for sustainable partner selection are determined. The approach is illustrated by means of an exemplary case study.

Keywords: Sustainable Supply Chain Management, Partner Selection, Supplier Selection, Recycling, AHP, Fuzzy, TOPSIS, Multi Criteria Decision Making.

1 Introduction

In view of the constantly increasing global volume of electronic waste more and more companies are joining recycling networks based on multilateral business-to-business contracts to ensure secure waste disposal on a mid-term or long-term basis. These networks are facing a variety of challenges, as e.g. a multitude of (new) legal environmental demands and regulations (WEEE, RoHS Directive) as well as norms and standards (Energy Star Computer Program), extended reporting and publishing requirements (Sustainability Index, EMAS) and a shortage of natural resources. On top of this come the growing public interest in environmental protection (Green Logistics) and the employers' obligation to treat their staff responsibly (e.g. Ethical Trading Initiative (ETI) and Supplier Ethical Data Exchange (SEDEX)) – for example, employees must be sufficiently protected from the impact of hazardous substances (PVC, chlorine-containing PCBs). Therefore, in order to achieve a balance between social and environmental goals on the one hand and the need for long-term profitability on the other hand, the management of recycling networks needs to draw on adequate methods, technologies, information and communication systems.

M. Nüttgens et al. (Eds.): Governance and Sustainability in IS, IFIP AICT 366, pp. 45–69, 2011.

In response to the general call for a more sustainable economy (cf. Carter and Rogers, 2008; Seuring and Müller, 2007) Sustainable Supply Chain Management (SSCM) extends the traditional concept of Supply Chain Management by adding environmental and social/ethical aspects.

This article aims at developing an integrated multi-criteria decision model (MCDM) that supports recycling partner selection in the electrics and electronics industry and takes financial, environmental and social dimensions into account.

2 Concept of Sustainable Supply Chain Management

SSCM is based on the adoption and extension of supply chain management concepts. According to Harland, supply chain management can be defined as "the management of a network of interconnected businesses involved in the ultimate provision of product and service packages required by end customers" (Harland, 1996). SSCM can be extended by the concept of sustainability, which encompasses social, environmental and economic aspects (Carter and Rogers, 2008). Shrivastava takes a more ecological rather than sociological view at sustainability, which he defines as "the potential for reducing long-term risks associated with resource depletion, fluctuations in energy costs, product liabilities, and pollution and waste management" (Shrivastava, 2007). In contrast, Sikdar takes a "macro-viewpoint" at sustainability that includes social, environmental and economic aspects. He calls sustainability "a wise balance among economic development, environmental stewardship, and social equity" (Sikdar, 2003).

In order to achieve a balance between environmental, social and economic dimensions (idea of the "triple bottom line" developed by Elkington, 2004) we decided to follow the definition of SSCM formulated by Carter and Rogers who describe it as the strategic achievement and integration of an organization's social, environmental, and economic goals through the systemic coordination of key inter-organizational business processes to improve the long-term economic performance of the individual company and its value network (Carter and Rogers, 2008).

Figure 1 illustrates the main components of SSCM, as well as the risks threatening it. The different dimensions of sustainability (environmental, economic and social performance of an organization) constitute three equally strong pillars that the building rests on, whereas risk and compliance management provide its foundation. The identification and mitigation of risks ensures long-term profitability. Laws, guidelines and standards serve as a basis for the implementation of SSCM throughout the supply chain.

Apart from that, SSCM includes values and ethics that need to be established in organizations. The concept also requires an efficient, flexible and "green" IT environment and the integration of the long-term goal of sustainable development into the corporate strategy. If these aspects are effectively combined, they can successfully protect the network against market, environmental and social threats and risks (cf. Figure 1).

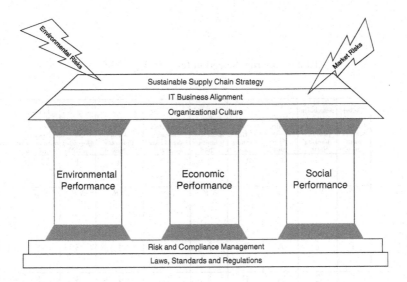

Fig. 1. House of SSCM (Wittstruck and Teuteberg 2010)

3 Method

The research method that this paper is based on can be characterized as design science research (Hevner et al., 2004) whereas the artefact developed in the following sections can be described as a holistic approach for sustainable partner selection in the electrics and electronics industry. The development of the model consists of the following phases:

3.1 Literature Review

A systematic literature review was conducted in order to determine the current state of research. The limitations of a systematic literature review lie in the paper selection process. However, we tried to minimize this risk by following a proven course of action for the creation of a literature review (Swanson, E.B., Ramiller, N.C. 1993, Webster, J. Watson, R., 2002). The restriction of the source material to high-quality articles leads to reliable results about the state of the art in SSCM research.

The search and the selection of the literature were carried out as follows: a systematic analysis of eleven high-quality journals was conducted. The oldest articles that were included date back to the year 1997. Table 1 shows the selected journals and how they have been evaluated in renowned international rankings. It becomes obvious from the table that only high-quality journals have been taken into account.

The following key words were used in order to achieve comprehensive search results: supply chain logistics, sustainability, green decision, multi objective, Analytical Hierarchy Process, Analytical Network Process, AHP, ANP, Fuzzy Logic,

Table 1. Journal Selection (cf. Harzing 2009)

	Cranfield University School of Management 2010	British Association of Business Schools (ABS) Ranking 2010	Wirt-schafts-universität Wien 2008	VHB Ranking 2008	Centre National de la Recherche Scientifique 2008	Australian Business Deans Council 2008	Aston University 2008	University of Queensland 2007	Erasmus Research Institute of Management Journals Listing 2006	WKWI 2008
Information Systems Research	4	4	A+	A+	1	A*	4	1	STAR	A
International Journal of Innovation and Sustainable Development	*N.R.*	*N.R.*	*N.R.*	C	*N.R.*	*N.R.*	*N.R.*	*N.R.*	*N.R.*	*N.R.*
Int. Journal of Logistics Management	3	2	A	D	3	B	1	3	S	*N.R.*
Int. J. of Physical Distribution & Logistics Management	3	2	A	B	4	C	1	3	S	*N.R.*
International Journal of Production Research	3	3	A	B	2	A	4	3	P	*N.R.*
Journal of Business Logistics	3	2	*N.R.*	B	*N.R.*	B	2	3	S	*N.R.*
Journal of Cleaner Production	*N.R.*	*N.R.*	*N.R.*	C	*N.R.*	*N.R.*	*N.R.*	*N.R.*	*N.R.*	*N.R.*
Logistics Research	*N.R.*	*N.R.*	*N.R.*	*N.R.*	*N.R.*	*N.R.*	*N.R.*	*N.R.*	*N.R.*	*N.R.*
MIS Quarterly	4	4	A+	A	1	A*	4	1	STAR	A
Naval Research Logistics	*N.R.*	3	A	B	3	B	*N.R.*	*N.R.*	S	*N.R.*
SCM: An International Journal	3	3	*N.R.*	C	4	A	3	4	S	*N.R.*
Rank Interpretation *N.R.*: Not ranked	4: World leading 3: Top international	4: Top journal 3: Highly regarded journal 2: Well regarded journal	A+: Top A: World-wide distributed	A+: Highest A...D E: Lowest	1*: Highest quality 1-3: Intermediate 4: Lowest quality	A*: Leading A: Highly regarded B: Well regarded C: Recognized	4: World leading 3: Internationally excellent 2: Recognized internationally	4: World leading 4: Lowest Quality 1: Highest quality 2-4: Intermediate 4: Lowest Quality	STAR: Top P: Best S: Recognized academic reputation	A: Top

Data Envelopment Analysis, Promethee, TOPSIS, Technique for Order Preference by Similarity to Ideal Solution, Operational Competitiveness Rating, OCRA, Stochastic Frontier Analysis, SFA, Free Disposable Hull, FDH, Cross Efficiency Analysis, Recycling, and Recycling Networks. The inclusion of many synonyms and/or semantically very similar expressions led to more exhaustive search results. Each identified article was checked for its relevance to the topic by reading the respective abstract and introduction. Subsequently, according to the framework of literature analysis the main approaches, criteria, trends and validation methods of partner selection were analyzed. To improve the quality of the analyses, both authors of this paper were involved in reviewing and coding the analyzed articles. The inter-rater reliability was good (inter-rater percentage agreement: > 92 % in all analyses).

3.2 Partner Selection

Because recycling companies can be both supplier (providing recycled materials for production) and customer (by purchasing used electronic devices) the term "partner selection" is preferred in this analysis to other known terms, e.g. 'supplier selection' or 'vendor 'selection' (Zarvić et al. 2010, Weber et al., 1991).

However, the selection of recycling partners focusing environmental, social and financial dimensions was not adequately tackled from the research community so far. In the section Development of a Partner Selection Method opportunities and limitations of these approaches regarding this topic are analyzed in order to develop an adequate holistic approach.

3.3 Identification of Partner Selection Criteria

First of all, existing partner selection criteria are identified on the basis of the systematic literature review. All criteria mentioned in the articles are extracted and tabulated. Table 3 also illustrates whether or not the criteria were validated in the research articles, and if yes, in what way.

3.4 Criteria Validation and Weighting

The criteria will be validated in the context of a survey among company representatives from recycling networks of the electrics and electronics industry. The experts will be asked whether the criteria mentioned in the literature seemed relevant to them. Also, they will be invited to name further criteria applied by their own or other companies. Subsequently, the participants will be asked to compare the criteria pairwise according to the AHP approach. A Fuzzy-AHP matrix will be generated on the basis of the participants' responses. Based on this matrix the criteria will be weighted by means of the software @Risk, resulting in an average relative weighting of the relevant criteria.

3.5 Design of the Study

The study is conducted by means of an online questionnaire and is carried out as follows:

Defining the Sample: Recycling networks of the German electrics and electronics industry will be selected to form the study sample. A special focus will be placed on products in the fields of entertainment electronics, telecommunication, computer hard-ware, medical technology or automotive IT. The reason for selecting these particular branches of production is that they cause particularly many ecological disturbances and, as a consequence, potential health problems. For example, some of the mentioned goods contain toxic substances and end up as e-waste on dumping grounds around the globe, e.g. in Asia or Africa, where they pollute the environment. Employees in production plants in China, Vietnam, Nigeria or India are not always sufficiently informed about the poisonous substances that they may be handling on a daily basis. Apart from these ecological considerations, the recycling of the above listed products (including disassembly, processing, separation, sorting of parts etc.) is almost as laborious as their production and causes the companies comparatively high costs (Walton, S.V. et al., 1998). In view of these problem complexes it becomes clear that the electrics and electronics industry is of special interest for researchers on SSCM, since it constitutes the primary target group for SSCM solutions.

Pre-Test: In February 2011, the questionnaire will be tested for comprehensibility in a pre-test with 10 participating business representatives.

Implementations: Between February and March 2011, experts will be invited to participate in the survey. These experts were mainly identified by searching the internet (search on "Xing" and "Linkedin"). A total of 3000 personal invitations to participate will be posted. We calculate a return rate of 3 %.

Analysis and Interpretation: An analysis phase will follow between March and April 2011. During this phase, the data will be consolidated evaluated by using AHP-Fuzzy-TOPSIS.

3.6 Model Validation

Implementation and Analysis: The individual steps from the Fuzzy AHP matrix and the weighted vectors to the final partner selection decision (by means of TOPSIS) are implemented in @Risk in order to test to what extent the model can be integrated into available standard software. For the selection of a recycling partner by means of the TOPSIS method, the data of ten electronic waste recycling companies will be stored in @Risk. The implementation of the model in @Risk is a first step to verify the usefulness of the approach for business practice. All data relevant for the evaluation of the criteria shall be retrieved by analyzing the recycling companies' websites.

Experiments: Experiments will be conducted in order to check whether the model influences the participants' decision making regarding sustainable partner selection.

4 Results from the Literature

At this point in time we have completed the third phase of our approach. The results gained on the basis of the systematic literature review are presented in the following section. In particular, the findings provide new insights regarding an adequate method for sustainable partner selection and relevant selection criteria.

4.1 Development of a Partner Selection Method

Important approaches for partner selection are summarized in Table 3. For our analysis, the following criteria were of particular interest:

- Approach: Which method was used?
- Focus on Sustainability: Does the article focus on financial, social and environmental issues?
- Industry Focus: What are the main results and topics?
- SCOR-Process: Which of the SCOR (Supply Chain Operations Reference Model) processes are considered?
- Purpose: What is the main objective?
- Findings: What are the findings?
- Major Limitations: What are major limitations?

Former research in the field of partner selection focused primarily on the "pre-stage" of the actual supply chain, that is, on direct suppliers (Ustun, O.; Demirtas, E.A., 2008); Kuoa, R. J.; Leeb, L. Y.; Huc, T.L., 2008); Kirytopoulos, K.; Leopoulos, V.; Mavrotas, G.; Voulgaridou, D., 2010). For the selection of recycling partners, however, this approach is insufficient because recycling companies can come into play both as a supplier and as a costumer the pre and post stage of the supply chain. For example, recycling companies can act as suppliers of recycled materials for the production of new goods or as buyers of electronic and other waste. Existing research works often focus on criteria like cost, time and quality (Zhu, Q.; Dou, Y.; Sarkis, J., 2010; Sarkis, J., 1998). Some authors also take environmental factors into account when discussing the issue of partner selection (Su, Y.; Jin, Z.; Yang, L., 2010; Sarkis, J., 1998; Sarmiento, R.; Thomas, A., 2010). However, a comprehensive view that integrates environmental, social and financial factors has been missing to date. Our study aims at filling this research gap.

Our Approach: Different methods for the weighting of criteria are suggested in the literature, the most popular ones being cost-utility analysis, quality function development and the AHP approach (Keeney, R.L.; Raiffa, H., 1993). Whereas quality function development is especially applied for the development of products

Table 2. Partner Selection Approaches

Approach	Authors, Year	Focus on Sustain ability	Industry Focus	SCOR-Process	Purpose	Findings	Major limitations
AHP	Sarmiento, R.; Thomas, A. (2010)	GreenSCM	No	Make	• The purpose of this paper is to discuss research gaps and the potential applications of analytic hierarchy process (AHP) in an internal benchmarking process used to identify improvement areas when firms attempt to adopt green initiatives with a supply chain perspective.	•The application of AHP to study the various themes mentioned above is not new. Nevertheless, no previous investigation has identified the limitations in those studies. Furthermore, previous paper has not proposed a multitier AHP approach to analyze the problems firms taking part in a supply chain might encounter when implementing green initiatives.	
	Liu, L.; Berger, P.; Zeng, A.; Gerstenfeld, A. (2008)	No	No	No	• The purpose of this paper is to show that there is a wealth of academic literature that qualitatively examines the outsourcing and offshoring from a go/no go perspective. The paper examines the complex "where to outsource" question by applying a quantitative approach called Analytic Hierarchy Process (AHP).	•The location selection decision is a component of the outsource supplier selection decision. •The AHP model effectively manages the complexity of the decision making process, incorporating all decision criteria harmoniously. •A method such as AHP, which is able to incorporate both qualitative and quantitative criteria into evaluations, would streamline the decision-making process. •The AHP process allows firms to look at a portfolio of choices and determine which firms are basically equal in qualifications.	•The interrelatio nship among criteria and the uncertainty of human decision making are not considered. •AHP supports a weighting of criteria/fact ors but gives only few hints how to find the supplier which meets these criteria best.
	Gaudenzi, B.; Borghesi, A. (2006)	No	No	Plan	•The aim of the research is to provide a method to evaluate supply chain risks that stand in the way of the supply chain objectives.	•The appreciation of the most critical supply chain risks comes from evaluations of the impacts and a consideration of the cause-effect relationships. The involvement of key managers is essential. In the case study the two most divergent evaluations were from the logistics manager and the sales manager.	
	Kahraman, C.; Cebeci, U.; Ulukan, Z. (2003)	No	White good manu-facturer	Make	•The aim of this paper is to use fuzzy analytic hierarchy process (AHP) to select the best supplier firm providing the most satisfaction for the criteria determined.	•The purchasing managers of a white good manufacturer established in Turkey were interviewed and the most important criteria taken into account by the managers while they were selecting their supplier firms were determined by a questionnaire. The fuzzy AHP was used to compare these supplier firms.	

Table 2. (*Continued*)

Approach	Authors, Year	Focus on Sustain ability	Industry Focus	SCOR- Process	Purpose	Findings	Major limitations
Fuzzy and AHP	Bottani, E.; Rizzi, A. (2005)	No	E- Procurement	Source	•The paper addresses the issues of how supplier selection criteria can be usefully adopted in real case applications to ponder and rank viable candidates.	•The hierarchy covers relevant issues related to e-procurement deployment •The framework seems adequate, since advanced MADM methods can be applied easily in order to rank potential candidates in terms of the "electronic transaction" criterion.	•The interrelation ships among criteria are not considered. •AHP supports a weighting of criteria/facto rs but gives only few hints how to find the supplier which meets these criteria best.
	Haq, A.N.; Kanaan, G. (2006)	No	Manu-facturing Company	Source	•This paper presents an integrated approach for supplier selection. •The approach is validated by a case study performed in an original equipment manufacturing company located in Southern India.	•A fuzzy analytical hierarchy process (FAHP) and genetic algorithms (GA) are presented and validated. •The approach supports decision making in built-to-order (BTO) supply chain environments.	
	Lu, L.Y.Y.; Wu, C.H.; Kuo, T.C. (2007)	GreenSCM	No	Source	•Developing a MODM-process for GreenSCM to help SC manager in measuring and evaluating suppliers' performance based on AHP decision-making method. •To reduce subjective bias in designing a weighting system, a fuzzy logic process is used to modify the AHP.	•This study presents a AHP and Fuzzy approach to enable managers to evaluate various projects and establish an environmentally benign product design.	
AHP, TOPSIS	Perçin, S. (2009)	No	No	Deliver	•The purpose of this paper is to provide a good insight into the use of a-two-phase AHP and TOPSIS approach that is a multi-criteria decision-making methodology in the evaluation of 3PL providers.	•This model provides decision makers with a simple, flexible, and easy-to-use approach to evaluate potential 3PL providers efficiently. Findings demonstrate that the proposed benchmarking framework, with minor modifications, can be useful to all firms in their 3PL provider selection decisions.	•The interrelation ship among criteria and the uncertainty of human decision making are not considered.

Table 2. (*Continued*)

Approach	Authors, Year	Focus on Sustai-nability	Industry Focus	SCOR-Process	Purpose	Findings	Major limitations
ANP	Bayazit, O. (2006)	No	No	Source	•The purpose of this paper is to provide a good insight into the use of analytic network process (ANP) in evaluating supplier selection problems.	•It is shown that ANP can be used as a decision analysis tool to solve multi-criteria supplier selection problems that contain interdependencies. •ANP is a complex methodology and requires more comparisons than the traditional AHP and it increases the effort.	•The uncertainty of human being decision making is not considered. •It is very time-consuming to use this complex approach in business practice.
	Kirytopoulos, K.; Leopoulos, V.; Mavrotas, G.; Voulgaridou, D. (2010)	No	No	Source	•The purpose of this paper is to provide a meta-model for supplier evaluation and order quantity allocation, based on a MCDM method, namely the Analytic Network Process (ANP) and a multiobjective mathematical programming method (MOMP), the AUGMECON.	•The proposed meta-model constitutes an efficient method that enables managers to actively participate in the decision making process and exploit the "qualitative value" of their suppliers, while minimizing the costs and the mean delivery times. In addition, it is proved to be suitable for the enterprise clusters, as it adapts a multiple sourcing strategy and enhances the partnership among the members.	
	Zhu, Q.; Dou, Y.; Sarkis, J.(2010)	Environmental	No	Source	•The purpose of this paper is to present the development of a methodology to evaluate suppliers using portfolio analysis based on the analytical network process (ANP) and environmental factors.	•The technique is useful and versatile. The paper clearly discerns various characteristics of the suppliers and produced recommendations on supplier management for an exemplary case scenario.	
	Sarkis, J. (1998)	Environmental	No	No	•This paper integrates these elements and their attributes into a strategic assessment and decision tool using the systems with feedback or analytical network process (ANP) technique first introduced by Saaty.	•The ANP technique, which has been sparingly investigated by researchers or applied by practitioners, is useful for modeling dynamic strategies systemic influences on managerial decisions.	

Table 2. (*Continued*)

Approach	Authors, Year	Focus on Sustainability	Industry Focus	SCOR-Process	Purpose	Findings	Major limitations
	Ustun, O.; Demirtas, E.A. (2008)	No	Plastic Molding Firms	Source	•The purpose of this paper is to choose the best suppliers. •Defining the optimum quantities among selected suppliers to maximize the total value of purchasing (TVP), and to minimize the total cost and total defect rate.	•The quality of final solutions obtained by ε-constraint, preemptive goal programming (PGP) and reservation level driven Tchebycheff procedure (RLTP) methods is compared by using an additive utility function. RLTP is better than the others according. •It is also possible to adapt this multi-period MOMILP model to multi-product case. This integrated approach can be improved to reflect decision maker's preferences with more accuracy.	
Fuzzy and DEA; Fuzzy and AHP	Kuoa, R. J.; Leeb, L. Y.; Huc, T.L. (2008)	No	Automotive	Source	•This study intends to develop a novel performance evaluation method, which integrates both fuzzy analytical hierarchy process (AHP) method and fuzzy data envelopment analysis (DEA) for assisting organizations to make the supplier selection decision.	•A Case study on an internationally well-known auto lighting OEM company shows that the proposed method is very suitable for practical applications.	•The interrelation ship among criteria and the uncertainty of human decision making are not considered.

and services, cost utility analysis has the disadvantage of not including the pairwise comparison of criteria. Instead, it is merely checked that the addition of all weighting factors does not result in a percentage higher than 100%. Therefore, in this paper the AHP approach is used as a basis for the recording and weighting of the criteria. The Analytic Hierarchy Process makes it possible to create a hierarchical structure for a multicriterial decision problem and to aggregate it at the different levels, but on the other hand it neglects the uncertainty and imprecision of human thought. The Fuzzy Set Theory is applied to overcome this limitation, for fuzzy logic can be used to describe fuzzy quantities. Hence, a combination of both approaches seems promising. Subsequently, the TOPSIS method can be applied to find out which alternatives best fulfill the identified criteria; i.e. TOPSIS is used to compare and rank recycling partners and their criteria values. This happens by means of a relative efficiency analysis in which two virtual alternatives are defined: the overall best and the overall worst one. The characteristics of the potential partners need to be compared to these alternatives (Mahmoodzadeh et. al. 2010).

In summary, this article differs from similar works in several ways: an integrated Fuzzy-AHP-TOPSIS approach is taken, all dimensions of sustainability are considered for the selection of partners, the criteria are systematically derived and empirically validated, the focus is on recycling networks of the electrics and electronics industry and the model is evaluated on the basis of an exemplary implementation and experiments.

4.2 Partner Selection Criteria

In the context of our literature review we identified 35 articles in which partner selection criteria were analyzed. Table 4 provides an overview of these criteria. The number of proposed criteria per publication varies between 4 and 18, with an average number of 9 criteria. The criteria were mostly derived from literature and not always validated by experts from professional practice. It becomes immediately obvious that quality and delivery criteria are by far the most frequently proposed ones. Out of these, process quality (23 occurrences), delivery time (22 occurrences) and product quality (19 occurrences) (Webber et al., 1991; Bos-Brouwers, 2010; Choy, Lee, 2003) received the most mentions. Financial criteria like price (18 occurrences) and financial capability (12 occurrences) were also very frequently mentioned (Ordoobadi, 2009; Kwong et al., 2000; Chan et al., 2008). IT and risk criteria received a medium number of mentions (Petroni, A. et al., 2000; Sarkis, J. et al., 2002) whereas social and environmental criteria were only rarely referred to. The know-how and the working conditions of the employees were mentioned as social criteria. Repeatedly suggested environmental criteria were the use of environmental management systems (EMAS) and the type of product packaging (Sarkis, J. et al., 2002; Simpson, M.P. et al., 2002).

Table 3. Review on Partner Selection Criteria

Main Criteria: **Social** — Sub-criteria and sum of mentioned criteria:
Working Conditions/Culture (6), Job Satisfaction (1), Workplace Safety (1), Code-of-Conduct (1), Stake-holder Communication (2), Health and Safety Standards (1), Education/Know-how (6).

Author	Domain	proposed Criteria	Validation of Criteria	Working Conditions/Culture	Job Satisfaction	Workplace Safety	Code-of-Conduct	Stake-holder Communication	Health and Safety Standards	Education/Know-how
Lu et al. (2007)	Supplier Selection	5	500 Companies							
Bayazit (2006)	Vendor Selection	8	No							
Ustun et al. (2008)	Supplier Selection	4	Interviews							
Kang et al. (2010)	Supplier Selection	4	8 Experts from universities and companies	1						
Wittstruck, Teuteberg (2011)	Recycling Networks	5	117 Companies of Electronic Industry	1						1
Dickson (1966)	Vendor Selection	11	Literature Review		1	1	1	1	1	
Webber et al. (1991)	Supplier Selection	10	Literature Review: 74 research arctiles							
Bos-Brouwers (2010)	SMEs	12	Semi-structured interviews							
Choy, Lee (2003)	Supplier Selection	9	Literature Review	1						1
Zhu et al. (2010)	Supplier Selection	10	Literature Review							
Ting, Cho (2008)	Supplier Selection	11	Literature Review	1						1
Ordoobadi (2009)	Supplier Selection	10	Literature Review							
Kwong et al. (2001)	Supplier Selection	7	Literature Review							
Chan et al. (2008)	Supplier Selection	18	Literature Review							
Sridhar (2010)	Supplier Selection	16	Literature Review							
Bevilacqua, Petroni (2002)	Supplier Selection	9	Literature Review	1						1
Bottani, Rizzi (2005)	Supplier Selection	6	Literature Review							
Towersa; Song (2010)	Supplier Selection	13	Literature Review							
Akarte et al. (2007)	Producer Selection	9	Literature Review							
Jain, V. et al. (2004)	Supplier Selection	6	Literature Review							
Li, S. et al (2002)	Supplier Selection	5	Empirical Study							
Craig, M. et al. (1997)	Supplier Selection	7	Literature Review							
Walton, S.V. et al. 1998	Supplier Selection	10	10 Experts							
Vonderembse, M. (1999)	Supplier Selection	4	Empirical Study							
Petroni, A. et al. (2000)	Supplier Selection	6	Empirical Study							
Sarkis, J. et al. (2002)	Supplier Selection	21	Literature Review	1				1		
Simpson, M.P. et al. (2002)	Supplier Selection	15	Exploratory Study							
Kannan, V.R. et al. (2002)	Supplier Selection	8	Empirical Study							
Muralidharan, C. (2002)	Supplier Selection	12	Literature Review							
Sharland, A. (2003)	Supplier Selection	5	Empirical Study							
Kim, D.Y. et al. (2010)	Supply Chain Partner	5	Literature Review							1
Dogan, I.; Sahin, U. (2003)	Supplier Selection	5	Literature Review							
Sun, S.Y. et al. (2009)	Supplier Selection	10	Empirical Study							1
Chan, Chan (2004)	Supplier Selection	5	Literature Review and Interviews							

Table 3. (*Continued*)

	Criterion		Lu et al. (2007)	Bayazit (2006)	Ustun et al. (2008)	Kang et al. (2010)	Wittstruck, Teuteberg (2011)	Dickson (1966)	Webber et al. (1991)	Bos-Brouwers (2010)	Choy, Lee (2003)	Zhu et al. (2010)	Ting, Cho (2008)	Ordoobadi (2009)	Kwong et al. (2001)	Chan et al. (2008)	Sridhar (2010)	Bevilacqua, Petroni (2002)	Bottani, Rizzi (2005)	Towersa; Song (2010)	Akarte et al. (2007)	Jain, V. et al (2004)	Li, S. et al (2002)	Craig, M. et al. (1997)	Walton, S.V. et al. 1998	Vondereuhse, M. (1999)	Petroni, A. et al. (2000)	Sarkis, J. et al. (2002)	Simpson, M.P. et al. (2002)	Kannan, V.R. et al. (2002)	Muralidharan, C. (2002)	Sharland, A. (2003)	Kim, D.Y. et al. (2010)	Dogan, I.; Sahin, U. (2003)	Sun, S.Y. et al. (2009)	Chan, Chan (2004)
Environmental	Materials Used	5	1				1			1	1													1												
	Energy Consumpt.	4	1							1	1													1												
	Solid residues	3	1							1														1												
	Liquid residues	3	1							1														1												
	Recycling processes	2								1														1												
	carbon balance	3	1							1														1												
	Residues	1																						1												
	Environm. Mgmt. Systems and Certific.	5											1							1				1									1	1		
	Green Image	2					1																	1												
	Geographical Location	7										1	1		1	1	1	1						1												
	Packaging ability	5										1	1	1										1				1								
Financial	Price	18		1						1	1	1	1	1	1	1					1	1	1						1	1	1		1	1	1	1
	Top Mgmt. Capability	11		1						1	1	1	1	1	1														1	1	1		1			
	Manufacturing Capabilities	12									1		1		1						1	1	1						1	1			1	1	1	1
	Personnel Capabilities	3		1											1																	1				
	Financial Capability	12		1			1					1	1	1	1	1	1	1											1				1	1		
	Market Share	3		1												1								1												
Risks	Customer Complaints	3			1																							1						1		
	Process Assurance	5								1			1							1													1	1		

Table 3. (*Continued*)

	Author	Lu et al. (2007)	Bayazit (2006)	Ustun et al. (2008)	Kang et al. (2010)	Wittstruck, Teuteberg (2011)	Dickson (1966)	Webber et al. (1991)	Bos-Brouwers (2010)	Choy, Lee (2003)	Zhu et al. (2010)	Ting, Cho (2008)	Ordoobadi (2009)	Kwong et al. (2001)	Chan et al. (2008)	Sridhar (2010)	Bevilacqua, Petroni (2002)	Bottani, Rizzi (2005)	Towersa; Song (2010)	Akarte et al. (2007)	Jain, V. et al. (2004)	Li, S. et al (2002)	Craig, M. et al. (1997)	Walton, S.V. et al. 1998	Vonderembse, M. (1999)	Petroni, A. et al. (2000)	Sarkis, J. et al. (2002)	Simpson, M.P. et al. (2002)	Kannan, V.R. et al. (2002)	Muralidharan, C. (2002)	Sharfaud, A. (2003)	Kim, D.Y. et al. (2010)	Dogan, I.; Sahin, U. (2003)	Sun, S.Y. et al. (2009)	Chan, Chan (2004)
Political Stability and Exchange Rates	2													1	1																				
Delivery Delay	10											1	1		1			1	1		1	1		1	1								1		
Warranties	6						1					1	1		1		1							1											
Product Innovation	9						1										1	1	1		1			1	1									1	1
Product Quality	19			1		1	1				1		1	1	1	1	1	1	1			1	1	1			1	1		1		1	1		
Process Quality	23			1				1	1	1	1	1	1	1	1	1	1	1	1		1			1			1	1		1	1		1	1	1
Process Innovation and Flexibility	16		1	1							1	1			1		1	1	1		1			1	1					1		1	1		1
Process Capability	7		1	1		1	1								1		1							1											
Geometric Capability	1																1																		
Customer Service / Responsiveness	17									1		1	1	1	1	1	1		1	1				1	1	1	1		1		1		1		
Delivery Time	22		1	1			1		1		1		1	1	1		1	1	1	1		1	1	1	1	1	1	1		1		1	1	1	
General Image	2						1								1																				
IT, Interfaces, Communication Systems	10				1	1								1	1		1							1			1	1	1			1			
Software	3																		1								1					1			
IT - Capability	15					1	1			1				1	1	1	1			1			1	1	1		1		1		1			
Economies of Scale	4			1								1	1																						
Delivery Costs	6											1			1		1							1	1										
Production Costs	5											1			1		1							1											
Cost structure	8											1		1	1		1		1					1											1

In view of all this, which criteria seem to be the most significant ones for the selection of recycling partners? According to the triple bottom line concept, the criteria should cover financial, environmental and social factors. Also, we want to account for the special characteristics of recycling companies. In accordance with the authors of the analyzed articles (as e. g. Ordoobadi, 2009; Kwong et al., 2000; Chan et al., 2008) we define price and financial capabilities as important criteria. In the context of this study, a recycling company's financial capability is regarded as a critical factor for its long-term capability to survive. In turn, the recycler's long-term survival is of high significance because electronic products often have a lifespan of several years, which means that cooperative relationships in the field of recycling must necessarily be long-term. Hence, we suggest the following selection critiera:

- Price
- Financial Capability

The main purpose of cooperating with a recycling company is to ensure the proper disposal of production materials and electronic waste. If required, the recycling company should be capable of recycling or disposing of large quantities of material and complex products (Dogan et al., 2003; Sun, et al., 2009). Hence, we suggest the following selection critiera:

- Recycling Capability
- Quality of Recycling Processes

Also, compliance with laws, guidelines and standards regarding the recycling and disposal of waste (WEEE, EuroStar etc.) constitutes a particular challenge for recycling companies because all these directives have a direct impact on their core business. Environmental Management Systems support the holistic management of environmental laws, guidelines and standards (Simpson et al., 2002; Kannan, et al., 2002). Thus, we suggest another selection criterion:

- Effective Implementation of Environmental Management Systems

Some of our electronic waste ends up at dumping grounds in Africa or in the Far East where health and safety measures are far less strict. If an international recycling company succeeds in communicating that it adheres to equally high safety standards for employees handling electronic waste at each of its locations, this can be a decisive competitive advantage (Bos-Brouwers, 2010). This correlation can be captured by means of the following criteria:

- Standardized Health and Safety Conditions
- Sustainable Image

It must also be pointed out that recycling partners only receive their raw materials after they have been used by the customer. This temporal delay results in the need for especially careful coordination and planning way before the actual utilization of the recycling service. The producer and the recycler need to exchange particularly detailed information regarding the exact composition of the product to be recycled. Such an exchange of information enables recyclers to prepare for the specific recycling methods that new products may require. It is therefore very important to provide configurable IT interfaces that enable the exchange of information (Chan et al., 2008; Sridhar, 2010). As a result, we define another selection criterion:

- Efficient IT-Interfaces

Furthermore, recycling companies are often positioned at a pre-stage of the supply chain. They provide processed materials for further production and also act as consultants to producers regarding sustainable production methods and eco-friendly product composition (Ordoobadi, 2009; Sridhar, 2010; Bevilacqua, Petroni, 2002). Therefore, we add the following criterion to our catalogue:

- Know-how in Electronic Materials and Manufacturing Processes

All in all, we have suggested nine criteria, which correspond to the average number of criteria mentioned in related research articles. In business practice, these criteria could be used as a starting point for the solution of sustainable partner selection problems.

5 An Exemplary Case Study

At the current phase of our research project we are preparing an empirical study in order to validate our approach. However, we will illustrate our approach by means of an exemplary case study based on fictive data. We assume a decision maker who wants to evaluate three recycling partners by means of the Fuzzy-AHP-TOPSIS approach. The procedure can be summarized as follows (Saaty, 1980; Mahmoodzadeh et al., 2007):

1. *Formulating hierarchy:* The hierarchy is structured into different levels: the goal, the criteria and the alternatives level. The goal of our study is to select the most adequate partner. On the criteria level we model the selection criteria presented in the chapter on Partner Selection Criteria. Finally, on the alternatives level we model three alternative recycling companies. The hierarchy of our case study is presented in Figure 2.

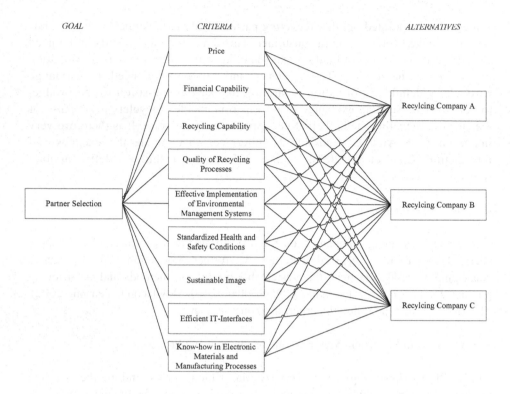

Fig. 2. Decision Hierarchy

2. Modeling Fuzzy Importance: A fuzzy set is a class of objects with a continuum of grades of membership. Such a set is characterized by a membership function, which assigns a grade of membership to each object that ranges between zero and one (Mahmoodzadeh et al., 2007). A triangular fuzzy number obtains three parameters that characterize the smallest possible value, the most promising value and the largest possible value. Table 4 provides an overview of the linguistic scale and the triangular fuzzy numbers assumed in this case study.

Table 4. Linguistic Scale

Linguistic Scale	Triangular Fuzzy Number
Absolutely more important	(5/2,3,7/2)
Very strongly more important	(2,5/2,3)
Strongly more important	(3/2,2,5/2)
Weakly more important	(1,3/2,2)
Equally important	(1/2,1,3/2)
Just equal	(1,1,1)

Figure 3 shows a Triangular Fuzzy Function μ(p). For instance, the linguistic scale "strongly more important" is determined by p1= 3/2, p2=2 and p3=5/2.

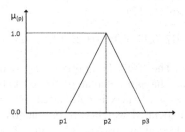

Fig. 3. Triangular Fuzzy Function

3. *Creating an Evaluation Matrix:* AHP uses pairwise comparisons to weight and rate the criteria. In our example the decision maker compares nine criteria with each other. Table 6 shows the exemplary evaluation matrix.

Table 5. Evaluation Matrix

	Price	Fin. Capability	Recycling Capability	Quality of Recycling Processes	Effective Impl. of EMIS	Standardized H&SC	Sustainable Image	Eff. IT Interfaces	EMMP Know-how
Price	1	(1,3/2,2)	(1/2,2/5,1/3)	(1,3/2,2)	(1,3/2,2)	(1/2,1,3/2)	(1/2,1,3/2)	(3/2,2,5/2)	(1,3/2,2)
Financial Capability		1	(1,2/3,1/2)	(1/2,2/5,1/3)	(1,3/2,2)	(1,3/2,2)	(2,5/2,3)	(1/2,1,3/2)	(1,3/2,2)
Recycling Capability			1	(1/2,2/5,1/3)	(2,5/2,3)	(1,3/2,2)	(1,3/2,2)	(2,5/2,3)	(1,3/2,2)
Quality of Recycling Processes				1	(5/2,3,7/2)	(2,5/2,3)	(5/2,3,7/2)	(1/2,1,3/2)	(1/2,2/5,1/3)
Effective Implementation of EMS					1	(1,3/2,2)	(1/2,1,3/2)	(1,3/2,2)	(1/2,1,3/2)
Standardized H&SC						(1,2/3,1/2)	(5/2,3,7/2)	(1,3/2,2)	(3/2,2,5/2)
Sustainable Image							1	(2,5/2,3)	(1/2,1,3/2)
Efficient IT Interfaces								1	(2,5/2,3)
Know-how in EMMP									1

4. *Calculating Normalized Weighting Factors:* The normalized weighting factor reflects the relative importance of the partner selection criteria. It can be concluded from the following normalized weighting factor W that "price" (0.21) is the most important selection criterion, followed by "quality of recycling processes" (0.13) and "efficient IT interfaces" (0.12):

$$W = \{0.21, 0.13, 0.08, 0.07, 0.17, 0.14, 0.02, 0.12, 0.05\}$$

5. *Evaluating Alternatives:* The TOPSIS approach is used to identify the optimal partner. To this end, after having calculated the normalized decision matrix, the weighted normalized decision matrix is calculated by multiplying the normalized decision matrix by its associated weights. Subsequently, the separation measures are calculated using the Euclidean distance (Mahmoodzadeh et al., 2007). Finally, the relative closeness to the ideal solution is calculated and a ranking of the three alternative companies is derived. As you can see from Table 6 Recycling Company B achieves the best score.

Table 6. Final Ranking of Recycling Partner

Partner	Score
Recycling Company A	0.2156
Recycling Company B	0.7321
Recycling Company C	0.0103

6 Conclusion

6.1 Implications

Due to the increasing number of electric devices being produced, the recycling of these materials will become more and more important. Thus, the selection of recycling partners with a view to environmental and social issues will become a significant topic for supply chain managers. The approach proposed in this paper considers the complexity of the supplier selection problem and includes financial, environmental and social dimensions. The model is intuitive and can be easily computerized. The results indicate that the Fuzzy-AHP-TOPSIS approach can be used as a decision making instrument for supply chain managers who need to select recycling partners. Both tangible and intangible factors can be incorporated into the model. In addition, assessment bias in pairwise comparison is reduced by combining AHP with fuzzy logic.

However, there are limitations to the approach. For instance, interrelationships among factors are not considered. If there are feedbacks and interdependencies among the factors, an unimportant factor may turn out to be far more important than even the most important one. The interdependencies that play a role in real-life partner selection problems are not captured in our study. Furthermore, the so-called Rank Reversal Problem has been pointed out by critics (Macharis et al., 2004). The term denotes that a ranking which is based on a comprehensive evaluation can be completely reversed by adding another alternative. For example, if criterion A is ranked higher than criterion B, the addition of a third criterion C might change the ranking to C>B>A. It is disputable whether there is an inherent logic to this phenomenon.

6.2 Further Research

Several research questions are still open at this stage: What do decision makers think of the suggested criteria? Will they consider them relevant? In what way does the holistic approach influence the decision making process?

These questions are will be part of our further research. As a next step we will verify the proposed criteria by interviewing experts from business practice. To this end an online questionnaire will be created. Subsequently, the approach will be implemented in @Risk in order to provide a software tool for sustainable partner selection. The instrument will then be tested by means of experiments which will also serve to investigate to what degree the approach influences the participants' decisions regarding sustainable partner selection. All these steps are currently in preparation.

Acknowledgement. The authors are indebted to Ms Anja Grube and the anonymous reviewers for fruitful discussions and substantive comments relating to this paper.

This research is funded by the European Regional Development Fund (ERDF). The authors are pleased to acknowledge the support by ERDF and all involved project partners.

References

Akarte, M.M., Ravi, B.: Casting product–process–producer compatibility evaluation and improvement. International Journal of Production Research 45(21), 4917–4936 (2007)

Bayazit, O.: Use of analytic network process in vendor selection decisions; Benchmarking. An International Journal 13(5), 556–579 (2006)

Bevilacqua, M., Petroni, A.: From Traditional Purchasing to Supplier Management. A Fuzzy Logic-based Approach to Supplier Selection. International Journal of Logistics Research and Applications. A Leading Journal of Supply Chain Management 5(3), 235–255 (2002)

Bos-Brouwers, H.E.J.: Corporate sustainability and innovation in SMEs. evidence of themes and activities in practice. Business Strategy and the Environment 19(7), 417–435 (2010)

Bottani, E., Rizzi, A.: A fuzzy multi-attribute framework for supplier selection in an e-procurement environment. International Journal of Logistics Research and Applications. A Leading Journal of Supply Chain Management 8(3), 249–266 (2005)

Chan, F.T.S., Chan, H.K.: Development of the supplier selection model¬ a case study in the advanced technology industry. Proceedings of the Institution of Mechanical Engineers - Part B - Engineering Manufacture 21(8), 1807–1824 (2004)

Chan, F.T.S., Kumar, N., Tiwari, M.K., Lau, H.C.W., Choy, K.L.: Global supplier selection. a fuzzy-AHP - approach. International Journal of Production Research 46(14), 3825–3857 (2008)

Carter, C., Rogers, D.: A framework of sustainable supply chain management: moving toward new theory. International Journal of Physical Distribution and Logistics Management 38(5), 56–68 (2008)

Choi, T.Y., Hartley, J.L.: An exploration of supplier selection practices across the supply chain. Journal of Operations Management 14(4), 333–343 (1996)

Chou, S., Shen, C., Chang, Y.: Vendor selection in a modified re-buy situation using a strategy-aligned fuzzy approach. International Journal of Production Research 45(14), 3113–3133 (2007)

Choy, K., Lee, W.: A generic supplier management tool for outsourcing manufacturing. Supply Chain Management. An International Journal 8(2), 140–154 (2003)

Dibbern, J., Goles, T., Hirschheim, R., Jayatilaka, B.: Information systems outsourcing: a survey and analysis of the literature. The DATA BASE for Advances in Information Systems 35(4), 6–102 (2004)

Dickson, G.W.: An analysis of vendor selection systems and decisions. Journal of Purchasing 2(8), 5–17 (1966)

Dogan, I., Sahin, U.: Supplier selection using activity-based costing and fuzzy present-worth techniques. Logistics Information Management 16(6), 420–426 (2003)

Elkington, J.: Enter the triple bottom line. In The Triple Bottom Line: Does It All Add up? In: Henriques, A., Richardson, J. (eds.) Earthscan, London, pp. 1–16 (2004)

Gaudenzi, B., Borghesi, A.: Managing risks in the supply chain using the AHP method. International Journal of Logistics Management 17(1), 114–136 (2006)

Gustin, C.M., Daugherty, P.J., Ellinger, A.E.: Supplier Selection Decisions In Systems/Software Purchases. The Journal of Supply Chain Management 33(4), 41–46 (1997)

Harland, C.M.: Supply chain management: relationships, chains and networks. British Journal of Management 7(1), 63–80 (1996)

Harzing, A.W.: Journal quality list, 34th edn. (2009), http://www.harzing.com (accessed January 30, 2011)

Haq, A.N., Kannan, G.: Design of an integrated supplier selection and multi-echelon distribution inventory model in a built-to-order supply chain environment. International Journal of Production Research 44(10), 1963–1985 (2006)

Hevner, A.R., March, S.T., Park, J., Ram, S.: Design Science in Information Systems Research. MIS Quarterly 28(1), 75–105 (2004)

Jain, V., Tiwari, M., Chan, F.: Evaluation of the supplier performance using an evolutionary fuzzy-based approach. Journal of Manufacturing Technology Management 15(8), 735–744 (2004)

Jain, V., Wadhwa, S., Deshmukh, S.G.: Supplier selection using fuzzy association rules mining approach. International Journal of Production Research 45(6), 1323–1353 (2007)

Javalgi, R.G., Jain, H.K.: Integrating multiple criteria decision making models into the decision support system framework for marketing decisions. Naval Research Logistics 35(6), 575–596 (1988)

Kahraman, C., Cebeci, U., Ulukan, Z.: Multi-criteria supplier selection using fuzzy AHP. Logistics Information Management 16(6), 382–394 (2003)

Kang, H.Y., Lee, A.H.I., Yang, C.Y.: A fuzzy ANP model for supplier selection as applied to IC packaging. Journal of Intelligent Manufacturing 21(1), 1–12 (2010)

Kannan, V.R., Tan, K.C.: Supplier Selection and Assessment. Their Impact on Business Performance. The Journal of Supply Chain Management 38(4), 11–21 (2002)

Keeney, R.L., Raiffa, H.: Decisions with Multiple Objectives; Preferences and Value Tradeoffs. Cambridge University Press, Cambridge (1993)

Kim, D., Kumar, V.K.A.U.: Performance assessment framework for supply chain partnership. Supply Chain Management. An International Journal 15(3), 187–195 (2010)

Kirytopoulos, K., Leopoulos, V., Mavrotas, G., Voulgaridou, D.: Multiple sourcing strategies and order allocation. an ANP-AUGMECON meta-model. Supply Chain Management. An International Journal 15(4), 263–276 (2010)

Kuoa, R.J., Leeb, L.Y., Huc, T.-L.: Developing a supplier selection system through integrating fuzzy AHP and fuzzy DEA - a case study on an auto lighting System Company in Taiwan. Production Planning & Control 21(3), 468–484 (2008)

Kwong, C.K., Ip, W., Chan, J.: Combining scoring method and fuzzy expert systems approach to supplier assessment - a case study. Integrated Manufacturing Systems 13(7), 512–519 (2002)

Lee, A.H.I.: A fuzzy AHP - evaluation model for buyer–supplier relationships with the consideration of benefits, opportunities, costs and risks. International Journal of Production Research 47(15), 4255–4280 (2009)

Li, S., Madhok, A., Plaschka, G., Verma, R.: Supplier-Switching Inertia and Competitive Asymmetry. A Demand-Side Perspective. Decision Sciences 37(4), 547–576 (2006)

Liu, L., Berger, P., Zeng, A., Gerstenfeld, A.: Applying the analytic hierarchy process to the offshore outsourcing location decision. Supply Chain Management. An International Journal 13(6), 435–449 (2008)

Lu, L.Y.Y., Wu, C.H., Kuo, T.C.: Environmental principles applicable to green supplier evaluation by using multi-objective decision analysis. International Journal of Production Research 45(18-19), 4317–4331 (2007)

Macharis, C., Springael, J., De Brucker, K., Verbeke, A.: PROMETHEE and AHP. The design of operational synergies in multi-criteria analysis. Strengthening PROMETHEE with ideas of AHP. European Journal of Operational Research 153(2), 307–317 (2004)

Muralidharan, C., Anantharaman, N., Deshmukh, S.: A Multi-Criteria Group Decisionmaking Model for Supplier Rating. The Journal of Supply Chain Management 38(4), 22–33 (2002)

Nassimbeni, G., Battain, F.: Evaluation of supplier contribution to product development. Fuzzy and neuro-fuzzy based approaches. International Journal of Production Research 41(13), 2933–2956 (2003)

Ordoobadi, S.: Application of Taguchi loss functions for supplier selection. Supply Chain Management. An International Journal 14(1), 22–30 (2009)

Pagell, M., Wu, Z.: Building an more complete Theory of Sustainable Supply Chain Management Using Case Studies of 10 Exemplars. Journal of Supply Chain Management 45(2), 37–56 (2009)

Park, D., Krishnan, H.A.: Understanding supplier selection practices. Differences between U.S. and Korean executives. Thunderbird International Business Review 43(2), 243–256 (2001)

Perçin, S.: Evaluation of third-party logistics 3PL providers by using a two-phase AHP and TOPSIS methodology. Benchmarking. An International Journal 16(5), 588–604 (2009)

Petroni, A., Braglia, M.: Vendor Selection Using Principal Component Analysis. The Journal of Supply Chain Management 36(2), 63–69 (2000)

Pochampally, K.K., Gupta, S.M.: Reverse Supply Chain Design. A Neural Network Approach. In: Wang, H.-F., Hua, T. (eds.) Web-Based Green Products Life Cycle Management Systems. Reverse Supply Chain Utilization, pp. 283–300 (2009)

Ramanathan, R.: Supplier selection problem. integrating DEA with the approaches of total cost of ownership and AHP. Supply Chain Management. An International Journal 12(4), 258–261 (2007)

Saaty, T.L.: The analytic hierarchy process. McGraw-Hill, New York (1980)

Sarkis, J.: Evaluating environmentally conscious business practices. European Journal of Operational Research 107(1), 159–174 (1998)

Sarkis, J., Talluri, S.: A Model for Strategic Supplier Selection. The Journal of Supply Chain Management 38(1), 18–28 (2002)

Sarmiento, R., Thomas, A.: Identifying improvement areas when implementing green initiatives using a multitier AHP approach. Benchmarking. An International Journal 17(3), 452–463 (2010)

Sharland, A., Eltantawy, R.A., Giunipero, L.C.: The Impact of Cycle Time on Supplier Selection and Subsequent Performance Outcomes. The Journal of Supply Chain Management 39(3), 4–12 (2003)

Shrivastava, S.K.: Green supply-chain management: a state-of-the-art literature review. International Journal of Management Reviews 9(1), 53–80 (2007)

Sikdar, S.K.: Sustainable development and sustainability metrics. AIChE Journal 49(8), 1928–1932 (2003)

Simpson, P.M., Siguaw, J.A., White, S.C.: Measuring the Performance of Suppliers. An Analysis of Evaluation Processes. The Journal of Supply Chain Management 38(1), 29–41 (2002)

Sridhar, C.N.V., Vijayakumar Reddy, K., Venugopal, R.V.: Investigations on Supplier Selection for e-Manufacturing. A Case study. International Journal of Business Insights and Transformation 3(2), 63–77 (2010)

Su, Y., Jin, Z., Yang, L.: System Dynamics Modeling for Strategic Management of Green Supply Chain. In: Hunter, M.G. (ed.) Strategic Information Systems. Concepts, Methodologies, Tools, and Applications, pp. 2617–2649 (2010)

Sun, S., Hsu, M., Hwang, W.: The impact of alignment between supply chain strategy and environmental uncertainty on SCM performance. Supply Chain Management. An International Journal 14(3), 201–212 (2009)

Swanson, E.B., Ramiller, N.C.: Information systems thematics: submissions to a new journal. Information Systems Research 4(4), 299–330 (1993)

Ting, S., Cho, D.I.: An integrated approach for supplier selection and purchasing decisions. Supply Chain Management. An International Journal 13(2), 116–127 (2008)

Torabi, S.A., Hassini, E.: Multi-site production planning integrating procurement and distribution plans in multi-echelon supply chains - an interactive fuzzy goal programming approach. International Journal of Production Research 47(19), 5475–5499 (2009)

Towers, N., Song, Y.: Assessing the future challenges in strategic sourcing commodity from China. a case-study analysis. Asia Pacific Business Review 16(4), 527–544 (2010)

Tsai, W., Hung, S.: A fuzzy goal programming approach for green supply chain optimisation under activity-based costing and performance evaluation with a value-chain structure. International Journal of Production Research 47(18), 4991–5017 (2009)

Ustun, O., Demirtas, E.A.: An integrated multi-objective decision-making process for multi-period lot-sizing with supplier selection. Omega 36(4), 509–521 (2008)

Vonderembse, M.A., Tracey, M.: The Impact of Supplier Selection Criteria and Supplier Involvement on Manufacturing Performance. The Journal of Supply Chain Management 35(3), 33–39 (1999)

Walton, S.V., Handfield, R.B., Melnyk, S.A.: The Green Supply Chain. Integrating Suppliers into Environmental Management Processes. The Journal of Supply Chain Management 34(2), 2–11 (1998)

Wang, E.J., Chen, Y.C., Wang, W.S., Su, T.S.: Analysis of outsourcing cost-effectiveness using a linear programming model with fuzzy multiple goals. International Journal of Production Research 48(2), 501–523 (2010)

Weber, C.A., Current, J.R., Benton, W.C.: Vendor selection criteria and methods. European Journal of Operational Research 50(1), 2–18 (1991)

Webster, J., Watson, R.: Analyzing the past to prepare for the future: writing a literature review. Management Information Systems Quarterly 26(2), 13–23 (2002)

Wittstruck, D., Teuteberg, F.: Sustainable Supply Chain Management in Recyclingnetzwerken der Elektro- und Elektroindustrie. In: Schumann, M., Breitner, M.H., et al. (eds.) Proceedings of Multikonferenz Wirtschaftsinformatik, Goettingen, pp. 1029–1043 (2010)

Zarvić, N., Seifert, M., Thoben, K.-D.: A task-resource dependency perspective on partner selection during the formation of networked business constellations. International Journal of Networking and Virtual Organisations 7(5), 399–414 (2010)

Zhu, Q., Dou, Y., Sarkis, J.: A portfolio-based analysis for green supplier management using the analytical network process. Supply Chain Management. An International Journal 15(4), 306–319 (2010)

Towards Sustainable IT by Teaching Governance Practices for Inter-Organizational Dependencies

Carl Stolze, Matthias Boehm, Novica Zarvić, and Oliver Thomas

Katharinenstraße 3, 49074 Osnabrück
Tel.: +49 541 9694810
{carl.stolze,matthias.boehm,novica.zarvic,
oliver.thomas}@uni-osnabrueck.de

Abstract. The issue of sustainability has been among the top concerns of IT practitioners for some time now. Although sustainability of and through IT can only be reached if all stakeholders work together, current teaching and on-the-job training approaches do not provide the required understanding of how to govern the cooperation. Furthermore, there is a general gap between IS academia and practice regarding skill teaching, stakeholder informing and contributions towards sustainable business practices. In this paper, we adopt a design science research methodology to develop and evaluate a first approach to close this threefold gap.

Keywords: Governance, Sustainability, Green IT, Alignment, Teaching, Inter-Organizational Dependencies, Information Technology.

1 Introduction

Today's business and information technology (IT) environment is more dynamic and competitive than ever before (LaFrance 2010; Lee et al. 2002; Wingreen et al. 2009). Increasing public awareness for the environmental impact of IT as well as rising energy prices made sustainability become one of the top concerns for the IS/IT function of many organizations – it is even viewed as a competitive factor now (Sarkar and Young 2009; Vykoukal et al. 2009). Practitioners and academics alike have been discussing mainly energy consumption-related questions under the term Green IT for some time (McBrayne 2007; Watson 2010). In more recent discussions, the focus started to shift towards a broader understanding of sustainable information systems (IS) – including its design as well as leveraging the design of IS for a more sustainable enterprise (El-Gayer and Fritz 2006; Gartner Inc. 2009; Melville 2010; Woodruff and Mankoff 2010).

Creating such an environment of IT that is sustainable in itself (Sustainable IT) as well as fostering sustainability throughout the organization (Sustainable through IT) requires the integration and informing of numerous stakeholders inside and outside one's organization (Watson 2010). Therefore, we are dealing, additionally and next to the intra-organizational relationships, with inter-organizational relationships (Bachmann and van Witteloostuijn 2009). Factors such as technological and organizational

M. Nüttgens et al. (Eds.): Governance and Sustainability in IS, IFIP AICT 366, pp. 70–88, 2011.

change, globalization, climate change and a sustainability movement create an environment, in which companies and individuals have to cope with changing and differing approaches, requirements and technologies as well as unprecedented volatility in their work, required knowledge and skills (Lee et al. 2002; Osorio and Bulchand 2011; Schambach and Blanton 2002). Especially IS professionals, and in particular those at the beginning of their career, have to strive for permanent personal growth regarding skill and knowledge (Schambach and Blanton 2002).

The traditional role of universities has been the fostering of critical thinking without adherence to specific approaches (Adams and Zanzi 2004). Within a specific discipline, such as Information Systems, the task is to create knowledge (through research) and distribute knowledge (through teaching) (Gill and Bhattacherjee 2009). It is reported that there is a threefold gap between IS academia and IS practice: First, knowledge and skills required for IS jobs are not taught satisfactorily (Lee et al. 2002). Second, IS research is not sufficiently informing its key stakeholders (Gill and Bhattacherjee 2009), so that methods and approaches for enabling a better knowledge transfer between practice and academia are required (Wilson and Guzdial 2010). And third, the discipline's contribution towards sustainable business practices has been described as insufficient so far (Melville 2010; Watson 2010). Although there are plenty of IS curricula for undergraduate and graduate degrees in Information Systems (Downey et al. 2008; Plice and Reinig 2009; Topi et al. 2010), integrated and holistic academic programs for on-the-job training of IS professionals are missing – especially ones that also integrate questions of inter-organizational relationships (IORs) and sustainability.

2 Research Method

In this paper, we aim at developing one possible conception to overcome the before described threefold problem adopting IS design science research (DSR) methodology. DSR aims at improving the environment with the help of theory and knowledge for action (Hevner et al. 2004; Carlsson et al. 2010; Kuechler and Vaishnavi 2008). We understand DSR in the sense that the development of practically applicable knowledge for designing and realizing diverse IS should be the outcome of the research endeavor (Carlsson et al. 2010; Kuechler and Vaishnavi 2008). Good DSR should start with the identification and presentation of relevant problems in an actual application domain (Hevner 2007; Kuechler and Vaishnavi 2008). This relevance has to be balanced with rigor, whilst following a circle of design and evaluation to propose a problem-solving novel contribution (Hevner 2007; Kuechler and Vaishnavi 2008).

In the course of this paper, we first introduce the concept of IORs together with the need for their governance and how sustainability efforts create new IORs. The relevance of our research is supported by a survey regarding IT governance and IORs. Afterwards, we explore currently offered on-the-job training courses in the IS domain as a basis for our own conception. The presentation of the results begins with an illustration of the requirements for an integrated and holistic teaching approach. Based on this, our approach with a specific focus on inter-organizational relations in the context of sustainable IT is presented. After we will have evaluated a first course in form of an experiment, we discuss the main findings, limitations and give an outlook.

3 Background

3.1 Inter-Organizational Relations and IT Governance

Throughout a single enterprise, departments and individuals are dependent on each other at various levels. For instance, in order to fulfill follow-up activities inside an intra-organizational business process, we often depend on an outcome provided by a colleague (Thompson 1962). Also, we can depend on the support that IT is supposed to provide us. The IT itself must be well-aligned with the business processes and the overall business strategy of the company (Henderson and Venkatraman 1993), resulting in new interdependencies that may influence the overall outcome. Therefore, interdependencies are a very important aspect and omnipresent in our working life (Kanter 1994). As a consequence they need to be managed and coordinated to assure the success of any business (Malone and Crowston 1994). When cooperating or collaborating with other companies and stakeholders (Kumar and van Dissel 1996), interdependencies are inter-organizational relationships (IORs) – business arrangements that cross the boundaries of an individual enterprise (Bachmann and van Witteloostuijn 2009). This in turn makes the challenge of managing and coordinating such inter-organizational collaborations (Chi and Holsapple 2005) and specifically the resulting inter-organizational dependencies (IODs) more complicated, because we firstly do not have a single decision point in such network arrangements and, secondly, we are dealing with dependencies that comprise different individual enterprises and thus have an inter-organizational character.

Since the late 1990s the concept of IT Governance emerged as the distinct conceptualization of steering the use of IT within a company (van Grembergen 2010). Business-IT Alignment and IT Governance can be understood as complementary and deeply intervened concepts (Tiwana and Konsynski 2010; Weill and Ross 2004). Most authors share the common understanding that IT Governance is the top management concern of controlling the strategic impact of IT and its value delivery to the business (Becker et al. 2009; Simonsson and Johnson 2006). These facts have – among others – an enormous impact for both Business-IT Alignment and IT Governance activities (Zarvić et al. 2010a), which need to be viewed as interrelated and coherent research topics in the IS research and teaching domain.

According to de Haes and van Grembergen (2004) all relational mechanisms are a very important aspect of governance. The biggest problem to be avoided is that business and IT do not understand each other and/or do not complement each other's work. In order to achieve effective IT Governance "two-way communication and a good participation/collaboration relationship between business and IT people" (de Haes and van Grembergen 2004) is needed. Hence, we are dealing with communication and collaboration issues. We can distinguish with respect to these two issues ex-ante and ex-post relational mechanisms, because several mechanisms should already be planned before IOR formation, and later monitored, controlled and adapted during the operation of an IOR (Dekker 2004). In Table 1, an overview on main relational mechanisms for inter-organizational governance is given.

Table 1. Relational mechanisms for inter-organizational governance

	Two-way communication	*Collaboration relationship*
Ex-ante mechanisms	• Set-up of communication standards, rules, schedules and plans that are relevant for communication aspect (Kumar and van Dissel 1996).	• Setting IOR goals (Dekker 2004). • IOR formation and partner selection on the basis of IODs (Zarvić et al. 2010b)
Ex-post mechanisms	• Measuring and evaluating communication intensities (Eschenbächer et al. 2010). • Determining communication maturity (Luftman 2005). • Mutually adjusting communication mechanisms, especially in the case of reciprocal inter-dependency (Kumar and van Dissel 1996).	• Strategic alignment maturity model (Luftman 2005). • ICoNOs MM: IT-enabled Collaborative Networked Organizations Maturity Model (Santana Tapia 2009). • IT Governance maturity model (IT Governance Institute 2010).

Nevertheless, according to Camarinha-Matos (2007), the trend of forming Collaborative Networks will further continue – especially in light of sustainability endeavors. This claim has been confirmed in a survey about IT governance and interorganizational relationships within our global research network. Based on completed questionnaires (n=18), equating to a response rate of 21.7%, we assessed the relevance of the investigated topic among researchers and practitioners alike to be sure to have identified a problem of interest for multiple entities (Offermann et al. 2009). The respondents came from Germany, The Netherlands, Poland, Brazil, Spain, Slovenia, Italy and USA. Half of the respondents are from research and academia and the other half works in consulting, logistics or IT-related industries, therefore answers are not biased by a specific industry affiliation. A proxy for competence of the respondents are their academic degrees: 16.6% hold a doctoral degree, 66.7% a Master degree (or equivalent), 11.2% a Bachelor degree, and only 5.5% of the respondents do not hold any academic degree.

Table 2 shows the main empirical results of our small survey with the five most important statements. Our questionnaire is based on a simple four-level Likert scale for the answers with values from 1 to 4. A value of 1 is used to represent complete disagreement whilst a value of 4 stands for complete agreement with a statement.

Table 2. Survey results about IT governance and IORs

#	Statement	Average
1	IT Governance is not important for inter-organizational relationships	1.13
2	Inter-organizational relationships need specific IT governance structures.	3.17
3	Business-IT Alignment is much more difficult in an inter-organizational context than in individual companies.	3.33
4	Inter-organizational dependencies (e.g. relying on business partners and their processes and systems) represent an important aspect with respect to IT Governance.	3.06
5	Do you think the importance of inter-organizational relationships and dependencies will increase in the future?	3.39

The respondents negate statement 1, as negative statement; therefore IT Governance should be seen as absolutely important for IORs. Answers to the second and fourth statement outline the intervened nature between IT Governance and IORs and IODs respectively. Together with statement 3 we draw the conclusion that specifically designed and adjusted Business-IT Alignment and IT Governance concepts have to be utilized for inter-organizational collaboration arrangements, especially for the integration of the different stakeholders in a sustainable IT arrangement. Statement 5, the importance of inter-organizational relationships and dependencies in the future, received a high median value as well, which is no surprise when the trend towards a more sustainable IT together with its new IORs is looked at.

3.2 Sustainable IT Creating IORs and IODs

The steady increase in computing power required an advancement in energy supply and cooling of IT infrastructure, thereby directing the focus of Green IT to technical components (Brooks et al. 2010; Ehrenfeld 2001; McBrayne 2007; Melville 2010; Schmidt et al. 2010; Watson 2010). By doing so, the sustainable development of the enterprise as a whole was often neglected. To make matters more complicated, in most organizations outside the IT industry there is a lack of expertise regarding the planning, realization and operation of IT infrastructure (Farhoomand 2005; McBrayne 2007; Schmidt et al. 2010), since they usually obtain IT as well as the related heating and air-conditioning equipment from specialized vendors. Besides facility management and energy, suppliers also provide products and services needed to run a company's IT infrastructure. To overcome these limitations towards a truly sustainable IT, an integrated approach is needed, an approach that integrates all stakeholders and thereby creates inter-organizational relations and dependencies (Melville 2010; Schmidt et al. 2010; Vykoukal et al. 2009). An example for such relations and dependencies is depicted in Fig. 1.

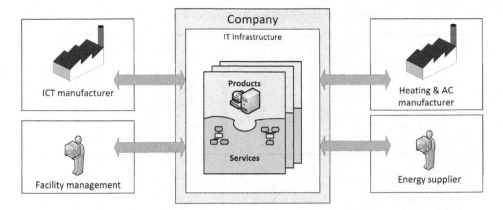

Fig. 1. Inter-organizational relations and dependencies for sustainable IT infrastructure

The focal company's IT infrastructure in the center of Fig. 1. consists of products and services. Although not explicitly shown, as those are intra-organizational dependencies, the IT and its infrastructure provide and consume services to and from the rest of the company. The depicted four dependencies and relations link the company with the ICT manufacturer, heating and air-condition manufacturer, a facility management company and last but not least with the energy supplier. All four provide vital parts for the IT infrastructure and therefore need to be included in every integration attempt towards more sustainability. Also, this integration creates a higher degree of interdependency as suppliers cannot be replaced as easy as before.

3.3 Training Approaches

As any successful change, the endeavor towards a more sustainable IT has to go through the head of any employee involved – first, to create awareness and understanding to eventually change behavior (Jenkin et al. 2010). This requires acquisition of knowledge and skills for present tasks – or in a simple word: training. According to Fitzgerald (1992), training is a tool to help individuals contribute to the organization and be successful in their current positions. Therefore, it is a means to an end. One can further discern general training and specific (on-the-job) training (Nguyen et al. 2010). In any case, it should result in changed behavior, meaning the newly acquired knowledge and skills are actually accompanied by the necessary competences to be applied (Fitzgerald 1992; Osorio and Bulchand 2011).

Literature describes different training programs for different purposes within the IT/IS domain (cf. Table 3). A common characteristic is the separation of required knowledge and competencies into two different segments. On the one side, there are technical skills, such as business and IT skills. Those should be taught. On the other side are personal skills, like the interpersonal skill of collaboration. It is noticeable that foundational IT skills and interpersonal skills are named most in literature. Although there are plenty of IS curricula for undergraduate and graduate degrees in Information Systems (Downey et al. 2008; Plice and Reinig 2009; Topi et al. 2010), integrated and holistic academic programs for on-the-job training of IS professionals are missing.

Table 3. Selected Teaching Approaches in Literature

Author(s)	Technical skills				Personal skills				
	Business skills	Foundational IT skills	IS analysis and design	Methodological know-how	Analytical ability	Interpersonal skills	Project management	Problem-based thinking	Learning techniques
Smid (2001)	x		x	x				x	x
Mohe (2006)		x		x	x	x	x	x	
Plice and Reinig (2009)		x				x			
Luftman and Ben-Zvi (2010)	x	x				x			
Pratt et al. (2010)		x		x	x	x			x
Gallagher et al. (2010)		x	x			x	x	x	

Next to the general descriptions of required knowledge and competencies as depicted in Table 3, there are more concrete lists of modules that IS courses should offer (cf. for example (Kim et al. 2006; Smith and McKeen 2006; Topi et al. 2010)). Modules on information management, corporate (IT) governance, IS strategy, security and other soft skills are named for example. Gorman (2010) criticizes that these approaches create a gap between "hard" IT training and "soft" HR skills training. In order to overcome this problem, Plice and Reinig (2009) investigated the requirements of an IS program (for undergraduate or graduate students) from an IT professional's point of view:

- Opportunities for the development of interpersonal communications skills.
- Coverage of a broad range of technical topics rather than in-depth coverage of specific hardware or software environments or programming languages.
- Acquisition of a core competency in systems development, project management as well as business and managerial skills.

4 Current Offers for on-the-Job Training

To assess the currently offered programs for on-the-job training, we examined 33 programs in the IT management area within German-speaking Europe. Although they all cover the same area, their organization and content as well as targets are diverging. Some claim that graduates will be able to plan, sell and implement complex IT projects or determine the organizational setting. In other courses, the focus is more on the technical and data processing level. And even others emphasize a scientific approach, independent working or the support for improving soft skills. However, most aim at qualifying successful future businesses leaders.

A selection of some characteristics of the investigated offerings can be found in Table 4. Overview on the Investigated Offerings. We found (out) that in more than half of the courses relatively recent graduates with one to five years of professional experience are targeted. Only 36.6% of the offers want to reach middle management. The range of fees varies from € 2,000 to more than € 50,000. However, the fees can be grouped into three clusters (low, medium and high fees). When it comes to the persons, who actual conduct the teaching, mainly professors are in charge. Only two courses have been found, that also involve practitioners. As certification, in 69.7% of the cases a classical master degree is awarded and 21.2% promote a MBA degree. Other certificates are only given by three courses. In 69.7% of the cases, a written examination is to achieve one of the certificates. Other forms of methods are rarely utilized. From this overview on existing offerings, one can see the necessity for offering on-the-job training courses, that are conducted by professors and practitioners, offer a certain certificate and utilize appropriate teaching methods by carefully choosing an appropriate fee system.

Table 4. Overview on the Investigated Offerings

Variable	Value	Absolute	Percent
Target group	Graduates with 1-5 years of professional experience	19	57.6%
	Professionals (middle management)	12	36.4%
	n/a	2	6.1%
Fee	€ 2,000-10,000	8	24.2%
	€ 10,001-30,000	12	36.4%
	€ 30,001-50,670	3	9.1%
	n/a	10	30.3%
Tutor	Professors	24	72.7%
	Professors and practitioners	2	6.1%
	n/a	7	21.2%
Certificate	Master (of Science or of Arts)	23	69.7%
	MBA	7	21.2%
	Other certificate	3	9.1%
Teaching method	Written examination	23	69.7%
	Presentation, group work	3	9.1%
	Participation	1	3.0%
	n/a	6	18.2%

Altogether, more than 60 different modules have been found in the 33 investigated curricula. As many of them cover similar topics and issues, each unit has been investigated according to its content, outline and objectives. Finally, the two kinds of modules (methodology and personal skills), which have been described in literature already, have also been discovered in this study. The methodological modules can be grouped further into seven units, namely Management in the Information Age, IS Fundamentals, IT Consulting, Enterprise Architecture Management, Business Process Management, Managing Security, Compliance and Risk as well as Sustainability and Ethics. The personal skill modules, which have been found, are grouped into Interpersonal skills and Project Management skills.

Based on these findings, one can derive requirements for an integrated teaching approach. The following points, which serve as the basis for our approach, have to be covered:

- Academia and practice knowledge exchange: It is important for any training, but especially for courses within highly dynamic environment like IT management to transfer knowledge from academia into practice and vice versa. Therefore, practitioners also have to be invited to teach scientists as well as other practitioners on specific topics.
- Structured procedure: Because of the diversity of offerings, certificates and organizational issues, IT training offerings have to be structured according to widely accepted procedures in order to ensure a useful and practicable training effect.
- Concentration on relevant issues: Based on defined objectives and the target group, the selection of relevant modules is vital. But also their connection with each other should be mentioned and outlined. This is especially true for teaching the governance of IORs in the context of sustainable IT.

5   Integrated Approach for Teaching

The aim of our approach is to derive and implement a program that captures a holistic view on relevant issues within the field of IT management with a special attention towards sustainable IT. The interaction between academia and practice is most important in order to ensure the theoretical foundation and the practical application of the taught material. For this objective, we follow the model shown in Fig. 2. which follows the ideas of collaborative practice research (Mathiassen 2002). Accordingly, practitioners and researches work together in order to share their information to the participants while both receive feedback on their actions. From the perspective of the participants, they do not only receive information on current technology and trends, but they also get to know others who are in similar situations as they are. Networking between them is therefore a side effect of our approach. Hence, this model ensures the knowledge transfer between academia and practice.

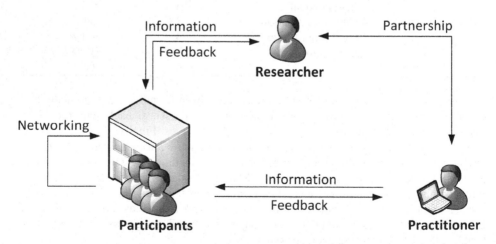

Fig. 2. Model of Researcher-Practitioner Collaboration

5.1 Framework and Modules

The framework of our approach is structured in form of a house (cf. Fig. 3.). The essential support functions of infrastructure management and teaching staff management build the base. Together with strategy at the top, evaluation and evolution as well as the operational management can be found in the roof. These activities ensure the successful implementation and the adherence to legal, political or other external requirements. Within the body of the house, the core modules can be found in two groups. First, methodology courses cover functional and technical content in the seven modules found during the assessment of existing offerings. Second, in the personal skills modules, interpersonal skills, leadership and conflict management as well as project management have to be taught.

These core activities respectively modules are framed with the relevant stakeholders. On the left-hand side, participants and tutors can be seen as the input side. On the right-hand side, companies, especially small and medium sized enterprises (SME), consulting firms and universities profit from the outcome of the training.

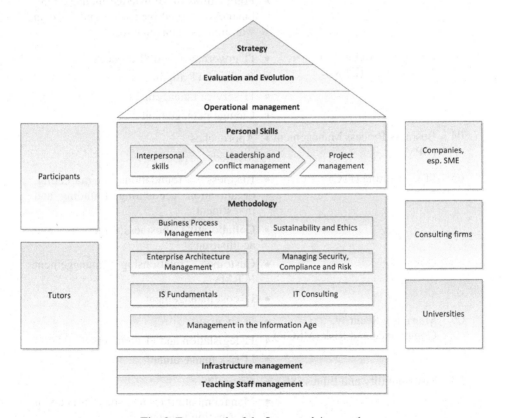

Fig. 3. Framework of the Integrated Approach

Table 5. Overview on the Methodology Modules

#	Module (Abbr.)	Content
01	Management in the Information Age (MIA)	• Internet economics • Management basics • English business language skills • Inter-organizational relations (IORs)
02	IS Fundamentals (ISF)	• IT basics and IT controlling • Enterprise software, like enterprise resource planning (ERP) • Foundations of knowledge management, business intelligence and data warehouses, data analytics
03	Enterprise Architecture Management (EAM)	• IT governance and IT strategy • Business-IT alignment • IT service management • Change management
04	Business Process Management (BPM)	• Approaches • Methods
05	IT Consulting (ITC)	• Business foundations: marketing, organization, accounting, founding and investment • Collaborative business, mergers and acquisitions • Customer relationship management (CRM) • IT cost management
06	Managing Security, Compliance and Risk (MSCR)	• IT security • IT legislation and IT contracts • IT risk management
07	Sustainability and Ethics (SE)	• Green IT • Management ethics and social aspects of information management • Intercultural studies

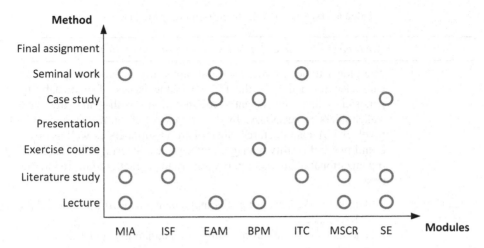

Fig. 4. Teaching Methods for each Methodological Module

In order to get a deeper insight into the actual content that is taught within the course, Table 5 gives an overview of the content of the methodology modules. For each module, a specific set of teaching methods, like case study teaching (Hackney, McMaster, and Harris 2003), is required (Beard and McPherson 1996). The assignment of methods for modules is depicted in Fig. 4. For each module (x-axis), specific methods (y-axis) have been chosen, which best facilitate learning (Beard and McPherson 1996).

Before discussing the holistic approach to teach IT governance practices for IORs in the context of sustainable IT, the personal skills modules should be briefly explained. A module regarding project management has to be included because projects are a major form of organization in IT. The interpersonal skills module teaches techniques for presentation and moderation. Although the leadership and conflict management module has not been found explicitly in literature, we think that these skills are crucial for managers on the way to a sustainable enterprise. In opposite to the methodological modules, the personal skills modules are taught in block seminars accompanied by two trainers for two days while a maximum of fourteen participants is allowed to attain one seminar. This practice ensures that every participant will learn as much as possible from the seminar.

5.2 Description of the Concept to Teach Governance Practices for IORs in the Context of Sustainable IT

A topic such as governance practices for IORs in the context of sustainable IT spans across multiple aspects and therefore modules in our framework. Therefore, we describe in Table 6 how such an interdisciplinary and important topic can be taught with the help of our framework. In the following, the content of the accountability class (class no. 5) is used to evaluate our approach.

Table 6. Description of the Interdisciplinary Module

	Governance Practices for IORs in the Context of Sustainable IT
Description	The global trend towards more sustainability in business practices calls also for action in the IT. To tackle issues of sustainability persistent and consistent collaboration with all involved stakeholders is necessary. In the context of IT infrastructure, this involves ICT manufacturers, air-condition suppliers as well as power utilities and facility management services. Steering of these inter-organizational relations requires governance practices tailored to the area.
Underlying classes	1. The networked economy (Management in the Information Age (MIA) module) 2. The call for more sustainability (Sustainability and Ethics (SE) module) 3. Sustainable IT – from Green IT to sustainability through IT (SE module) 4. Aligning business & IT (Enterprise Architecture Management (EAM) module) 5. Accountability and IT governance practices (EAM module)
Learning objectives	• Being aware of the issues of sustainability. • Enabling the design of sustainable IT. • Understanding accountability as important aspect of sustainability and governance. • Being able to design and implement governance practices on IORs that foster sustainable behavior.

6   Evaluation and Results

To test our approach, we conducted an experiment in a post-graduate teaching assignment on Enterprise Architecture Management – namely in the underlying class 5 "accountability assignment". The assignment of accountability to executive roles and the fulfilling persons is one of the key elements of establishing IT Governance practices. Magnusson stated recently that IT Governance is carried out by top executives (Magnusson 2010). We therefore considered in our experiment about an accountability matrix only top executives (CxOs) because "IT Governance should be an integral part of an enterprise governance and, in this respect, a primary concern of the board of directors that is responsible for governing the enterprises" (de Haes and van Grembergen 2004). IT Governance implementations should therefore not be an issue only within IT, but business executives should take a leading role as well (van Grembergen 2010).

Seven teams of two to three students were formed and given about 45 minutes of time at their disposal to assign different job descriptions to predefined enterprise architecture levels, whereby each enterprise architecture level was represented by one dependency category representing a generalization of diverse layered architecture style frameworks (Zarvić et al. 2010a). The main focus of the experiment was a detailed competency mapping of selected job descriptions according to the so-called competence pyramid (cf. Wieringa et al. 2009). In addition, the post-graduate students also treated the aspect of responsibility of the selected job descriptions as well as of top executive roles on the basis of the RASCI model (Paul et al. 2010). The results of accountability spans for the different CxOs are depicted Fig. 5.

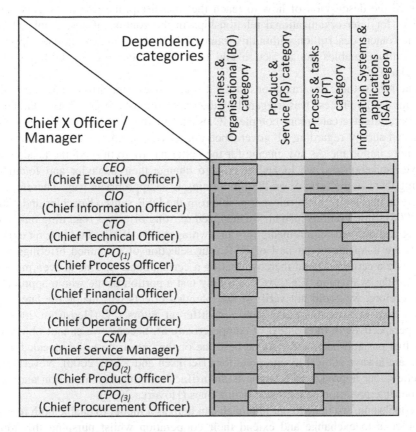

Fig. 5. Accountability Matrix for different top executives

As the resulting accountability matrix lines out, we can conclude with respect to the design of governance practices in the context of sustainable IT that these students understood the underlying concepts of accountability, IT governance and accountability assignment and their relations quite well. Also, the different accountability span of different roles was quite well understood.

7 Discussion and Conclusion

In our research, guided by the DSR paradigm, we conceptualized an integrated and holistic approach for teaching post-graduate professionals. Our approach as a whole is an artifact that consists of several distinct parts in its design: The model of researcher-practitioner collaboration aims at facilitating and improving exchange between academia and practice. It is the underlying rationale for the design as well as the structure for enabling interaction between the stakeholders. The framework as second model is the visual trademark representation of our approach. Furthermore, we presented the description of how to teach the interdisciplinary topic of governance practices for inter-organizational relationships in the context of sustainable IT as a specific content description within this framework. In this sense our holistic approach as an artifact enables human action and is thereby following the DSR paradigm (Hovorka 2010).

Nonetheless, there are limitations in the design process, the artifact and the evaluation. Our design process was triggered by the realization of the fact that sustainability endeavors might create more complex IODs and thereby IORs. From a previously conducted survey regarding IT governance and IODs we knew they would become even more important. As any change for the better has to go through the heads of the involved stakeholders, we looked at how to change their behavior and found that teaching them in the form of on-the-job training is an appropriate way. Therefore, we are certain that we tackle a relevant problem in the DSR sense (Kuechler and Vaishnavi 2008). Based on this insight, we analyzed existing offerings regarding on-the-job training and derived requirements for our own approach. Whilst building on existing knowledge is an important part of DSR, our selection of examined offerings could only cover a certain set and thereby creating a certain context. This is even more obvious for the evaluation: First, we could only test a portion of the whole approach so far. Therefore, we could not verify if the intended effects will match the later experienced ones or how this varies between different actors (cf. (Hedström 2003) for those perspectives in the context of computerization). Second, we cannot objectively prove that our approach is the single best one or the only truth to be revealed as our results are always subject to interpretation (Heriksen and Kautz 2006). Nevertheless, we believe our approach as a whole is an artifact enabling human action and being from our interpretation better than existing ones (Hovorka 2010).

In conclusion, we believe our approach can help as a model to enable both research and practice to exchange and extend their cooperation whilst pursuing the aim of sustainable IT. For the future, we aim at constantly evaluating and iteratively evolving the approach based on feedback – especially in light of changing educational demands and environments (Osorio and Bulchand 2011). Thereby, we hope to contribute, one step at a time, towards a better use of IT to build a sustainable future.

Acknowledgement. This paper was partially written in the context of the research project IMUCON which is funded by the European Regional Development Fund (ERDF). The authors are pleased to acknowledge the support by ERDF and all involved project partners. Furthermore, we would like to thank the anonymous reviewers for their insightful and helpful comments.

References

Adams, S.M., Zanzi, A.: Academic development for careers in management consulting. Career Development International 9(6), 559–577 (2004)

Bachmann, R., van Witteloostuijn, A.: Analyzing Inter-Organizational Relationships in the Context of Their Business Systems. European Societies 11(1), 49–76 (2009)

Beard, C., McPherson, M.: Design and Use of Group-based Training Methods. In: Wilson, J.P. (ed.) Human Resource Development: Learning & Training for Individuals & Organizations, pp. 285–306. Sterling, London (1996)

Becker, J., Pöppelbuß, J., Stolze, C., Cyrus, A.: Developing a Framework for IT Governance in the Post-Merger Integration Phase. In: Proceedings of the 17th European Conference on Information Systems (ECIS 2009), Verona, Italy, pp. 3137–3149 (2009)

Brooks, S., Wang, X., Sarker, S.: Unpacking Green IT: A Review of the Existing Literature. In: Proceedings of AMCIS 2010, Paper 398 (2010)

Camarinha-Matos, L.: Collaborative Networks in Industry - Trends and Foundations. In: Cunha, P., Maropoulos, P. (eds.) Digital Enterprise Technology - Perspectives and Future Challenges, pp. 45–56. Springer, New York (2007)

Carlsson, S.A., Henningsson, S., Hrastinski, S., Keller, C.: Socio-technical IS design science research: developing design theory for IS integration management. Information Systems and e-Business Management 9(1), 109–131 (2010)

Chi, L., Holsapple, C.W.: Understanding computer-mediated interorganizational collaboration - a model and framework. Journal of knowledge Management 9(1), 53–75 (2005)

De Haes, S., van Grembergen, W.: IT Governance and Its Mechanisms. Information Systems Control Journal (1) (2004)

Dekker, H.: Control of inter-organizational relationships: evidence on appropriation concerns and coordination requirements. Accounting, Organizations and Society 29(1), 27–49 (2004)

Downey, J.P., McMurtrey, M.E., Zeltmann, S.M.: Mapping the MIS Curriculum Based on Critical Skills of New Graduates: An Empirical Examination of IT Professionals. Journal of Information Systems Education (19) (2008)

Ehrenfeld, J.: Designing 'Sustainable' Product/Service Systems. In: Proceedings of International Symposium on Environmentally Conscious Design and Inverse Manufacturing, December 11-15. IEEE Computer Society, Los Alamitos (2001)

El-Gayer, O., Fritz, B.D.: Environmental Management Information Systems for Sustainable Development - A Conceptual Overview. Communications of the AIS (17), article 34 (2006)

Eschenbächer, J., Zarvić, N., Thomas, O., Thoben, K.-D.: Measuring and Evaluating Communication Intensities in Collaborative Networks. In: Camarinha-Matos, L.M., Boucher, X., Afsarmanesh, H. (eds.) PRO-VE 2010. IFIP AICT, vol. 336, pp. 527–536. Springer, Heidelberg (2010)

Farhoomand, A.: Managing (e)business transformation: a global perspective. Palgrave Macmillan, Basingstoke (2005)

Fitzgerald, W.: Training Versus Development. Training & Development 46(5), 81–84 (1992)

Gallagher, K.P., Kaiser, K.M., Simon, J.C., Beath, C.M., Goles, T.: The Requisite Variety of Skills for IT Professionals. Communications of the ACM 53(6), 144–148 (2010)

Gartner Inc. Gartner Identifies the Top 10 Strategic Technologies for 2010 (2009), http://www.gartner.com/it/page.jsp?id=1210613 (retrieved 2010-08-07)

Gill, G., Bhattacherjee, A.: Whom Are We Informing? Issues and Recommendations for MIS Research from an Informing Sciences Perspective. MIS Quarterly 33(2), 217–235 (2009)

Gorman, M.F.: A Case Study in Effectively Bridging the Business Skills Gap for the Information Technology Professional. Journal of Education for Business 86(1), 17–24 (2010)

Hackney, R., McMaster, T., Harris, A.: Using Cases As A Teaching Tool In IS Education. Journal of Information Systems Education 14(3), 229–234 (2003)

Hedström, K.: The Socio-Political Construction of CareSys. In: Daamsgard, J., Henriksen, H.Z. (eds.) Networked Information Technologies - Diffusion and Adoption, pp. 1–18. Kluwer Academic Publishers, New York (2003)

Henderson, J.C., Venkatraman, N.: Strategic Alignment: Leveraging Information Technology for Transforming Organisations. IBM Systems Journal 32(1), 272–284 (1993)

Heriksen, H.Z., Kautz, K.: An Analysis of IFIP TC 8 WG 8.6. In: Avison, D., Elliot, S., Krogstie, J., Pries-Heje, J. (eds.) The Past and Future of Information Systems: 1976-2006 and Beyond, Santiago, Chile, August 21-23. IFIP 19th World Computer Congress, TC-8, Information System Stream, pp. 143–152. Springer, Boston (2006)

Hevner, A.R.: The Three Cycle View of Design Science Research. Scandinavian Journal of Information Systems 19(2), 87–92 (2007)

Hevner, A.R., March, S.T., Park, J., Ram, S.: Design Science in Information Systems Research. MIS Quarterly 28(1), 75–105 (2004)

Hovorka, D.S.: Incommensurability and Multi-paradigm Grounding in Design Science Research: Implications for Creating Knowledge. In: Pries-Heje, J., Venable, J., Bunker, D., Russo, N.L., DeGross, J.I. (eds.) IFIP WG. IFIP AICT, vol. 318, pp. 13–27. Springer, Heidelberg (2010)

IT Governance Institute 2010, Board Briefing on IT Governance, 2nd edn. (2010), http://www.itgi.org/

Jenkin, T., Webster, J., McShane, L.: An agenda for "Green" information technology and systems research. Information and Organization 21(1), 17–40 (2010)

Kanter, R.: Collaborative advantage - The art of alliances. Harvard Business Review 72(4), 96–108 (1994)

Kim, Y., Hsu, J., Stern, M.: An Update on the IS / IT Skills Gap. Journal of Information Systems Education 17(4), 395–403 (2006)

Kuechler, W., Vaishnavi, V.: The emergence of design research in information systems in North America. Journal of Design Research 7(1), 1–16 (2008)

Kumar, K., van Dissel, H.G.: Sustainable collaboration - managing conflict and cooperation in interorganizational systems. MIS Quarterly 20(3), 297–300 (1996)

LaFrance, G.: Bridging the IT Skills Gap Through Industry and Academic Collaboration. Employment Relations Today 36(4), 25–30 (2010)

Lee, S., Koh, S., Yen, D., Tang, H.-L.: Perception gaps between IS academics and IS practitioners: an exploratory study. Information & Management 40(1), 51–61 (2002)

Luftman, J.: Key Issues for IT Executives 2004. MIS Quarterly Executive 4(2), 269–285 (2005)

Luftman, J.N., Ben-Zvi, T.: Key Issues for IT Executives 2010: Judicious IT Investments Continue Post-Recession. MIS Quarterly Executive 9(4) (2010)

Magnusson, J.: Professional Analysts and the Ongoing Construction of IT Governance. International Journal of IT/Business Alignment and Governance 1(2), 1–12 (2010)

Malone, T.W., Crowston, K.: The interdisciplinary study of coordination. ACM Computing Surveys 26(1), 87–119 (1994)

Mathiassen, L.: Collaborative practice research. Scandinavian Journal of Information Systems 14(1), 57–73 (2002)

McBrayne, C.: 'Green IT' - the next burning issue for business. IBM Global Technology Services, London (2007)

Melville, N.P.: Information Systems Innovation for Environmental Sustainability. MIS Quarterly 34(1), 1–21 (2010)

Mohe, M.: What Do Consulting Firms Expect from Graduates and Universities? Empirical Insights from the German Consulting Market. In: Deelmann, T., Mohe, M. (eds.) Selection and Evaluation of Consultants, pp. 53–68. Rainer Hampp, Munich (2006)

Nguyen, T.N., Truong, Q., Buyens, D.: The Relationship between Training and Firm Performance: A Literature Review. Research & Practice in Human Resource Management 18(1), 36–45 (2010)

Offermann, P., Levina, O., Schönnherr, M., Bub, U.: Outline of a design science research process. In: Proceedings of the 4th International Conference on Design Science Research in Information Systems and Technology (DESRIST), pp. 1–11. ACM, Philadelphia (2009)

Osorio, J., Bulchand, J.: Moving towards 2020: A Tentative Approach to ITEM. In: Tatnall, A., Kereteletswe, O.C., Visscher, A. (eds.) ITEM 2010. IFIP AICT, vol. 348, pp. 104–112. Springer, Heidelberg (2011)

Paul, D., Yeates, D., Cadle, J.: Business Analysis, 2nd edn. British Informatics Society Limited, Chippenham (2010)

Plice, R., Reinig, B.: Leveraging Alumni and Business Community Relations to Assess the Information Systems Curriculum. Journal of Education for Business 84(3), 142–150 (2009)

Pratt, J.A., Hauser, K., Ross, S.C.: IS Staffing During a Recession: Comparing Student and IS Recruiter Perceptions. Journal of Information Systems Education 21(1), 69–85 (2010)

Santana Tapia, R.: Assessing business-IT alignment in networked organizations, Ph.D., University of Twente (2009)

Sarkar, P., Young, L.: Managerial Attitudes Towards Green IT: An Explorative Study of Policy Drivers. In: Proceedings of PACIS 2009, Paper 95 (2009)

Schambach, T., Blanton, J.E.: The professional development challenge for IT professionals. Communications of the ACM 45(4), 83–87 (2002)

Schmidt, N.-H., Erek, K., Kolbe, L. M., Zarnekow, R.: Predictors of Green IT Adoption: Implications from an Empirical Investigation. In: Proceedings of AMCIS 2010, Paper 367 (2010)

Simonsson, M., Johnson, P.: Defining IT governance – a consolidation of literature. Royal Institute of Technology (KTH) - EARP Working paper MS103, Stockholm, Sweden (2006)

Smid, G.: Consultants' Learning within Academia: Five devices for the design of university-based learning opportunities for management consultants. Studies in Continuing Education 23(1), 55–70 (2001)

Smith, H.A., McKeen, J.D.: IT in 2010: The next frontier. MIS Quarterly 5(3), 125–136 (2006)

Thompson, J.: Organizations in action. McGraw-Hill, New York (1962)

Tiwana, A., Konsynski, B.: Complementarities Between Organizational IT Architecture and Governance Structure. Information Systems Research 21(2), 288–304 (2010)

Topi, H., Valacich, J.S., Wright, R.T., Kaiser, K.M., Nunamaker Jr., J.F., Sipior, J.C., de Vreede, G.J.: IS 2010 - Curriculum Guidelines for Undergraduate Degree Programs in Information Systems. In: Association for Computing Machinery and Association for Information Systems (2010)

Van Grembergen, W.: From IT Governance to Enterprise Governance of IT: A Journey for Creating Business Value Out of IT. In: Cellary, W., Estevez, E. (eds.) Software Services for e-World. IFIP AICT, vol. 341, p. 3. Springer, Heidelberg (2010)

Vykoukal, J., Wolf, M., Beck, R.: Does Green IT Matter? Analysis of the Relationship between Green IT and Grid Technology from a Resource-Based View Perspective. In: Proceedings of PACIS 2009, Paper 51 (2009)

Watson, R.T.: Information Systems and environmentally sustainable development: energy informatics and new directions for the IS community. MIS Quarterly 34(1), 23–38 (2010)

Weill, P., Ross, J.W.: IT Governance: How Top Performers Manage IT Decision Rights for Superior Results. Harvard Business School Press, Boston (2004)

Wieringa, R., van Eck, P., Steghuis, C., Proper, E.: Competences of IT Architects, 2nd edn., Netherlands Architecture Forum for the Digital World (2009)

Wilson, C., Guzdial, M.: How to make progress in computing education. Communications of the ACM 53(5), 35–37 (2010)

Wingreen, S.C., Lerouge, C., Blanton, J.E.: Structuring Training for IT Professionals and the Firm: An Application of the Q- Methodology. International Journal of Global Management Studies 1(1), 53–67 (2009)

Woodruff, A., Mankoff, J.: Environmental Sustainability. IEEE Pervasive Computing 8(1), 18–21 (2010)

Zarvić, N., Fellmann, M., Thomas, O.: Towards Dependency-based Alignment for Collaborative Businesses. In: Klink, S., et al. (eds.) Proceedings of EMISA 2010, GI edn., pp. 53–67. Gesellschaft für Informatik, Karlsruhe (2010a)

Zarvić, N., Seifert, M., Thoben, K.-D.: A task-resource dependency perspective on partner selection during the formation of networked business constellations. International Journal of Networking and Virtual Organisations (IJNVO) 7(5), 399–414 (2010b)

Sustainability Aspects of Barrier-Free Information and Communication Technology (ICT) in the Private Sector

Daryoush Daniel Vaziri

University of applied science Bonn-Rhein-Sieg, D-53757 Sankt Augustin, Germany
Tel.: +49 (0) 2241 865123
Daryoush.Vaziri@h-brs.de

Abstract. This paper will examine sustainability aspects of accessible information and communication technology for the private sector. First, the introduction highlights the current barriers against and drivers for barrier-free ICT. Second, the ICT scope for the further examination will be declared. Common accepted usability design clusters will be used to illustrate accessibility design principles. Regarding the impact of barrier-free ICT on sustainability aspects, three dimensions will be determined. For each dimension several positive effects, initiated by the implementation of accessible ICT, will be demonstrated.

Keywords: Accessibility, ICT, Accessible ICT, barrier-free ICT, Sustainability, Barrier-free design, Accessible Design.

1   Introduction

With the latest information and communication technology (ICT), disabled people are able to undertake a variety of tasks that would otherwise be difficult or impossible. They have the opportunity to participate in everyday life as well as in daily business. However, this new quality of life is significantly dependent on enterprise decisions made at the beginning of specific IT-projects. According to paragraph 11 of the equality act for disabled people in Germany, carriers of public governance are compelled to design barrier-free information technology (Department of justice 2007). Similar efforts can be found in the legislative texts of e. g. the United Kingdom (Directgov 2010) or the United States (Department of justice 2009). Even though the abovementioned paragraphs indicate, that the governments will work towards, to prevail on commercial enterprises to design accessible IT, the current involvement seems nominal.

A study, executed by Bloor research in the year 2009, examined the current and planned accessibility status of organizations' ICT Systems. Referring to the 141 completed surveys, significant increases cannot be expected. Barriers to improve accessibility, mentioned by the participants, are illustrated in figure 1 (Abrahams 2009).

The poor support and commitment of the senior management results in an insufficient budget available for improving accessibility, which is in fact the reason for the major lack of understanding / training and the inadequate condition of development and testing tools.

M. Nüttgens et al. (Eds.): Governance and Sustainability in IS, IFIP AICT 366, pp. 89–102, 2011.
© IFIP International Federation for Information Processing 2011

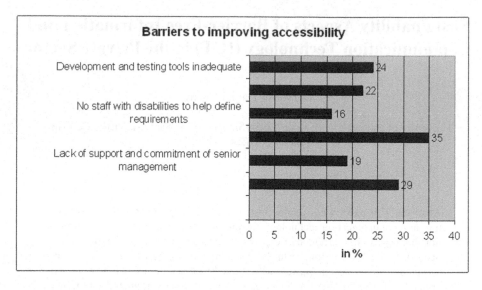

Fig. 1. Barriers to improving accessibility[1]

In contrast, the aforementioned study also revealed important drivers to improve accessibility, demonstrated in figure 2[2] (Abrahams 2009).

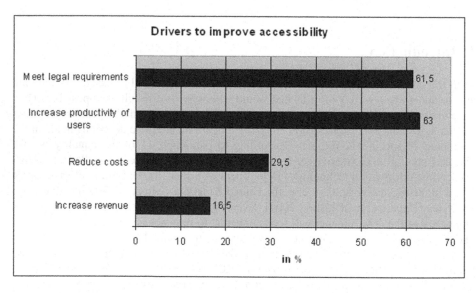

Fig. 2. Drivers to improve accessibility[3]

---

[1] Self provided figure.
[2] Data is based on an averaging of the original study.
[3] Self provided figure.

The minor importance of accessibility as a driver for cost -cutting and sales increases seems to be a decisive reason for the poor support and commitment of the management level. Legal requirements and user productivity as the most frequently mentioned drivers for accessibility do not seem to have a major impact on management decisions (Abrahams 2009).

This emphasizes the need to sensitize the management for the holistic advantageousness of an accessible IT-Infrastructure from an economic, ecological and social point of view.

2 ICT Scope for Barrier –Free Design and Development

Within this paper the sustainability of barrier-free business application software will be examined. Therefore business application software can be defined as a package of essential tools to increase efficiency and effectiveness of business processes by supporting employees or customers and enabling parallelization, digitalization and automation of business transactions (Verma 2009). Furthermore the examination will focus on enterprise websites as a communication channel to the customer and thus as an essential platform for generating revenues. Within this article the presentation and process logic of business applications and enterprise websites are of special importance.

3 Design Principles for Barrier –Free ICT

There are many types of disabilities which have a bearing on the development of accessible ICT. Some of them are listed below (Galitz 2002):

* Visual disabilities
* Hearing disabilities
* Physical movement disabilities
* Speech or language disabilities
* Cognitive disabilities
* Seizure disorders

To regard all of these disabilities, several design principles have been compiled and published.

As we mainly examine the sustainability of barrier-free ICT, the design principles will only be explained briefly. Therefore the principles are aggregated into established clusters of usability depicted in figure 3. This classification can be derived from various resources, concerning with usability engineering (W3C 2008; Agarwal et al. 2010; Lidwell et al. 2010; Lányi et al. 2007).

Perceptibility

Perceptibility implies that content presented on a website or within an application is perceivable for every user regardless of his disability (Pühretmair, Miesenberger 2005). To fulfil this criterion, developers can integrate additional functionalities like scalability or the two-channel principle. The latter is used to provide multiple

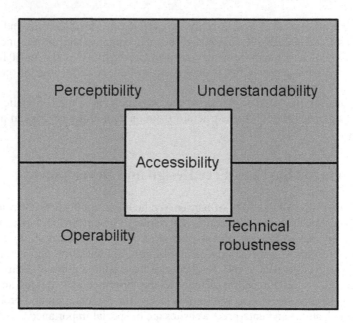

Fig. 3. Clusters for accessibility design principles[4]

opportunities for the user to succeed a specific task (Wegge, Zimmermann 2007). Furthermore the content can be enriched by alternative tags, which replenishes non-textual content with descriptions. Another crucial, often underestimated, criterion is the colour contrast of content. Users with visual disabilities for example might have a dyschromatopsia and therefore would not be able to differentiate between red and green content. Imagine a top manager, afflicted with dyschromatopsia, reviewing operating numbers that are represented in a usual traffic light-system.

Understandability

This criterion intends to make text content readable and understandable as well as to make the application processes appear and operate predictable. Therefore developers can for example programmatically determine the default language of the application or label unusual words and abbreviations. A Screen-Reader, used by many disabled people to read the content presented on a website or within an application, can only help the user when text or text parts are labelled correctly.

To render application processes predictable to the user it is an advantage to highlight any focused components. Furthermore navigational mechanisms that are repeated on multiple web pages or application screens should be consistent if possible. Components that share the same functionality should use a same identifier like a symbol or name (W3C 2008).

---

[4] Self provided figure.

Operability

To make applications operable for disabled people all functionality should be trigger-able through a keyboard. Some people afflicted by physical movement disabilities are not able to use a computer mouse. The only way for them to navigate through the content of a web site or application is to use the tabulator-key of the keyboard. Focus order and focus visibility are important and have to be considered. Hence, developers should avoid keyboard traps, which would kill the operability at a stroke. Generally the user should be provided with enough time to use, read and process the content. Seizure disorders also have to be taken into account when developing a website or application. So, rapidly flashing content should be avoided [0].

Technical robustness and technical openness

Website or application content must be robust enough, so that a variety of assistive technologies can interpret the content reliably. Compatibility of current and future technologies has to be ensured. In addition, fulfilling this principle prohibits redundant data and multiple versions. Special features of robust content are listed below (W3C 2008):

- Elements have complete start and end tags
- Elements are nested according to their specifications
- Elements do not contain duplicate attributes
- Any ID's are unique (specific exceptions allowed)

For detailed information on accessible designing principles the author references the interested reader to the resources, mentioned above.

There are some more aspects, which might come into consideration, when designing accessible ICT, e.g. maintainability, efficiency, memorability, learnability. The author decided only to describe the most frequently mentioned principles found in literature (W3C 2008; Agarwal et al. 2010; Lidwell et al. 2010; Lányi et al. 2007), as this paper mainly focuses on sustainability aspects of barrier-free ICT. Nevertheless, these additional aspects can have impact on sustainability as well and therefore should not be disregarded when designing accessible ICT.

4   Sustainability Aspects of Barrier –Free ICT

Information and communication technology is one of the most significant promoters to sustainability in everyday life as well as in daily business. Due to ICT many transactions, even whole processes, can be accomplished automatically or/and with minimal effort. Besides economy that experienced a robust growth, environment and society can be declared as beneficiaries as well (World economic forum 2009). Therefore the following examination of the sustainability of accessible ICT will be illustrated from a business economic, ecological and social point of view. These sustainability dimensions are derived from several sources, which cover a wide topic area (Nga, Soo 2010; Madruga 2002; European commission 2001; Lehtonen 2004). Hence, the author applies these dimensions to append this topic to a familiar classification of sustainability dimensions.

None of the following paragraphs can be regarded isolated. Instead they feature intermeshed fields, which can profit by implementing accessible ICT.

4.1 Business Economic Aspects

If we imply the purpose of running a business is to earn profit by supplying the demand of customers with products or services that are generated with optimal allocated resources, under the consideration of competitors' activities and stakeholders' interests, then we can abstract a specific scope of data to measure the success of that business[5]:

- Market share
- Image / Reputation
- Costs
- Revenues

The following examples will demonstrate how barrier-free ICT can positively impact the abovementioned fields. Figure 4 provides a graphical overview of this section.

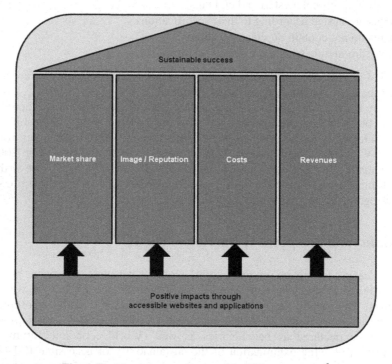

Fig. 4. Positive impacts of accessible ICT components[6]

---

[5] No claim to completeness.
[6] Self provided figure.

Market share

The process of globalization significantly amplifies the national and international competition for enterprises. As the supplement rises, customers find a variety of alternative products at lower prices. However, globalization also results in a rise of demand. Through ICT, products can be sold to any customer at any time around the globe. Increasing market share becomes essential for enterprises to persist in such a competitive landscape (Rüttimann 2007).

If we define an enterprise website as a firm's representation on the Internet with the opportunity to diffuse information, to acquire new customers and to offer and sell products and services this would definitely be one efficient way to increase market share.

Therefore the website must be available and accessible to as many Internet users as possible. Worldwide there are about 650 million people with disabilities (United Nations enable 2007). Europe numerated approximately 500 Mio inhabitants in the year 2009 (Marcu 2009). 67.1 percent out of those 500 Mio inhabitants were declared as working-age population (Eurostat 2010). 15.7 percent, respectively 52.7 Mio people of that working population either have a long-standing health problem or a disability (Eurostat 2003). Every fourth European declares, having a member of their family affected by a disability (The European research Group's 2001). Those people usually are not able to use common inaccessible websites easily and thus approximately more than a fifth of the spending power in Europe is not used efficiently. Figure 5 provides a graphical presentation of the proportion between working-age population and people with long-standing health problems or disabilities within that working-age population.

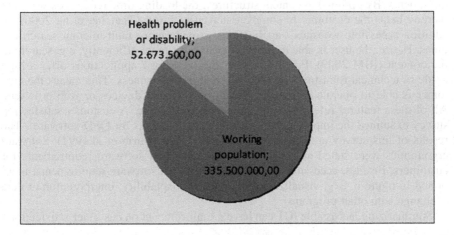

Fig. 5. Proportion between working-age population and health problems/disabilities

All this data and the aforementioned fact, that many enterprises in the private sector still are quite reserved in terms of investing in accessible ICT, leads into one logic consequence:

To increase market share and to benefit from idle revenue potential, investing in barrier-free ICT is a serious option.

Accessible ICT supports the realization of certain success factors crucial to a growth in market share.

- Findability

  Accessibility offers some inherent benefits for search engine optimization. Google, MSN or Yahoo for example use specific rules called algorithms to find and rank web sites. These algorithms could be the most frequent disabled user on a website. They show some important behaviour, similar to these of certain disabled people. Search Engine algorithms are blind, navigate with JavaScript disabled and stop cold if a link is not operable. One of the principles of accessibility is to ensure, that a blind user, who is unable to use Javascript, can navigate and understand the website. Therefore, fulfilling this accessibility principle increases the findability of a website and thus can increase market share (Thatcher et al. 2006).

- Customer Satisfaction

  As nowadays "Time is Money", customers always seek for the fastest, easiest and most convenient way to fulfil their tasks on the internet. Accessible websites or applications provide a properly written source code. Therefore the content structure is optimized and enriched by specific tag words, which help the user to find and understand content more comfortable (Clark 2002). As the development of accessible websites / applications considers and evaluates criteria like, the font size, colour contrasts, text colours and more, the perceptibility for the customer is improved. Furthermore, the customer is able to adapt the website or application to its requirements. By optimizing content structures, the loading time reduces as well and thereby helps the customer to complete activities faster (Thatcher et al. 2006). In addition accessible websites / applications provide more fault-tolerant search engines. Hence, the user is able to fulfil specific tasks more efficiently, e.g. searching the content (IBM 2009). Finally, barrier-free websites / applications offer a high grade of technical robustness respectively technical openness. This means the customer is able to operate within the system by different devices or web browsers. All of these features refer to a software ergonomic nature. A customer satisfaction survey examined the importance of customer requirements for QFD-software[7]. The results of this survey are illustrated in figure 6 (Herzwurm et al.1997). Software ergonomics were stated as one of the most important software requirements for customers. Besides, accessible ICT affects additional software requirements, mentioned in figure 6, e. g. visualization, individual adaptability, interpretation or data exchange with other programs.

  Summarizing, accessible ICT can have a major impact on customer satisfaction.

- Conversion rate

  As the website can generate more satisfied users, some of them might remember the website and return to it. Over time the conversion rate could increase and the customer base could be expanded.

---

[7] Quality function deployment software.

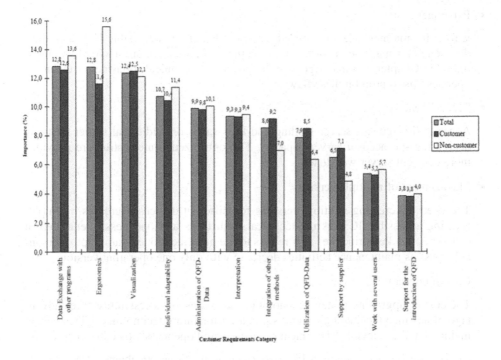

Fig. 6. Customer requirements for QFD-software (Herzwurm et al. 1997)

- Device independence

  As mentioned in chapter 3, accessible websites / applications provide a higher grade of technical robustness and openness. So, the access to the website / application is available for more browsers and devices, e.g. Safari Browser and Apple iphone. Therefore more customers with various technologies are able to use the website / application efficiently (Thatcher et al. 2006).

Image / Reputation

Providing accessible ICT will affect in a positive image and a growth in reputation, as the enterprise attends to the interests and needs of disabled people and thus considers inherent social desires of people without disabilities (OneVoice 2010). From a strategic point of view, accessible ICT provides to fulfil Corporate Social Strategy (CSR) objectives, which are essential to improve an enterprises' image and reputation within the society (De Andrés et al. 2009).

Costs

Investing in accessible ICT often results in improved technical performance. Many organizations can realize direct cost savings by improving their technical performance through barrier-free ICT (Thatcher et al. 2006). Some of the cost savings are listed below (Thatcher et al. 2006).

- Personnel costs

  Efforts for maintenance are reduced when implementing accessible ICT, as redundant data and multiple versions of the website / application are avoided. As mentioned in Chapter 3, a major goal of the principle "technical robustness / technical openness" is to prohibit these flaws.

- Server capacity

  Accessibility reduces server loading and thus saves on additional server costs by decreasing the need of server capacity. The optimized content structure provides more efficient server workloads.

- Management of multiple versions

  The need for creating multiple versions for different devices decreases by implementing accessible ICT, as the technical robustness and openness, mentioned in chapter 3, is a key principle. This relates to the aforementioned paragraph "personnel costs" as maintenance activities decrease with only one operating version.

- Cost of upgrading

  The cost of upgrading to new technologies decreases, as accessibility takes advantage of advanced technologies and is prepared for future technologies. This is also included in the principle "Technical robustness and openness", listed in chapter 3.

The cost criterion also contains additional aspects, mentioned in chapter 3, like maintainability or efficiency. These aspects can greatly benefit by investing in accessible ICT and might have a major affect on ICT costs.

Revenues

The revenue potential can increase by the improvement of abovementioned fields. Increasing market share and reputation will expand the customer base and raise revenues, while simultaneously will ensure a major constant liquidity. Cutting direct costs through accessible ICT enables the enterprise to optimize allocation of financial resources and to transfer them to promising business units.

4.2 Ecological Aspects

Citizens of developed countries, in their role as consumers, are becoming increasingly aware of problems associated with the deterioration of the environment due to the functionality of the market. As a result they exhibit preferences for green products and processes, revealed in an increased willingness to pay for them (García-Gallego, Georgantzís 2011). "The code of conduct" on data centres energy efficiency, published by the European institute for energy, reveals the environmental problems of increasing energy consumption. According to that article, it is extremely recommended to optimize power distribution, cooling infrastructure, IT equipment and IT output to increase energy efficiency and thereby to minimize energy consumption (Institute for energy 2008).

Accessible ICT reduces traffic and server capacities, by providing an optimized data and process structure. Thus energy consumption will deplete (Djokic 2010). Additionally, accessible ICT decreases location bound operations for everyone. This can result in a lower use of technologies causing CO_2 emissions. Implementing barrier-free ICT is one step to transport a firms' ecological awareness to the consumer.

4.3 Social Aspects

Accessible ICT provides many social aspects, especially for people with disabilities. To participate in everyday life as well as in daily business is a crucial key factor for disabled people to be equally acknowledged within the society. But not only disabled people can benefit from accessible ICT. Therefore some hypotheses will be constructed in the following paragraphs:

- Workforce potential increases

  Enterprises that offer an accessible working environment will be able to choose their employees from a major pool. Expertise of older, experienced people as well as disabled "hidden potentials" can be acquired and deployed as valuable manpower. Accessible ICT makes the work more comfortable and reduces illnesses / injuries related to a software ergonomic nature. Older and disabled people do both benefit from this. Especially the principles "perceptibility" and "operability" provide the appropriate criteria, which will be stated in the paragraph "labour conditions increase".

- Adaptation to demographic transition

  By 2050, the proportion of the world's population aged over 65 will be twice as high as currently. Estimations illustrate an increase from 7.6% currently to 16.2%. This would make about 1 billion people aged over 65 (Standard & Poors 2010). In contrast, the portion of people ages 16-24 is decreasing. Referring to a study, executed by "USA Today", this age segment declined, from 66% in the year 2000, to 55% in the year 2010 (Cauchon 2010). This persistent tendency leads to a decreasing working-age population (Population reference bureau 2010). Enterprises have to face a dwindling workforce potential, while the quantity of older personnel is ascending. This circumstance requires specific adaptations of future business applications to fit the requirements of elderly employees and to prevent negative health effects from the entire staff, induced by software usage. As mentioned in section 4.1 accessible ICT improves software ergonomics and thereby provides more comfortable working environments for elderly people as well as for disabled people.

- Labour conditions increase

  Improvements in labour conditions can be acquired for people with and without disabilities. As we mentioned issues related to a software ergonomic nature before, some examples for improving labour conditions, respectively software ergonomics will be stated below:

  — Adjustments of font size
  — High contrasts

— Reduced loading times
— Different colour schemes
— Voice recognition and command
— Touchscreen operation
— Assistant / help functionalities
— Error avoidance functionalities

Many more aspects of accessible websites / applications would improve labour conditions.

• Gap between people with and without disabilities

According to a study concerning the American territory, executed by the Kessler foundation, only 21% of disabled people are employed. In comparison, 59% of people without disabilities have an employment. In terms of internet access, only 54% of people with disabilities can use the World Wide Web, while 85% of people without disabilities are able to use this platform (Kessler, Catts 2010). Accessible ICT will help to close this gap and will ensure equal conditions for disabled people.

5 Conclusion

This article demonstrated the reluctance of enterprises when deciding about accessible ICT. Drivers for and barriers against accessible ICT were identified. Application software and enterprise websites were declared as the ICT Scope for the investigation. Design principles for barrier-free ICT, sorted into usability clusters, illustrated opportunities to develop accessible ICT. Three dimensions of sustainability were defined and the positive impact of accessible ICT on these dimensions was examined.

The current literature mainly covers the accessibility of web sites, so the author applied these sources. Nevertheless, the accessibility of applications can be derived from these sources as well, as web applications are considered by the latest accessibility requirements.

The inquiry showed that investing in accessibility can be worthwhile and wider might be essential for enterprises to survive in the near future.

References

Abrahams, P.: Survey of attitudes to accessible ICT. Bloor Research, 2–9 (July 2009)

Agarwal, B.B., Tayal, S.P., Gupta, M.: Software engineering and testing: An introduction, p. 105. Jones and Bartlett Publishers, Massachusetts (2010)

Cauchon, D.: American workforce growing grayer, published in: USA today (2010), http://www.usatoday.com/money/workplace/2010-12-14-older-workers-employment_N.htm?csp=usat.me

Clark, J.: Building accessible websites, p. 96 et seq. New Riders publishing, Indiana (2002)

De Andrés, J., Lorca, P., Martínez, A.B.: Economic and Financial Factors for the Adoption and Visibility Effects of Web Accessibility:The Case of European Banks. Journal of the American society for Information science and technology 60(9), 1769–1770 (2009)

Department of Justice (Germany). Equality Act for disabled people. Paragraph 11 (December 2007)

Department of Justice (USA). Americans with Disabilities Act (January 1, 2009),
http://www.ada.gov/pubs/adastatute08.htm

Directgov. Disabled peoples's rights in everyday life (2010),
http://www.direct.gov.uk/en/DisabledPeople/
RightsAndObligations/DG_4019061

Djokic, D.: Web Accessibility in the European Union, 11th Libre Software Meeting, Bordeaux, p. 18 et seq. (2010),
http://bearstech.com/media/Web%20Accessibility%20in%20the%
20EU%20-%20FINAL.pdf

European commission, Agriculture directorate general. A Framework for indicators for the economic and social dimensions of sustainable agriculture and rural development, p. 3 (February 2001),
http://ec.europa.eu/agriculture/publi/reports/sustain/
index_en.pdf

Eurostat, European commission. population structure and ageing (2010),
http://epp.eurostat.ec.europa.eu/statistics_explained/
index.php/Population_structure_and_ageing

Eurostat, research results. 2003. Cited in OSSATE Accessibility Market and Stakeholder Analysis (2005)

Galitz, W.O.: The essential guide to user interface design, pp. 579–584. John Wiley and sons, Inc., New York (2002)

García-Gallego, A., Georgantzís, N.: Good and Bad Increases in Ecological Awareness: Environmental Differentiation Revisited. Strategic Behavior and the Environment 1, 71–72 (2011)

Herzwurm, G., Mellis, W., Schockert, S., Weinberger, C.: Customer oriented evaluation of QFD Software tools, p. 5 (1997),
http://www.qfd-id.de/en/articles/evaluation_tools/
qfd-tools.pdf

IBM. Accessibility in Web 2.0 technology (2009),
http://www.ibm.com/developerworks/web/library/
wa-aj-web20/index.html

Institute for energy, European commission. Code of conduct for data centres energy efficiency Version 1.0, pp. 3–7 (2008),
http://ec.europa.eu/information_society/activities/
sustainable_growth/docs/datacenter_code-conduct.pdf

Kessler, E. B., Catts, R. Survey of Americans with Disabilities (2010),
http://www.2010disabilitysurveys.org/indexold.html

Lányi, S.C., Forrai, S., Czank, N., Hajgató, A.: On developing validator software xvalid for testing home pages of universal design. In: Stephanidis, C. (ed.) Universal Access in Human-Computer Interaction, Coping with diversity, p. 285 (2007)

Lehtonen, M.: The environmental social interface of sustainable development: capabilities, social capital, institutions. Ecological Economics #49, 199–214 (2004)

Lidwell, W., Holden, K., Butler, J.: Universal principles of design, revised and updated: 125 ways to enhance usability, influence perception, increase appeal, make better design decision, p. 16. Rockport publishers, Massachusetts (2010)

Madruga, R.P.: The social dimension of sustainable development. United Nations expert meeting on National and International Cooperation for social development: Sharing of experiences and practices in social development, p. 2 (June 2002),
http://www.redem.buap.mx/pdf/ramon/pichs5.pdf

Marcu, M.: The EU-27 population continues to grow. In: Eurostat 2009, Population and social conditions (2009),
http://epp.eurostat.ec.europa.eu/cache/ITY_OFFPUB/
KS-QA-09-031/EN/KS-QA-09-031-EN.PDF

Nga, J.K.H., Soo, N.W.M.: The influence of personal attributes on perceptions of economic, social and environmental dimensions of sustainability. In: 2nd International Conference on Business and Economic Research, Paper # 72, p. 2 (2010),
http://www.internationalconference.com.my/proceeding/
icber2010_proceeding/PAPER_072_PersonalAttributes.pdf

OneVoice for accessible ICT. Accessible ICT – Benefits to Business and Society (2010),
http://www.onevoiceict.org/pdfs/Accessible%20ICT%20-
%20Benefits%20to%20Business%20and%20Society.pdf

Population Reference Bureau. 2010 World population Data Sheet (July 2010),
http://www.prb.org/Publications/Datasheets/2010/2010wpds.aspx

Pühretmair, F., Miesenberger, K.: Making sense of accessibility in IT Design - usable accessibility vs. accessible usability. In: Proceedings of the 16th international Workshop on Database and Expert Systems Applications (DEXA 2005), 1529-4188/05, p. 2. IEEE Computer society, Los Alamitos (2005)

Rüttimann, B.G.: Modelling Economic Globalization: A Post-Neoclassic View on Foreign Trade and Competition, pp. 17–20. Monsenstein and Vannerdat, Muenster (2007)

Standard & Poors. Global Aging 2010: An Irreversible Truth (2010),
http://www.standardandpoors.com/products-services/articles/
en/us/?assetID=1245229586712

Thatcher, J., Burks, M.R., Heilmann, C.: Web Accessibility –Web standards and regulatory compliance, p. 42 et seq. Springer, New York (2006)

The European Research Group's. Eurobarometer, 54.2/2001 (2001)

United Nations enable. Nations Convention on Rights of Persons with Disabilities (2007),
http://www.un.org/disabilities/default.asp?id=150

Verma, N.: Business Process Management: Profiting from Process, pp. 1–4. Global India publications pvt ltd., New Delhi (2009)

Wegge, K.P., Zimmermann, D.: Accessibility, Usability, Safety, Ergonomics, Concepts, Models and Differences. In: Stephanidis, C. (ed.) HCII 2007, Part I. LNCS, vol. 4554, pp. 294–301. Springer, Heidelberg (2007)

World economic forum. ICT for economic growth: A dynamic ecosystem driving the global recovery, pp. 1–7 (2009),
https://members.weforum.org/pdf/ict/ICT%20for%20Growth.pdf

W3C. Web Content Accessibility Guidelines (WCAG) 2.0 (December 11, 2008),
http://www.w3.org/TR/2008/REC-WCAG20-20081211/

Part III
Design Themes

Make Kitsch the Enemy: The "Monstrous Carbuncle" of the UK's Vetting and Barring Scheme

David Wastell[1] and Sue White[2]

[1] Nottingham University Business School, Nottingham, UK
Tel.: +44 (0) 7810522749
david.wastell@nottingham.ac.uk
[2] School of Social Policy, Institute of Applied Social Studies, University of Birmingham, UK
Tel.: +44 (0) 7974196716
s.white.3@bham.ac.uk

Abstract. In architecture, the primacy of function over form was one of the core tenets of the Bauhaus School of Design. In Information Systems, function is critical, yet so many systems fail to deliver hoped for benefits. Badly designed, acquired imitatively for their symbolic, magical power, they represent a form of kitsch. To illustrate this, we describe a major national IS initiative in the UK, the Vetting and Barring Scheme (VBS). Set up to ensure that only "suitable" adults would ever work with children and vulnerable adults, the Scheme became subject to increasing criticism for its intrusiveness and illiberality, and was suspended at the point of implementation in 2010. Here we expose the kitsch-ness of the Scheme as a meretricious imitation of the sort of diagnostic test used in medicine. We show how its inevitable dysfunctions outweighed its hypothetical benefits, which were largely magical and symbolic in nature. That the VBS attracted such little critical comment from IS scholars is significant, suggesting two biases (pro-business and pro-technology) in IS research which should be put right. We argue that kitsch can be combatted by practising design along principles akin to those of the Bauhaus. Our field can contribute to this, but our infatuation with theory, in itself a form of kitsch science, stands in the way of a closer relationship with practice.

Keywords: Design, kitsch, public services, Bauhaus, information systems, magic.

1 Prelude: From Bauhaus to Our House

In great design, form and function come together seamlessly. Every part contributes to the whole in a way that seems inevitable. So too in a great system. Hence I've coined the term beautiful system (Peters, 2005, p. 54)

Peters is right, aesthetics is more than a simple question of appearances: the well-designed artefact is a pleasure to use, be it high-tech or mundane. What matters is fitness-for-purpose, of form following function. In a cautionary tale, Norman gives the example of a friend, trapped in a set of swinging doors in a Boston hotel (Norman, 1998). Designed for visual appeal, with no visible pillars or hinges, his friend was

M. Nüttgens et al. (Eds.): Governance and Sustainability in IS, IFIP AICT 366, pp. 105–118, 2011.
© IFIP International Federation for Information Processing 2011

pushing against the hinge: "Pretty doors. Elegant. Probably won a design prize", the friend comments ruefully. The primacy of function in design, though hardly a new idea, was most notably espoused in modern times by the Bauhaus design school, especially under the leadership of its second director, Hannes Meyer (1928-30): "They rejected art... art is composition, but since building [is] only means to an end, building could never be an art form" (Droste, 2010, p. 69). Meyer's functional design philosophy is well reflected in the following quotation (van Leeuwen, 2005, p.71):

1. sex life, 2. sleeping habits, 3. pets, 4. gardening, 5. personal hygiene, 6. weather protection, 7. hygiene in the home, 8. car maintenance, 9. cooking, 10. heating, 11. exposure to the sun, 12. services - these are the only motives when building a house. We examine the daily routine of everyone who lives in the house and this gives us the functional diagram - the functional diagram and the economic programme are the determining principles of the building project.

As le Corbusier famously said, the house as "machine for living". Functionalism prospered in the Bauhaus and its influence on architecture has been profound, remarkably so for a small school which flourished for but a flash of time. Architectural functionalism has many critics, not least the novelist and acerbic essayist Tom Wolfe (Wolfe, 1981). Most would now agree that aesthetics, in the conventional sense of beauty, is important for buildings; they should be pleasing to the eye, not carbuncular! But for information systems, function is all, an anti-aesthetic if you like. What then does the record say, how well have we done in our house? Not so well, it would seem from the high rate of failure which continues to bedevil attempts to develop and deploy IT-based systems in organizations (Wastell, 2011). The problem is a chronic one. Writing 25 years ago, Reinermann (1986) comments on the widespread of "dissatisfaction with EDP[1] infrastructure" prevalent at the time. Interestingly, he goes on to proselytize the application of Bauhaus concepts to the design of information systems to redress this disquiet. He notes several "positive associations" between IS design and Bauhaus philosophy, singling out the following Bauhauser precepts as particularly relevant: a positive orientation to "modern technology"; the paramount emphasis on "user needs" and functionalism; concern with the "entirety of design", i.e. the need for all elements to fit together in "the great building"; the striving for standardization of modules and products; and finally, the need for designers to be equipped with "solid knowledge of modern technologies... only architects and designers who really know about the properties of materials and production methods are able to utilize their full potential".

Regarding functionalism, it is worth quoting Reinermann (with a little paraphrase) at length:

The Bauhaus favoured a grassroots approach: having new materials and production methods at our disposal, isn't there a different way to fulfill the functions of a product? "Form without ornament", "form follows function", no more "Kitsch for the rich", those were typical Bauhaus phrases. They led to courageous, resolute, sometimes radical approaches to new designs... [T]he analogy to information systems is obvious. Very often we have put administrative procedures on the computer as they

---

[1] Electronic Data Processing, in the terminology of yesteryear.

had been carried out traditionally... It is probably not too wrong to compare today's information systems to the time when gasoline engines were "added" to stage coaches....(ibid, p.75)

Kitsch for the rich is an apt phrase indeed, given the vast expenditure made by organizations on IT systems which so often fail to deliver. In thinking about IS design, the idea of kitsch will be explored further in this paper. Although, the term was originally used in connection with art, to distinguish between mass-produced imitations and original works of great quality, nowadays we use it to refer to anything second-rate and tasteless, the tacky stuff of gift shops and the like. But kitsch is not confined to the gift shop; it is ubiquitous. Launer (2008) talks for instance about medical kitsch, using the example of cognitive-behavioural therapy (CBT). He notes CBT's popularity with politicians as a cheap, quick fix for depression, and the public benefit it thereby confers in reducing unemployment and social security bills (Launer, 2008). Launer characterizes kitsch as "the mindless confusion of what is banal, glossy, easy to produce and cheap, with what is complex, subtle, painstaking and unique" (p. 111). The idea that a short course of treatment given by people with minimal training can yield long-term transformation of people's lives is pure kitsch. But it is difficult to resist, in giving us what we want in a simple prescription; who could be against it?

A well-designed Information System should inspire admiration and delight, but so often they don't, and as we have noted, the literature abounds with "atrocity stories" of design calamities. In this paper, we will explore the recent failure of a major national IS initiative in the UK, namely the Vetting and Barring Scheme (VBS). We have two aims in mind in telling this particular tale. The first is to explore the idea of kitsch and its remedies. The second is to provoke a little reflexive thought within the IS "discipline" itself, in particular on its proper object of study. Although the VBS is an information system and a consequential one to boot, it has received no critique from IS scholars, outside some cursory comments by ourselves. This omission suggests a serious "attentional disorder" within our research community, a form of techno-myopia, which we will briefly reflect on, considering how it might be redressed through a broadening of the research agenda and an eschewal of what we shall call "kitsch science".

2 The Fiasco of the Vetting and Barring Scheme

Madame Sosotris, famous clairvoyante,
With a wicked pack of cards. Here, said she,
Is your card, the drowned Phoenician sailor.
T.S. Eliot, The Wasteland

2.1 The Rise and Fall of the VBS

Those of us in the UK will remember the Soham murders only too well, but we will begin with a brief recapitulation of the case. In August 2002, two ten-year-old girls,

Holly Wells and Jessica Chapman, were drawn into the home of Ian Huntley, in the village of Soham (Cambridgeshire). We do not know why, but they may have thought his girlfriend, Maxine Carr (a teaching assistant in Holly and Jessica's class at primary school) was inside, but she was not and the children were brutally killed. The reasons for the murder have never been established, though sexual motives were implied at the trial. That Huntley was a caretaker at Soham Village College (located adjacently to the victims' school) caused public disquiet; it appeared he had been investigated in another part of the country (Humberside) for sexual offences involving girls under the age of consent, but this information had not emerged during the police vetting check when Huntley was appointed as caretaker.

In December 2003, a public enquiry was instigated led by Sir Michael Bichard to investigate the apparent failings of record keeping, vetting practices and information sharing that had occurred, and to make policy recommendations accordingly. Central to Bichard's recommendations was the setting up of a single, central body, with exclusive responsibility for administering the registration of all those wishing to work with children or vulnerable adults. A period of public consultation began on what became known as the Vetting and Barring Scheme (VBS) to be operated by an Independent Safeguarding Authority (ISA). Crucially this new body had the power to bar as well as vet. In a glossy document, published in March 2010, the key features of the Scheme are trumpeted as follows:

The Scheme aims to protect children and vulnerable adults by ensuring that people who are judged to present a risk of harm are not allowed to work with them. In the past, barring decisions have been taken by Ministers and civil servants. They are now made by an independent body of experts, the Independent Safeguarding Authority, and follow a clear and structured judgment process, which is about assessing the risk of future harm based on the information that is known about the individual (Home Office, 2010, p. 6).

The quote brings out a critical aspiration of the new scheme; the phrase "risk of future harm" implies the ability to predict. The concept of "future harm" is invoked on 22 further occasions throughout the 73 pages of the document, in three basic guises, as something posed, assessed or reduced. Yet nowhere is it defined or operationalized. What risk? What harm? The document itself has a strong kitschy quality in terms of its visual presentation, full of glossy images, generally of smiling, contented folk, "vulnerable people" in hospitals and schools, now made safe by the Scheme. This has the immediate smack of the "political kitsch" we readily associate with communist regimes: of May-day parades, simple slogans, sentimental images of happy workers in a workers' paradise, political party posters evoking idyllic folkloric scenes (Božilović, 2007). Lugg (1998, p. 4) speaks of kitsch as a powerful political construction: "designed to colonise the receiver's consciousness. As such Kitsch is the beautiful lie. It reassures and comforts the receiver … through readily understood symbolism". There are 25 such images in the main body of the document, some taking up a full page; a collage of three is shown in figure 1. Reading the crude semiotics of such visual propaganda, surely no-one can be in any doubt that the Scheme will work!

Announcing the Scheme in April 2008, Sir Roger Singleton (ISA's Chairman) said: "The Independent Safeguarding Authority will provide a ground-breaking vetting and barring service... allow[ing] us to ensure an improved level of safeguarding as well the development of better information sharing systems." Despite such worthy claims, the inception of the scheme in October 2009 was greeted with dismay on many sides given its scale and range. Over 11 million people would be covered, and it seemed that relatively minor contact with children in a voluntary capacity would require registration (e.g. parents helping with lifts to school sports events) and anyone seeking formal employment would also have to pay a significant fee. Crucially, soft data (e.g. evidence of drug misuse reported to social services) as well as hard data (criminal convictions) would be gathered. School leaders in particular were worried that the Scheme was overly bureaucratic and disproportionate, and that it would deter volunteers. Such concerns led to the VBS being scaled back, although the adjustments were relatively minor with 9 million individuals still caught in the net. The key date was set of November 2010 by which time anyone working in a "regulated activity" must be registered. Criticism rumbled on though throughout 2010. Civil liberties groups protested and the Royal College of Nursing also called for a judicial review. In June 2010, shortly after coming to power, the Home Secretary of the new Coalition Government announced that the Scheme would be put on hold and reviewed, describing it as draconian: "You were assumed to be guilty until you were proven innocent".

Fig. 1. Collage of images from the Vetting and Barring Scheme Guidance, March 2010

2.2 To Bar or Not to Bar, That Is the Question

In this section, we attempt to give a flavour of how the ISA's decision-making process was intended to work, constructed from a Guidance Note it published in

February 2009. It is difficult, but we will try to resist the temptation for lampoonery! The Note reaffirms the purpose of the Process as "to ensure that all barring decisions follow a standard process which affords a fair, rigorous, consistent, transparent and legitimate assessment of whether an individual should be prevented from working with children and/or vulnerable adults".

Organizationally, such decisions were to be made by a body of 100 or so administrative grade case-workers based at a single "central" location, in Darlington in the north east of England. As well as hard data regarding criminal convictions, the ISA's database would garner a range of softer information not just from statutory bodies and employers, but from any "informal source", including "for example, a newspaper article which gives cause for concern". From this hotpotch of material, so-called "facts" would be determined. How such facts would be produced is notable, keeping in mind that this is desk work conducted from a remote location. For instance, regarding evidence from employers the Guidance Notes states:

Referral information is received from employers which have dealt with individuals through their internal disciplinary procedures. The conclusions reached by employers are reviewed to establish, on a balance of probability, the facts. It is the facts of the case that determine whether the case requires further consideration and not the conclusions that the employer reached.

The Note also encourages case-workers to be vigilant for "cumulative behaviour":

You must look out for instances of behaviour which, although not in themselves determinative of the potential for risk, give rise to concerns when looked at cumulatively that someone may pose a risk of harm to children or vulnerable adults.

Having assembled the "facts", a "Structured Judgement Process" (SJP) is then applied focusing on "risk factors linked to future harm". These factors are divided into four broad areas. The first, for instance, is designated as "Harm-Related Interests/Intrinsic Drives", defined as behaviour "driven by or motivated out of a specific interest in, and/or fantasy about, harmful behaviour". How were the case-workers to identify such an "intrinsic drive". The SJP instructs case workers as follows:

Within this context, consider how far the case material reflects the presence or absence of the following risk factors (not exhaustive): Sexual preference for children; Excessive/obsessive interest in sexual activity; Personal gratification derived from thoughts/acts of violence or violent fantasy; Personal gratification derived from thoughts of being in control over others.

And to reiterate, this risk assessment is purely a desk exercise! Having weighed up the evidence, the case-worker then has to decide whether she is "minded to bar" or not. If the former, the individual is invited "to make representations". If no challenge is made, then the decision stands. How such "beating your wife" representations are handled is somewhat vague, although one thing is clear, it is not an independent procedure. The implication is that disputed decisions are resolved within the ISA's line management system; only a minority of cases are expected to reach the level of the ISA's Board (to be decided by the Director of Operations) but this is still part of the organization itself. The moral hazard is obvious. How likely it is that decisions will be over-turned when to do so would intrinsically undermine the validity of the organization's own, much vaunted, decision-making process?

2.3   Critique – More Harm Than Good

As a major, national information system, the fiasco of the VBS makes fascinating and instructive reading, and we wrote a pamphlet in 2010 excoriating the systemic deficiencies of the Scheme (White and Wastell, 2010). We put forward the hypothetical case of a 16 year old youth, with a fractured family background, who becomes involved in a fracas with another boy in a taxi queue, after a night on the town. The police are called, he is cautioned; because the other boy was 15, a violent assault against a "minor" is now on his record. Over the next few years, there are other minor non-violent crimes (e.g. shoplifting) as our protagonist struggles with drug use, but in his early twenties, he settles down determined to make something of himself. He volunteers to work in a third sector young person's service, aiming to train to be social worker, and is vetted. The ISA case-worker reviews his application; they do not meet him but evaluate his "electronic self" in the database, following their "clear and structured judgment process". What else could be decided other than "minded to bar", especially in an agency set up to extirpate risk. The wicked card is dealt; all are informed, the applicant and the agency. He may protest (how likely in this case?) but the damage has been done... ironically to the sort of young, vulnerable person the Scheme was designed to protect!

Aside from the social harm the scheme will inevitably produce, illustrated by this vignette, will it actually work in protecting children? We were highly skeptical. Most salient of all, it is hard to see how it would have protected Holly and Jessica. Yes, it would have excluded Huntley from the caretaker's job, but this was at another school; his connection with the children came via his girlfriend, and even the Scheme's intrusive tentacles do not stretch as far as checking partners. It may not have stopped Huntley, though it might have hindered him; it certainly would not have stopped Humbert Humbert, the ogre of Nabokov's "subversive comedy". Speaking of Lolita's mother, H. H. ponders monstrously:

I did not plan to marry Charlotte in order to eliminate her in some vulgar, gruesome and dangerous manner... Other visions of venery presented themselves to me swaying and smiling. I saw myself administering a powerful sleeping potion to both mother and daughter so as to fondle the latter through the night with perfect impunity (Nabokov, Lolita, pp. 70-71)

Though the hideous plan was ultimately superfluous, it's the thought that counts. Had the Scheme's architects perused that novel, some pause might have been given to their grandiose ambitions; but it seems not. Other absurdities derive from the definition of the activities to be regulated by the Scheme. Car park attendants and kitchen staff in the health service, for instance, would be covered. Not so a self-employed music instructor working with a child alone in their own home, making one of the images in our collage (figure 1) profoundly ironic. We drew particular attention to the publication of a "Myth-buster" web-page by central government, intended to defuse adverse media critique. Such criticisms, described as "Myths", were systematically refuted by the marshaling of so-called Facts, such as "the VBS will make it much harder for anyone known to pose a risk to gain access to children through paid or unpaid work". This is in no sense a fact, how can it be until the Scheme becomes an evaluated reality. We described such self-styled facts as magical thinking, that wishing something necessarily makes it true. Such magical thinking is typical of the language used throughout to describe the VBS; as we have seen, there is an unshakeable certainty that it will produce the desired effect.

The Scheme's apparent ignorance of the nature and circumstances of child abuse, particularly sexual abuse, was especially concerning. We noted how the Internet had exponentially increased the exposure of children to predatory adults outwith the gaze of the VBS. Add to this the vast numbers of workers from overseas in the UK's public services whose history cannot be traced. And so on, the complications multiply as the myths of the Scheme meet the facts of the real world. Putting all this together, we argued that such inconsistencies betrayed the real motives of the Scheme as less about protecting children than protecting government from the lynch-mob of public outrage in anticipation of future adverse events. The purpose of the Scheme was like that of all political kitsch, to soothe, to pacify, to make people feel secure; the Benign State has acted, and all may now sleep safely.

3 Back in the Bauhaus: The "Right Stuff" of IS Design

The breaking of a wave cannot explain the whole sea (Nabokov)

The VBS exemplifies many salient features of Beck's Risk Society: the application of "scientific models of hazard assessment" (Beck, 1998 p. 17) to control risks which are fundamentally incalculable; manufactured uncertainty (the production of risk by the effort to control it); and bureaucracy as a form of organized irresponsibility. The VBS depends crucially on the idea that the "risk of future harm" is something that can be predicted. It is one thing to exclude an individual from a job on the basis of their past record; certainly, had Huntley's unsavoury history been known, he would rightly have been appraised as unsuitable for the school job. It is quite another to predict the future, as the Scheme purports, using the language of risk. The idea that salient "facts" can be determined and processed through an algorithmic process to produce some sort of "calculable probability" is magic pure and simple. But this is what the Scheme purports to do: it provides "a clear and structured judgement process, which is about assessing the risk of future harm". To see the absurdity of such a claim, let us compare the VBS with a situation where such an actuarial approach is possible, the use of diagnostic testing in medicine. Writing in the year Wikipedia celebrates its tenth birthday, let's consult it for an example. Wikipedia, kitsch – we'll take the risk! Wikipedia gives the example of the faecal blood test to screen for bowel cancer and we shall use this to introduce key concepts and terminology. Consider the results presented in table 1 regarding the predictive efficacy of this test. The table show the test to yield 184 correct results, 2 "true positives" (TP) and 182 "true negatives". Errors fall into two categories: "false negatives" (FN) when a case is missed when the disease is present (FN=1), and the generally more prevalent "false positive", i.e. when there is a false alarm (FP=18).

Table 1. The faecal blood test to screen for bowel cancer

	Bowel cancer confirmed (by endoscopy)	No cancer present	Total
Positive test outcome	2	18	20
Negative outcome	1	182	183
Total	3	200	203

Two statistics are used to summarize the performance of binary tests: sensitivity (the proportion of predicted cases where the disease is actually present), and specificity (the proportion of cases where no disease is present and this is accurately indicated by the test). Formally, we have:

Sensitivity = TP / (TP + FN) = 2/3 = 66.7%
Specificity = TN/ (FP + FN) = 182/(18+182) = 91%

Both parameters are required to give a full appreciation of how well the test performs and mean different things. Sensitivity reflects how well the test predicts the disease whilst specificity reflects how effectively it indicates its absence. A high false positive rate compromises the latter, spuriously indicating the present of the disease. Here, sensitivity is relatively low, 1 of the 3 cancers is missed by the test, whereas specificity is high, 91%. High specificity is what we want in a screening test; its prime purpose is to provide reassurance. Here only 19 individuals are alarmed unnecessarily, compared with 182 who are correctly informed that they have no reason to fear. The distinction between sensitivity and specificity is crucial; for a screening test like this, it is specificity which is important: the purpose is to provide reassurance to those without the disease with a minimum of unnecessary distress (and expense) from false alarms. When a positive result is returned, this will be the occasion for a second stage of more rigorous investigation. Whether 91% is satisfactory is not the point; the point is that the figures allow rational decisions to be made about the value of the test.

In IS, we would not normally think of such diagnostic tests as information systems, but they certainly are, and again we need to ask ourselves why they fall outside our purview. In many ways, it could be argued that such systems represent something of an IS gold standard, the genuine article, the right stuff. What else do they do but provide information, and high quality, proven information to boot? Diagnostic tests are information systems whose design is informed by rigorous research (itself an information system) to establish the key properties of their performance, their predictive validity in particular. The faecal blood test is an IS whose efficacy has been materially appraised in terms of objectively defined and measurable properties and credible non-magical claims can be made regarding its performance. It is truly scientific, unlike the "kitsch science" which underpins so much social policy, including the VBS. Commenting acerbically on the "notoriously low predictive power" of social science, Lugg argues that it functions as a "kitsched version of science". She gives the example of the economic predictions made by such august bodies as the Federal Reserve:

These predictions are generally based on economic theory and statistical modelling (and contain an air of science), yet such musings run uncomfortably close to tea-leaf reading, as some professional economists will cheerfully concede.... Scientific-sounding prognosticians are met with great anticipation and reverence. Yet the actual merits of this national ritual, bolstered by kitsched science, go largely unquestioned (Lugg, 1999, p. 76)

Turning to the VBS, its kitsch-ness should now be self-evident. It purports to be scientific, to operate like the predictive, diagnostic tests of medicine. But it is an imposter, it is no such thing. There is no data whatsoever to appraise its efficacy. No idea of its sensitivity, or specificity, the likely false positive or hit rate. At the very least, one would have expected some piloting of the Scheme; its reliability could certainly have been appraised by submitting a sample of cases twice, checking for agreement. More fundamentally, is it actually possibly to make the type of judgements it is set up to make in a systematic way, to infer with any degree of confidence the presence of harmful drives and instincts from a mish mash of electronic data? Surely, such "diagnoses" require rigorous face-to-face investigation by highly-skilled clinical professionals. Empirical evidence that the "clear and structured judgement process" produced consistent results would be reassuring and important to demonstrate. Carrying out an analogous evaluation to that of the clinical screening test would, of course, be difficult, if not impossible. The equivalent of "the cancer" would be the occurrence of a case of serious harm to a vulnerable person. But unlike cancer, there is no definitive "endoscopic" investigation that can be carried out at the time of the test. Serious harm can only be known once it has happened; then it is too late, and cause-effect attributions can only be inferred with considerable caution. But no evaluation was even attempted. Worse still, the need for evaluation seems never to have occurred to policy-makers. One doubts the nuances of sensitivity and specificity ever troubled the consciences of the Scheme's votaries; a magical belief in its efficacy was quite enough.

4   Rocking the Boat

[Kitsch] is easy and syrupy. It does not postulate an observer with an active mind, with the imagination and creativity to grasp a work's potentialities (Edelman, 1995, p. 33)

We had two aims in mind in writing this paper. We will begin with the second, the neglect of the VBS by IS scholars and the implications of this for our field. Why did such a major and consequential system as the VBS, a project which developed over many years and was so often in the public eye, pass without critical scrutiny? One factor may be the continuing bias within our scholarship and research towards commercial organizations. Yes, there is certainly a smattering of IS research in the public domain, but it remains a minority genre, despite the vast investments on IT in the public sector, the burgeoning of e-Government as a global phenomenon, and the highly prominent failure of many major IT projects in the public sphere.

Another factor may simply be its low-tech nature, the fact that it was not explicitly talked about as an IT project. Yet IT certainly forms an integral part of the system, facilitating the flow of data from peripheral agencies to the nerve-centre of the Scheme, where databases and other electronic technology would store, process and report that information. In many ways, it is more of an information system than many of the systems which the majority of IS colleagues study. Properly speaking, these are not information systems at all, at least in the pure sense, as their primary goal is not the production of information. To use a handy phrase of Alty (2008), they are "IT-reliant work systems"; examples include: fulfillment systems for physical goods, package delivery systems, highly automated manufacturing systems. Information is important, but the primary production goal is something else, e.g. the manufactured article. In contrast, Alty defines a true information system as:

a system in which human participants and/or machines perform work using information, technology and other resources to produce informational products.

This is exactly what the VBS does: it is fundamentally a socio-technical system producing informational products involving the garnering of a range of data about individuals, some hard and some soft, and making decisions based on this about their suitability to work with children. That is its sole raison-d'etre. That it almost completely escaped our attention suggests that we may have become rather too enthralled with technology; because the technology of the VBS was not emphasized, we missed it. As simple, and as tragic, as that. Galliers's exhortation (Desouza et al., 2007) "to raise our sights beyond the IT artifact" would seem to be a timely injunction, to be heeded before it is too late. More generally, Galliers advocates a broader, more catholic prospectus for the "discipline":

We need to make the boundaries of our field more porous, to open up to the wider social science community. I use the term trans-disciplinary to describe this approach. It is the spaces between disciplines that require investigation and from which new knowledge will emerge. (pp. 267-8)

We would like to think that the work presented here, as the collaboration of an IS academic and a social work professor, provides a good example of what Galliers had in mind. Techno-myopia is one problem, but perhaps we also spend too much of our time doing the wrong things, writing self-referential journal papers, for instance, when we should be speaking out and entering the public debate, as we did here with our pamphlet on the VBS. We strongly concur with Desouza et al (2007) that the determination to make an impact, to make IS "really matter", needs to replace the obsession with publication in soi-disant "top-quality" journals, which no-one but ourselves reads. How absurd is that! More kitsched science…

Turning now to IS design, we again encounter Kitsch. The VBS provides just one more example of IS kitsch, albeit a spectacular one, once its true colours are revealed. Its "Structured Judgment Process" in particular is pure kitsch, a meretricious copy of the real thing, the medical diagnostic test. The SJP makes a complete mockery of the idea of expert professional decision making. Is it really possible to decide from a desk in Darlington, from data not specifically gathered for that purpose, whether an individual harbours harmful fantasies? This is preposterous. The VBS is an "ugly lie", providing meaningless reassurance that all will be well and avoiding confrontation with unpalatable truths, that some children do die in appalling circumstance, and perhaps there is little that we can do about it. Its publicity, like so much other official documentation of the day, is even more obviously kitsch: glossy and sloganistic, chocker-block with sentimental images. Propaganda is another name for it!

Kitsch is ubiquitous, like a rash. How apt a phrase it is for organisations that spend lots of money on technology, without doing the hard graft of design to produce something which works and is of genuine value. Brown & Hagel (2003) contend that the productivity paradox, the dissociation between investments in technology and actual benefits, reflects the failure of many organisations to use technology to innovate their business practices: "Companies that mechanically insert IT into their businesses will only destroy IT's economic value. Unfortunately, all too many companies do this" (p. 2). Kitsch for the rich! Magic, the fetishization of material objects, seems drive this faith in technology, this desire for kitsch solutions. Markus and Benjamin write of the enchantment of technology across all business sectors, and the need to break its spell:

Many IT-enabled change projects fail, …. we have argued that [this] stems from mistaken beliefs about the causes of change, belief in IT as a magic bullet. IT is not a magic bullet. Change in human behavior cannot take place at a distance but requires direct personal contact between change agents and targets…. Successful change takes good ideas, skill, and plain hard work — but it does not need magic (Markus & Benjamin, 1997, pp. 66-7)

If organisations are to gain real benefits from technology, kitsch must be eschewed. In medicine, Launer advocates "good, painstaking science" as the antidote to kitsch and its "plausible slogans". What is needed is a sound design approach utilizing "the positive aspects of the Bauhaus" (Reinermann, 1986, p. 80): no more adding "gasoline engines to stage coaches"! Though not all would approve, those Bauhausers certainly knew a thing or two about design and there is much we post-moderns can learn, especially in the world of information systems where appearance matters so much less than function. An IS should be fit-for-purpose above all else.

There are important implications in this for practice, and not just for IS practitioners. Elsewhere, we have argued that managers need to play a more central role in designing systems (Wastell, 2011). By "system", we mean "the work system", defined by Alter (2008) as "a system in which human participants and machines perform work using information, technology, and other resources to produce specific products and/or services". The definition is important. So-defined, it should be self-evident why we assert the design of such systems to be the manager's primary task, i.e. to configure the work-system under their jurisdiction as efficiently and effectively as possible. What else could "management" possibly mean? A change of managerial mind-set is thus needed; managers at all levels need to see themselves as designers, abjuring the magical and the meretricious. In the austere times ahead in the public services in the UK, and doubtless other parts of the world, such a "design attitude" (Boland and Collopy, 2004; Wastell, 2010) will become ever more pertinent as managers and the value they add, are apt to come under increasing scrutiny, and the pressures increase to do more with less. Let designing be the "day job", be it radical innovation, continuous improvement, or the mundane fine-tuning of existing designs, keeping form and function in alignment (Wastell, 2011).

Given the current vogue for evidence-based management (Baskerville, 2009; Wastell, 2010) there are important opportunities for IS scholars to seize. The time is ripe for our field. Our "design knowledge-base" is certainly formidable, ranging from practical design methods and tools, knowledge of particular classes of artefact and their impact, knowledge of the design process itself and its potential dysfunctions. This is especially the case for the "design science" wing of the field, which can look forward to a lustrous future. But the gap between theory and practice is still a wide one, with little of our knowledge-base making the cross-over into practical application. What is needed is a different dissemination approach and ethos, to make the knowledge accessible and actionable for the practitioner community. In this endeavor, care must be taken to avoid kitsch science. We have enough already: the plethora of TAM studies, for instance, each accounting for much the same 10% of variance, always leaving the remaining 90% unexplained! The test for kitsch in an applied discipline is whether anyone uses our theories in practice.

Finally, kitsch cannot be mentioned without invoking Milan Kundera, the Czech writer. For Sabina, the painter-protagonist in the Unbearable Lightness of Being, "kitsch was her image of home, all peace, quiet and harmony, and ruled by a loving mother and a wise father.... The less her life was like that sweetest of dreams, the more sensitive she was to its magic". Sabina thus proclaims kitsch as the enemy of her creativity, and those involved in the design of information systems, and IT-based systems more broadly, should do likewise:

Precisely by deflecting the creative and the uncertain, kitsch advances the repetitive, the secure and the comfortable, supplying the reassurance that what is to come will resemble what has gone before, that the hazards of innovation and uncertainty are far away, and that one is safe and secure in the routines of an unadventurous genre. (Binkley, 2000, pp. 135-6)

References

Alter, S.: Defining information systems as work systems: implications for the IS field. European Journal of Information Systems 17, 448–469 (2008)

Baskerville, R.: Preparing for evidence-based management. European Journal of Information Systems 18, 523–525 (2009)

Beck, U.: Politics of Risk Society. In: Franklin, J. (ed.) The Politics of the Risk Society, pp. 9–22. Polity Press, Cambridge (1998)

Binkley, S.: Kitsch as a Repetitive System: A Problem for the Theory of Taste Hierarchy. Journal of Material Culture 5, 131–152 (2000)

Boland, R.J., Collopy, F.: Managing as designing. Stanford Business Books, Stanford (2004)

Božilović, N.: Political kitsch and myth-making consciousness. Philosophy, Sociology and Psychology 6, 41–52 (2007)

Brown, J.S., Hagel, J.: Does IT matter? An HBR debate. Harvard Business Review (letters to the editor), 1–17 (June 2003)

Desouza, K.C., Ein-Dor, P., McCubbrey, D.J., Galliers, R.D., Myers, M., Watson, R.T.: Social activism in information systems research: making the world a better place. Communications of the Association for Information Systems 19, 261–277 (2007)

Droste, M.: Bauhaus. Taschen, Hohenzollernring (2010)

Edelman, M.: From art to politics. University of Chicago Press, Chicago (1995)

Home Office. The vetting and barring scheme guidance, Home Office report (March 2010) ISBN: 978-1-84987-202-7

Launer, J.: Medical kitsch. Postgraduate Medical Journal 8, 111–112 (2008)

Lugg, C.: Political kitsch and educational policy. In: Proceedings of the AERA Annual Convention, San Diego, pp. 1–25 (1998)

Lugg, C.: Kitsch: from education to public policy. Falmer Press, NewYork (1999)

Nabokov, V.: Lolita. Penguin Books, London (1955)

Norman, D.A.: The design of everyday things. Basic Books, New York (1998)

Peters, T.: Design - innovate, differentiate, communicate. DK Publishing, New York (2005)

Pfeffer, J., Sutton, R.I.: Evidence-based management. Harvard Business Review, 63–74 (January 2006)

Reinermann, H.: The design of information systems for local administrations: from Bauhaus to Rathaus. Computers, Environment and Urban Systems 11, 73–80 (1986)

Van Leeuuwen, T.: Introducing social semiotics. Routledge, Abingdon (2005)

Wastell, D.G.: Managing as designing: opportunity knocks for the IS field? European Journal of Information Systems 19, 422–431 (2010)

Wastell, D.G.: Managing as designing in the public services: beyond techno-magic. Triarchy Press, Axminster (2011)

Wastell, D.G., White, S.: Facts, myths and thought-styles.... and a rallying call for civic engagement. Journal of Strategic Information Systems 19, 307–318 (2010)

White, S., Wastell, D.G.: Catching Sex Offenders: Vigilance is the Best Safeguard. In: Why We Should Scrap the Vetting Database, pp. 13–19. Manifest Club Report, London (2010)

Wolfe, T.: From Bauhaus to Our House. Picador, New York (1981)

The Design – Reality Gap: The Impact of Stakeholder Strategies on IS Implementation in Developing Countries

Ranjan Vaidya, Michael D. Myers, and Lesley Gardner

Department of Information Systems & Operations Management, University of Auckland
Business School, Owen G Glenn Building, 12 Grafton Road, Auckland, New Zealand 1010
Tel.: +64 22587644, +64 9 373 7599, Ext.: 87468,
Tel.: +64 9 373 7599, Ext.: 86638
{r.vaidya,m.myers,l.gardner}@auckland.ac.nz

Abstract. A deep understanding of stakeholder strategies can be a powerful tool in helping IS researchers understand the realities of IS design and implementation in developing countries. We discuss the strategies used by stakeholders during the implementation of the first state government owned agricultural marketing information system project in India. Our main findings are that, while some stakeholder strategies were consistent with the implementation of the new system, most stakeholder strategies were not. Our findings may have important implications for the design and implementation of information systems in other developing countries.

Keywords: Stakeholder theory, Stakeholder strategy, information systems, interpretive case study, developing countries.

1 Introduction

The failure of ICT projects is a dominant theme within the ICT for development (ICT4D) research stream (Avgerou, 2008). Studies have related IS failure with stakeholder issues such as stakeholder expectations, impact on stakeholder interests and their involvement in IS design and implementation (Bailur, 2006; Bhatnagar, 2007; Krishna & Walsham, 2005; Kumar & Best, 2006; Lyytinen, 1988; Lyytinen & Hirschheim, 1987; Scholl, 2002; Walsham & Sahay, 2006).

Stakeholder issues have received considerable attention in IS, but the question that how stakeholders achieve their objectives through various strategies has been a neglected theme in information systems in developing countries (ISDC) research. This is in spite of the fact that study of stakeholder strategies provides useful insight on areas of IS intervention. Our research question is how stakeholder strategies impact ICT4D projects in developing countries.

We attempt to answer this question by the model proposed by Frooman (Frooman, 1999; Frooman & Murrell, 2005) as the theoretical basis for studying the stakeholder strategies in IS implementation at an agricultural marketing board in India. The board initiated the implementation in 2003 with an objective of connecting the various government agricultural markets of the state. The project involves four primary stakeholders; the farmers, government officers, the traders and the private partner company

M. Nüttgens et al. (Eds.): Governance and Sustainability in IS, IFIP AICT 366, pp. 119–134, 2011.

implementing the information system. We discuss the strategies of these stakeholders in relation to the success or failure of the information system.

The paper proceeds as follows. In the next section we briefly review the stakeholder strategies in the background of stakeholder theory. In section three we discuss the interpretive case study method used in the current research. Section four presents the case study. In section five we present our analysis of the study. The final section is the discussion and conclusion.

2   Stakeholder Strategies in Is Implementation

Stakeholder theory provides a theoretical framework for understanding stakeholders. Conflicting stakeholder interests provide the premises for the stakeholder theory and its ultimate concern is improvement in organizational ethics (Kaler, 2002; Phillips, Freeman, & Wicks, 2003). There are three distinct approaches to the stakeholder theory namely descriptive, instrumental and normative. The descriptive approach is concerned with the description of stakeholders and their conflicting interests. The instrumental approach views the stakeholders as a means for achieving the organizational objectives. The normative approach concerns itself with moral and ethical issues of stakeholder management and is at the core of both the descriptive and instrumental approaches (Kaler, 2002; Phillips, et al., 2003). According to Frooman (1999) stakeholder theory provides a framework for answering there basic stakeholder questions namely; who are the stakeholders? what are their interests? And how do they achieve these interests? Each of these questions has led to the development of separate research streams namely stakeholder identification, stakeholder interests and stakeholder strategies. While the first two questions have received adequate attention from researchers, the third has been left largely unexplored (Frooman & Murrell, 2005). Hence the contribution of this paper is that it studies the stakeholder strategies in ICT4D setting.

In the stream of management, this limitation in stakeholder theory research has been recognized and attempts have been made to provide theoretical frameworks for studying stakeholder strategies (Frooman, 1999; Frooman & Murrell, 2005; Hendry, 2005). These attempts are primarily based on the model proposed by Frooman (1999). In this model the choice of stakeholder strategy is determined by the resource relationship between the organization and stakeholders. Through control of various resources (physical, financial or informational) the stakeholders influence each other's decision making. The stakeholders may use direct strategies or indirect strategies. In direct strategies the stakeholders withhold the resources and force their dictates to the organization. In indirect strategies the decision making is influenced through involvement. The attributes proposed by Mitchell et al (1997) namely power, legitimacy and urgency may be used to understand the claims of the stakeholders on resources.

Frooman (1999) reviews the various strategies that are used by stakeholders such as boycotts and proxy resolutions, coercion or compromise, divestures, formation of coalitions, usage and withholding of resources, vendettas, use of allies, etc. Figure 1 below presents the model proposed by Frooman (1999) and presents the power dynamics between the organization and the stakeholder, while the figure 2 presents the strategy used by the stakeholder.

Typology of Resource Relationships			
		Is the stakeholder dependent on the firm	
		No	Yes
Is the firm dependent	No	Low interdependence	Firm power
on the stakeholder	Yes	Stakeholder power	High interdependence

Fig. 1. Frooman (1999) typology of resource relationship

Typology of Influence Strategies			
		Is the stakeholder dependent on the firm	
		No	Yes
Is the firm dependent	No	Indirect/ withholding	Indirect/ usage
on the stakeholder	Yes	Direct/ withholding	Direct/ usage

Fig. 2. Frooman (1999) typology of choice of strategy

The model proposed by Frooman (1999) has some limitations. We highlight these as follows:

1. First, the unit of analysis in Frooman's model is organization. This is highlighted by the use of the term "stakeholder theory of firms" in place of "stakeholder theory" in various studies (Brenner et al in Mellahi & Wood, 2003). A general criticism of the stakeholder theory is that it has been applied to a formally constituted collective such as an organization with its suppliers. According to Preston & Sapienza (1990) "the stakeholder model is an organizational construct". However ICT4D projects often involve stakeholders that lack a clear organizational structure such as traders, villagers, farmers, urban poor, city dwellers, etc. There are various examples of research studies that present examples of such informally existing groups such as poor women, farmers, pensioners, school teachers, drivers and vehicle owners, students, etc (Best & Kumar, 2008; Ciborra, 2005; Heeks & Arun, 2010; Kumar & Best, 2006; Lewis & Madon, 2004). Stakeholder literature often regards such stakeholders as secondary in spite of the fact that they are the primary stakeholders in these projects (Zietsma & Winn, 2008). We suggest that the unit of analysis for stakeholder strategies should not be limited to the organization, but expanded to include other kinds of collectives such as farmers.

2. Second, Frooman's model is based on a single construct i.e. resource dependence. It has been accepted by Frooman (Frooman & Murrell, 2005) that resource dependence is just one construct as is mentioned "Specifically, we test whether one component of a firm's relational setting—its resource relationships with

stakeholders—is a determinant of the choice of strategies stakeholders use to influence a firm". Moreover other studies have shown that the strategies that stakeholders choose are not based on resource requirements only (Mellahi & Wood, 2003). Cultural factors may also play an important role in influencing the decision making (Walsham & Sahay, 1999).

3. Third, empirical studies have indicated that the model proposed by Frooman is a parsimonious model but does not account for the use of multiple strategies simultaneously (Hendry, 2005).

In this paper we try to overcome these limitations by studying the strategies for each stakeholder and we do not bind ourselves to the construct of resource dependence alone. Also our objective in this paper is not to present a refined model of stakeholder strategies and the conditions in which a particular strategy is chosen. Instead we discuss the strategies from the point of view of their impact on the success of information system. Our theoretical contribution is twofold. First we demonstrate that strategies are a means for understanding the complex reality in ICT4D projects. Second we attempt to identify the attributes of strategies that negatively impact IS success. The theoretical model that we propose for information system development, implementation and use is presented in figure 3 below. The model presents stakeholder strategies as a mediating construct between IS design & implementation and social reality. The bidirectional arrow between stakeholder strategies and social reality suggests that stakeholder strategies both cause and are caused by social realities and hence reflect the realities of IS design and implementation. The other bidirectional arrow suggests that IS design and implementation and stakeholder strategies should inform each other.

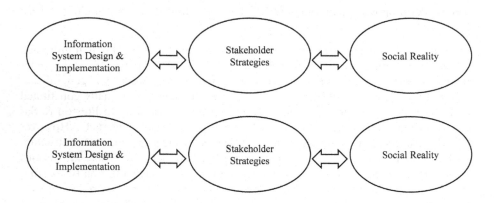

Fig. 3. Stakeholder strategy based model for IS design and implementation

3 Research Method

Our overall approach in the present study has been qualitative, as qualitative research helps the researchers to understand the behaviour of people in the light of their context and values (Myers, 2009). Our epistemological stance is interpretive (Klein

& Myers, 1999; Nandhakumar & Jones, 1997; Orlikowski & Baroudi, 1991). One reason for choosing an interpretive approach is that interpretive research does not require the formulation of constructs a priori (Cavaye, 1996). Moreover interpretive case studies are well suited for studying the phenomenon in context (Cavaye, 1996; Klein & Myers, 1999; Walsham, 2006).

The data for the study was collected by one of the authors for a six month period in 2009 and 2010. The data was collected from semi structured interviews, observations, field notes and government records. Overall 27 interviews were conducted with far-mers, government officers, private partners and traders. Table 1 presents the distribu-tion of interviews:

Table 1. List of stakeholder Strategies

Stakeholder	Interviews
Government employees	7
Private partners	9
Traders	2
Farmers	9

The interviews with the government officers and private partners were undertaken at different levels of hierarchy. The interviews with the farmers and traders were undertaken at market yards as well as their villages. These interviews and field visits were carried out at six different yards in the state. The interviews lasted from between 30 minutes to 2 hours. The interviews with all the respondents were undertaken in Hindi language. The interviews with the farmers were recorded while notes were taken for the interviews with other stakeholders. The data was analysed with NVivo software. Certain documents and reports such as project reports, yard details, Perfor-ma, reports generated by IS, etc were collected both from the office of the private partners as well as the government offices.

4   Case Description

This case study describes the implementation of an information system at an agricul-tural marketing board in one of the states of India. The project is unique as it is the first effort by state government in India to integrate the government owned market yards through the use of information and communication technologies (ICT). These yards are a common meeting platform for the traders and the farmers.

4.1 The State

The state under study is one of the twenty eight states of India. The total population of the state is over 60 million of which over seventy percent is rural. There are over fifty thousand villages in the state and agriculture is a major source of livelihood. The state is a leading producer of various agricultural commodities in India namely soybeans, grams, oilseeds and pulses. Local farmers sell their commodities to the traders in the government owned market yards. These yards are managed by a committee comprising of the traders, farmers and government officers.

4.2 History of Market Yards

The agricultural commodity markets in India were regulated through the Bombay Cotton Market Act of 1927. The act specified the establishment of certain open yards where un-baled cotton of the farmers could be marketed (Singh, 2007). This resulted in creation of market yards where the farmers sold their commodities to the traders through commission agents. Initially these yards were completely autonomous bodies but in early seventies the state government created a state level agricultural marketing board for controlling the yards. This saw some changes in the yard administration. A common exemplary code of rules was prescribed for all yards of the state, the process of commissioning was banned and the middle and upper management employees of the yard were absorbed as board employees.

4.3 Agricultural Marketing Board

The Agricultural Marketing Board is the apex organization in the state responsible for providing marketing support to the farmers. The board can be viewed as a three level organization. The first level comprises of the market yards where the trade transactions take place. At the second level are the regional offices that control and monitor the yards. At the third level is the head office which is located in the state capital. At present there are over two hundred yards in the state.

4.4 Process of Trade Transactions

The trade transactions at the yard includes processes of auctioning of the commodities, weighing of the commodities, payments to the farmers and depositing of the service charges by the traders. These are described in steps below:

- **Step 1:** The farmers enter the yards and are issued an entry slip.
- **Step 2:** After entry farmers display their commodities for sale to traders at designated spots. A yard employee such as an inspector conducts the auction in front of the traders and the farmers.
- **Step 3:** After the auction is over the commodity is weighed by the contractual labourers and the weight is certified by a weight certificatory.
- **Step 4:** The farmer collects payment from the trader.

- **Step 5:** The trader is required to deposit the service charges payable to the yard committee. The service charge is two percent of the payment value[1] . After the service charge is deposited, the trader is issued a 'no objection certificate' by the yard authorities. The trader is required to show this certificate for transporting the commodities to other states.

4.5 Problems in Manual System

The process of selling and buying at the yard is one which involves various sub processes such as auctioning, weighing, etc. This is exacerbated by complicated documentation that needs to be reconciled for the calculations of service charges payable by the traders. Often the data may not reconcile and this is a major embarrassment for the government employees. Such a situation is exploited by the traders who manipulate the trader records and under report their transactions. Furthermore, the farmers travel long distances to reach the market yards. Often the rates are unfavourable and they end up with losses. There are conflicts between the various stakeholders on issues related to quality of the commodity, payments to farmers, etc. Thus the exploitation of the farmers provided the overall rationale for initiating the computerization project in 2003.

4.6 Computerization of Yards

The project aimed at capturing the data of all the processes electronically through computer terminals, hand held electronic terminals and electronic weigh bridges. At each yard the data is uploaded to a central server and is redistributed to various yards, inter-state check posts and the board head office. The data is also displayed on the website of the board. At each computerized yard, the processed data (auction rates, etc) are displayed on TV sets. The project is being implemented in phases and presently the data is captured from over sixty market yards.

The project has been conceived and executed by the board and a consortium of organizations. The entire investment on hardware, software, manpower and maintenance has been done by the private partners. The board pays the vendor a percentage of the total service charges collected.

An evaluation by the Department of Information Technology, Ministry of Information and Communication Technology, Government of India in 2008 indicates that the project has been successful in providing timely payments to the farmers, reducing the errors in transactions and providing an overall improved quality of services (DIT, 2008 pp 92). Empirical evidence however suggests that there are certain issues with IS implementation.

5 Case Analysis

The farmers, government officers, traders and the private partners are the primary stakeholders on the basis of the dimensions of *power, legitimacy* and *urgency*

---

[1] A further 0.20 percent fee is charged from the traders and is contributed in the fund for the homeless people. Thus a trader pays a total fee of 2.20 percent.

(Mitchell, et al., 1997). These stakeholders have different contexts and requirements. A poor farmer for example approaches the yard when there is a need to repay some loan or there is a social function in his family. The government officer gets his income from the income of the yard. The private partner's revenue is based on certain percentage share of the yard income. The trader obviously makes his profit through the yard and thus has immense stakes in the working of the yard.

These stakeholders use various strategies to serve their interests in the yard. These strategies have positive, *negative* or *neutral* impacts on the success of information systems. Table 2 below lists the various positive, negative and neutral strategies adopted by the stakeholders. One the left hand side of the table the impact of the strategy is presented *as negative, positive* or *neutral*. Corresponding to the four stakeholders, each of the negative, positive and neutral strategy is presented. For example the farmers use negative impact strategies or *quality manipulations* and *signing multiple contracts*. The positive impact strategies of the farmers include *stocking and mortgaging of commodities*. The neutral strategies include *exercise of patience* and *agitations*.

Table 2. List of stakeholder Strategies

Stakeholders / Strategy impact	FARMERS	TRADERS	PRIVATE PARTNERS (PP)	GOVERNMENT OFFICERS
NEGATIVE	Quality Manipulations	Smuggles Commodity	Deploys inadequate staff	Ignores the rules/regulations
	Signing multiple contracts	Under reporting	Deploys untrained staff	Apathetic to subordinate needs
POSITIVE	Stocking	Stocking	Facilitates free communication	Observes suspicious traders
	Mortgages the commodity	Lesser margins and higher transactions	Conveys to employees the differences in govt & PP	Resorts to clauses of contract in dealing with PP
NEUTRAL	Maintains patience in some processes	Advance payments	Maintains its work culture	Replies to internal notices diplomatically
	Agitations	Blames the government	Blames the government	Levies penalty on the traders

Given space limitations, we will discuss only those strategies that have a negative impact on the information system below. Of course, it is the negative strategies that cause most of the difficulties with the implementation of the system.

5.1 Farmer Strategies

Often the farmers manipulate the commodity quality by mixing the old harvest with the new. By doing so their commodity is sold at higher rates. Sometimes such quality manipulations are detected by the traders and this is a major source of conflict at the yard. These manipulations are sometimes intentional and sometimes because of contextual factors. One of the farmers explained the context of these quality manipulations as under:

"See in this field you will observe that the wheat crop is not homogenous. Some grains have grown tall while others are stunted. The farmer here has mixed different seed varieties. He might not have enough money to buy new seeds. Or maybe his intention is to sell the commodity in the yard. So if the higher quality grains are mixed with the lower quality, there are chances that the commodity can be sold for higher rates." According to a private partner employee:

"Often the farmers have old stock of commodity. Such stock has lost its lustre and the farmers know that it won't yield them a good price. So the crafty farmers sometimes mix the old stock with the new. Sometimes various farmers share the lorry and their produce gets mixed up and results in a mixed quality".

One government officer described a typical situation arising out of such quality manipulation:

"A farmer brought some chillies for selling. The sample that was shown to the trader had a very good quality. The trader quoted a rate of 4000 rupees a quintal. But beneath the good quality there was the very poor quality. When the commodity was weighed a conflict arose, the trader refused to pay the rate of 4000 rupees. The farmer then called some goons in the yard premises and they started threatening the trader"

The immediate outcome of such a quality manipulation is a conflict between farmers and traders. Such conflicts are resolved through the intermediations of the government officers. In the long term however, such manipulations result in a trust deficit between the stakeholders as well as the information systems. The current project implementation ignores quality manipulations by the farmers and hence no quality assessment mechanism has been introduced. This was aptly mentioned by a government officer who mentioned that:

"The farmer does not have grading equipment for these different commodities. So if we can install these different grading machines in the yard. Such conflicts will be reduced. So computerization should look into these aspects also".

Also the farmers sometimes sign auction contracts with more than one trader. An auction contract is a binding agreement between the trader and the farmer. Farmers sign multiple contracts and sell the commodity to the trader that offers the best rate. Various contextual factors force the farmers to choose this strategy. Sometimes because of the huge crowd, the auctions are conducted in haste by the government officers and farmers do not get sufficient time to consider the suitability of the rates. Often farmers are not aware about their right to cancel the auction contract in situations of unsatisfactory rates. Moreover, the process of cancellation requires that the farmers write an application. Given their literacy levels, most of the farmers are uncomfortable with writing such applications. Also the process of cancellation is a bureaucratic procedure and the already exhausted farmer naturally desists from it. This strategy has a negative impact on the success of the information system as it results in massive data reconciliation problems. This is because multiple contracts are issued but only few fulfilled. One government officer explained this as under:

"It is quite common here that the farmers do not respect their auctions contracts. If the prices increase they re-auction their commodity and don't cancel their previous contracts. This has implications on the other yard processes as two contracts exist for single transaction".

In the long run this results in the trust deficit between the stakeholders which has negative impact on the information system.

5.2 Trader Strategies

Apart from the farmers, the traders also resort to various strategies that have a negative impact on success of information system. They smuggle the commodity in the adjoining states without paying appropriate service charges for them. One of the private partner respondents explained how the traders implemented this strategy:

"See the traders usually export common commodities such as wheat, soya bean, etc to the adjoining states. They pay all the service charges and taxes for these commodities. But often within these commodities they keep a few bags of commodities that are highly priced such as poppy seeds. The check post inspectors neither have the time nor the resources to verify each commodity bag. They just ensure that the vehicles have all required documents. Thus the high priced commodities are smuggled to the other states without any service charge or tax paid on them".

The current information system does not have the ability for physical verification of the commodities at the check posts. The strategy has a negative impact on the success of information system as the government officers are helpless in curbing the smuggling by the traders.

Another strategy of the traders that has direct negative impact on IS success is under reporting of their trade transactions. This reduces their service charge payments. Such a strategy has a negative impact on information system as it creates massive problems of data reconciliation. A private partner employee described the mechanism of under reporting by the traders as under:

"It's common in the yards that traders do not accurately report the commodity prices. The traders need a tax paid certificate in order to sell the commodity forward. This certificate is issued for the quantity of a commodity. The traders report that the commodity was purchased at a very low cost and show a higher stock. Such manipulations get highlighted only when we scrutinise the computerised record. It's only then we realise that the trader had purchased, for example, only 50 quintal of a commodity but has exported 80 quintals. For example the usual rate of garlic is around 1800 rupees a quintal. But those who do the manipulations of weight and commodity, they report the rate at around 300 to 400 rupees per quintal. They show an increased stock to adjust their unrecorded transactions".

There are certain contextual factors that allow the traders to continue with such strategies. The policy of the board requires that income of the employees should be generated through their respective yards. The income of the yards directly depends on the service charge payments of the traders. This makes the government officers vulnerable to corruption. Secondly the yards had been operated manually for a long time. The crowd situations in the yards have made it very difficult to monitor all the transactions of the traders. Consequently the traders have become habituated to submit records as per their will. The current information system changes this situation as the records of traders are available with the click of the mouse. Obviously the traders have opposed the introduction IS in certain yards. One of the private partner employees mentioned that:

"In some yards the commodities with high monetary values are traded and we need to exercise a lot of vigilance and caution there. At some occasions our employees were physically threatened. If you try to help them (*traders*) understand the rationale of computerization, they say that we are least interested in understanding this. They say we do not want to know about your system. They want that the documentation should be done as per their will. They submit the records as they want, and care least about the rules, regulations and law".

Also the traders have strong links with the other power groups such as politicians and the press. This accentuates their power and motivates them further to use negative-impact strategies. Overall the employment of such strategies results in a lack of sense of ownership amongst the stakeholders. The trust deficit further motivates the stakeholders to use negative impact strategies thereby jeopardising the success of IS.

5.3 Private Partner Strategies

The private partners that are implementing the information system also employ various negative impact strategies. The private partner's objective is profit maximization through service delivery. Cost reduction contributes to it. One ways to reduce the cost is to deploy fewer human resources. Another way is to deploy lowly skilled human resources. The private partners use both these strategies. This has serious negative implications on the success of information system because the fundamental tasks such as data entry are not done properly. According to one government officer, often the private partner does not provide the number of employees as agreed in the contract. The government officer explained this as under:

"The commodities of the farmers are weighed at the weigh points. I have over fifty such weigh points in this yard. If the private partners need actual data from the field, they have to employee around fifty people with the hand held terminals here to capture the live data. Moreover they will need some people at the auction spot. This will create a requirement of around 60 people here. But they have deployed only 10-12 people. So they deploy lesser staff and use our records for entering the data".

Another employee described this situation as under:

"Contractors in India usually have a tendency to minimise the expenditure irrespective of its impact on the quality. So that's what happening here with the private partner. They are minimising their cost by staffing lower quality of staff and lesser number of employees."

Another strategy of the private partner is to misinterpret the reports generated by the IS. This has negative impact on the overall trustworthiness of the information systems. The managers obviously question credibility of the information generated from the information system. This was explained by one of the government officer as under:

"I will give you one more example of the kind of tricks that private partners play to prove the effectiveness of the IS. The traders submit their records of the transaction usually after ten days. For instance for the trade done between the 1st and 10th of a month, the trader submits the record on 11th. Similarly for the next 10 days, the records are submitted after 20th. Obviously if you check the computerized records on the fifteenth, it will show that some traders have not paid their service charges. So the private partner reports a recovery from the trader, when in effect the truth is that the trader has not yet submitted the records. So the private partners do such false reporting to show that the IS has been successful in recovering the service charge payments".

The choice of such negative strategies results in trust deficit between the government officers and the private partners. This has negative consequences on the success of information system.

5.4 Government Officer Strategies

In dealing with the other stakeholders, particularly the traders and farmers, the government officer's decision making is influenced by factors that are above the rules and regulations of the market. Over the years the officers have developed a strategy of first acquiring the knowledge about the background of the person and then dealing with his concerns. The issues are not resolved as per the applicable rules. The impact of such a strategy is that the expectation of *transparency* due to IS intervention is lost. One of the government officers was frank to admit this and mentioned that:

"This organization presents a classic case of working of a government functionary. Any person is scot free here. He can behave the way he likes to. Here if there is slightest problem in any process such as auction or weighing, then the person comes here to fight with me. They know that they are talking to a government officer and so he can be suppressed. They can make my complaint any time and so they come here and start fighting. So what I have to do is that I need to look at the overall background of the person and then I have to deal with him. If he has a political background, he needs to be treated differently. So I have to look at the background of the person first and the booklet on the rules and regulations of market is kept aside. See we run this place with our tact and not with the Act".

Often the senior government officers have developed a strategy of dealing their subordinates with apathy. This was mentioned by one government officer as under:

"So in India no one thinks about these matters. Our work is not even analyzed, forget about appreciation. I am almost going to complete about two years in this yard and in this duration none of my seniors have given me any feedback about my work."

This has negative impact on IS implementation as the organizational prerequisites of structural changes are not met. The rigid bureaucracy results in a lack of sense of belonging and ownership. This creates a trust deficit and further motivates the stakeholders to employ negative impact strategies. The recursive relationship between these factors and negative impact strategies is presented in Figure 4 below:

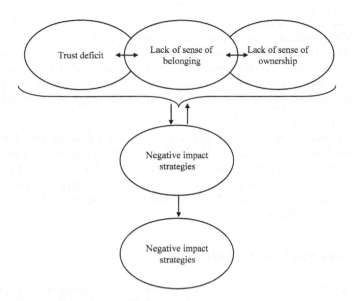

Fig. 4. Recursive relationship between negative impact strategies and trust deficit, sense of belonging and ownership

5.5 Attributes of Negative Impact Strategies

We have seen that the stakeholders use various strategies that have a potentially nega-tive impact on IS success. These range from smuggling the commodities to showing apathy to the subordinates. We next present some attributes that are common in the various negative impact strategies:

1. **Crowd Situations:** Negative impact strategies are employed in crowd/ haste situa-tions. For example in the current study, it is observed that due to huge crowd at the entrance/ exit gate of the yard, it often becomes difficult to track the entries/ exit of the commodities from the yard. This situation is exploited by the traders to under report their commodities. This attribute has direct application in ICT4D projects as most of such projects are implemented in crowd situations. For the IS to be suc-cessful, it becomes important that such crowd situations should be avoided by em-phasis on queue management techniques.
2. **Time value of commodity:** The choice of a negative impact strategy is also de-termined to some extent by the future value of the commodity. If a positive/ neutral strategy, such as stocking, involves a commodity that loses its economic value with the passage of time, then a stakeholder is likely to choose a negative impact strate-gy. Farmers, for example, often stock their commodities. In some commodities such as soy bean and wheat, stocking results in the loss of lustre of the commodity. The commodity thus loses its value. In such cases farmers manipulate their quali-ties by mixing the old stock with the fresh stock. In *agricultural marketing information systems*, this attribute is of particular interest.
3. **Non-Retractability and involvement of other stakeholders:** Negative impact strategies are either not completely retractable or retractable only after considerable

resources have been exhausted. For example, a farmer who mixes two different commodities of wheat cannot retract. The retraction is possible, only by deploying considerable effort or technological resources. Moreover this retraction requires involvement of other stakeholders. A farmer may sign multiple auction contracts but if he chooses to get these cancelled; he needs to submit an application to the government officers. It is only after their approval that such contracts can be cancelled.

Of these attributes some are of immense practical significance. For example the attribute related to *crowd situations*. Earlier studies from developing countries have revealed that queue management does have a positive impact on IS implementation (Bhatnagar, 2007 pp 22). Retraction of negative impact strategies requires the involvement of other stakeholders. Thus it is important to identify processes that involve multiple stakeholders.

6 Discussion and Conclusions

Information systems projects in developing countries have a record of being implemented in an ad hoc manner (Bailur, 2006). In ICT4D projects that involve multiple stakeholders, an understanding of these strategies can provide an effective tool in understanding how these strategies can have positive or negative impacts on the success of the system. It is to be noted that the most of the negative impact strategies not only seem to be against the existing rules and regulations but also are unethical. In the current case various strategies such as smuggling of the commodities, under reporting the trade transactions, quality manipulations, etc have not been fully brought under the scope of IS. Given that this project is the first government owned agricultural marketing information system project in India and that other states are likely to follow its implementation, one idea would be to design the IS so as to curb the negative impact strategies of the stakeholders.

We acknowledge various limitations of the current study. First, the study is India specific. Though past studies on agricultural marketing in developing countries reveal common issues (FAO, 2001; A. Shepherd, 2005; A. S. Shepherd, 1997), yet agriculture in India may have some unique characteristics. Second, the results from the study are specific to agricultural marketing information systems. Urban ICT4D projects will have different stakeholders and hence there will be variations in the strategies. However, we believe that the overall approach of studying stakeholder strategies might well be relevant for the design and implementation of ICT4D projects in other countries and different industries.

References

Avgerou, C.: Information systems in developing Countries: a critical research review. Journal of Information Technology 23, 133–146 (2008)

Bailur, S.: Using Stakeholder Theory to Analyze Telecenter Projects. Information Technologies and International Development 3(3), 61–80 (2006)

Best, M., Kumar, R.: Sustainability Failures of Rural Telecenters: Challenges from the Sustainable Access in Rural India (SARI) Project. Information Technologies and International Development 4(4), 31–45 (2008)

Bhatnagar, S.: Impact Assessment Study of Computerised Service Delivery Projects from India and Chile. IT at World Bank, Staff Working Paper (42147), 2 (2007)

Cavaye, A.L.M.: Case study research: a multi-face-ted research approach for IS. Information Systems Journal 6, 227–242 (1996)

Ciborra, C.: Interpreting e-government and development: Efficiency, transparency or governance at a distance? Information Technology and People 18(3), 260–279 (2005)

DIT. Draft Report on Impact Assessment of e-Governance Projects. Depertment of Information Technology, Government of India, New Delhi (2008)

FAO. Information and communication technologies servicing farm radio: New contents, new partnerships. Paper presented at the International Workshop on Farm Radio Broadcasting, Rome, Italy (February 19-22, 2001)

Frooman, J.: Stakeholder Influence Strategies. Academy of Management Review 24(2), 191–205 (1999)

Frooman, J., Murrell, A.J.: Stakeholder Influence Strategies: The Roles of Structural and Demographic Determinants. Business Society 44(3) (2005)

Heeks, R., Arun, S.: Social outsourcing as a development tool: The impact of outsourcing it services to women's social enterprises in Kerala. Journal of International Development 22(4), 441–454 (2010)

Hendry, J.R.: Stakeholder Influence Strategies: An Empirical Exploration. Journal of Business Ethics 61, 79–99 (2005)

Kaler, J.: Morality and Strategy in Stakeholder identification. Journal of Business Ethics 39, 91–99 (2002)

Klein, H., Myers, M.: A set of principles for conducting and evaluating interpretive field studies in information systems. MIS Quarterly 23(1), 67–93 (1999)

Krishna, S., Walsham, G.: Implementing public information systems in developing countries: Learning from a success story. Information Technology for Development 11(2), 123–140 (2005)

Kumar, R., Best, M.: Impact and Sustainability of E-Government Services in Developing Countries: Lessons Learned from Tamilnadu, India. The Information Society 22, 1–12 (2006)

Kumar, R., Best, M.L.: Impact and sustainability of E-government services in developing countries: Lessons learned from Tamil Nadu, India. Information Society 22(1), 1–12 (2006)

Lewis, D., Madon, S.: Information systems and nongovernmental development organizations: Advocacy, organizational learning, and accountability. Information Society 20(2), 117–126 (2004)

Lyytinen, K.: Expectation failure concept and systems analysts view of information system failures: Results of an exploratory study. Information & Management 14(1), 45–56 (1988)

Lyytinen, K., Hirschheim, R.: Information failures—a survey and classification of the empirical literature. Oxford Surveys in Information Technology 4, 257–309 (1987)

Mellahi, K., Wood, G.: The Role and Potential of Stakeholders in "Hollow Participation": Conventional Stakeholder Theory and Institutionalist Alternatives. Business & Society Review 108(2), 183–202 (2003)

Mitchell, R.K., Agle, B.R., Wood, D.J.: Toward a theory of stakeholder identification and salience: Defining the principle of who and what really counts. Academy of Management Review 22, 853–886 (1997)

Myers, M.: Qualitative Research in Business & Management. Sage publications, London (2009)

Nandhakumar, J., Jones, M.: Too close for comfort? Distance and engagement in interpretive information systems research. Info Systems Journal 7, 109–131 (1997)

Orlikowski, W.J., Baroudi, J.: Studying information technology in organizations: research approaches and assumptions. Information Systems Research 2(1), 1–28 (1991)

Phillips, R., Freeman, R.E., Wicks, A.C.: What Stakeholder Theory Is Not. Business Ethics Quarterly 13(4), 479–502 (2003)

Preston, L.E., Sapienza, H.J.: Stakeholder management and corporate performance. Journal of Behavioral Economics 19(4), 361–375 (1990)

Scholl, J.H.: E-government: A Special Case of ICT-enabled Business Process Change. Paper presented at the Proceedings of the 36th Hawaii International Conference on System Sciences (2002)

Shepherd, A.: Bringing market information to farmers: opportunities through FM radio, vol. 9. Agricultural Support Systems Division, FAO, Rome (2005)

Shepherd, A.S.: Market Information Services: Theory and Practice Rome: FAO (1997)

Singh, B.: Whither Agriculture in India. N. R. Agrawal & Company, India, Agra (2007)

Walsham, G.: Doing interpretive research. European Journal of Information Systems 15, 320–330 (2006)

Walsham, G., Sahay, S.: GIS for district-level administration in India: Problems and opportunities. MIS Quarterly: Management Information Systems 23(1), 39–66 (1999)

Walsham, G., Sahay, S.: Research on Information Systems in Developing Countries: Current Landscape and Future Prospects. Information Technology for Development 12(1), 7–24 (2006)

Zietsma, C., Winn, M.I.: Building chains and directing flows: Strategies and tactics of mutual influence in stakeholder conflicts. Business and Society 47(1), 68–101 (2008)

Understanding the Role of Information Technology for Organizational Control Design: Risk Control as New Control Mechanism

Manuel Wiesche, Michael Schermann, and Helmut Krcmar

Boltzmannstr. 3, 85748 Garching, Germany
Tel.: +49 (0) 89 289 19532
{wiesche,michael.schermann,krcmar}@in.tum.de

Abstract. Organizational control is one of the fundamental functions of management. Although controls come along with performance constraints, organizations rely on control mechanisms to direct attention, motivate, and encourage organizational members to act according to organizational goals and objectives. Managers build their decision on control design on the degree of knowledge about the value creation process and the predictability of the outcome. In this paper, we enhance a popular theoretical framework for organizational control design by enclosing IT-enabled controls. We explore the framework empirically in a multiple case study on Governance, Risk management, and Compliance information systems (GRC IS), a popular new trend in organizational control design. Our findings provide evidence that IT-enabled controls enable a new control mechanism, risk control, for situations with perfect knowledge about the transformation process and high ability to measure output. As research implication, we recommend an extension of organizational control theory to incorporate the effects of information technology on control design. As practical implication, we provide decision support for the selection of GRC controls, depending on situational factors and the expected value proposition. In sum, this research enhances the body of knowledge on organizational control design with a risk-based perspective.

Keywords: Risk Control, Organizational Control, Risk Management, Compliance, Governance, GRC, Uncertainty.

1   Introduction

Organizational control refers to management mechanisms to direct attention, motivate, and encourage organizational members to act according to organizational goals and objectives (Cardinal et al. 2004; Eisenhardt 1985; Lange 2008; Ouchi 1979; Tannenbaum 1962). The dominant model of organizational control design (Ouchi 1979) suggests certain control mechanisms, depending on the dimensions availability of outcome measures and knowledge of the transformation process. The framework allows managers to decide between input control (e.g. employee selection, training), behavior control (e.g., specific procedures for certain tasks), and output control

M. Nüttgens et al. (Eds.): Governance and Sustainability in IS, IFIP AICT 366, pp. 135–152, 2011.

(e.g. quality assurance). However, research criticizes the framework as too static (Cardinal et al. 2004), implementing wrong informal controls (Kirsch et al. 2002), and lacking performance and integration (Liu et al. 2010).

In this paper, we find that the existing organizational control mechanisms decision framework omits the rising uncertainty in organizations and the IT-enabled possibilities of automation and mass-data processing. This leads to the following research question: *How does Information Technology affect organizational control design?* To answer this question, we derive two hypotheses from IS and control literature to reveal the effects of IT on organizational control theory. We evaluate our hypotheses in practice through analyzing the current trend of IT-enabled organizational control design, called Governance, Risk management and Compliance (GRC). We argue that IT enables a new control mechanism for situations with perfect knowledge about the transformation process and high ability to measure output. We propose a new control mechanism, based on extensive knowledge about business processes and management's ability to gather dubious information early enough to permit time for countermeasures.

The remainder of this paper is organized as followed: The next section gives an overview over the current state of GRC IS. The following section reviews prior literature on organizational control. Subsequently, hypotheses are presented, followed by the description of the research methodology and an overview of the empirical results. The paper ends with a discussion of the results, implications for research and practice, and concluding remarks.

2   Current State of GRC IS

Looking at the current practical developments in control design, the Sarbanes–Oxley Act (SOX) in 2002 and its equivalent regulations in other nations (Wiesche et al. 2011) caused the development of new, IT-enabled controls which can be found under the label of GRC IS, which today is certainly prominent in practice (Dittmar 2007; Parry 2004). For this research, we understand GRC as the integrated Governance, Risk, and Compliance perspective on organizational controls for management (Volonino et al. 2004). GRC IS provide a variety of controls ranging from procedures to monitor user access to information systems, to monitor process performance and provide enterprise-wide risk management. Besides controls, GRC also implements mechanisms to report on compliance and to manage existing business processes (Heiser 2010).

In the disciplines of audit and consulting, GRC is discussed as the automation and observation of controls (Doyle et al. 2007; Parry 2004). Research furthermore focuses on control deficiencies (Ashbaugh-Skaife et al. 2008) and the effects on the financial outcome (Doyle et al. 2007). Research on GRC in governance literature includes the IT-business alignment and adequate and efficient coordination of tasks (Chan 2002). Compliance-related discussions rather focus on effective controls (Jensen 1993), cost reduction (Wagner et al. 2006) and the integrity of information systems (Volonino et al. 2004). Literature on software-based control discusses effectiveness of measures (Nolan et al. 2005). Software development companies selling GRC solutions focus on segregation of duty and process control (Heiser 2010). From an Information Systems perspective, research on GRC IS focuses on frameworks for the design of GRC IS (Beneish et al. 2008; Racz et al. 2010).

3 Theoretical Foundation

Before elaborating on control mechanisms and situational conditions, it is helpful to recapitulate organizational control theory. Following Tannenbaum's understanding of organizational control as interpersonal influence relations within organizations, organizations are arrangements of individual human interactions (Tannenbaum 1962). Control enables idiosyncratic behavior and compliance with the strategic plan and is therefore fundamental for any organization. For a broad summary of the various understandings of organizational control refer to Lange (2008) and Walsh et al. (2006). Although there has been criticism (Eisenhardt 1985; Nilakant et al. 1994), Ouchi's organizational control framework (1979) is still the most prominent in current research (Nixon et al. 2005) and will be introduced in the following.

3.1 Different Control Mechanisms

To control relations within organizations, several control mechanisms exist. All control mechanisms are based on two underlying control strategies (Lange 2008). The first, formal control strategy forces coercion and manipulates rewards and sanctions. This control strategy requires explicit, formal rules, procedures, and policies to both monitor and reward organizational performance. This requires the continuous collection and aggregation of information. The second, informal control strategy aims at minimizing the divergence of personal and company goals. To establish an internal, value based control strategy, the principal has to define norms, values, and culture to ensure goal congruence with the agent. Using e.g. careful recruitment and company-wide beliefs, and norms, the principal can align the agent's behavior to suit the organization's goal. The following four control mechanisms are implementations of the two control strategies (Lange 2008).

When implementing output control mechanisms, the principal monitors the agent's achievements at the end of the given tasks. The monitoring of the output of the value creation process implements the formal control strategy through analyzing the output of the performed tasks. Implementing output control requires a clear understanding of the results of the value creation process and the ability to evaluate the outcome (Das et al. 2001; Ouchi 1979).

Behavior control implements control mechanisms that help the principal to evaluate the agent's behavior. It implements the formal control strategy through evaluating the tasks that are performed by the employee on appropriateness and alignment with the overall strategy. Behavior control requires knowledge of the transformation process and understanding of the involved resources (Das et al. 2001; Ouchi 1979).

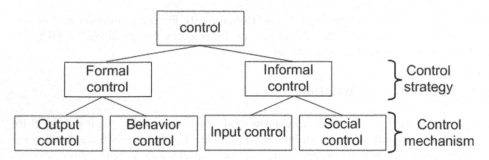

Fig. 1. Control Typology

Input control refers to the selection of appropriate agents who reveal goal congruence with the principal. Input control is a way to implement the strategy of socially aligning goals through selecting good employees who share goals that suit the organizational strategy. Implementing input control requires the ability to measure the agent's alignment with the principal's goals and furthermore the existence of agents who have the required characteristics (Ouchi 1979).

Social control refers to the development of shared beliefs, values and norms through guidelines and top management commitment. Implementing social control requires the ability to influence the agent's alignment with the principal's goals through guidelines and code of conducts (Ouchi 1979). For further examples for control mechanisms refer to Kirsch (1997) and Lange (2008).

In the following section we will introduce factors, influencing the decision for either control mechanisms. For now, we assert that behavior control is effective but output control the more efficient choice (Ouchi 1979). Management should commonly prefer behavior control to output control due to the ability to implement the right countermeasures before the end of the value creation process. Input control requires the lowest operational costs and should be chosen if the turnover within the organization is low (Ouchi 1979). Due to phenomena like the ongoing war for talent (Chambers et al. 1998) it might sometimes not be possible to either design effective input controls or find the right candidates.

3.2 Decision Model for Control Mechanisms

To decide which control mechanism suits the current organizational decision situation, the underlying information characteristics of the agency situation are important (Ouchi 1979). Depending on the characteristics of the situation, the principal can decide which control mechanism to use. Literature suggests that the ability to design certain controls depends on the principal's knowledge of the transformation process and principal's ability to measure the result of the value creation process early or at a later stage of the process (Figure 2).

The dimension knowledge of the transformation process refers to the principal's knowledge how the value creation tasks have to be performed by the agent (Ouchi 1979). If the principal exactly knows which tasks the agent has to accomplish, the knowledge of the transformation process is high. When the principal does not know, which factors influence the value creation and therefore the necessary tasks the agent has to perform, the knowledge of the transformation process is low.

The dimension ability to measure refers to the principal's ability to determine the result of a certain task. While literature agrees on knowledge of the transformation process, the second dimension is discussed controversially: It is argued that the suggested dimension output lacks the integration of uncertainty and controllability as fundamental factors influencing the decision (Eisenhardt 1985; Nilakant et al. 1994). Especially modern, complex organizations struggle with uncertainty about the outcome of the value creation process (Weick et al. 2007). Decisions are based on uncertain information, e.g. forecasts or assumptions of employees. Complexity, interdependencies and quick changes in market and other surrounding areas lead to non-predictability of the process outcome and its market success.

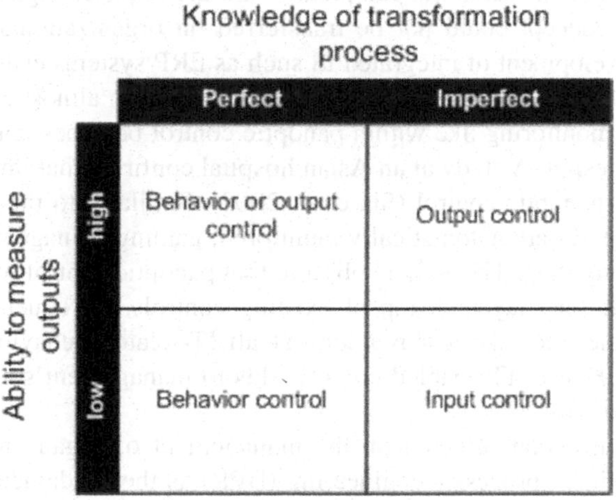

Knowledge of transformation process

		Perfect	Imperfect
Ability to measure outputs	high	Behavior or output control	Output control
	low	Behavior control	Input control

Fig. 2. Organizational Control Framework (Ouchi 1979)

The author argues that the developed dimensions provide decision support for specific managerial situations (Ouchi 1979). Although this is true for three quadrants of the matrix (Figure 2), the framework does not provide decision support for situations with high ability to measure output and perfect knowledge of the transformation process, e.g. the suggested "Apollo program". Although the author suggests that in this situation, "the lower cost alternative will be preferred" (Ouchi 1979), the framework lacks decision support for the situation with high ability to measure output and perfect knowledge of the transformation process:

"We can completely specify each step of the transformation process which must occur in order for a manned capsule to get to the surface of the moon and back to earth, thus giving us the possibility of behavior control. However, we also have an unambiguous measure of output: either the capsule gets there and back, or it doesn't. Thus we have a choice of either behavior control or of output control." (Ouchi 1979)

4   Effects of IT on Organizational Control

Since GRC IS, as the current trend in organizational control design, focuses on the integration of IT, we will discuss the effects of IT on organizational control design in the following.

IT-enabled control mediates direct supervision of the agent through electronic surveillance and therefore adds to management's knowledge on the value creation process. With the evolving of ERP systems in companies, a new form of control emerged: the panoptic control. The panoptic control refers to what Bentham suggested for prison design in the early nineteenth century (Foucault 1977). The prison is built with a central tower that enables guards to see all prisoners from one position. This type of visibility creates an indirect situation of ubiquitous inspection and surveillance (Clegg 1998). Due to its complexity and the required high effort of manual monitoring, this concept could not be transferred on organizational control design. However, the development of integrated IS such as ERP systems enables such panoptic controls (Quattrone et al. 2005). Since IT is integrated in almost every employee's task, continuous monitoring like within panoptic control becomes feasible for organizational control design. A study at an Asian hospital confirms that implementing ERP software enables panoptic control (Sia et al. 2002). Similarly to the panoptic prison, all business processes are automatically monitored, gaining management access to all process steps at any time. The authors observe that panoptic control was automatically added as an additional layer on top of existing controls. Introducing ERP systems enables management to take a closer look at all IT-related behavior, performed by their employees. Hence, IT-enabled control adds to management's knowledge of the transformation process.

There has been extant research on the management of organizational processes. Starting with business process reengineering (BPR) as the fundamental redesign and radical new development of the whole organization or the core processes (Hammer et al. 1993), process management evolved to a less radical and more focused management of organizational processes (Davenport 1993). Literature finds that one of the major reasons for process management is the documentation and visualization of existing processes (Gunge 2000). Introducing IT-enabled control extends this documentation perspective for organizational controls. With the combination of the knowledge on the necessary value creation tasks and IT-enabled control, management is able to closely monitor and control the organizational value creation process. Hence, IT enables the visibility of company processes and creates transparency among procedures and tasks. This leads to the following hypothesis, which adds to organizational control theory:

Hypothesis 1: The adoption of IT increases the knowledge of the transformation process in organizational control situations.

IT-enabled automation allows the processing of mass data. Using IT enables the principal to gather and evaluating high amounts of data efficiently (Orlikowski 1991). Focus can be laid on either value creation related tasks or not value creation related behavior.

Since management is able to evaluate not business process related behavior, non-compliant behavior can be recognized earlier (Fisher 2007). The automatic and intelligent pre-selection through thresholds and alerts helps management gather dubious information early enough to permit time for countermeasures. Before the introduction of IT-enabled controls it was not efficient to react on every vague, uncertain possible threat: organizational decision makers focused on precise information (Ansoff 1975). IT-enabled transparency within the organization allows the collection of specific information with reasonable effort. With the introduction of mass data processing and automation in control design, management can explore dubious, but vague information at an early stage and therefore develop better planned countermeasures.

IT-enabled data processing enables realtime and background data processing. Management can monitor their employees through automated IS which run in the background of the employee's working station. Hence, IT-enabled control does not reduce organizational performance, gives management easy access to vague failure data, and allows the implementation of early warnings (Ansoff 1975; Weick et al. 2007). Therefore, using IT to support organizational control mechanisms increases the amount of data that can be processed. Accordingly, the following hypothesis is proposed:

Hypothesis 2: Using IT to support organizational control mechanisms increases management's ability to measure output.

In sum, the reviewed literature suggests that the impact of IT on organizational control design affects especially situations with high ability to measure output and perfect knowledge of the transformation process. IT allows new controls through its ability to create transparency and process mass data. In the following, we will provide empirical evidence, revealing the need to extend the existing organizational control decision framework (Figure 2).

5 Research Methodology

For scrutinizing the theoretical foundation of IT-enabled controls, a multiple case study was chosen (Yin 2008). This approach seemed appropriate to understand how GRC IS influences control design and its impacts on control efficiency. We conducted qualitative data analysis (Strauss et al. 1998) on 14 expert interviews.

We derived hypotheses from literature before analyzing the case data, not to imitate quantitative research, but to test these hypotheses from various perspectives on the topic of GRC. This approach allows theory building (sampling logic) and model development (generalization) (Yin 2008). To develop the model we built on existing research on organizational control and derived additional influencing factors.

Since this case builds upon existing theory, the focus of selecting comparison groups for theory building was on maximizing diversity (Glaser et al. 2001). Maximizing diversity increases the possibility of finding different and varying data belonging to one sample. The differences support category building and summing up the data.

5.1 Sampling and Data Collection

To achieve highest diversity, a broad view on GRC was chosen, including all perspectives that relate to IT-enabled controls within organizations (Table 1). The professions and disciplines relevant for this research included audit, consulting, governance, compliance, risk management, IT, and users in terms of GRC IS.

Table 1. Perspectives on GRC Controls and Interviewees

Perspective	Expert ID	Language	Length	Background	Experience
Audit	Auditor 1	German	1 h 04 min	Business	8 years
Audit	Auditor 2	German	1 h 04 min	Accounting	4 years
Consulting	Consultant 1	English	1 h 25 min	Business	10 years
Consulting	Consultant 2	German	0 h 59 min	Audit	23 years
Governance	Governance expert 1	English	1 h 02 min	Audit	16 years
Governance	Governance expert 2	English	1 h 15 min	Compliance	10 years
Usage	Company expert 1	German	0 h 51 min	Computer Science	6 years
Usage	Company expert 2	German	1 h 13 min	Computer Science	12 years
Compliance	Compliance expert 1	English	1 h 07 min	Finance	16 years
Compliance	Compliance expert 2	German	1 h 49 min	Finance	22 years
Software	IT professional 1	German	1 h 22 min	Accounting	17 years
Software	IT professional 2	German	1 h 59 min	Computer Science	11 years
Risk	Risk manager 1	German	1 h 04 min	IS	14 years
Risk	Risk manager 2	English	1 h 02 min	Risk Management	3 years

Since the different perspectives on GRC provide different focal points, we interviewed two experts from each perspective using convenience sampling. We met experts on GRC workshops in Germany and used professional discussion groups and blogs to identify potential respondents. All experts had between 3 and 23 years of experience in their profession; the average experience was more than 12 years. Although having different backgrounds, we grouped the expert's perspective according to their current job description (Table 1). We conducted the interviews using guidelines with semi-structured questions, including questions about GRC systems as well as questions regarding the developed IT-enabled controls. We tailored the interview guidelines to the hypotheses on the impact of IT control design. The interviews were open-ended phone interviews, the interview with compliance expert 2 was held face-to-face. We conducted nine interviews in German. The interviews with the governance and risk experts, compliance expert 1, and consultant 1 were held in English.

5.2 Data Analysis Procedure

We tape-recorded, transcribed, and anonymized all interviews. We integrated the transcripts from the 14 interviews into a hermeneutic unit comprising 67,761 words and 58 pages of text using the software ATLAS.ti. The coding procedure was conducted following Glaser and Strauss' (2001) guidelines. First, the first author read and coded the interview transcripts line by line, using phrases from the transcripts that describe the phenomenon (open coding). Similar he tagged phenomena with the same phrase. This resulted in a list of 129 codings and 563 phrases. Following the coding by the first author, the second author likewise coded the transcripts independently. We discussed and agreed on the differing codes. In the next iteration (axial coding), we grouped the developed phrases to concepts. We put the derived concepts in coherence and then aggregated them regarding their effect on control.

6 Results

Controls in the context of GRC range from segregation of duty to policies and code of conduct. Prominent controls include behavior control mechanisms, referred to as process control. This incorporates the automation of internal control management for SOX-compliance as well as similar requirements and integration with risk management solutions. GRC incorporates further behavior control to monitor certain organizational risks with the integration of various participants and stakeholders. Experts gave several examples ranging from the energy sector to risk management solutions for IT companies, providing automated testing of controls. Further, ethical guidelines and codes of conduct exist and provide examples of social control mechanisms. In terms of output control, existing quality assurance solutions were integrated in the organization's GRC portfolio. Such controls are often implemented too late in the value creation process and therefore meet only regulatory compliance aspects. In the context of ERP solutions, the most prominent control is segregation of duty, called access control. Access control includes automation of end-to-end access and authorization management with strong integration within the access control solutions. Such controls can be implemented early in the organizational value creation process and provide first insights on fraud or other undesirable behavior. Controls like access control are enabled by IT, making it possible to process masses of data in real time.

"With GRC concepts, companies can implement controls which [...] support the early processing of information and providing information on possible company risks which might be blurred, but if ignored might result in serious to the organization." *(Governance expert 1)*

6.1 The Role of IT in Increasing Knowledge of the Transformation Process

An aspect which persistently appeared in the study was the ability to create transparency through ubiquitous controls, which run in background of existing IS. The different GRC perspectives reveal certain reasons for creating transparency. From an audit and compliance perspective, transparency accelerates audits and therefore reduces costs. Practitioners actually operating GRC solutions use transparency for decision support and compliance reasons. From the IT-perspective, the main reason was for decision support. The functional units report on their situation and management uses this information as basis for their decisions. Therefore, this information needs to be reliable. Before the development of IT-enabled controls, management had to rely on their input and social control mechanisms, not guaranteeing reliable results. With the development of IT-enabled controls, management is able to verify the given information and to equally compare different reports. Consistent with hypothesis 1, interviewees argued that with IT-enabled controls, management can enhance knowledge of the transformation process:

"Management had to rely [on] reports and estimations with different quality and hierarchical level from various functions across the organization. At the end of the day, they had to decide [...] based on this information. The new approach enables management to have transparency through reporting structures and work tasks. I am convinced that it creates transparency and better knowledge of the employee's tasks." (IT professional 2)

From management perspective, this issue becomes even clearer. Before the implementation of IT-enabled control, management had to rely on their employee's engagement. Organizations were not able to know about all tasks performed on each hierarchical level. Therefore, they had to trust their employees and could only monitor the results at a reasonable level of costs. Automated, IT-enabled control mechanisms are able to process high amounts of data and provide information in real time. This enables management to get information on certain, maybe critical processes with reasonable efforts and supports hypothesis 1.

"As a manager, you should know how your company works. [...] He has to know which tasks have to be performed to create a certain value. The implementation of GRC systems helps him to gain this knowledge context-specific [...] and gain information [to] found his decisions on." (Company expert 2)

From governance perspective, governmental regulations and the eager to found decisions on good data motivate management to define certain rules and procedures to provide this information. Management requests real time information on the risks, the organization is currently facing. This knowledge is gained from risk management at the operational level of the organization. Therefore the organization needs transparency from a top-down perspective. Especially for performance based controls it is important to develop integrated controls with similar measures.

Extending the process oriented value creation perspective, GRC enables optimization of the companies value creation tasks. Consultant 1, an interviewee with more than 20 years of experience in the field of IT consulting, argues that GRC is the natural successor of process management. Historically, IS design moved from mainframe to functional computing. Following that, the integrated process perspective, BPR and business process management (BPM) arose, enabling more control for management. The last years revealed serious shortcomings in this process oriented ERP based solution. SOX and other regulatory guidelines demanded formal aspects, sometimes questioning the usefulness of compliance rules and organizational benefit. The expert argues that GRC enables a new focus on business process optimization from a control perspective. The new trend of GRC controls helps companies meet this new type of requirements and increases management's knowledge of their value creation processes. Other experts confirm this argument, claiming that process control increase transparency and therefore increase the knowledge of the transformation process.

"Beyond governance and legal issues, [with the rise of GRC] there is a trend to-wards process optimization. It enables companies to directly optimize their portfolio and their internal structures." (Consultant 2)

"Process control applications optimize [...] business operations and help ensure compliance and mitigate risk by centrally monitoring key controls for business processes and cross-enterprise IT systems." (Risk expert 2)

Overall, the study illustrates the hypothesis that IT-enabled controls increase the knowledge of the transformation process. There are various reasons for creating transparency, but they all lead to the aim that the principal enhances his knowledge on the tasks performed by the agent and therefore the knowledge on the transformation process.

6.2 The Role of IT in Enhancing Management's Ability to Measure Output

Regarding hypothesis 2, the study results revealed clear evidence that IT-enabled controls increase the ability to integrate weak signals. In organizations, there are often enough warnings that, if correctly interpreted, could prevent certain negative outcomes from happening. To understand why these warnings are often ignored, the existing control mechanisms give an understanding of this shortcoming (figure 3). Input and social controls do not provide reliability on certain happenings. Output control provides this reliability, but too late to implement correcting measures on this specific output to prevent the negative outcome. In a setting of outcome certainty, where all outcome-influencing factors are known and determinable, process control enables reliability on the desired outcome.

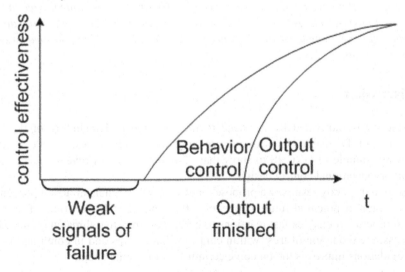

Fig. 3. Temporal Perspective on Control Mechanisms

However, today's organizational settings become more complex and intricate and it is often impossible to monitor all influencing factors and control the necessary tasks. Although there has always been early information on possible negative outcomes, there was hardly any possibility to examine all indicators and derive preventing measures. The implementation of IT-based controls enables management to continuously monitor and rate weak signals that possibly lead to negative outcomes. Automation helps both, mass data processing and reduction of reaction time.

"[...], whistle blower mechanism can be automated, in addition to improving the amount of data processed within GRC solutions." (Compliance expert 1)

„So, companies would surely not document [transparency] with such detail and rigor, if there were no governmental regulations, forcing them to provide evidence." (Auditor 1)

This indication for the second hypothesis is further supported by arguments from the interviewees. Although there are various control mechanisms, the interviewees implicitly ranked their examples according to certain criteria. The experts claimed that control quality depends on control effectiveness. Deepening this argumentation, the study reveals that control effectiveness depends on two factors: point in time and certainty. Ideal controls would be applied early in the organizations value creation process and the effects of the controls would be entirely clear. Since there are no such controls, the experts stated that the tradeoff is either late usage or high uncertainty. In some cases (by the experts referred to as process control), the certainty is relatively high and it can be done early in the value creation process. As soon as there is higher uncertainty, the controls can either just be at the final product or service (quality management) or early with high effort and some uncertainty on the effects of the situation and possible controls (e.g. access control).

„You generally develop various controls. [...] Firstly, access controls (technically, reporting tools) which give an overview on the situation. Secondly, you develop guidelines for your employees and monitor that. Thirdly, you have to measure your results." (Consultant 2)

7 Discussion

This study was motivated by the need to improve the understanding of the value proposition of IT-enabled control on organizational control design. We used the prominent example of GRC IS to show that IT-enabled control reveals new perspectives on organizational control design.

Based on the study results, we propose a new control mechanism to support an early anticipation of potential future happenings that endanger the outcome of the value creation process. It enables fast reactions to early warnings that threaten organizational success, the reduction of trust within control relationships and in combination with legal regulations improves the outcome certainty of the value chain.

7.1 IT Enables Organizational Controls

The results confirm the assumption that in today's heterogeneous organizational environment a combination of various control mechanisms is necessary (Meiselman 2007; Orlikowski 1991). Especially auditors and consultants confirm that there are different GRC IS application contexts. These different goals imply different expectations and results. Management can decide between various controls, depending on the underlying organizational situation (Liu et al. 2010). The results furthermore reveal that management increasingly relies on IT-enabled controls.

As presumed above, the found IT-enabled controls do not fit in the described classifications in literature (Table 2). As behavior and output control can only implemented within the value creation process, IT-enabled controls are implemented without clear connection to these pure functional process but rather with an object oriented perspective. Since input and social control do focus on the organizational unit but are informal, the found IT-enabled controls cannot be classified within the existing frameworks.

Table 2. Classification of control types with new type risk controls

control mechanism	type	organizational integration	strengths	weaknesses	necessary conditions
input control	in-formal	organizational unit	- low supervision costs - reliability due to goal congruence	- high level of trust necessary - highly qualified agents necessary	- availability of qualified agents - low turnover
social control	in-formal	organizational unit	- low setup costs - no supervision costs - suits unknown situations	- high level of trust necessary - hard to evaluate - unreliable effects	- ongoing trainings necessary - continuity - low turnover
output control	formal	functional process	- low costs of supervision - unambiguousness - clear scale of measurement	- requires full knowledge on process output - point in time of measurement might be too late	- concrete definition of value creation - ability to measure output
behavior control	formal	functional process	- possibility to change direction during the process - monitor agent's task performance	- high supervision costs - reduces task performance - no clear measurement scale	- transformation process must be known - behavior needs to be measureable
risk control (IT-eabled)	formal	organizational unit	- early warning of success threats - interpreting weak signals	- high degree of interpretation - mass of information - high costs	- business intelligence - mass data processing

7.2 Introducing an IT-Enabled Control Mechanism: Risk Control

The results reveal that IT enables new and fundamental controls within organizational control design. Since these controls combine characteristics that cannot be found in literature, we propose a new control mechanism called risk control. The controls introduced by the GRC experts, e.g. information systems for access control and risk management, are characterized by their focus on organizational unit rather than functional processes and allow implementing early warning systems to interpret ex-ante signal before incidents occur. Due to integration of IT, risk controls can process a high amount of data from various sources within the organization.

Risk control refers to the principal's early understanding of the uncertain, surprising, or non-assessable future happenings that endanger the outcome of the value creation process. As seen in the current approaches in practice, organizations use risk management to gain transparency, interpret early warnings and hence provide decision support. Using IT-enabled risk management, principals can control situations with high knowledge of the transformation process and high ability to measure output.

Risk control implies the tedious collection of high amounts of data and the careful analysis of this data with respect to signals of organizational failure. It is useful in vital and complex environments. It enables organizations to react early and possibly prevent major negative consequences at an early stage of the process (Ansoff 1975). It turns organizational control from reactive to proactive actions. Risk control allows performance-steadiness through ubiquitous monitoring of agents. It is based on effective risk management and IT support. Risk management allows the prediction of strategic surprises and threats to value creation processes (Ansoff 1975). This is possible through the integration of IT in the organizational control design. IT enables data collection across various functions at a reasonable amount of time and costs. To create resilience and prevent negative surprises, risk control provides early help in uncertain environments. The study reveals several control mechanisms that can be applied in situations with low outcome certainty and high knowledge of the transformation process. Access control, information systems for risk management or whistle blowing are examples for risk control mechanisms.

Although risk controls create transparency about organizational units and allow ex-ante management of possible threats, they have the disadvantage of being cost intensive and interpretation dependent.

7.3 Placing Risk Control in the Organizational Control Framework

Existing literature on organizational controls does not provide decision support on control design for high knowledge of the transformation process and high ability to measure output (Ouchi 1979). The author uses additional indicators (costs) to suggest the most suitable control mechanism. The suggested control mechanism risk control uses IT to enable early information retrieval on a wide data basis but needs both, high ability to measure outputs and perfect knowledge of the transformation process (figure 4). Within the suggested decision framework (Ouchi 1979), the suggested control fits in the upper left corner with perfect knowledge of the transformation process and high ability to measure output. Its characteristics of using automation and mass data processing allow handling high amounts of data at an early point in time. It is further characterized by processing not only process related data, as it was characteristic for formal controls before, but allows integrating data relating to specific organizational units. Hence, the suggested risk control is the most suitable control mechanism for organizational situations with perfect knowledge of the transformation process and high ability to measure output.

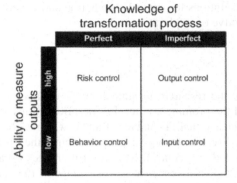

Fig. 4. Adopted Organizational Control Framework (Ouchi 1979)

7.4 Implications and Limitations

This research contributes to organizational control theory by integrating the effect of IT-enabled controls on organizational control design. We explain the benefits from automation and transparency through implementing IT-enabled controls within GRC IS. We propose risk control as a new control mechanism, incorporating weak signals within organizational control. Based on the assumption of higher goal incongruence and performance ambiguity, we argue that risk control mechanisms help to identify weak signals and prevent future threats to the organization. The adopted organizational control framework gives additional decision support for designing organizational controls through being the optimal alternative for situations with high ability to measure output and perfect knowledge of the transformation process. Within GRC IS, risk control is frequently implemented, e.g. through information systems for access control and risk management.

However, there are several limitations to take into account. First, it should be conceded that this study is based on only 14 interviews. Although it's exploratory nature and the aim of maximizing diversity allows certain broadness at the expense of depth, selecting only two experts from each GRC perspective could bias the findings through their personal opinion or specific experience. Although we used a broad sample from various organizations, it might be possible that the suggested concept of risk control is not suitable in all organizational settings. Especially in settings of emerging organizations or loose structures (Cardinal et al. 2004), risk controls have to be explored. Furthermore, we might have overlooked additional GRC stakeholders and hence additional value propositions.

In addition, although being the most obvious, organizational control theory might not be the appropriate theoretical lens for researching GRC IS. As it is more output oriented, goal-setting theory might also be an alternative (Locke et al. 2002). Instead of using theories from management and organizational science, we could also have used theories from computer science or IS which can be extended to accounting information systems as well. For example, the theory of technology dominance (Arnold et al. 1998) might also help in assessing the impact of IT on control especially in terms of decision support. We also focused on exploiting existing control potentials.

We focused on GRC solutions for control automation and coherence and hence lack a self-contained perspective on exploration.

8 Conclusion

In this paper, we ask the research question how IT changes organizational control design. We examined the prominent control trend GRC to answer the research question. We provided evidence that IT-enabled controls within GRC IS change organizational control design. We extend organizational control theory by proposing a new control mechanism called risk control. Risk control enables organizations to prevent possible major negative consequences at an early stage of the value creation process. It allows reduction in variance and performance-steadiness through ubiquitous monitoring of agents. Risk control allows managers to react early and possibly prevent major negative consequences at an early stage of the process. It helps managers to interpret weak signals but requires a high degree of interpretation and the ability to deal with high amounts of data.

References

Ansoff, H.I.: Managing strategic surprise by response to weak signals. California Management Review 18(2), 21–33 (1975)

Arnold, V., Sutton, S.G.: The Theory of Technology Dominance: Understanding the Impact of Intelligent Decisions Aids on Decision Makers' Judgments. Advances in Accounting Behavioral Research 1, 175–194 (1998)

Ashbaugh-Skaife, H., Collins, D., Kinnery, W.R.: The effect of SOX internal control deficiencies and their remediation on accrual quality. The Accounting Review 83(1), 217–250 (2008)

Beneish, M., Billings, M., Hodder, L.: Internal control weaknesses and information uncertainty. The Accounting Review 83(3), 665–703 (2008)

Cardinal, L.B., Sitkin, S.B., Long, C.P.: Balancing and Rebalancing in the Creation and Evolution of Organizational Control. Organization Science 15, 411–431 (2004)

Chambers, E.G., Foulon, M., Handfield-Jones, H., Michaels, E.G.: War for Talent. McKinsey Quarterly 3, 44–58 (1998)

Chan, Y.E.: Why haven't we mastered alignment? The importance of the informal organization structure. MIS Quarterly Executive 1(2), 97–112 (2002)

Clegg, S.: Foucault, Power and Organization. In: McKinley, A., Starkey, K. (eds.) Foucault, Management and Organization Theory, pp. 29–48. Sage, London (1998)

Das, T., Teng, B.: Trust, control, and risk in strategic alliances: An integrated framework. Organization Studies 22(2), 215–283 (2001)

Davenport, T.H.: Process innovation: reengineering work through information technology, p. 365. Harvard Business School Press, Boston (1993)

Dittmar, L.: Demystifying GRC. Business Trends Quarterly 4, 16–18 (2007)

Doyle, J., Ge, W., Mcvay, S.: Determinants of weaknesses in internal control over financial reporting. Journal of Accounting and Economics 44(1-2), 193–223 (2007)

Eisenhardt, K.M.: Control: Organizational and Economic Approaches. Management Science 31(2), 134–149 (1985)

Fisher, J.: Compliance in the Performance Management Context: What technologies could simplify compliance and automate information gathering? Bank, Accounting & Finance 20(4), 41–49 (2007)

Foucault, M.: Discipline and Punishment: The Birth of the Prison, p. 318. Vintage, New York (1977)

Glaser, B.G., Strauss, A.L.: The discovery of grounded theory: Strategies for qualitative research. Aldine de Gruyter, Hawthorne (2001)

Gunge, S.P.: Business Process Reengineering and The New Organization. In: Knights, D., Willmott, H. (eds.) The Reengineering Revolution: Critical Studies of Corporate Change, pp. 114–133. Sage, London (2000)

Hammer, M., Champy, J.: Reengineering the corporation: A manifesto for business revolution. Harper Business, New York (1993)

Heiser, J.: Hype Cycle for Governance, Risk and Compliance Technologies (2010)

Jensen, M.: The modern industrial revolution, exit, and the failure of internal control systems. Journal of Finance 48(3), 831–880 (1993)

Kirsch, L.J., Sambamurthy, V., Ko, D.-G., Purvis, R.L.: Controlling Information Systems Development Projects: The View from the Client. Management Science 48, 484–498 (2002)

Kirsch, L.S.: Portfolios of Control Modes and IS Project Management. Information Systems Research 8(3), 215–239 (1997)

Lange, D.: A Multidimensional Conceptualization of Organizational Corruption Control. The Academy of Management Review 33(3), 710 (2008)

Liu, L., Yetton, P., Sauer, C.: A normative theory of organizational control: Main and interaction effects of control modes on performance. In: Proceedings of the 18th European Conference on Information Systems (ECIS), Verona, Italy (2010)

Locke, E.A., Latham, G.P.: Building a Practically Useful Theory of Goal Setting and Task Motivation. American Psychologist 57(9), 705–717 (2002)

Meiselman, J.: Risk, Governance and Compliance Trends for 2007. Risk Management 54(2), 40 (2007)

Nilakant, V., Rao, H.: Agency Theory and Uncertainty in Organizations: An Evaluation. Organization Studies 15(5), 649–672 (1994)

Nixon, W., Burns, J.: Management control in the 21st century. Management Accounting Research 16(3), 260–268 (2005)

Nolan, R., McFarlan, F.W.: Information technology and the board of directors. Harvard Business Review 83(10), 96–106 (2005)

Orlikowski, W.: Integrated Information Environment or Matrix of Control? The Contradictory Implications of Information Technology. Accounting, Management, and Information Technologies 1(1), 9–42 (1991)

Ouchi, W.G.: A Conceptual Framework for the Design of Organizational Control Mechanisms. Management Science 25(9), 833–848 (1979)

Parry, E.: SOX Wars: CIOs share ideas, fears on Sarbanes-Oxley compliance, SearchCIO.com:7 (2004)

Quattrone, P., Hopper, T.: A 'time–space odyssey': management control systems in two multinational organisations. Accounting, Organizations and Society 30(7-8), 735–764 (2005)

Racz, N., Weippl, E., Seufert, A.: A Frame of Reference for Research of Integrated Governance, Risk and Compliance (GRC). In: Communications and Multimedia Security, pp. 106–117. Springer, Heidelberg (2010)

Sia, S., Tang, M., Soh, C., Boh, W.: Enterprise resource planning (ERP) systems as a technology of power: empowerment or panoptic control? ACM SIGMIS Database 33(1), 23–37 (2002)

Strauss, A., Corbin, J.: Basics of Qualitative Research Techniques and Procedures for Developing Grounded Theory Sage. Sage, London (1998)

Tannenbaum, A.S.: Control in Organizations: Individual Adjustment and Organizational Performance. Administrative Science Quarterly 7(2), 236 (1962)

Volonino, L., Gessner, G.H., Kermis, G.F.: Holistic Compliance with Sarbanes-Oxley. Communications of the Association for Information Systems 14 (2004)

Wagner, S., Dittmar, L.: The unexpected benefits of Sarbanes-Oxley. Harvard Business Review 84(4), 133 (2006)

Walsh, J.P., Meyer, A.D., Schoonhoven, C.B.: A Future for Organization Theory: Living in and Living with Changing Organizations. Organization Science 17(5), 657–671 (2006)

Weick, K.E., Sutcliffe, K.M.: Managing the Unexpected: Assuring High Performance in an Age of Complexity. John Wiley and Sons, San Francisco (2007)

Wiesche, M., Berwing, C., Schermann, M., Krcmar, H.: Patterns for Understanding Control Requirements for Information Systems for Governance, Risk Management, and Compliance (GRC IS). In: CAiSE Workshop on GRCIS, London, UK (to appear, 2011)

Yin, R.K.: Case Study Research: Design and Methods, 5th edn. SAGE Publications, Thousand Oaks (2008)

Part IV
Customer and User Integration

A Meta-analysis of the Unified Theory of Acceptance and Use of Technology (UTAUT)

Yogesh K. Dwivedi[1], Nripendra P. Rana[1], Hsin Chen[2], and Michael D. Williams[1]

[1] School of Business & Economics, Swansea University, Swansea, UK
{ykdwivedi,nrananp}@gmail.com, M.D.Williams@swansea.ac.uk
[2] Business Systems Department, University of Bedfordshire, UK
hsin.chen@beds.ac.uk

Abstract. The originating article of the Unified Theory of Acceptance and Use of Technology (UTAUT) has been cited by a large number of studies. However, a detailed examination of such citations revealed that only small proportion (43 articles) of these citations actually utilized the theory or its constructs in their empirical research for examining IS/IT related issues. In order to examine whether the theory is performing consistently well across various studies, this research aims to undertake a statistical meta-analysis of findings reported in 43 published studies that have actually utilized UTAUT or its constructs in their empirical research. Findings reveal the underperformance of theory in subsequent studies in comparison to the performance of UTAUT reported in the originating article. The limitations experienced while conducting the meta-analysis, recommendations, and the future scope for the further research in this area have also been briefly explained in concluding section.

Keywords: Adoption, Diffusion, UTAUT, TAM, Meta-analysis, Information Systems.

1 Introduction

UTAUT was proposed as a theoretical advancement over existing theories used to examine adoption and diffusion related research. Venkatesh et al. (2003) reviewed, mapped and integrated constructs from following eight theories and models: theory of reasoned action (TRA), technology acceptance model (TAM), motivational model (MM), theory of planned behavior (TPB), a combined theory of planned behavior/technology acceptance model (C-TPB-TAM), model of PC utilization (MPCU), innovation diffusion theory (IDT), and social cognitive theory (SCT). By doing so the authors aimed to develop a unified view by eliminating redundancy and repetitions as several constructs in these theories were common.

Like its majority of predecessors' theories and models in the area of adoption and diffusion of IT/IS, UTAUT facilitates in examining user's intentions to use an information system and consequent usage behavior. The variance in intentions can be explained by measuring effect of four key independent constructs, namely, performance expectancy (PE), effort expectancy (EE), social influence (SI), and facilitating

M. Nüttgens et al. (Eds.): Governance and Sustainability in IS, IFIP AICT 366, pp. 155–170, 2011.

conditions (FC) as direct determinants of usage intention and behavior (Venkatesh et al. 2003). The effect of independent variables on dependent variables is moderated by following four moderating variables: gender, age, experience, and voluntariness of use (Venkatesh et al. 2003).

Two of its constructs are similar to TAM constructs: PE can be mapped to perceived usefulness (PU) whereas EE can be mapped to perceived ease of use (PEOU). The remaining two constructs (SI and FC) are from TPB. Due to the similarity (in terms of constructs and relationships) of UTAUT with TAM and TPB, the current and future adoption and diffusion studies might be favouring use of UTAUT. This is particularly more likely as many scholars in the recent past have criticized over exploitation of TAM which ultimately affecting development of alternative theories and models in this area. However, it is difficult to demonstrate that if UTAUT is replacing TAM in empirical studies as there is no review of previous empirical studies that have utilized UTAUT. Also, there is no study that has surveyed or reviewed performance of UTAUT subsequently – so, there is a lack of information regarding reliability and consistency of performance of this theory in different situations.

Many literature reviews and meta-analyses have been conducted on UTAUT's popular precursor theories and models such as TAM and TPB. For example, use of TAM by a large number of studies caught researchers' attention to analyze trends, patterns of use, and the actual performance of the model through systematic review and meta-analysis technique. The successful efforts towards the systematic review were performed by Lee et al. (2003), and Legris et al. (2003), whereas, the meta-analysis for measuring the performance of TAM was carried out by Deng et al. (2005), King and He (2006), and Ma and Liu (2004). The similar meta-analytic approach was also performed for TPB, and TRA by other previous studies (Hausenblas et al. 1997; Sheeran and Taylor 1999).

A large citation counts for UTAUT's originating article, its use in many empirical studies, an inconsistent performance of the theory, and a lack of reviews and meta-analysis related to it necessitate determining the past and current trends of its use by conducting systematic reviews and meta-analysis of articles that have either cited or utilized it as theoretical basis in their empirical research. Considering above discussions, this study aims *to conduct a review and meta-analysis of articles that have cited the originating article* (i.e. Venkatesh et al. 2003) *and have utilized UTAUT (or its constructs) for undertaking empirical research on adoption and diffusion of IT/IS*. According to King and He (2006, p. 741) "Meta-analysis allows various results to be combined, taking account of the relative sample and effect sizes, thereby allowing both insignificant and significant effects to be analyzed. The overall result is then undoubtedly more accurate and more credible because of the overarching span of the analysis." This outlines contribution of this paper by conducting meta-analysis which might present more accurate and credible performance of the UTAUT theory.

The remaining paper is organized as follows: The next section will provide an overview of the research method utilized. The findings will then be presented and discussed in subsequent sections. The last section of this paper will outline conclusions, limitations and future research directions.

2 Research Method

As the aim of this research is to analyze and synthesize existing findings on use of the UTAUT theory, a combination of profiling review and meta-analysis methods (Deng et al. 2005; King and He 2006; Lee et al. 2003; Legris et al. 2003; Ma and Liu 2004) was considered as the most appropriate one for this purpose. This research utilized data collected from studies that cited UTAUT's originating article (Venkatesh et al. 2003). These citations were identified by employing *Web of Science*[@] database. The demographic data (such as year of publications, and source of publications) related to all cited studies were first collected from *Web of Science*[@] database. The citations for fully available articles were downloaded for the purpose of extracting further details from the cited articles.

There were total of 870 studies that cited UTAUT, out of which 450 studies were available to be downloaded as full articles. A detailed examination of 450 available studies led to identify 43 studies that used UTAUT (or its constructs) in their empirical studies. The remaining 407 studies just cited the originating article on UTAUT (Venkatesh et al. 2003) and did make full or partial use of the theory in their empirical research. In order to observe modifications, adaptations and integration of external variables with UTAUT by adopting an approach from the research of Legris et al. (2003), this study also analyzed 43 studies to identify the external variables, and external theories they used along with UTAUT.

A further and more detailed analysis of 43 studies (that have used UTAUT) was conducted which revealed that only 27 studies used the quantitative research method (similar to the originating article) and therefore subjected to the meta-analysis. The remaining 16 studies used UTAUT with some different research methods (for example qualitative or other statistical measurement technique) and hence was not considered for meta-analysis. Although 27 studies seem relatively fewer in counts, it was considered adequate in number for conducting the meta-analysis. A similar number of studies were also utilized in previous meta-analyses research (Deng et al. 2005; Legris et al. 2003; Ma and Liu 2004). For example, Legris et al. (2003) successfully conducted meta-analysis on TAM by extracting statistical data from three studies. Ma and Liu (2004) employed data from 26 empirical papers and Deng et al. (2005) collected data from 21 studies. Since these studies are published in respected peer reviewed journal, we considered 27 studies as an appropriate number for this research.

Adopting approach from previous meta-analysis studies (Deng et al. 2005; King and He 2006; Legris et al. 2003; Ma and Liu 2004), the following types of data were collected from 27 studies for the purpose of meta-analysis: reliability of the constructs (Chronbach's α), sample size, correlation coefficient, and overall variance explained (or adjusted R2).

Meta-analysis is a statistical method by which information from individual studies is assimilated (Field 2001). Aforementioned summary data from each study applied to calculate an effect size for the study. An effect size is a number that exhibits the extent of the affiliation between two variables. The p-value is often used as a surrogate for the effect size, with a considerable p-value taken to entail a significant effect and a non-significant p-value taken to imply a marginal effect (Borenstein cited in Cooper et al. 2009). Once the mean effect size has been computed, it can be articulated in terms of standard normal deviations (a Z score) by dividing it by the standard error of the mean.

A significance value (i.e. the probability, p, of obtaining a Z score of such magnitude by chance) can then be calculated. Alternatively, the magnitude of the average effect size can be deduced from the boundaries of a confidence interval constructed around the mean effect size (Field 2001). Meta-analysis is used as a way of trying to establish the true effect sizes (i.e. effect sizes in a population) by combining effect sizes from independent studies. There are two ways to conceptualise this process: fixed effect and random effect models. In reality, the random effect model is probably more realistic than the fixed effect on widely held occasions especially when the findings are not restricted only to those studies included in the meta-analysis but used to make general conclusions about the research domain (Field 2001). Considering the above facts, this study has also made use of random effect model for the meta-analysis.

3   Findings

3.1   Demography of Citations

Citations by Source

MIS Quarterly emerged as the leading journal with the largest number of citations (C=36) followed by *Lecture Notes on Computer Science* as the second most published outlets with 30 citations, this followed by other leading journals such as: *Information & Management* (28 citations), *Computer in Human Behavior* (27 citations), *European Journal of Information Systems* (27 citations), and *Journal of Computer Information Systems* (22 citations); *Journal of the American Society for Information Science and Technology* (17 Citations), *IFIP Conferences* (16 Citations), *International Journal of Human-Computer Studies* (16 Citations), *Computers & Education* (14 Citations), *Journal of The Association For Information Systems* (14 Citations), *Information Systems Research* (13 Citations), *Decision Support Systems* (12 Citations), *IEEE Transactions on Engineering Management* (11 Citations), and *Journal of Information Technology* (10 Citations).

Citations by Year

The analysis of citation year indicates that citations of the originating article have constantly increased since 2004 when six studies cited it. Thereafter, 62 citations appeared in the year 2005, 91 in 2006, 141 in 2007, 214 in 2008, and 228 citations in 2009. The trend appears to be ongoing as 128 papers already cited the originating theory at the time of writing this paper in mid-2010. The trend suggests that the originating article has quickly gained acceptance and popularity amongst IS/IT researchers.

Theories, Models and External Variables Used with UTAUT

The aim of this aspect of our analysis is to identify external variables, external theories, and the relationship of external variables with the independent and dependent constructs of UTAUT for all 43 studies which have used UTAUT.

Use of External Theories

Table 1 lists the seven out of the 43 UTAUT-based studies that used external theories in their research model analyses. Our analysis reveals that TAM is the most frequently used theory alongside UTAUT – being utilized on four occasions, followed by Task Technology Fit (TTF) twice, and one instances each of IDT, and SCT.

Table 1. Summary of External Theories

Reference	External Theory
Aggelidis and Chatzoglou (2009)	TAM, TAM2
Baron et al. (2006)	TAM
He et al. (2007)	IDT, TTF
Tsai (2009)	SCT
van Biljon and Kotze (2008)	TAM
van Biljon and Renaud (2008)	TAM
Zhou et al. (2010)	TTF

LEGEND: IDT: Innovation Diffusion Theory; SCT: Social Cognitive Theory; TAM: Technology Acceptance Model; TAM2: Extended TAM; TTF: Task Technology Fit

Use of External Variables

The findings from our external variables analysis reveal that only 22 out of 43 studies have used external variables in their investigations. The remaining 21 used only the original constructs of UTAUT. Although age, gender, experience, and voluntariness of use are moderating variables in the original UTAUT (Venkatesh et al. 2003), these moderators are treated as external constructs in some of the studies. Attitude, anxiety, trust, self-efficacy, PEOU, PU, perceived risk, and perceived credibility are some of the most common external variables employed. Studies which did not use external variables indicated that they were applying the original theory without altering it to achieve their objectives. Table 2 lists only those studies which used external variables.

The analysis of relationship amongst UTAUT constructs and external constructs (as listed in Table 2) reveals that attainment value, utility value, trust, attitude, perceived ease of use, perceived usefulness, computer self-efficacy, gender, perceived risk, income, and experience have a significant impact on behavioral intention (BI). However, anxiety, training, age, perceived credibility, and social isolation do not have a significant impact and self-efficacy, subjective norm, and objective norm have mixed influence. Furthermore, trust, belief and credibility have a significant and mixed impact on performance expectancy (PE). Similarly, computer anxiety, computer self-efficacy, resistance to change, and relevance have positive impact while credibility has a non-significant impact on effort expectancy (EE). Conversely, social influence (SI) is negatively impacted by credibility. Nevertheless, IT knowledge has a positive impact on facilitating conditions (FC). As far as intention to use (IU) or usage (U) is concerned, it is impacted positively by variables from task-technology fit models, and experience but impacted insignificantly by trust, and internet experience. Apart from these external constructs, income has been shown as a moderating variable on BI.

Table 2. Summary of External Variables

Reference	External Variables
Abu-Shanab and Pearson (2009)	Self-Efficacy, Anxiety, Perceived Trust, Perceived Risk, Personal Innovativeness, Locus of Control
Aggelidis and Chatzoglou (2009)	Attitude, Self-efficacy, anxiety, Perceived usefulness, Ease of use, Training
Chiu et al. (2010)	Trust, Past Transactions, Gender, Age, Internet Experience
Chiu and Wang (2008)	Computer Self-Efficacy, Attainment Value, Utility Value, Intrinsic Value (Playfulness), Social Isolation, Anxiety, Delay in Responses, Risk of Arbitrary Learning
Curtis et al. (2010)	Voluntariness of Use, Anxiety, self-efficacy
Dadayan and Ferro (2005)	Compatibility, Computer Anxiety, Computer Attitude, Acceptance Motivation, Organizational Facilitation
He et al. (2007)	Individual Innovativeness, Compatibility, Task Technology Fit
Jong and Wang (2009)	Attitude, Self-efficacy, Anxiety
Kijsanayotin et al. (2009)	Voluntariness, Experience, Knowledge
Laumer et al. (2010)	Subjective Norm, Objective Norm
Lin and Anol (2008)	Online Support Expectancy, Online Social Support
Loo et al. (2009)	Perceived Credibility, Anxiety
Luo et al. (2010)	Trust Belief, Perceived Risk, Self-Efficacy, Disposition to Trust
Nov and Ye (2009)	Result Demonstrability, Computer Self-Efficacy, Computer Anxiety, Resistance to Change, Screen Design, Relevance, Terminology
Schaupp et al. (2010)	Optimism Bias, Trust of e-file system, Perceived Risk
Shin (2009)	Trust, Self Efficacy, Perceived Security
van Biljon and Kotze (2008)	PEOU, PU, Human Nature Influence, and Cultural Influence Demographic Factors, Socio-Economic Factors, and Personal Factors
van Dijk et al. (2008)	Age, Gender, Educational Level, Societal position, Family position, Digital Media Preference, Digital Media Access, Digital Media Experience, Attitude towards use, Knowledge of Services
Ye et al. (2008)	Computer Self-Efficacy, Risk aversion, Social influences, Breadth of use, Satisfaction, Relative Advantage, PEOU, Perceived Security
YenYuen and Yeow (2009)	Perceived Credibility, Anxiety, Self-Efficacy, Attitude towards using IBS
Yeow et al. (2008)	Perceived Credibility, Anxiety, Self-Efficacy, Attitude towards using OBS
Zhou et al. (2010)	Task Technology Fit

3.2 Meta-analysis

This section aims to investigate the corresponding relationships between constructs, measure their average reliability, the combined correlations between the constructs and their significance, and the major limitations of the studies. The findings from detailed analyses are presented in the following sub-sections.

Sample Size

Table 3 illustrates the sample sizes from 27 studies that used UTAUT. Two studies by Duyck et al. (2010) and Laumer et al. (2010) have used more than one representative sample to present and compare cases in different scenarios.

Table 3. Sample Sizes

Reference	Sample Size	Reference	Sample Size
van Dijk et al. (2008)	1225	Nov and Ye (2009)	271
Kijsanayotin et al. (2009)	1187	Schaupp et al. (2010)	260
Abu-Shanab and Pearson (2009)	878	Laumer et al. (2010)	255
Tsai (2009)	759	Zhou et al. (2010)	250
Al-Gahtani et al. (2007)	722	Wang and Shih (2009)	244
Jong and Wang (2009)	606	Hung et al. (2007)	233
Chiu et al. (2010)	412	Sapio et al. (2010)	181
Curtis et al. (2010)	409	Chang et al. (2007)	140
Duyck et al. (2010)	362	Luo et al. (2010)	122
Aggelidis and Chatzoglou (2009)	341	Gupta et al. (2008)	102
Lin and Anol (2008)	317	van Biljon and Kotze (2008)	57
Ye et al. (2008)	306	Alapetite et al. (2009)	39
Shin (2009)	296	Huser et al. (2010)	18
Chiu and Wang (2008)	286		

Relationships between UTAUT Constructs

Table 4 represents the relationships between UTAUT constructs in terms of significant, non-significant, and not applicable categories. The category is specified as not applicable when the relationship between the constructs are not talked off at all may be because of the obvious reason of the study being qualitative or partially discussing the correlation where the relationship in question is not taken into consideration in that particular study. A number of studies have fallen in the 'not applicable' category because correlations between the constructs were not specified in such studies. Moreover, there is relatively a very few number of relationships categorised within non-significant category. Performance expectancy shows the highest number of significant relations with behavioral intention, followed by social influence, effort expectancy, and facilitating conditions.

Although relatively a larger numbers of studies have shown significant impacts of facilitating conditions on usage (as per the original model of UTAUT), there are still some studies which have analyzed impact of facilitating conditions on behavioral intention as well. Moreover, only eight out of 43 studies have shown the relationship between behavioral intention and usage.

Table 4. Relationships with UTAUT constructs (approach adapted from Lee et al. 2003)

Relationship Type	PE▶BI	EE▶BI	SI▶BI	FC▶BI	FC▶U	BI▶U
Significant	25	19	22	9	14	8
Non-Significant	0	5	3	2	2	0
Not Applicable	18	19	18	32	27	35
Total	43	43	43	43	43	43

Reliability of UTAUT Constructs

Table 5 lists Chronbach's alpha (α) values for indicating reliability of UTAUT constructs across all such studies (18 studies) which have used this theory. Two of the studies have got more than one set of reliabilities because they have been applied to two different set of samples. The remaining nine studies (Alapetite et al. 2009; Duyck et al. 2010; Hung et al. 2007; Jong and Wang 2009; Lin and Anol 2008; Sapio et al. 2010; Shin 2009; Tsai 2009; van Biljon and Kotze 2008) did not provide Chronbach's alpha (α) values for any of its constructs. As per Santos (1999), Chronbach's (α) determines the internal uniformity or average correlation of items in a survey mechanism to measure its reliability. Alpha coefficient varies in the value from zero to one and may be employed to explain the reliability of factors obtained from dichotomous and/or multi-point designed opinion or dimension. The higher the value, the more trustworthy the created dimension is (Santos 1999). Nunnaly (1978) pointed out 0.7 to be a standard reliability coefficient. So, the average reliability for each construct more than 0.7 (as illustrated in table 5) indicates that all of them are falling under the acceptable reliability levels.

UTAUT Correlations

Figure 1 shows the original UTAUT theory with all its key constructs and their corresponding relationships. The combined correlation of the constructs has been shown in the figure with respect to the individual □-values of the constructs. This combined effect of correlation has been calculated using the comprehensive meta-analysis software.

Table 5. UTAUT constructs with reliabilities [*NS=Non-Significant] (adapted from King and He 2006)

Reference	PE	EE	SI	FC	BI	U
Abu-Shanab and Pearson (2009)	0.929	0.905	0.821	0.0825	0.895	-------
Aggelidis and Chatzoglou (2009)	-------	-------	-------	0.890	-------	-------
Al-Gahtani et al. (2007)	0.900	0.900	0.950	0.770	0.760	0.850
Chang et al. (2007)	0.940	0.950	0.870	0.950	0.930	-------
Chiu and Wang (2008)	0.850	0.890	0.890	0.820	0.940	-------
Chiu et al. (2010)	-------	-------	-------	-------	0.970	-------
Curtis et al. (2010)	0.840	0.870	0.890	0.720	0.960	-------
Gupta et al. (2008)	0.814	0.812	0.812	0.809	0.839	-------
Huser et al. (2010)	0.871	0.849	-------	--------	0.752	-------
Kijsanayotin et al. (2009)	0.930	0.930	0.890	0.900	0.970	-------
Laumer et al. (2010)	0.736	0.795	-------	0.787	0.870	-------
	0.707	0.842	-------	0.587	0.883	-------
Luo et al. (2010)	0.890	--------	-------	--------	0.890	-------
Nov and Ye (2009)	0.880	0.870	-------	--------	0.960	-------
Schaupp et al. (2010)	0.740	0.830	0.800	0.740	--------	0.910
van Dijk et al. (2008)	0.750	0.830	0.150	--------	--------	-------
	*NS	--------	-------	--------	--------	-------
Wang and Shih (2009)	0.921	0.916	0.939	0.819	0.905	0.863
Ye et al. (2008)	-------	-------	0.870	--------	--------	-------
Zhou et al. (2010)	0.866	0.864	0.846	0.833	--------	0.857
Number of Studies	17	15	12	13	14	4
Average Reliability	0.798	0.870	0.811	0.747	0.895	0.870

The inputs given to the application for each construct were their individual β-values and sample size from the specific studies. The combined zero-order correlations for each pair of constructs indicate the significant relationship between them. The R2-value for BI and Usage has been calculated taking the average of R2-values of all the studies and found to be significant as well. Hence, the general concept of the relationship between the constructs is consistent with the original theory of UTAUT (Venkatesh et al. 2003).

Table 6 shows the correlation results for the five relationships for all its constructs (King and He 2006) calculated through comprehensive meta-analysis software. The result shows that PE-BI and BI-U are relatively strongly correlated than the other relationships. The p-values across all the relationships indicate that the correlations between constructs are significant and hence consistent with the original theory of

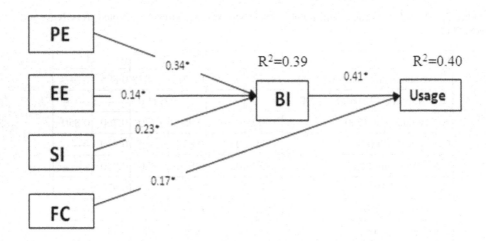

Fig. 1. UTAUT Constructs Combined Correlation with *p<0.05 (model adapted from Venkatesh et al. 2003)

Table 6. Summary of Zero-Order correlations between UTAUT constructs (approach adapted from King and He 2006; Source: Comprehensive Meta-Analysis Software[1])

Statistical Measurement	PE→BI	EE→BI	SI→BI	FC→U	BI→U
Number of Studies	8	8	10	8	3
Total Sample Size	4170	4170	4453	1846	1990
Average (β)	0.343	0.140	0.231	0.165	0.405
Z-value	21.699	2.201	4.945	7.103	4.097
p (Effect Size)	0.000	0.028	0.000	0.000	0.000
95% Low (β)	0.231	0.015	0.141	0.120	0.221
95% High (β)	0.446	0.261	0.317	0.209	0.562

UTAUT. The 95% confidence interval also supports the correlation values and likelihood of these values to fall in the given interval.

3.3 Major Limitations of Studies That Have Utilized UTAUT

Based on some of the common limitations encountered frequently across most of the studies, Table 7 has categorized limitations from individual studies into nine broader categories. Out of 43 studies, there are nine such papers which have not listed any limitations and Table 7 has listed them in a separate category called 'No Limitations Specified'. A considerable number of the studies have mentioned single IS, single subject, or cross-sectional studies as their major limitations. However, there are some studies which have referenced their limitations as: small number of samples, no application of actual usage, self-selection bias, and specialized single task difficult to generalize.

---

[1] Comprehensive Meta-Analysis Software: http://www.meta-analysis.com

Table 7. Summary of limitations of UTAUT studies (approach adapted from Lee et al. 2003)

Limitation	Papers (#)	Explanation	Examples
Self-Reported Usage	4	Does not assess the actual usage	Hung et al. (2007)
Single IS	8	Only use a single IS for research	Chang et al. (2007)
Student Samples	1	Not appropriate for working situation	Tsai (2009)
Single Subject	12	Only one community, organization, culture or country	Li (2010)
Cross Sectional Study	5	Measured at only one point of time	Chiu et al. (2010)
Measurement Problems	1	Conclusion from data analysis is difficult	Ye et al. (2008)
Single Task	3	Difficult to generalize the result	Wang and Shih (2009)
Others	20	Small sample size, self-selection bias, little reflection on cultural difference, short exposure time to adopt new IS	Schaupp et al. (2010)
No Limitations Specified	9	Limitations not mentioned in the studies	Curtis et al. (2010)

4 Discussions

The findings regarding the relationships between the constructs of UTAUT in Table 8 signify that most of the relationships exist between the constructs are consistently significant. These findings are in accordance with the findings of Venkatesh et al. (2003) in the original paper of UTAUT. However, there are still few relationships which are non-significant in nature and require further attention. Moreover, the relationship between FC and BI needs a further research consideration as most of the studies find this relationship as significant which is in disparity with original composition of the UTAUT (Venkatesh et al. 2003).

But, the findings of the combined effect of the overall relationship between the constructs demonstrated in Table 6 and Figure 2 measured through the meta-analysis software were found to be positive and significant. The comparison of construct correlations from the original theory and the combined effect is presented in Figure 2 below.

The comparison of the correlation values between the constructs from the original theory and the combined effect shows that the direct effects of PE and the direct effects and interaction terms from EE, SI, FC, and BI have got the larger values in original model than the model obtained from the meta-analysis. Although, all relationships appear to be significant in meta-analysis, a lower correlation coefficient (β) suggests less consistent performance of UTAUT in various contexts. This may be due to relatively less number of studies used in for the meta-analysis and the absence of moderators in majority of studies that have utilized the UTAUT model. Any future

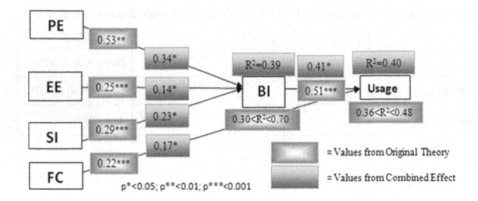

Fig. 2. Construct correlations and R2 from original theory and combined effect (Model adapted from Venkatesh et al. 2003; Data Source: Venkatesh et al. 2003; Comprehensive Meta-Analysis Software)

research wishes to apply UTAUT should apply it in its original form that means effect of moderating variables must not be excluded from the model.

The combined R^2-values are computed as an average of all the studies used for meta- analysis as the comprehensive meta-analysis tool does not provide the option for such input and it is found that the R^2-values for both BI and U fall between the original theory's (Venkatesh et al. 2003) value range of 'direct effects only' and 'direct effects and interaction terms values' and hence acceptable.

The findings for the average combined reliability through Chronbach's (α) in Table 5 represent that all the constructs except FC (with acceptable reliability of 0.735) are greater than or equal to 0.8, and therefore, highly reliable and these findings are similar to TAM meta-analysis findings measured by King and He (2006) across the various studies where they also considered the reliability of 0.8 as highly reliable. The findings regarding the limitations for the studies specified in Table 7 are in line with one used in Lee et al. (2003) for TAM studies' limitations and open up a further scope of future research in those areas. Most of the studies are analyzed either along single IS, single subject, or single task category where they are applicable only to a specific area of research. Hence, a serious research agenda is to make them compatible with the generic scenarios. Although most of the studies are cross-sectional in nature, it becomes a potential limitation for them sometimes as they do not provide a clear picture of adoption of the technology. Lee et al. (2003) argue that users' intent and opinion may change over the period of time and hence it is required to assess the adoption behavior at various points over longer period of time (Lee et al. 2003).

5 Conclusions

- The following significant points emerged from the findings and discussions presented in this study are:
- A number of empirical studies that utilized UTAUT were based on relatively very small sample size.

- There is an increasing trend of using external variables and external theories to-gether with the UTAUT.
- Relationships between external variables along with UTAUT constructs and beha-vioral intention were generally reported as significant or mixed significant.
- Reliability of UTAUT's survey instrument was found consistent in all citations that have utilized it.
- The overall effect of zero-order correlations between independent and dependent constructs of UTAUT was found significant.

The findings from this study also have relevance for technology adoption and diffu-sion research. The refined model of UTAUT based on meta-analysis that presented within this report may contribute to the area of IS/IT adoption and diffusion research as it raises many vital points related to the original model. For example, those studies that are utilizing UTAUT model generally ignore the effect of moderating variables which might be distorting the actual performance of the theory. It also highlights issue of integrating external variables without giving strong and logical justifications, for example, some studies have utilized both usefulness and performance expectancy and others have utilized both effort expectancy and ease of use. These constructs are es-sentially similar in nature and should not be employed in same study to avoid repeti-tions and redundancy.

5.1 Limitations and Further Research Directions

The first limitation is that some studies could not be taken into consideration because of the lack of privileged access rights for some journals such as European Journal of Information Systems, and Journal of Information Technology. The future researchers can look for the access more such UTAUT related studies in order to more accurately explore the meta-analysis. Secondly, the study does not take into consideration the analysis of moderating variables and their impacts on the constructs. The researchers can more elaborately analyze the effect of moderators such as age, gender, expe-rience, and voluntariness of use on the relationships of the constructs to get more effective outcome. Thirdly, the combined R^2-value for BI and U has not been com-puted using the meta-analysis tool as they do not have any such option for generating the combined effect for the same and hence represented just by taking the average of individual R2-values. The future researchers need to explore some more appropriate method to compute the combined R^2-value through some specific software tool or relevant statistical measurements. Fourthly, the study has not considered the structural relationship between UTAUT constructs where majority of researchers have been more fascinated about it as it helps them explicate individuals' adoption of new tech-nologies, than in the zero-order correlations (King and He 2006). This research could have been made more generalized by incorporating the structural relationships be-tween the constructs where most of the researchers are more interested about. Lastly, this study has not considered qualitative studies as a potential candidate for meta-analysis as King and He (2006) have done in the meta-analysis of TAM studies. The future research can also explore this kind of meta-analysis to be included along with quantitative one.

References

Abu-Shanab, E., Pearson, M.: Internet Banking in Jordan: An Arabic Instrument Validation Process. International Arab Journal of Information Technology 6(3), 235–244 (2009)

Aggelidis, V.P., Chatzoglou, P.D.: Using a modified technology acceptance model in hospitals. International Journal of Medical Informatics 78(2), 115–126 (2009)

Alapetite, A., Andersen, H.B., Hertzum, M.: Acceptance of speech recognition by physicians: A survey of expectations, experiences, and social influence. International Journal of Human-Computer Studies 67(1), 6–49 (2009)

Al-Gahtani, S.S., Hubona, G.S., Wang, J.: Information technology (IT) in Saudi Arabia: Culture and the acceptance and use of IT. Information & Management 44(8), 681–691 (2007)

Baron, S., Patterson, A., Harris, K.: Beyond technology acceptance: understanding consumer practice. International Journal of Service Industry Management 17(2), 111–135 (2006)

Borenstein, M.: Effect Sizes for Continuous Data. In: Cooper, H., Hedges, L.V., Valentine, J.C. (eds.) The Handbook of Research Synthesis and Meta-Analysis. Russell Sage Foundation, New York (2009)

Chang, I.C., Hwang, H.G., Hung, W.F., Li, Y.C.: Physicians' acceptance of pharmacokinetics-based clinical decision support systems. Expert Systems with Applications 33(2), 296–303 (2007)

Chiu, C.M., Wang, E.T.G.: Understanding Web-based learning continuance intention: The role of subjective task value. Information & Management 45(3), 194–201 (2008)

Chiu, C.M., Huang, H.Y., Yen, C.H.: Antecedents of trust in online auctions. Electronic Commerce Research and Applications 9(2), 148–159 (2010)

Curtis, L., Edwards, C., Fraser, K.L., Gudelsky, S., Holmquist, J., Thornton, K.: Adoption of social media for public relations by non-profit organizations. Public Relations Review 36(1), 90–92 (2010)

Dadayan, L., Ferro, E.: When technology meets the mind: A comparative study of the technology acceptance model. In: Wimmer, M.A., Traunmüller, R., Grönlund, Å., Andersen, K.V. (eds.) EGOV 2005. LNCS, vol. 3591, pp. 137–144. Springer, Heidelberg (2005)

Deng, X., Doll, W.J., Hendrickson, A.R., Scazzero, J.A.: A multi-group analysis of structural invariance: an illustration using technology acceptance model. Information & Management 42(5), 745–759 (2005)

Duyck, P., Pynoo, B., Devolder, P., Voet, T., Adang, L., Ovaere, D.: Monitoring the PACS Implementation Process in Large University Hospital-Discrepancies between Radiologists and Physicians. Journal of Digital Imaging 23(1), 73–80 (2010)

Field, A.P.: Meta-analysis of correlation coefficients: a Monte Carlo comparison of fixed- and random-effects methods. Psychological Methods 6(2), 161–180 (2001)

Gupta, B., Dasgupta, S., Gupta, A.: Adoption of ICT in a government organization in a developing country: An empirical study. Journal of Strategic Information Systems 17(2), 140–154 (2008)

Hausenblas, H.A., Carron, A.V., Mack, D.V.: Application of the theories of reasoned action and planned behavior to exercise behavior: A meta-analysis. Journal of Sport & Exercise Psychology 19(1), 36–51 (1997)

He, D.H., Lu, Y.B., Alfred, U.: An integrated framework for mobile business acceptance. Alfred Univ., Alfred (2007)

Hung, Y.H., Wang, Y.S., Chou, S.C.T.: User Acceptance of E-Government Services. Natl Sun Yat-Sen Univ., Kaohsiung (2007)

Huser, V., Narus, S.P., Rocha, R.A.: Evaluation of a flowchart-based EHR query system: A case study of RetroGuide. Journal of Biomedical Informatics 43(1), 41–50 (2010)

Jong, D., Wang, T.S.: Student Acceptance of Web-based Learning System. Acad. Publ., Oulu (2009)

Kijsanayotin, B., Pannarunothai, S., Speedie, S.M.: Factors influencing health information technology adoption in Thailand's community health centers: Applying the UTAUT model. International Journal of Medical Informatics 78(6), 404–416 (2009)

King, W.R., He, J.: A meta-analysis of the technology acceptance model. Information & Management 43, 740–755 (2006)

Laumer, S., Eckhardt, A., Trunk, N.: Do as your parents say?-Analyzing IT adoption influencing factors for full and under age applicants. Information Systems Frontiers 12(2), 169–183 (2010)

Lee, Y., Kozar, K.A., Larsen, K.R.T.: The Technology Acceptance Model: Past, Present, and Future. Communications of the Association for Information System 12, 752–780 (2003)

Legris, P., Ingham, J., Collerette, P.: Why do people use information technology? A critical review of the technology acceptance model. Information & Management 40(3), 191–204 (2003)

Li, W.: Virtual knowledge sharing in a cross-cultural context. Journal of Knowledge Management 14(1), 38–50 (2010)

Lin, C.P., Anol, B.: Learning online social support: An investigation of network information technology based on UTAUT. Cyber Psychology & Behavior 11(3), 268–272 (2008)

Loo, W.H., Yeow, P.H.P., Chong, S.C.: User acceptance of Malaysian government multipurpose smartcard applications. Government Information Quarterly 26(2), 358–367 (2009)

Luo, X., Li, H., Zhang, J., Shim, J.P.: Examining multi-dimensional trust and multi-faceted risk in initial acceptance of emerging technologies: An empirical study of mobile banking services. Decision Support System 49(2), 222–234 (2010)

Ma, Q., Liu, L.: The technology acceptance model: a meta-analysis of empirical findings. Journal of Organizational and End User Computing 16(1), 59–72 (2004)

Nov, O., Ye, C.: Resistance to Change and the Adoption of Digital Libraries: An Integrative Model. Journal of the American Society for Information Science and Technology 60(8), 1702–1708 (2009)

Nunnaly, J.: Psychometric theory. McGraw-Hill, New York (1978)

Santos, J.R.A.: Chronbach's Alpha: A Tool for Assessing the Reliability of Scales. Journal of Extension 37(2), 1–5 (1999)

Sapio, B., Turk, T., Cornacchia, M., Papa, F., Nicolo, E., Livi, S.: Building scenarios of digital television adoption: a pilot study. Technology Analysis & Strategic Management 22(1), 43–63 (2010)

Schaupp, L.C., Carter, L., McBride, M.E.: E-file adoption: A study of US taxpayers' intentions. Computers in Human Behavior 26(4), 636–644 (2010)

Sheeran, P., Taylor, S.: Predicting Intentions to Use Condoms: A Meta-Analysis and Comparison of the Theories of Reasoned Action and Planned Behavior. Journal of Applied Social Psychology 29(8), 1624–1675 (1999)

Shin, D.H.: Towards an understanding of the consumer acceptance of mobile wallet. Computers in Human Behavior 25(6), 1343–1354 (2009)

Tsai, Y.H., Lin, C.P., Chiu, C.K., Joe, S.W.: Understanding learning behavior using location and prior performance as moderators. Social Science Journal 46(4), 787–799 (2009)

van Biljon, J., Kotze, P.: Cultural Factors in a Mobile Phone Adoption and Usage Model. Journal of Universal Computer Science 14(16), 2650–2679 (2008) van Biljon, J., Renaud, K.: A Qualitative Study of the Applicability of Technology Acceptance Models to Senior Mobile Phone Users. In: Song, I.-Y., Piattini, M., Chen, Y.-P.P., Hartmann, S., Grandi, F., Trujillo, J., Opdahl, A.L., Ferri, F., Grifoni, P., Caschera, M.C., Rolland, C., Woo, C., Salinesi, C., Zimányi, E., Claramunt, C., Frasincar, F., Houben, G.-J., Thiran, P. (eds.) ER Workshops 2008. LNCS, vol. 5232, pp. 228–237. Springer, Heidelberg (2008)

van Dijk, J., Peters, O., Ebbers, W.: Explaining the acceptance and use of government Internet services: A multivariate analysis of 2006 survey data in the Netherlands. Government Information Quarterly 25(3), 379–399 (2008)

Venkatesh, V., Morris, M.G., Davis, G.B., Davis, F.D.: User acceptance of information technology: Toward a unified view. MIS Quarterly 27(3), 425–478 (2003)

Wang, Y.S., Shih, Y.W.: Why do people use information kiosks? A validation of the Unified Theory of Acceptance and Use of Technology. Government Information Quarterly 26(1), 158–165 (2009)

Ye, C., Seo, D., Desouza, K.C., Sangareddy, S.P., Jha, S.: Influences of IT Substitutes and User Experience on Post-Adoption User Switching: An Empirical Investigation. Journal of the American Society for Information Science and Technology 59(13), 2115–2132 (2008)

YenYuen, Y., Yeow, P.H.P.: User Acceptance of Internet Banking Service in Malaysia. In: Cordeiro, J., Hammoudi, S., Filipe, J. (eds.) Web Information Systems and Technologies, vol. 18, pp. 295–306. Springer, Berlin (2009)

Yeow, P.H.P., Yuen, Y.Y., Tong, D.Y.K., Lim, N.: User acceptance of Online Banking Service in Australia. Int. Business Information Management Assoc-Ibima, Norristown (2008)

Zhou, T., Lu, Y.B., Wang, B.: Integrating TTF and UTAUT to explain mobile banking user adoption. Computers in Human Behavior 26(4), 760–767 (2010)

Getting Customers' Motives: Lean on Motivation Theory for Designing Virtual Ideas Communities

Ulrich Bretschneider and Jan Marco Leimeister

Kassel University, Chair for Information Systems, Nora-Platiel-Str. 4, 34127 Kassel, Germany
Tel.: +49 (0) 561 804 2880
{bretschneider,leimeister}@wi-kassel.de

Abstract. Virtual ideas communities such as Dell's "Ideastorm" or Intel's "Ideazone" are very popular in practice. In such communities distributed groups of individual customers focus on voluntarily sharing and elaborating innovative ideas to support company's new products development. However, a look at existing ideas community leads to the conclusion that many of them are featured to the minimum necessary. Typically, they fail to provide technical components and organizational arrangements that are able to motivate customers to submit ideas. Based on insights from motivation theory it is known that such components and arrangements could serve as incentives for submitting ideas, as they activate customers' corresponding motives, which again lead to idea submission. In reverse, this means when knowing customers different motives one can systematically derive adequate components and arrangements from it. The aim of this paper is to derive components from customers' motives. Our research approach is two-folded. First, we applied an online survey among participants of the SAPiens ideas community. We empirically queried motives that lead participants to submit ideas. After that we come up with an empirical tested set of six motives (self-marketing, fun, altruism, recognition, product improvement and enhancement as well as learning). Second, we used these six motives in order to derive a set of adequate components from it. Our research will deliver important examples and insights how to arrange virtual ideas communities with technical and organizational components and arrangements in order to make them more effective, so that more customers are willing to submit ideas.

Keywords: virtual ideas communities, open innovation, user motivation, customer integration, motives.

1 Introduction

1.1 Open Innovation: Customer Integration into Innovation Activities

In the 20th century, many leading industrial companies generated, developed and commercialized ideas for innovations in self-reliance. Nowadays, companies are increasingly rethinking the fundamental ways of managing their innovation activities.

M. Nüttgens et al. (Eds.): Governance and Sustainability in IS, IFIP AICT 366, pp. 171–187, 2011.

According to Chesbrough's open innovation paradigm, overcoming companies' boundaries in order to open up for other resources for innovation becomes more and more important (Chesbrough 2003). In this context customers are seen as one of the biggest resource for innovations. Customer integration into innovation activities is a strategy of value creation in which customers are taking part in innovation value creating activities. Customers respectively product users often have rather high product expertise as well as knowledge and creativity potential, which they gained by regular product usage. However, this customer's knowledge is hardly accessible for companies. When integrating customer into the product innovation process companies profit by getting access to customer's product know-how.

In particular, when integrating customers into the early stages of the product innovation process, which focuses on generating innovations ideas, companies tend to get access to customer innovation ideas. On the one hand, ideas expressed by customers reflect their needs and wishes. On the other hand these ideas can represent suggestions describing how ideas can be transferred into marketable products. These so called "need information" and "solution information" constitute valuable input for the product innovation process (von Hippel 1994).

In literature and practice certain methods for integrating customers into the early stages of the innovation process are discussed. Von Hippel's "Lead-User-Approach" is a popular example of this understanding of customer integration (von Hippel 1986). The Lead-User-Method implies systematic identification of single innovative customers, so-called lead users, and their integration into workshops in order to generate ideas and concepts for new products or services together with companies' employees.

In literature and practice ideas competitions are described as another familiar practice to get access to customer ideas. An ideas competition can be defined as an invitation of a company to its customer base in order to submit innovation ideas to a certain topic within a certain short timeline and typically via an Internet platform. An idea-reviewers committee evaluates these contributions and selects the winner (Piller and Walcher 2006; Leimeister, Huber et al. 2009).

Recently, a novel method becomes relevant in practice. This alternative method can be constituted as "Virtual Ideas Communities". Ideas communities are initiated by companies and seek to offer customers a virtual forum for submitting innovation ideas. On the virtual community platform customers can post their ideas, vote for other participants' ideas and comment and/or discuss on other participants' ideas in order to help making ideas better in a collaborative manner.

While online user innovation communities in general are not a new phenomenon, as at least the open source software phenomenon demonstrates, with ideas communities there is an underlying difference. Firms run idea communities - from initial community building until continuous community management. This allows them to control the community in total and because of this to use its idea outcome non-restrictively. In contrast to that, so far known online user innovation communities, like open source communities or online communities of enthusiasts in basketball that share ideas for improving the design or other features of sport shoes (Füller, Jawecki et al. 2007), are run completely by and for users, which made it difficult for firms harnessing communities' outcome for new product development.

So, ideas communities, which we define as distributed groups of individual customers focused on sharing and elaborating innovation ideas supported by computer mediated community platforms as well as initiated and run by firms, are an emerging popular strategy in order to gain ideas for innovations from customers. Companies like Google, Intel, BMW, SAP, or Acrobat are only a few examples that run ideas communities.

1.2 Theoretical Background: Motivation Theory

Motivation psychology differentiates between the notion "motive" and "motivation". A motive is seen as an individual's psychological disposition (von Rosenstiel 2003). This disposition describes how important certain goals for an individual are. Some motives are inborn but a relatively stable set of motives is developed during an individual's socialization process (Heckhausen and Heckhausen 2006). This set of motives constitutes an individual's cognitive subsystem. Motivation describes the process how an individual's motives become activated. The basic principle of motivation is characterized in motivation psychology as follows: In a particular situational context, an adequate motive will be activated and subsequently cause certain behaviour. In such situational contexts certain things, that an individual perceives, will serve as incentive that stimulates corresponding motives. So motives can be seen as incitement to human act and behaviour (von Rosenstiel 2003). Von Rosenstiel (von Rosenstiel 2003) illustrates the activation of human behaviour in a simple model, shown in the following figure.

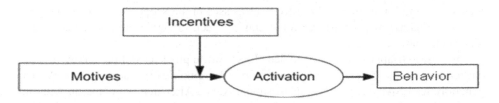

Fig. 1. Motivation model, adapted from Von Rosenstiel (2003)

One can distinguish between intrinsic and extrinsic motivation: There are certain activities and behaviors that some people naturally engage in, such as eating or drinking. Deci calls this intrinsic motivation, because the underlying motives are stimulated by an inborn feeling, such as hunger or thirst, not by a situational context as described above (Deci and Ryan 1985). Beside the motives that belong to the class of internal motivation there are several other motives, which do not arise from an individual's inborn desire. They arise directly from external stimuli that are perceived from above mentioned situational context. These motives can thus be categorized into the class of so called external motives (Deci and Ryan 1985).

For our research one can draw on this motivation model. So, adapted to the case of ideas communities certain components of ideas communities can be interpreted by a customer as a mentioned incentive that again activates this person's individual corresponding motive and then finally lead to idea submission.

1.3 Research Aim, Approach, and Methodology

Many ideas community offer only a limited range of attractive components, such as technical functionalities, tools or organizational arrangements. Typically, ideas communities only offer three, technical based core-elements. These are IT-based systems for idea up-loading, idea commenting, and idea evaluating. Certainly, the lack of attractive components and arrangements is a main reason why most ideas communities count only few ideas. However, providing more attractive components is the manipulating variable that firms can use in order to influence customers' willingness for idea submission, as can be learned from above mentioned motivation theory.

So, our research aimed at identifying much more attractive components and arrangements for virtual ideas communities than existing core elements. The underlying approach of our research in accordance to the above described motivation model is as follows: Knowing customers' motives one is able to determine adequate components and arrangements that serve as incentives for stimulating theirs corresponding motives and than in turn will make them submit ideas in a much more willing manner.

So, our research seeks to deliver technical- as well as organizational-based components and arrangements that are able to raise idea output in ideas communities. As Schneiderman (Shneiderman 2000) emphasized the necessity of efficient environments enabling innovation and creativity processes in the scope of customer integration, our findings will contribute for designing such effective environments within idea communities.

Our research approach is two-folded. First, we applied an online survey among participants of the SAPiens idea community. We empirically queried motives that generally lead SAPiens participants to submit ideas. After that we come up with an empirical tested set of six motives (self-marketing, fun, altruism, recognition, product improvement and enhancement as well as learning). Second, we used these six motives in order to derive a set of adequate components and arrangements from it.

1.4 Case Background: The SAPiens Ideas Community

SAPiens is an Internet based ideas community (www.sapiens.info) initiated and run by the ERP software producer SAP. SAPiens was launched in summer 2009 and targeted users of SAP software. Each submitted idea, phrased in an average length of five-line phrases, was visualised in an idea pool, a separate section of the online platform. Figure 2 shows the homepage of the SAPiens ideas community.

Until March 2010 156 SAP users became registered members of the SAPiens community. Of those users, 149 actively participated by submitting at least one idea. The rest participated by just scoring and commenting submissions of other users or simply lurk. The comments and user evaluations helped the ideas presenters to refine their ideas.

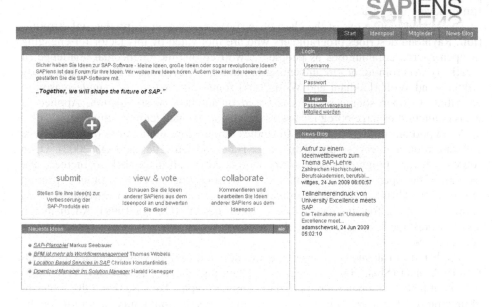

Fig. 2. Homepage of the SAPiens ideas community

2   Motives of Sapiens' Members

In order to research motives that make SAPiens members submitting ideas we query a set of eleven possible and adequate operationalized motives among SAPiens members with the help of an online survey. Before that, we extracted queried motives from an extensive literature review. After data collection we analysed empirical data with the help of factor analysis. All results are presented in the following sections.

2.1   Literature Review

Human motivation has been discussed prominently in the field of open source community research. Various motives are examined that make open source software programmers participate in open source software projects. As open source software communities are basically comparable to ideas communities it is worth to check if motives examined in the open source domain could be extracted to our case. So we conducted a literature review. We examined six empirical studies out of the field of open source research that deal with programmers' motives for participation in open source communities. We focused on its examined motivation factors and analyzed which of them are appropriable for the use of our own survey. Based on the insights of this research we applied 11 motives, which are briefly described as follows.

The first motive is fun. Fun is a prominent motive studied in several open source motivation studies, e.g., Hars and Ou (Hars and Ou 2002), Lakhani and Wolf (Lakhani and Wolf 2005), and Osterloh et al. (Osterloh, Rota et al. 2002). In open source context, the fun motive is described as having fun or enjoying one-self when programming. Applied to ideas communities the fun motive is manifested in having **fun** in developing ideas.

The second motive out of the class of intrinsic motivation is **intellectual stimulation**. Raymond describes programmers who are motivated by this factor for engaging in open source communities as people "...who enjoys the intellectual challenge of creatively overcoming or circumventing limitations" (Raymond 1996). In their study Lakhani and Wolf (Lakhani and Wolf 2005) found out that the top single reason to contribute to open source projects is based on intellectual stimulation. Applied to ideas communities developing ideas for participants is intellectually stimulating.

An important motive considered in studies that explore motivations of open source software programmers is "**altruism**", e.g., Hars and Ou (Hars and Ou 2002). Open source software programmers who are motivated by altruism seek to increase the welfare of the open software community by writing program code without expecting any reward. Altruism can be interpreted as the direct opposite to selfishness or as "doing something for another at some cost to oneself" (Ozinga 1999). Altruism can also be presumed to be a driver that motivates customers to participate in ideas communities.

Another intrinsic motive considered in open source motivation studies is "**reciprocity**". Shah (Shah 2005) as well as Lakhani and Wolf (Lakhani and Wolf 2005) found out that some open source programmers participate because they felt a sense of obligation to give something back to the open source community in return for the software tools it provides. This motive could also be assigned to the case of customer participation in ideas communities. So, some customer may feel obliged to SAP in return for the use of the SAP software.

One motive out of the class of external motives is the so called **recognition**, e.g., Hars and Ou (Hars and Ou 2002) or Hertel et al. (Hertel, Niedner et al. 2003). Recognition contains expected reactions of significant others, such as other programmers. Motivation to contribute to a open source community should be higher the more positive the expected reactions of significant others are, weighted by the perceived importance of these significant others. This relation is formally expressed as a multiplicative function. Applied to ideas communities participants expect positive reactions from other participants as well as the organizer. These reactions by thirds may be caused by the submitted ideas displayed on the Internet platform.

Furthermore, people may consider participating in ideas communities as an effective way to demonstrate their capabilities and skills shown through their submitted ideas. Their achievements in ideas communities can be used to demonstrate competence to the organizer of the ideas community or others. Reactions by thirds may be caused on the basis of submitted ideas. Participating in ideas community, therefore, can be a good channel for self-advertisement for those seeking new job opportunities, for example. This phenomenon is mainly discussed in the field of researching motivations of open source programmers as **self-marketing** motive, e.g., Hars and Ou (Hars and Ou 2002) or Hertel et al. (Hertel, Niedner et al. 2003).

In the context of open source communities identification is examined also as a motivational factor. Identification is a reason for programmers engaging in open source communities when other participants sharing someone's aims, ideals, etc. (Hars and Ou 2002; Osterloh, Rota et al. 2002; Hertel, Niedner et al. 2003; Lakhani and Wolf

2005). Kelly and Breinlinger (Kelly and Breinlinger 1995) as well as Simon et al. (Simon, Loewy et al. 1998) used identification in order to explain why people engage in social movements of specific social groups such as older people, women, etc. Applied to ideas communities, people may regard for participating because they feel aligned to the organising firm of the ideas community in a manner that marketing science characterizes as customer's brand loyalty or company awareness (Aaker 1997). So, **identification with the organizing firm** is a motivational factor worth to be include to our survey.

Insights from open source motivation research reveal that many open source programmers participate in open source projects because of their willing to improve functionality of the software or failures in the lines of code (Hars and Ou 2002). This could be also relevant for participants of ideas communities. By submitting an idea participants may accentuate the necessity for improving the functionality or a defect of the underlying product. So, **product improvement** is a motivational factor worth to be include to our survey.

Furthermore, in the open source software research the need motive is discussed. As several studies, e.g., Gosh et al. (Ghosh, Glott et al. 2002) reveal that programmers engage in open source communities because they have a personal need or just detect a need for a certain kind of software. They appeal to an existing community or even form a new open software community in order to implement their need. Applied to the SAPiens ideas community customers may motivate to submit an idea because they detect a certain personal need which they phrase into an idea. So, the **need** motive seems to be worth included in our study.

Another motive out of the class of extrinsic motivation is **learning**. Learning is also discussed in the field of open source motivation research. Hars and Ou (Hars and Ou 2002) found out that some open source programmers are motivated for participating in open source projects by the prospect of selecting learning experiences. This motivation factor can be adopted for the present study. So, customers may also participate in ideas communities to expand their personal skills, capabilities, and knowledge.

Different open source motivation studies found out that open source software programmers also seek for **contacts to peers** in order to make new friends or socialize with others (Hertel, Niedner et al. 2003). When applied to ideas communities we expect that customer also have this motive to contribute to ideas communities.

2.2 Survey

The survey seeks to explore the motives that make participants of the SAPiens ideas community contribute ideas. Since perceived motivation-related issues can be best expressed by the participants of the SAPiens community themselves, we conducted a standardized questionnaire survey. 29 items were formulated in order to measure the 11 motives (see table 1). Using a rating scale ranging from 1 (strongly disagree) to 5 (strongly agree), participants were asked to rate the degree to which extent each motive makes him or her submitting ideas to the SAPiens ideas community.

Table 1. Adapted motives

Motive	Reference
Fun	Contextualized from Hars/Ou (2002); Hertel/Niedner/Herrmann (2003); Lakhani/Wolf (2005); Shah (2005).
Intellectual stimulation	Contextualized from Lakhani/Wolf (2005).
Altruism	Contextualized from Hars/Ou (2002); Shah (2005).
Reciprocity	Contextualized from Ghosh et al. (2002); Lakhani/Wolf (2005); Shah (2005).
Recognition	Contextualized from Ghosh et al. (2002); Hars/Ou (2002); Hertel/Niedner/Herrmann (2003); Lakhani/Wolf (2005); Shah (2005).
Identifying with the organizing firm	Developed in this research by building on Hars/Ou (2002); Hertel/Niedner/Herrmann (2003); Lakhani/Wolf (2005); Osterloh/Rota/Kuster (2002).
Product improvement	Contextualized from Ghosh et al. (2002); Hertel/Niedner/Herrmann (2003); Shah (2005).
Need	Contextualized from Ghosh et al. (2002); Hars/Ou (2002); Lakhani/Wolf (2005); Shah (2005).
Learning	Contextualized from Ghosh et al. (2002); Hars/Ou (2002); Hertel/Niedner/Herrmann (2003); Lakhani/Wolf (2005).
Contact to peers	Contextualized from Ghosh et al. (2002); Hertel/Niedner/Herrmann (2003).

Table 2. Rotated component matrix

Items *I attended the SAPiens ideas community because...*	Components					
	1	2	3	4	5	6
1. Fun						
... I have fun in working out ideas and creative solutions. *(S1)*	0.065	**_0.660_**	0.268	0.065	0.117	-0.039
... I perceive composing creative ideas as a kind of self-realization. *(S2)*	0.043	**_0.630_**	0.026	0.209	0.325	0.176
... I take much pleasure in being creative. *(S3)*	0.255	**_0.785_**	0.203	0.107	0.118	0.030
2. Intellectual stimulation						
... I'm stimulated by generating creative ideas. *(IH1)*	*excluded as item did not achieve critical MSA value*					

Table 2. (*Continued*)

Items	Components					
I attended the SAPiens ideas community because…	1	2	3	4	5	6
… I'm intellectually challenged by developing creative ideas. *(IH2)*	0.190	**0.898**	0.065	-0.023	0.082	0.135
3. Altruism						
… I want to benefit others by contributing an idea. *(ALT1)*	-0.106	0.360	**0.569**	0.203	0.300	0.141
… I want to make my idea available to the general public without expecting any return. *(ALT2)*	0.058	0.106	**0.727**	0.141	-0.020	0.162
4. Reciprocity						
… I believe that SAP goes to the time and effort of developing the SAP software, so that I want to regive SAP my idea. *(REZ1)*	0.024	-0.050	0.468	0.161	0.261	0.508
… I want to reciprocate to SAP as I use the SAP software gratis. *(REZ2)*	*excluded as item did not achieve critical MSA value*					
… I want to give SAP my ideas as I return professional qualification through SAP. *(REZ3)*	*excluded as item did not achieve critical MSA value*					
… I want to benefit to SAP by submitting an idea as I benefit from my SAP skills. *(REZ4)*	*excluded as item did not achieve critical MSA value*					
5. Recognition						
… I hoped that other members would appreciate my idea(s). *(ANER1)*	0.423	0.236	0.048	**0.610**	0.087	0.120
… I hoped that other participants would honor my idea(s). *(ANER2)*	0.110	0.452	0.407	0.418	0.096	0.006
… I hoped that SAP would value my idea(s). *(ANER3)*	0.415	0.089	0.131	**0.710**	0.191	0.284

Table 2. (*Continued*)

Items *I attended the SAPiens ideas community because…*	Components					
	1	2	3	4	5	6
… I hoped that SAP would appreciate my idea(s). *(ANER4)*	0.046	0.094	0.210	**0.832**	0.253	0.071
6. Self-marketing						
… I hoped to show my skills and abilities through my idea(s) to potential employers. *(SM1)*	**0.624**	0.263	-0.080	0.229	0.400	-0.040
… I hoped to convince SAP of my skills and abilities through my idea(s). *(SM2)*	**0.762**	0.214	-0.121	0.337	0.160	0.216
… I hoped to demonstrate my skills and abilities through my idea(s). *(SM3)*	**0.853**	0.003	0.125	0.003	0.164	0.126
7. Identification with the organizing firm						
… I identify with the SAP brand. *(CI1)*	0.376	0.227	0.445	0.144	0.042	0.075
… I'm into SAP and because of that I wanted to support SAP. *(CI2)*	0.383	0.347	**0.588**	-0.009	0.313	0.099
8. Product improvement						
… I want to give a helping hand in improving existing SAP software. *(PV1)*	0.042	0.069	-0.023	0.164	**0.644**	0.183
… I detected a software bug and I wanted to help fixing it. *(PV2)*	*excluded as item did not achieve critical MSA value*					
9. Need						
… my idea mirrors a need that is not covered by existing SAP software applications, yet. *(BEDA1)*	0.086	0.205	0.312	0.360	**0.670**	-0.065
… I wish to tell SAP about my certain needs that are not covered by existing SAP applications, yet. *(BEDA2)*	0.141	0.120	0.444	-0.124	**0.590**	-0.100

Table 2. *(Continued)*

Items	Components					
I attended the SAPiens ideas community because...	1	2	3	4	5	6
... I detected a need for a certain SAP software application and put it into an idea. *(BEDA3)*	0.129	0.364	0.024	0.194	**0.578**	0.110
10. Learning						
... I hoped to get learning experiences through the feedback concerning my idea(s). *(L1)*	0.413	0.138	0.426	-0.011	-0.102	**0.677**
... I hoped to learn from discussions with other members of the SA-Piens community. *(L2)*	0.244	0.158	0.041	0.202	0.131	**0.785**
11. Contact to peers						
... I hoped to get in contact with other SAP software users in order to talk with them about my idea(s). *(KZG1)*	**0.644**	0.107	0.285	0.124	-0.099	0.231
... I hoped to get in contact with other SAP software users in order to share experiences and information. *(KZG2)*	0.482	0.348	0.314	0.222	-0293	0.057
Cronbach's Alpha	**0.857**	**0.860**	**0.772**	**0.852**	**0.779**	**0.804**

The questionnaire used in this study was structured, tested and consequently adapted to the needs of the target audience. The questionnaire was pre-tested by 10 experts pursuing doctoral and Master's degrees in information technology and business administration. The objectives of the pre-test were to ensure that none of the items were ambiguous as well as that the items adequately captured the domain of interest. Expert opinions' indicated that the content of the items was valid.

We run the online survey in March 2010. The questionnaire was implemented using the online-survey service "2aks". Each participant of the SAPiens ideas community that submitted at least one idea (N = 149) was provided with a personalized link to the online survey by eMail. The survey was administered over a period of four weeks. Eighty-seven participants provided adaptable answers to the questionnaire which represents a 58.39% response rate. 70.11 % of those adaptable answers were men (n = 61). 60.92 % (n = 53) of those adaptable answers were between 20 and 30 years old. As it concerns the occupation of these participants, with 55.17 % (n = 48) students were overrepresented in the sample. The rest were either SAP consultants or persons in charge that work with SAP applications once a day or at least a few times a week.

2.3 Results

We tested construct validity of our 11 motives and related 29 items based on an exploratory factor analysis. We analyzed the items with the help of the statistical software program SPSS 17.0. In order to check whether the data was appropriate for factor analysis we pre-analyzed the Measures of Sampling Adequacy (MSA) for the whole data structure as well as for individual items. The items REZ2, PV2, IH1, REZ4 as well as REZ3 showed MSA values that were lower 0.5. According to Cureton and D'Agostion's recommendation, who deemed that items achieve sampling adequacy if values are equal or exceed the criterion of 0.5 (Cureton and D'Agostino 1983), these items were excluded within six iterations. After the sixth iteration all remaining items were above 0.6 and exploratory factor analysis was applicable. Furthermore, we pre-checked the global MSA value after the sixth iteration in order to ensure applicability of explorative factor analysis. With a MSA of 0.729 Cureton and D'Agostion's (Cureton and D'Agostino 1983) stringent 0.5-criteria was met, too.

The factor analysis resulted in six factors with eigenvalues higher 1 (varimax rotation). All the six factors explain a total of 66.321 % variance. The first factor explained 14.149 % variance. It was mostly determined by all items that represent the expected motive self-marketing as well as the item KZG1. As the intention to seek for peers in order to get in contact can be seen as an assumption for self-marketing activities as well as peers constitutes the target audience of self-marketing activities the KZG1 loading on this factor can be accepted plausible. Because of this, we will call this factor as **"self-marketing"** (component 1 in figure 5). The second factor explained 13.887 % variance and mostly was determined by all "fun" items. Furthermore, the item IH2 also loads on this factor. As intellectual stimulation can be interpreted as a form of fun we will accept including this item in factor 2. Following this argumentation we will call this factor **"fun"** (component 2 in table 2).

The items ALT1 and ALT2 as well as CI2 load on another factor, which explained 11.066 % variance. As altruistic feelings only will be brought toward a certain person or organization with whom or which one can identify this seems plausible. Thus, the third factor can be called **"altruism"** (component 3 in table 2). On the fourth factor load 3 items that expected to explain **"recognition"** (component 4 in table 2), solely (10.040 % variance).

The fifth factor, which represents a 9.989 % expression of variance, we call **"product improvement and enhancement"** (component 5 in table 2) as all need items as well as one of two product improvement items load on it. Finally, the sixth factor which explained additional 7.190 % variance was mostly determined by the supposed learning items. As supposed, **learning** (component 6 in table 2) seemed to be an independent motive.

The items REZ1, ANER2, CI1 as well as KZG2 were excluded as their values are < 0.55 according to Hair et al.'s recommendation, who deemed that items achieve acceptable factor loadings if values are equal or exceed the criterion of 0.55 (Hair, Anderson et al. 1998). After this complex explanatory factor analysis its results support the contention that our model has adequate construct validity.

The reliability of the resulting factors was checked using Cronbach's alpha. A Cronbach's alpha of 0.7 or higher (Nunnally 1978) was used as an acceptable value for internal consistency of the measure. The Cronbach's alphas of the four factors range from 0.772 to 0.860 (compare table 2). These values support the contention that all the factors had adequate reliability.

As examination of validity as well as reliability of an underlying research model by solely applying explanatory factor analysis respectively Cronbach's alpha do not meet modern requirements (Bogazzi, Yi et al. 1991), according to Homburg and Giering's recommendation (Homburg and Giering 1996) we secondly tested our new model, based on its six remaining factors and its corresponding 20 items, by applying confirmatory factor analysis and using Amos 18.0. First, we checked the global fit of the new model. The Goodness of Fit Index (GFI) was 0.951 and the Adjusted Goodness of Fit Index (AGFI) was 0.933. These indices were well over the under threshold of 0.9, which indicates an adequate fit (Browne and Cudeck 1993). In order to check

Table 3. Values for Individual Item Reliability, Composite Reliability, and AVE

Factor	Item	Individual Item Reliability (>/= 0.4)	Composite Reliability (>/= 0.6)	AVE (>/= 0.5)
Self-Marketing	MO_SM_1	0.557		
	MO_SM_2	0.800	0.860	0.608
	MO_SM_3	0.564		
	MO_KZG_1	0.503		
Fun	MO_S_1	0.433		
	MO_S_2	0.577	0.871	0.639
	MO_S_3	0.828		
	MO_IH_2	0.647		
Altruism	MO_ALT_1	0.490		
	MO_ALT_2	0.493	0.778	0.552
	MO_CI_2	0.881		
Recognition	MO_ANER_1	0.677		
	MO_ANER_3	0.927	0.860	0.676
	MO_ANER_4	0.424		
Product Improvement and Enhancement	MO_BEDA_1	0.725		
	MO_BEDA_2	0.427	0.781	0.574
	MO_BEDA_3	0.647		
	MO_PV_1	0.418		
Learning	MO_L_1	0.725	0.698	0.536
	MO_L_2	0.626		

reliability of the model, we measured all Individual Item Reliabilities, which exceeded the minimum threshold of 0.4 (Homburg and Giering 1996). Hence, good reliability is confirmed (compare table 3).

Furthermore, all factors of our new model showed good values for Composite Reliabilities as well as good values for Average Variance Explained (AVE), so that convergent validity can be assumed (compare table 3). Values of 0.6 regarding the Composite Reliability and 0.5 for the AVE can be seen as minimum values for indicating a good measurement quality (Bagozzi and Yi 1988). The discriminant validity of the factors was checked by using the Fornell-Larcker criteria, which claims that one factor's AVE should be higher than its squared correlation with every other factor (Fornell and Larcker 1981). Tables 3 and 4 depict that discriminant validity can be assumed for the six factors of our new model.

Table 4. Squared Multiple Correlations

Squared Multiple Correlations						
	Self-Marketing	Fun	Altruism	Recognition	Prod Imp + Enh	Learning
Self-Marketing		0.00289	0.0729	0.2401	0.0729	0.2704
Fun	0.0289		0.0324	0.0225	0.00289	0.0324
Altruism	0.0729	0.0324		0.0729	0.1156	0.1444
Recognition	0.2401	0.0225	0.0729		0.1089	0.2116
Prod Im + Enh	0.0729	0.00289	0.1156	0.1089		0.0441
Learning	0.2704	0.0324	0.1444	0.2116	0.0441	

3   Deriving Components for Virtual Ideas Communities

The purpose of our motivation study was to explore customers' motives for submitting ideas to the SAPiens idea community. Overall, the results suggest that there are six motives (self-marketing, fun, altruism, recognition, product improvement and enhancement as well as learning). In this section we exemplary use four of these six motives in order to derive adequate technical and organizational components and arrangements from it. Our research will deliver important examples and insights how to arrange virtual ideas communities with more attractive technical and organizational components and arrangements in order to make them more effective, so that more customers are willing to submit ideas.

First of all, we detected **"Self-Marketing"** as a significant motive. Because of this, organizers of ideas communities should procure possibilities that optimally display and represent participants' skills and capabilities. For example, implementing a profile site for every participant on the Internet platform of an ideas community - that displays participants' vita, competencies etc. as known from social network communities like Xing - would be fruitful in this context.

As our results show, the motive **"Recognition"** also was relevant. This suggests that organizers should play an active part in ideas communities and get in contact with participating customers, for example by commenting or giving positive feedback to participants' ideas, or praising participants' ideas as much as possible. In order to display positive reactions by the firm, organizers should assign "trophies" for customers' contributions by branding high quality ideas with a star, for example. These collectible achievements may more likely cause again positive reactions from other participants of the community. In order to get recognition from other participants rating systems would be fruitful. With the help of rating systems other users can quickly leave their opinions on ideas, for example by labeling a row of stars on which users can rate each idea.

Our findings reveal **"Learning"** as a relevant motive, too. That means that customers also participate in ideas communities in order to expand their personal skills, capabilities, and knowledge. So, in order to raise the likelihood of ideas submissions organizers should implement environments, where participants can select learning experiences when developing ideas. For example, coining mentors or tutors assisting participants actively in developing or elaborating ideas would be a possible measure in this context.

In light of the motives "Recognition" as well as "Learning" it is also important to implement an atmosphere of cooperation amongst the members of the community, not only because the principle goal of ideas communities is that its members discuss and enhance innovation ideas. An atmosphere of interpersonal cooperation will also raise members' willingness to give recognition to other participants as well as members' willingness to share learning experiences to other participants. When there is any kind of competitive culture on the other side, as it can be observed in ideas competitions, it will cause a non-cooperative behavior and may even cause a schism within the community. So, in order to implement a collaborative culture the organizers have to take appropriate organizational measures in the scope of current community management.

Furthermore, when building and running ideas communities firms should take into account that **fun** is an important motive that leads to ideas submission. Thus, firms have to establish organizational structures or design artifacts that serve customers' fun during an individual's process of generating ideas. For example, external mentors that will support participants in the manner of a ghost-writer would be an adequate design element in this context. Furthermore, the community platform should offer a personal site where members can display their collection of ideas. Spending time in creating ideas, managing, sharing, and curating the individual collection will give pleasure to the members. Furthermore, in terms of the recognition motive the owner's individual ideas collection is validated and recognized when other members comment, rate or even just view the displayed ideas in the collection. Furthermore, such an ideas collection can serve as self-marketing tool as the displayed ideas mirrored indirectly owner's competences, creativity potential etc. In this context, owners may be seen as an expert in the area of interest, which enhances its reputation and in turn increases the likelihood of submitting more ideas of good quality.

4 Future Research and Limitations

Our results provide only a few examples for components that can be derived from our empirical tested motives. Certainly, there are a lot more to explore. As these components are derived by plausibility efforts, they have to be evaluated in a further step.

Only when tested empirically one can make sure that hypothetically derived components are really leading to idea submissions. So, future research has to develop and apply empirical tests that prove effectiveness of each component in accordance to its corresponding motive.

One of the major limitations of this study involves the sample of the motivation survey. First, the sample size was relatively small. Despite the fact that the size was absolutely adequate for applied factor analysis as well as regressions analysis our results would be more meaningful with a higher sample size. Second, the proportion of students included in the sample is relatively high. Despite the fact that students can be considered as users of the SAP software applications, our results might impose some limitations concerning the generalizability. Future research should test and validate the model by collecting more data sets as well as data from a different composition of subjects consisting of more "typically" SAP users, like SAP consultants or accounting clerks working with SAP applications.

References

Aaker, J.: Dimensions of Brand Personality. Journal of Marketing Research 34(3), 347–356 (1997)

Bagozzi, R.P., Yi, Y.: On the evaluation of Structural Equatation Models. Journal of the Academy of Marketing Sciences 16(1), 74–94 (1988)

Bogazzi, R., Yi, Y., et al.: Assessing Construct Validity in Organizational Research. Administrative Science Quarterly 36, 421–458 (1991)

Browne, M.W., Cudeck, R.: Alternative ways of assessing model fit. In: Bollen, K.A., Long, J.S. (eds.) Testing Structural Equation Models. Sage, Newbury Park (1993)

Chesbrough, H.: The era of open innovation. Sloan Management Review 44(4), 35–41 (2003)

Cureton, E.E., D'Agostino, R.B.: Factor Analysis: An Applied Approach. Hillsdale, New Jersey (1983)

Deci, E.L., Ryan, R.M.: Intrinsic Motivation and Self-Determination in Human Behavio. Springer, Heidelberg (1985)

Fornell, C., Larcker, D.F.: Evaluating Structural Equation Models with Unobservable Variables and Measurement Error. Journal of Marketing Research 18(2), 39–50 (1981)

Füller, J., Jawecki, G., et al.: Innovation Creation by online Basketball communities. Journal of Business Research 60(1), 60–71 (2007)

Ghosh, R.A., Glott, R., et al.: The Free/Libre and Open Source Software Developers Survey and Study – FLOSS, International Institute of Infonomics, University of Maastricht (2002)

Hair, J.F., Anderson, R.E., et al.: Multivariate Data Analysis. Prentice-Hall, Upper Saddle River, NJ (1998)

Hars, A., Ou, S.: Working for free? Motivations for participating in open-source projects. International Journal of Electronic Commerce 6(3), 25–39 (2002)

Heckhausen, J., Heckhausen, H.: Motivation und Handeln. Springer, Heidelberg (2006)

Hertel, G., Niedner, S., et al.: Motivation of software developers in open source projects: An internet-based survey of contributors to the Linux kernel. Research Policy 32(1), 1159–1177 (2003)

Homburg, C., Giering, A.: Konzeptionalisierung und Operationalisierung komplexer Konstrukte: Ein Leitfaden für die Marketingforschung. Marketing Zeitschrift für Forschung und Praxis 18(1), 5–24 (1996)

Kelly, C., Breinlinger, S.: Identity and injustice: exploring women's participation in collective action. Journal of Community and Applied Social Psychology 5, 41–57 (1995)

Lakhani, K.R., Wolf, B.: Why Hackers Do What They Do. Understanding Motivation and Effort in Free/Open Source Software Projects. In: Feller, J., Fitzgerald, B., Hissam, S., Lakhani, K.R. (eds.) Perspectives on Free and Open Source Software. The MIT Press, Cambridge (2005)

Leimeister, J.M., Huber, M., et al.: Leveraging Crowdsourcing: Activation-Supporting Components for IT-Based Ideas Competitions. Journal of Management Information Systems 26(1), 197–224 (2009)

Nunnally, J.C.: Psychometric Theory, New York (1978)

Osterloh, M., Rota, S., et al.: Open Source Software Production: Climbing on the Shoulders of Giants, MIT Working Paper. MIT, Cambridge (2002)

Ozinga, J.: Altruism. Praeger, Westport (1999)

Piller, F.T., Walcher, D.: Toolkits for Idea Competitions: A Novel Method to Integrate Users in New Product Development. R&D Management 36(3), 307–318 (2006)

Raymond, E.S.: The New Hacker's Dictionary. The MIT-Press, Cambridge (1996)

Shah, S.K.: Motivation, Governance & the Viability of Hybrid Forms in Open Source Software Development, Working Paper, University of Washington (2005)

Shneiderman, B.: Creating Creativity: User Interfaces for Supporting Innovation. ACM Transactions on Computer-Human Interaction 7(1), 114–138 (2000)

Simon, B., Loewy, M., et al.: Collective identification and social movement participation. Journal of Personality and Social Psychology 74, 646–658 (1998)

von Hippel, E.: Lead users: a source of novel product concepts. Management Science 32(7), 791–805 (1986)

von Hippel, E.: Sticky information and the locus of problem solving. Management Science 40(4), 429–439 (1994)

von Rosenstiel, L.: Grundlagen der Organisationspsychologie. Schäffer-Poeschel, Stuttgart (2003)

Diffusion of Open Source ERP Systems Development: How Users Are Involved

Björn Johansson

Department of Informatics, School of Economics and Management,
Lund University, Sweden
Tel.: +46 46 222 80 21
Bjorn.johansson@ics.lu.se

Abstract. Open Source receives high attention among organizations today, and there is also a growing interest on Open Source Enterprise Resource Planning (OS ERP) systems. Open source development is often considered having a high level of involvement from stakeholders in adopting organizations. However, it depends on for the first what is meant by stakeholders, but also what is meant by involvement. In the area of ERP development stakeholder involvement is defined as to what extent users of the system are involved in the development of the standardized software package. The way this is done differs between different vendors but it can be summarized as dealing with management of requirements. In this paper we explore how requirements management is done in development of OS ERP. To do this, we use a theoretical base on requirements management in the ERP field from which we investigate stakeholder involvement in four organizations and the development of it's respectively OS ERP system. The basic question asked was: how are end-users of OS ERPs involved in the development of OS ERP. From the investigation we present a general picture of the requirements management process in the OS ERP area. The main conclusion is that end-users are not involved to the extent first expected and when comparing with proprietary ERP development a tendency towards a similar approach to requirements management in OS ERP development was discovered.

Keywords: Requirements Engineering, Enterprise Resource Planning, ERP, Open Source, Standard systems, user involvement.

1 Introduction

Many organizations implement enterprise resource planning (ERP) systems from the view that they will obtain an advantage over its competitor (Verville et al., 2007), by for instance getting better and faster access to information stored. However, there are organizations that are resistant because ERP implementation takes time and costs a lot of money, while there is also a high risk that it may fail (Daneva, 2007; The Standish Group, 1995; Verville et al., 2007). This has created an interest in developing ERPs in the open source (OS) area. The open source ERP development could be seen as an

M. Nüttgens et al. (Eds.): Governance and Sustainability in IS, IFIP AICT 366, pp. 188–203, 2011.

alternative to traditional ERP proprietary systems available today. Rapp (2009) suggests that OS have grown large and states that it continues to grow strongly as more and more organizations become interested in how they can benefit from OS in their organization. However, the same thing can also be stated about ERPs. But, the question is then if combing open source and ERPs is that a doable and beneficial combination for organizations. It can be claimed that if it should be, development probably needs to be done with closeness to its users. An interesting question to ask is therefore to what extent and how users are involved in OS ERP development.

According to Fitzgerald (2006) open source development differ from "ordinary" software development since the first phases of planning, analysis and design usually has no clear borders, and is performed by a single developer or a small group of developers. This is explained in a survey by Zhao and Elbaum (2003), showing that a large proportion of projects in OS are developed by self-interest and only a small part are developed in response to different organizational needs. Lemos (2008) states that OS ERP is a growing market, and that there is a growing commercial interest in it. Fitzgerald (2006) argues that since OS projects will be more commercial, a greater level of structure and control in development is needed. Sommerville (2007) supports this by observing that in development of large systems, such as ERPs, the high complexity is a major problem. Young (2001) provides the following view of requirements management in software development: "We often record requirements in a disorganized manner, and we spent far too little time verifying what we do record. We allow change to control us, rather than establishing mechanisms to control change. In short, we fail to establish a solid foundation for the system or software that we intend to build ".

From this discussion the question which is discussed in this paper is: How are end-users involved in the development of Open Source ERPs? To answer this, a description of four OS ERP developer organizations and their respectively OS ERP system are presented (section 2). Section 3 then presents an analysis on how requirements management is done in the four organizations. The final section then presents some conclusions on the question how end-users are involved in development of OS ERP and some future research directions in that area.

2 Four ERP Developer Organizations and Their OS ERP System

This section reports from an investigation done in four organizations that have the commonality that they all develop what is marketed as open source ERP systems. Data was collected in semi-structured interviews with representatives from the organizations. Respondents were selected from the perspective of having high level of knowledge about how development is done in respectively organization. In addition to the interviews, data was gained by investigating documents from respectively organization's websites. The interviews were tape-recorded and then transcribed. Follow up questions was asked in order to clarify some uncertainties. Investigated organizations were: Project Open, Night Labs, Openbravo and Open Source Strategies, and the interviewee has the following role: Founder, CEO, product manager, and product manager.

2.1 Project Open

Project Open develops an OS ERP system with the same name. They also offer various types of consulting services relating to adaptation of the system within organizations (beyond normal support).

Project Open's development is highly controlled and are usually based on customer requirements and direct funding from customers. The main source for requirements is individual customers. However, they also take into account requirements from potential customers. Project Open has a limited scale of development that starts from self-initiated projects without involving a customer. These projects are based on experience from past client projects. Some requirements also arise internally from own ideas, and to a limited extent requirements are gained from the community around Project Open. Prioritization of stakeholders was described as:

> "Well, you know everybody who basically finance and sponsor development, will be considered in the first place." (Founder of Project Open)

The majority of requirements are gathered in meetings with representatives of the customer and users related to a specific customer project. During these meetings, they usually organize a workshop at the customer organization place for development of requirements with users. Requirements are also partly obtained from the community forums on sourceforge.net, but, since the community does not provide any funding, this source of requirement is not of high priority. At the moment Project Open also works with building a repository of requirements from four other projects, and plans to post them on a website to avoid having to start from scratch with future similar requirements. During customers' workshops, cost estimates on requirements are created. After this Project Open develops and uses prototypes to visualize requirements which they later on discuss with the customer. It usually leads to decisions about how to continue. If there is a need for requirements prioritization due to various constraints, the customer always has the last word. In situations where they feel they need more feedback about a specific requirement within a short period of time, they tend to repeat the workshop activities, as described by the founder of Project Open in the following way:

> "In some very rare cases we sometime would need to organize like a second workshop to dive deep into particular questions that have come up during this stage and only then these are required - when we talk about more complex extensions, configuration of workflows and so on."

Project Open visualize requirements through prototypes, besides this they also describe them in conjunction with a form of use cases. This is done to make sure that requirements are understood correctly, and to make it possible to have feedback on requirements from the customer. During the requirements engineering process changes in requirements are managed through an iterative process. During requirements engineering activities documentation of requirements are done in parallel, by formulating requirements in a specific document. This documentation is then used as a manual for the system.

2.2 Night Labs

Night Labs is an organization that develops OS products and offers consulting services in the OS software development field. They develop an OS ERP system called JFire. Night Labs provide their own support and adjustments of their own developed systems.

Software development by Night Labs is divided into different projects, each project having its own requirements management process. Requirements are gained by talking to the customer. This is the major source of requirements, the idea is to have customers to describe requirement from the context of usage. Requirements are also obtained from a community forum where developers and users can discuss and also provide feedback on requirements. Requirements are also gained from discussions within Night Labs. They also analyze requirements in competing systems. Night Labs put great importance to investigate whether requirements are specific to a specific customer or if it is possible to adjust them to fit more customers. Recycling of requirements is done by analyzing requirements of modules that they already have developed for a specific customer. They then investigate whether it is possible to implement the system and making it useful for another customer, with or without changes. The CEO of Night Labs says:

"Of course it happens sometimes, that we think: 'Ah, this is very specific´ then we implement it specifically and then maybe later someone else comes with more of the same thing, and only sometimes minor changes and then of course we go back and take the previous project, and analyze what can we pull out".

Night Labs state that dependent on the development situation there is to some extent different demand on management of requirements. An individual project often gathers a larger amount of requirements in the beginning. After receiving some feedback the major changes primarily relates to contextual changes because it was misunderstood from the beginning. If several projects run in parallel, it could mean that requirements to a higher extent will be gained during the projects because of overlaps between the projects' requirements. It is also stated that requirements continuously comes from the community. Once Night Labs have gathered a variety of requirements for a project, they try to investigate how the requirements can be implemented and provide feedback to customers aiming at resolving uncertainties. At Night Labs they argue that customers usually do not provide adequate information about their demands so they could implement requirements directly. The CEO states that:

"In this situation we basically have most of the requirements analysis at the beginning and then we have during the project only analyses of maybe misunderstanding and adapting to the requirements, to fit the needs of the customer better".

To handle this situation they therefore develop use cases which they use when discussing requirements with customers. These use cases are then used to verify that all requirements are consistent with what the customer wants and expects. This activity takes place regularly. The CEO, however, said that there often is confusion and it is important to work closely with the customer throughout the process to quickly ensure that they are on the right track. Night Labs also present prototypes consisting of an early version of implemented requirements for the customer, to obtain feedback confirming that their understanding of the requirement is correct. If constraints arise regarding implementation of a number of requirements within the same project, Night Labs conduct priority activities focusing on deciding on what requirements to be implemented first. They present the situation for the customer, after which the customer should select the items to be prioritized. However, sometimes they need to do the requirements prioritization by themselves. The prioritization is then based primarily on the basis of what benefits the project most and what implemented requirement benefits the largest number of users. The CEO says:

"So we have to invest from our own money, so we have to decide if this is a benefit for the project in general, for us as a company, whether it benefits" a wide range of users or whether if it is a very, very individual thing".

Developed use cases have the roles as both contract and documentation between Night Labs and the customer. Regarding communication within the community forums this communication is automatically saved and stored on a wiki. Customers may self-prioritize requirements they consider most important in their projects but Night Labs has to interact and say what is possible, considering all necessary constraints. The CEO describes this in the following way:

"Of course we make constraints, if he says: 'I want something' and we know that for this something, something else needs to be done and he says: 'Ah, but this I want later' then we have to tell him: 'Yeah, sorry, but you can't build the roof without first building the house'."

Night Labs in a similar way involve the community by constantly showing were in the process of implementing a requirement they are and collecting feedback from the community in that matter. Changes on requirements are handled in what is termed as "Change Request". These changes are handled differently depending on what stage the project are in when they are discovered. If changes occur before implementation has started they are according to Night Labs not a big problem. But, if there is a change in requirements that have already been implemented, it is a bigger problem. Night Labs then solve this problem by dealing with it in the next version of the system.

2.3 Openbravo

Openbravo is an organization that develops the OS ERP system Openbravo ERP. Special customization and other services around Openbravo ERP are done by partners who are scattered around the world.

Depending on type of development there is a variation on how requirements are gathered. Requirements come from partners, the community related to Openbravo, as well as internally. Partners are seen as the main source of requirements for future development of Openbravo ERP. Requirements management is done through close contact with the originator of the project and is constantly ongoing. All sources, however, plays a role, a product manager at Openbravo describes it as:

"Our Requirements are driven of what the partner's need, but also" in a large part by what we believe need to be done to strategically move the product forward and provide a best of breed platform for developers."

If there is a partner involved in future development of requirements, this is discussed in meetings and/or forums with the partner. Another way of requirements gathering is by monitoring community forums. After the specific context for the requirements is described, requirements are visualized by various forms of prototyping in order to produce feedback, and to confirm that the resulting requirements are correct. These are then presented either for customers or for the whole community, through meetings, forums and blogs. The prototypes are mainly based on requirements from external stakeholders. However, on some occasions, prototypes are developed from internally gained requirements; based on what developer at Openbravo think users want to see in the system. The prototypes in that case also aim at generating feedback from potential users. The product manager gave the following description of the process:

"We actually start our requirements gathering from the perspective of what will the user see, what interface, what screen the user will be presented with and the workflows, and we work backwards from there."

Prioritization of requirements is sometimes done by a partner. This is the case if the partner provides money for specific functionality to be implemented. If so, there is a discussion with the partner in order to reach an agreement over what should be done. But, in most cases requirements prioritization are based on what they believe is best for users, however, sometimes they let users vote on what requirements should be implemented. Openbravo is working on what they call its backlog which is a list of requirements and its priority. This backlog consists of three pillars: the first pillar is "maintain" that aims at constantly keep Openbravo far ahead among the competitors, which is described by the product manager as:

"One is that we want to maintain our competitive edge and also that with our partners."

The second pillar is "Delight" which aims at increasing ease of use for users of Openbravo ERP. Described by the product manager as:

"That is we want to develop features and functionality that would delight our users (...)".

The last pillar is "Monetize" which aims to provide an economic value to the product, which is described by the product manager in the following way:

"These are features that allow Openbravo and its partners to make money."

When a partner is involved a specification of the requirements are developed before implementation begins. The specifications are posted on a forum where feedback can be obtained and were Openbravo developers are able to direct questions about the requirement to the partner. Documentation of requirements continues the whole time during the project and is done in parallel with development. Openbravo is aware of the fact that requirements changes and therefore has Openbravo, according to the product manager, a flexible approach to managing change. However, when implementation has started changes become more complex. Changes are handled through the forum, where developers and other stakeholders, according to the product manager, can have a dialogue about change:

"And we have a very interactive approach in defining the requirements for our customers, and while that is going on, any change is permissible, until the point that we start development (...)".

2.4 Open Source Strategies

Open Source Strategies is an organization that develops Opentaps and whose purpose is to promote OS development in general. They also provide consulting services, mainly related to adjustments of Opentaps, but also on evaluating, testing, certification, training in development and integration of the software.

The main sources for requirements are, according to a product manager for Opentaps, users of the system and the Opentaps related community. However, some requirements are gained internal, during own development when the system is used by themselves. Opentaps also have customer projects where customers are responsible for presenting requirements. These customer projects have the highest priority. Gathering of requirements are in part concentrated to the start of the project. The major part of requirements is collected at the beginning by discussions with the customer and its users. All requirements from the collection add up to what the product manager termed as an issue-tracker. However, the product manager adds that new requirements arise during the project, primarily through the monitoring of community forums, but also internally during the time they develop the system. The gathering of requirements is done in various ways, for instance by being contacted by users who produce their own needs; these are then discussed to develop a stringent set of demands. The product manager said:

"Then basically we would go to the user and discuss exactly what they're looking for, and we would put it usually on an issue tracker to describe what their requirements are."

Sometimes Opentaps create prototypes that are presented to the community and based on these prototypes experience on requirements is gained. In addition Opentaps sometimes also use scenarios describing the context as they have understood it during discussions with users. They then use the scenarios to achieve feedback on requirements and its context. Reuse of requirements is also an aspect of their requirements management, which is described by the product manager in the following way:

"In this way it's a bit like a city: each building in the city represents the requirements of its residents at one point, and the buildings are reused and modified over time to meet new requirements".

At Opentaps changes in requirements are handled by introducing changes in the system, which then undergoes testing and thereafter are documented. This may be due to the iterative process they use, which the product manager describes as:

"It is just an iterative process of the system being used of people and shown to people and their feedback gets incorporated and the system is modified."

Requirements are undergoing discussions and various tests with the customer to ensure that requirements are correctly understood. Stakeholders in the community forums also provide feedback through the various scenarios presented in the forums. The requirements prioritization that takes place depends on various factors based on whether it is a customer project or not. For customer projects, the customer has the final say regarding what requirements should be prioritized. If not, prioritization of requirements is done from the number of users that Opentaps believe would have the function, or depending on the number of users who have contacted them and asked for a specific function. The product manager said:

"So for example, a lot of people will come to us and say 'you know we would like this" and that, if it is something we think will benefit a lot of users we will give it a higher priority".

Documentation of Opentaps then takes place after the functionality has been implemented. This documentation is then used as user manuals and to preserve requirements for future use. This is described by the product manager in the following way:

"Usually after the feature has been implemented, for the purpose of allowing other people to use the feature and also documenting the requirements for later use".

3 Analysis and Discussion

The following section highlights both similarities and differences in how end-users are involved in development of the four organizations respectively OS ERP system. The description above is analyzed and discussed from literature around software requirements under the following headings: 1) requirements elicitation, 2) requirements analysis and negotiation, 3) requirements documentation, 4) requirements validation, and 5) requirements changes.

3.1 Requirements Elicitation

It is possible to distinguish similarities and differences in how the different organizations collect requirements. Three of the organizations have a more concentrated collection of requirements at the start of the project. However, there is then an ongoing less extensive requirements elicitation in all cases. Openbravo differs from the other organizations since it has a continuously requirements gathering process where they constantly repeat their activities to gather requirements. The requirements management process in all four organizations suggest that they take into account changes on requirements related to its context, just like Hickey and Davis (2003) as well as Kotonya and Sommerville (1998) state being necessary. This is also in line with the statement from Eriksson (2008) who argues that it is difficult to gather all requirements at one single point. All interviewees claim that the organizations focus a lot on customers when gathering requirements, just like Davis (2005) describes as the key stakeholders in a system development project. However, it is only Open Source Strategies, which explicitly says that they interact directly with users when they discuss requirements. The other organization seems to more indirectly discuss requirements with other stakeholders and not directly involve end-users. It is also stated that requirements are gained internally within the organizations, except in the Project Open case. All organizations use community forums to develop standards to some degree, however, the extent of their importance as a source for requirements differ between the different organizations. Project Open does not involve the community in the requirements gathering to any large extent, while others take more account of different communities. There is no clear idea of what types of stakeholders that are involved in the community forums. But, it is possible to speculate that it probably involves different groups of stakeholders, including users. This may explain why organizations do not directly approach the users to gather requirements. The community may also consist of developers and other stakeholders. It can be assumed that a high interest in the system is needed for any stakeholders to be active in the community. Therefore, there is possibly a mismatch between various stakeholders involved on the forums. The prioritization of stakeholders is consistent within the organizations, since all are taking the greatest account of the one that provides funding. Group Meetings is also a regular feature of the organizations, however, Project Open uses workshops instead. Both activities were based on individual group meetings with discussions between stakeholders and developers. Furthermore, it is possible to distinguish differences in what activities and technologies that they choose in their requirements elicitation process. These differences can be explained from Jiang et al. (2005) who argue that the choice of techniques may be different because of stakeholders' knowledge, or from Hickey and Davis (2003) as well as Zowghi and Coulin (2005), whom argue that selection of technologies is based on the context for the requirements. Reuse of requirements is done only in three of the organizations. Recycling is most pronounced in Project Open, which has built storage of requirements from previous projects, to avoid repeating the process to develop similar requirements. This is in line with Robertson and Robertson (2006) who argue that recycling can be the basis for new requirements. Night Labs only reuse requirements from already implemented modules, however, despite that changes are usually required to be made on the requirement. Their reuse demands insights into parts of the system. Reuse of Open Source Strategies takes place over time, without any specific plan. In Openbravo reuse is not a widespread activity, the reuse of requirements that is done is done primarily through the reuse of code. Table 1 provides an overview of requirements elicitation in the different organizations.

3.2 Requirements Analysis and Negotiation

The use of prototypes is one way among the organizations to analyze requirements. The prototypes are presented to various stakeholders to identify problems. This is consistent with the view that Kotonya and Sommerville (1998) give on the analysis and negotiation phase. However, Night Labs differ since they do not use prototypes. Within all organizations there are also other activities designed to create discussion about requirements. Three of the organizations are following group meetings, while Project Open uses workshops to discuss the same issue. Both activities promote discussion of requirements but they differ to some extent. Workshops are seen as a more formal and structured activity than group meetings, however, both types of discussion activities are designed to arrive at agreement on requirements. All organizations use a systematic approach to analyze requirements and describe the context for requirements, but also to find out if they have developed legally ok requirements. This is consistent with one of the main activities in the analysis phase that Sommerville and Sawyer (1997), Kotonya and Sommerville (1998) as well as Wiegers (1999) chooses to emphasize, claiming that this are distinctive part of the analysis and negotiation phase in requirements management. It is common for developer to prioritize customer requirements in the projects they are involved in. The organizations involved in internal projects gives priority based on what would benefit a major part of users. This statement is consistent with Karlsson (1996) who describes, the importance of stressing customer satisfaction when prioritize requirements. Prioritization in Openbravo is mainly based on what they call "Monetize", which basically means that requirements that allow Openbravo and its partners to make a profit should be prioritized. The negotiating process in the described organizations is consistent with the structure Kotonya and Sommerville (1998) present in which a discussion, prioritization and agreement are included. Table 2 gives an overview of how the analysis and negotiation of requirements are done at the various organizations.

Table 1. Requirements elicitation

Organization	Project Open	Night Labs	Openbravo	Open Source Strategies
Description	Requirements gathering begins with a high number of requirements gathered from the customer at the beginning of the project. The community plays no significant role in gathering of requirements.	Requirements gathering take mainly place in the beginning of customer projects with customers and their users, but there is also an ongoing gathering of requirements from the community.	Requirements gathering take mainly place in the beginning of customer projects with customers and their users, but there is also an ongoing gathering of requirements from the community.	Requirements gathering take place in an ongoing fashion. However, the majority of requirements are collected, at the beginning of projects.
Activities/ Techniques	Workshops, prototypes, community forums.	Group meetings, use cases, community forums.	Group meetings, prototypes, community forums.	Group meetings, community forums.
Reuse of requirements	Building up a stock of ready-made requirements from previous projects that must be used when having related demands, to avoid the need to repeat the process. However, changes are often required.	Re-use of requirements is done by analysis of previous projects with similar requirements. Requires usually small changes.	No reuse of requirements.	Some reuse exists when requirements change. Previous requirements can be the basis for new demands.
Where do demands come from?	Customers, potential customers, internal, community.	Customers, internal, community, market analysis	Partners, community, internally	Customers, users, community

Table 2. Requirements analysis and negotiation

Organization	Project Open	Night Labs	Openbravo	Open Source Strategies
Description	Analysis of requirements is done through discussions with the customer, as part of the workshops conducted when gathering requirements.	By holding discussions with stakeholders sorting out confusion on requirements. Takes place when a variety of requirements has been developed.	When a prototype is produced, they present it to the community and partners who provide feedback.	Discusses and shows the customer functions in a prototype, collect feedback. This is done after a set of demands is developed.
Activities / Techniques	Prototypes, workshops	Group Meetings	Group meetings, prototypes, community forums and blogs	Group meetings, prototypes.
Prioritization of requirements	Customer focused, the customer prioritizes the requirements of the projects.	Customer prioritizes their requirements. Night Labs has a large number of parameters which they use when they prioritize in their own projects.	Partner priority, when a partner is involved and pay. Otherwise priority of requirements is based on the three pillars.	Customers prioritize requirements for their projects. OpenTaps prioritize according to what benefits the most users.

3.3 Requirements Documentation

Requirements documentation in Project Open, Night Labs and Openbravo is done in an ongoing fashion during development projects. The ongoing documentation is a way of dealing with changes among requirements and to be more flexible. The documentation process in Open Source Strategies differs, and documentation is done first after requirements have been implemented. The aim of the documentation varies between the organizations. However, all organizations except Openbravo are using the documentation as a base for user manuals. Night Labs documentation is also used as a contract between them and their customers. Openbravo are using the documentation as a support to developers. The way documentation is done also differs to some extent, however, they all document requirements in what they call a requirements specification. Night Labs in addition also document requirements in use cases, which is in line with what Eriksson (2008) describes as one way of using use cases. An overview of requirements documentation in the organizations is shown in Table 3.

Table 3. Requirements documentation

Organization	Project Open	Night Labs	Openbravo	Open Source Strategies
Description	Documentation is ongoing and consists of specifications.	Documenting everything on the system that runs. The record is done by use cases.	Documentation is ongoing with the project. Specification of projects linked to a discussion forum.	The documentation is done after requirements have been implemented in projects.
Purpose	Documentation is used as a manual for the system.	Documentation serves as the contract for the customer and help for the user.	To provide support for the developer to communicate changes.	To ensure the requirements and provide assistance to users.

3.4 Requirements Validation

All organizations except Open Source Strategies use prototypes to get feedback on requirements they have developed. Project Open does not address the community in relation to feedback on developed requirements, while the rest do so. Even if all, except Open Source Strategies, use prototypes the way they use prototypes differs. What differs is the way they present a specific prototype. Three of the organizations have validation activities that are repeated during the requirements engineering process, which is in line with Wiegers (1999) as well as Loucopolous and Karakostas (1995) description of doing validation activities throughout the entire requirements engineering process. However, Open Source Strategies differs since they perform this activity only at the end of the development project. All organizations have a discussion with the customer aiming at validating requirements. The community is also involved in validation of requirements, except in Project Open, which consistently excludes the community from the entire requirements management process. A common feature of organizations is that they perform the various activities in order to check whether they have got the requirements right, which is consistent with the view that Kotonya and Sommerville (1998), and Sailor (1990) describes as one characteristic of the validation phase. Table 4 provides an overview of how organizations deal with requirements validation.

3.5 Requirements Changes

All organizations are working continuously to cope with changes that occur during the requirements engineering process, which is consistent with the picture Kotonya and Sommerville (1998) give as necessary when dealing with requirements. This suggests that all organizations are aware of that the context of requirements is changing, as several authors point out (Davis, 2005; Eriksson, 2008; Kotonya and Sommerville, 1998). All organizations are taking account of changes if they occur before the development is initiated, while there are clear discrepancies in how they work to manage these changes later in development. It is possible to distinguish the two organizations, Labs Night and Openbravo, from the other since they have distinct techniques to manage changes and change requests. Project Open and Open Source Strategies does not have an explicit technique to manage change. However, they deal with changes by having an iterative approach. Table 5 gives an overview of the process of requirements changes in the organizations.

Table 4. Requirements validation

Organization	Project Open	Night Labs	Openbravo	Open Source Strategies
Description	Collect feedback on requirements and discuss it with the customer in an ongoing fashion.	Collect feedback and discuss it with the customer and the community regularly during the project.	Partners are close-ly involved in the development, and through frequent contact with the community, feedback on requirements is discussed frequently.	Through discussion with the customer and the community. This is done at the end of the requirements management process.
Activities / Techniques	Review, prototypes, use cases.	Community forums, reviews, prototypes, use cases.	Community forums, reviews, prototypes.	Community Forum, Review, test-case.

Table 5. Requirements changes

Organization	Project Open	Night Labs	Openbravo	Open Source Strategies
Description	Changes occurring early in the development project are taken into account more or less directly. After development has started only minor changes are considered.	Changes are considered if related requirement not have been im-plemented, otherwise changes are managed in the next version of the system. Change request is used to manage changes.	Changes are generally allowed be-fore development starts. Then it's up to the one who request the change on requirement to take decisions. The forums are used to manage changes.	The work is done in an iterative process that allows that changes in requirements can be handled. Changes are implemented directly in the system.

Summing up the description above which was based on the interviews, but also on the analysis of similarities and dissimilarities also presented above, give the following summary. Regarding requirements elicitation, it can be stated that concentrated requirements gathering takes place at the beginning of the projects. But, there are also an ongoing requirements gathering during development of the projects. Involved stakeholders are customers, community, and internal stakeholders. Customers of the developed product are the prioritized stakeholder group. The major technique used for requirements elicitation is group meetings and workshops, and community forums. There is also to some extent a reuse of requirements from previous projects.

During the analysis and negotiation phase group meetings and workshops, and prototypes are used to analyze requirements. In customer projects the prioritization is done by the customer. In internal projects the prioritization is done from the perspective of what will be most beneficial for the biggest part of users. Negotiating activities are done during the analysis of requirements. All companies consult stakeholders, both through structured discussion activities, and through more informal approaches.

Requirements documentation is ongoing in many parts of the requirements management process. The documentation is then often used as a user manual or act as a base for the user manual. To a high extent the documentation builds on requirements specifications.

Requirements validation is an ongoing process, Reviews of requirements and prototypes are used to validate requirements. In the process the community and users are involved.

Regarding requirements changes is this done continuously until the development is initiated and has started.

3.6 Conclusions and Future Research

The research presents a representation of requirements management processes in Open Source ERP development. From this some conclusions can be drawn on the question asked in the paper, which are: How are end-users involved in the development of Open Source ERPs?

Requirements elicitation is done as a concentrated collection of requirements in the beginning of the development project, followed by a concurrent less extensive requirement collection during the project. There is also a reuse of requirements from previous projects. From the question on end-users involvement it can be concluded that users are involved but not to a higher extent than in other standardized software package development. There is a tendency that end-users are involved to a higher extent than in proprietary ERP development. However, if critical reflect on this it can be said that this tendency is to a very high extent similar to involvement in customization/configuration of proprietary ERP software package.

There are a number of different ways in which stakeholders are involved. The most common techniques consist of personal meetings with customers, aiming at creating discussions about requirements. Community forums are used to stimulate dialogue about context of requirements and produce feedback on specific requirements. Prototypes are used to show stakeholders how work is progressing and to ensure that the requirements corresponding to stakeholder needs. Requirements are then visualized to users and analyzed through close meetings in which they also are negotiated upon.

It can also be concluded that to some extent are end-users involved in prioritization of requirements, however, interesting to notice is that prioritization to a high extent builds on what the developing OS ERP organizations see as beneficial for them. In other words, if the customer pays for implementation of the specific requirement or if they see that they will earn money from the implementation in another way, for instance gaining a competitive advantage in relation to competitors in the OS ERP space, the specific requirement will be prioritized.

The research shows that there is a structured requirements management process in the development of open source ERPs. Future research on how this process is related to the often stated benefit, flexibility of Open Source ERPs, would be interesting to conduct.

Acknowledgement. I would like to thank my former students Alexander Persson and Oscar Sjöcrona at department of Informatics, Lund University for their assistance with helping me collecting the data for this research.

References

Daneva, M.: Understanding Success and Failure Profiles of ERP Requirements Engineering: an Empirical Study. In: 33rd EUROMICRO Conference on Software Engineering and Advanced Applications (EUROMICRO 2007) (2007)

Davis, A.M.: Just enough requirements management: where software development meets marketing. Dorset House Publishing, New York (2005)

Eriksson, U.: Requirements engineering for IT-systems (in Swedish: Kravhantering för IT-system), 2nd edn. Studentlitteratur, Lund (2008)

Fitzgerald, B.: The Transformation of Open Source Software. MIS Quarterly 30(3) (2006)

Hickey, A.M., Davis, A.M.: Elicitation technique selection: how do experts do it? In: 11th IEEE International Requirements Engineering Conference (2003)

Jiang, L., Eberlein, A., Far, B.H.: Combining Requirements Engineering Techniques - Theory and Case Study. In: 12th IEEE International Conference and Workshops on the Engineering of Computer-Based Systems, ECBS 2005 (2005)

Karlsson, J.: Software requirements prioritizing. In: The Second International Conference on Requirements Engineering (1996)

Kotonya, G., Sommerville, I.: Requirements engineering: Processes and techniques. John Wiley & Sons, Chichester (1998)

Lemos, R.: Open Source ERP grows up. CIO.com (2008), http://www.cio.com/

Loucopoulos, P., Karakostas, V.: System requirements engineering. McGraw-Hill, Berkshire (1995)

Rapp, J.: Increased Interest for Open Source (in Swedish: Ökat intresse för Open Source.) Logica (2009), http://www.logica.se

Robertson, S., Robertson, J.: Mastering the requirements process, 2nd edn. Addison-Wesley, Upper Saddle River (2006)

Sailor, J.D.: System Engineering: An introduction. In: Thayer, I.R.H., Dorfman, M. (eds.) System and Software Requirements Engineering, pp. 35–47. IEEE Computer Society Press, Washington (1990)

Sommerville, I.: Software Engineering, 8th edn. Pearson Education Limited, Harlow (2007)

Sommerville, I., Sawyer, P.: Requirements engineering: a good practice guide. John Wiley & Sons Ltd., Chichester (1997)

The Standish Group. CHAOS Report (1995),
   http://www.projectsmart.co.uk/docs/chaos-report.pdf
Verville, J. J., Palanisamy, R., Bernadas, C., Halingten, A.: ERP Acquisition Planning: A Criti-
   cal Dimension for Making the Right Choice. Long Range Planning 40(1) (2007)
Wiegers, K.E.: Software Requirements. Microsoft Press, Redmond (1999)
Young, R.R.: Effective Requirements Practices. Addison-Wesley, Boston (2001)
Zhao, L., Elbaum, S.: Quality assurance under the open source development model. The Journal of Systems and Software 66(1) (2003)
Zowghi, D., Coulin, C.: Requirements Elicitation: A survey of techniques, approaches and
   tools. In: Aurum, I.A., Wohlin, C. (eds.) Engineering and Managing Software Requirements,
   pp. 19–46. Springer, Berlin (2005)

Part V
Future Subjects

Improving the Applicability of Environmental Scanning Systems: State of the Art and Future Research

Jörg H. Mayer[1], Neon Steinecke[2], and Reiner Quick[2]

[1] University of St. Gallen, Mueller-Friedberg-Strasse 8, 9000 St. Gallen, Switzerland
Tel.: +41 (0) 71 224 2190
joerg.mayer@unisg.ch
[2] Darmstadt University of Technology, Hochschulstrasse 1, 64289 Darmstadt, Germany
Tel.: +49 (0) 6151 16 3423, +49 (0) 6151 16 3423
neon.steinecke@stud.tu-darmstadt.de
quick@bwl.tu-darmstadt.de

Abstract. The 2008/2009 economic crisis provided a sustainable impulse for improving environmental scanning systems (ESS). Although a rich body of know-ledge exists, concepts are not often used in practice. This article contributes a literature review addressing six findings for ESS design to become more applicable than the state of the art. They are structured by the elements of information systems (IS) design theories. Addressing the lack of a sound requirements analysis, our first finding proposes 360-degree ESS for executives' "managing a company" task and presents how to select just the most important scanning areas to keep focus. Three other findings cover the IS model perspective focusing on a better "grasp" of weak signals: define concrete indicators and use IT to identify relevant cause-effective-chains, leverage IT to automate day-to-day routines and monitor the variety of indicators' movements, and—as a fourth finding—leverage expert experience with an impact matrix and translate indicators' impact into a balanced opportunity-and-threat portfolio. From the methods perspective on ESS, we propose to more closely incorporate scanning results into executives' decision-making process by generating scenarios from a set of environment assumptions as well as to use retrospective controls to continuously update the ESS and collaborate to share the scanning findings day-to-day.

Keywords: Corporate management, balanced chance and risk management, information and communication technology (ICT), literature review.

1 Introduction

Environments' increasing volatility is a growing concern for companies. Executives worry about not being prepared for environmental shifts or—even worse—not being able to parry them. The 2008/2009 economic crisis gave a sustainable impulse for focusing earlier on emerging threats and opportunities (Hopwood 2009; Makridakis et

M. Nüttgens et al. (Eds.): Governance and Sustainability in IS, IFIP AICT 366, pp. 207–223, 2011.
© IFIP International Federation for Information Processing 2011

al. 2010). *Environmental scanning*—ideally, IT-based within a corporate business intelligence (BI) architecture (Wixom et al. 2010)[1] —can help to manage this challenge. Companies that do so will have brighter prospects than those that do not (Ansoff 1980).

With Ansoff's (1975) article "Managing Strategic Surprise by Response to Weak Signals" as an example, a rich body of knowledge exists, but it often goes unused. Practitioners perceive the task as a difficult one per se (Lesca et al. 2008). Some may not even know how to start (Albright 2004). They experience *difficulties* in designing, implementing, and operating environmental scanning systems (ESS). The objective of this article is therefore to design such information systems (IS) that are more applicable than the state of the art (Sec. 5.2).

As this work represents a first step in a larger research project, we start with a review of related work for big picture thinking and define future research to follow for more applicable ESS. Generally based on the Webster and Watson (2002) approach to literature review, we follow vom Brocke et al.'s (2009) five-step procedure. *Definition of review scope*: We motivate this article by reporting gaps between the rich body of knowledge and survey results suggesting that these concepts are often not used in practice. *Conceptualization of topic*: After revisiting foundations (Sec. 2), we show the need of ESS (Sec. 3). Hereafter we derive a framework for categorizing the literature (Sec. 4). *Literature search and analysis*: We then lay open our literature search process (Sec. 5.1). Out of 80 publications surveyed, we describe the most important ones providing accepted knowledge (Sec. 5.2). *Literature synthesis*: Based on the findings, we develop a future research agenda (Sec. 6). We close with a summary, the limitations of our work and ongoing research (Sec. 7).

2 Foundations

A company's environment could be defined as the relevant physical and social factors within and beyond the organization's boundary (Duncan 1972). While operational analysis focuses on internal difficulties in the implementation of strategic programs with the aim of fully leveraging identified potential, strategic environmental scanning, in turn, aims at anticipating (long-term) environmental shifts and analyzing their potential impact.

This research concentrates on the latter referred to as "*environmental scanning*". Its main function is to gather, interpret, and use pertinent information about events, trends, and relationships in an organization's environment that would assist management in planning the future course of action (Aguilar 1967).

As an IS label to support *managerial* decision making, management support systems[2] (MSS) are proposed in literature. They cover decision support systems

---

[1] BI is a broad category of technologies, applications, and processes for gathering, storing, accessing, and analyzing data to help its users make better decision (Wixom et al. 2010).

[2] Both, MSS (Clark Jr. et al. 2007) and DSS (Arnott et al. 2008) have been proposed as labels for IS intended to provide IT support for managerial decision making. Since DSS evolved from a specific concept that originated as a complement to MIS and was overlapped in the late 1980s with EIS, we refer to MSS on hand (Power 2008).

(DSS), management information systems (MIS), executive information systems (EIS), more recently knowledge management systems (KMS), and BI systems (Clark Jr. et al. 2007). ESS, in turn, have their roots in management literature focusing on the executives' task to be aware of environmental trends (Aguilar 1967). They specify the sectors to-be scanned, monitor the most important indicators that may create opportunities or threats for the organization, cover the IS-based tools to be used (Yasai-Ardenaki et al. 1996), incorporate the findings of such analyses into executives' decision making, and often assign responsibilities to support environmental scanning (not covered in this article, but in Lenz et al. 1986).

Two information collection modes are distinguished (Choudhury et al. 1997): In contrast to the reactive mode in which information is acquired to resolve a problem, we follow the *proactive mode* in which the environment is scanned for upcoming changes that represent opportunities and threats (Fahey et al. 1977). As a result, this article aims at ESS, which are conceived as structured, reticulated IT-based IS to allow executives to scan their environment from an overall perspective for a proactive corporate management.

3 Need for Improving Environmental Scanning Systems

Regulatory needs: Environmental scanning is not just "nice to have", as Kajüter (2004) shows in his multicountry comparison. In the wake of several cases of fraud around the turn of the millenium that were neither detected by internal controls nor by auditors, legislators expressed a need for a more detailed risk management approach. Best known is the U.S. Sarbanes-Oxley-Act. In particular Section 404, requires companies listed on the New York Stock Exchange to extensively document internal controls, establish independent audit committees, and have internal controls' effectiveness audited mandatory (Sherman et al. 2009). Furthermore, financial statements are normally prepared on the assumption that a company will continue in operations for the foreseeable future (IASB Framework 4.1; ISA 1.25). This requires predictions of at least one year (Choo 2009). In the wake of the 2008/2009 economic crisis, the assessment of this "going-concern" has gained an increased importance.

Empirical evidence: Fuld (2003) showed the lack of an early warning system in 97% of the U.S. companies he surveyed. Interviews with 140 corporate strategists found that two-thirds had been surprised by as many as three high-impact competitive events in the past five years. Following Krystek & Herzhoff (2006), 30% of European chemicals companies do not have strategic ESS in place. 15% said that the instruments available are not sufficiently accepted to be used in practice. Day & Schoemaker's (2005) survey of global managers found that 81% perceived their future need for peripheral vision to be greater than their current capacity. Similar findings are reported from companies within the Financial Times "Europe 500" report (Mayer 2010): most of the executives consider environmental-scanning concepts to be too complex and even too difficult to implement. Therefore, results are not a substantial part of executive decision-making process.

4 Framework for Literature Systematization

Following Webster and Watson (2002) a literature review is concept-centric. Elements of IS design theories in combination with the research method used offer a framework for structuring the literature (Figure 1).

4.1 Elements of IS Design Theories

According to Walls et al. (1992), IS design theories consist of three elements: (1) *Requirements* can be defined as prerequisites, conditions, or capabilities needed by users of software systems to solve a problem or achieve an objective (IEEE610.12-1990). They delineate what IS should do, both from the functional and non-functional perspective (Kotonya et al. 1998). Functional requirements address "what" IS should or must do (purpose of the IS). Non-functional requirements, in contrast, reflect "how well" IS perform within the given environment as it fulfills its function, e.g. response time and reliability (Paech et al. 2004).

Designing ESS is not a Greenfield approach. For that reason, IS design theories cover guidelines for bringing the system to life. They contribute to methods and models. (2) *Models* outline concrete systems, features, or combinations of these (Gregor 2006). We distinguish between forecasting as the first generation of ESS, indicator-based systems as the second one, and environmental scanning using weak signals as the third generation. (3) *Methods* cover the process of environmental scanning. We differentiate between information gathering ("scanning"), analytical techniques to identify latent or pending changes; and the incorporation of the scanning results into executives' decision-making process.

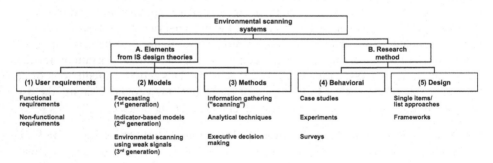

Fig. 1. Framework for literature systematization

4.2 Research Methods

The type of research method is another dimension in our framework for systematizing the literature. Their distinction is important as it influences the granularity of requirements and design principles: from abstract findings by a survey regarding "appropriate technology" to detailed IS features from an in-depth case study such as "drill-down functionality to an upstream ERP" (Urbach et al. 2009).

(4) Papers with a *behavioral focus* explain phenomena from practice. Therefore, they rely on observations and focus on some type of empirical method. We differentiate between case studies to learn from single design, experiments, and surveys (Urbach et al. 2009). (5) *Design approaches* involve ideas and frameworks for creating a better world and provide more direct recommendations for IS (Walls et al. 1992). We go on differentiating between single items and broader "list" approa-ches that specify sets of requirements, design principles and frameworks that focus on the relationship between requirements and design principles.

5 Literature Analysis

Generally based on the Webster and Watson (2002) approach to literature review, we introduce our search strategy (Sec. 5.1). Then, we systematize the results to discuss the most important publications at a glance (Sec. 5.2). The synthesis of findings follows in Sec. 6.

5.1 Search Strategy

Following vom Brocke et al. (2009), we first perform a journal search. We focus on leading IS research outlets and select six of the most relevant IS journals[3] reflecting their ranking[4] and impact factor[5] (Webster et al. 2002). Furthermore, we expand our list with proceedings from the two A-ranked international conferences listed by WKWI (2008): the International and European Conferences on IS (ICIS, ECIS). Second, we use EBSCO host, Google scholar, Science Direct, and Wiley Inter Science to access the journals. Third, the keywords "environmental scanning system" and "early warning system, weak signal, leading indicator" produce 14 relevant hits in total. Fourth, by doing a backward and forward search, we add the keywords "man-agement support systems" and "business intelligence" to our search string, leading to additional 13 IS articles. Finally, we did the same search on strategic management literature[6] coming up with another 53 hits. So, we end up with 80 relevant publica-tions in total (Figure 2, in detail Table A1).

5.2 Results

Figure 3 presents the 80 publications identified as relevant within the framework we derived before. The most revealing publications are discussed below. The insights then allow us to develop the findings for ESS more applicable than the state of the art (Sec. 6).

---

[3] MIS Quarterly, Decision Support Systems, Information & Management, Journal of Manage-ment Information Systems, European Journal of Information Systems, and Information Sys-tem Management.

[4] Based on journal rankings of AIS (2010); VHB (2008); WKWI (2008).

[5] We considered impact factors from http://www.elsevier.com.

[6] Strategic Management Journal (SMJ), Long Range Planning (LRP), Journal of Management Studies (JMS), Technology Analysis and Strategic Management (TASM), Academy of Man-agement Review (AMR), Harvard Business Review (HBR).

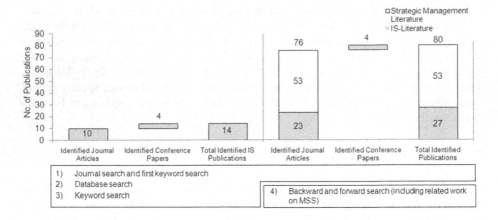

Fig. 2. Selection of the relevant publications

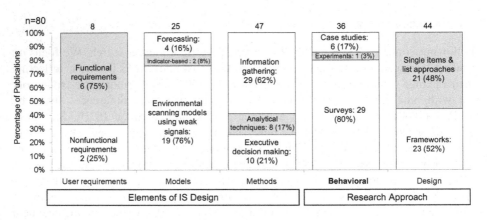

Fig. 3. Classification of the publications

User requirements

Just six out of 80 publications focus on functional requirements and an even minor number of two on non-functional ones. Of particular relevance is Xu et al. (2003). To develop a Corporate Radar, these authors conducted a cross-industry study and found that *task-related environmental* areas are perceived to be more important than far-general environmental in-formation. For example, in the computer and electronics industry the supplier sector was assessed as a fundamental area for environmental scanning.

Another five studies reviewed functional requirements of executives by their scanning practices. For example, Yasai-Ardenaki & Nystrom (1996) emphasize a link between scanning areas and *strategy*. Especially in volatile industries, the *"periphery"*—a metaphor, describing latent changes that can come e.g. from political movements—should be considered for environmental scanning (Day et al. 2004). Regarding Daft et al. (1988) the periphery should cover at least science, politics, law and justice and international relationships. Focusing the non-functional perspective, El Sawy (1985) dealt with executives scanning requirements and suggests that a successful solution should have just a *limited number of scanning areas and sources.*

Models

Out of our 80 articles, 25 publications cover models for environmental scanning. They can be divided into three generations: Early warning systems were first mentioned in the late six-ties by Cohen & Zinbarg (1967). These key-figure-oriented approaches are based on thresholds that define the range of tolerance. If a critical value is exceeded, an alert is triggered. Forecasting advances this technique using time series, not only for planned and actual data, but also planned and *extrapolated as-is data.*

Second generation ESS identify latent risks and chances. Such an indicator-based model is described by Davies et al. (2006). Their *key risk indicators* (KRI) are standardized indicators that focus on potential problems, e.g., staff turnover could signal inadequate human resources performance. Since random or natural fluctuations occur, they *recommend reference values and ranges of tolerance* to avoid overreactions.

After companies failed to act proactively on the oil-crisis, Ansoff introduced the concept of *weak signals* in 1975. An example is the World Wide Web (www) changing the private and business communication or the spread of carbon fibre. The latter's usage for example has increased steadily in recent years and its potential to serve as a substitute for steel represents a strategic issue for steelmakers. As we see nowadays, weak signals do not always work out. They often lack "grasp" for direct interactions. But Ansoff's concept is still topical in recent literature. In fact, 76% of publications about models use his approach. Narchal et al. (1987) promise that a *systematic scanning and monitoring* is more effective than ad hoc scanning in giving a prognosis of future developments. Hereby, they stress descriptors indicating relevant developments, trends, and events in the environment. They explain and quantify dynamics within the scanning areas.

Methods

Aguilar (1967) was the first to examine four different modes of scanning, namely undirected viewing, conditional viewing, informal search and formal search. Attaining strategic advantages by *information gathering* have been of high interest and therefore 62% of articles on methods refine the concept.

Several *analytical techniques* for environmental scanning are distinguished in literature and covers 17 % of the publications researched: mathematical methods facilitate a systematic integration of quantifiable figures into ESS. But, the 2008/2009 economic crisis showed that they had significant scarcities for ordinary users. Often premises were too complicated (Ma-kridakis et al., 2010) or the use of confidence intervals in value-at-risk models excludes improbable, high-impact events (Fuld, 2003). Taleb et al. (2009) also criticize these models, because even small errors in the assumptions underlying the distributions can be devastating. Heuristic approaches are alternatives (Ansoff 1980). For example, the *delphi method* comprises three features: First, responses from experts to a topic are anonymous, usually using formalized questionnaires. Second, in several iterations, feedback is given to the experts. Third, after a few iterations, when the results stabilized, group response is aggregated (Dalkey 1969). Narchal et al. (1987) recommend *influence diagrams* focusing on levers and their influence on the most important environmental indicators. In order to model dependencies between single items, *cross-impact matrices* evolved (Fontela 1976). It is also argued that such matrices can contribute to find a most probable *scenario* of the future.

One dimensional performance measurement systems often do not suffice to meet the complete information need. More important, Fuld (2003) showed that companies often fail to act on generated environmental scanning information, either by measuring the impact of identified opportunities and threats on (financial) performance indicators *or incorporating the results of ESS in executives' decision making process* per se. Frolick et al. (1997) argue to embed EIS into the environmental scanning process. EIS can enhance identifying issues, establishing means of scanning, delineating sources of external information and decision making. Finally, they can help to incorporate anticipated changes in the planning and reporting.

MSS and environmental scanning

To complement our results, we also consider findings from contemporary related MSS work. Gleißner & Füser (2000) propose *artificial neural networks* to support early warning capabilities in corporations. In contrast to humans, they are not limited by psychological barriers. Moreover they can deal with many different variables coincidentally—as needed to handle the potential span of indicators. They are adaptive and robust models. Thus, they are widely used for fraud detection (Ngai et al. 2011), but not used in environmental scanning.

Using *value at risk* (VaR, Chen et al. 2011) and unstructured data from BI can predict financial market risk and thus should contribute to environmental scanning. Recent developments in the www, namely *web 2.0*, and incorporated social networking, provide useful in-formation on customers and competitors. For example, customers that judge their goods bought offer useful strategic information on products quality and future offers (Chen et al. 2011). Besides the internet, also *capital markets* provide useful information on customers, suppliers, competitors, and the economic development (Plambeck & Weber 2010). They can deliver future perspectives, e.g. on growth rates of economies or net sales of organizations.

Understanding BI in a broader sense, Goul and Corral (2007) ask for *data warehouses* (DWH) to include information about external issues such as competitors or regulations and to provide measurability of the strategic advantages. Lönnqvist and Pirttimäki (2006) performed a literature review to evaluate existing methods for measuring the *value of BI* within the organization. For example user satisfaction gives an insight. Those measurement approaches should be checked for applicability to evaluate ESS.

6 Synthesis

The literature systematization in Sec. 5 reveals major gaps in research to overcome for more applicable ESS. Interpreting them, we go on with six findings for a reworked

IS (also Mayer 2011). Herein, we incorporate first ideas from Narchal et al. (1987) and Mayer and Wurl (2011). The latter refer to it as the *Corporate Radar*. An instantiations at a large, international companies in the basic materials sector (Europe, sales: USD 56 bn; employees: 174,000) helped us to make the findings more concrete.

6.1 User Requirements: Lack of Sound Requirements Analysis

Just six out of 80 publications focus on functional requirements and an even smaller number of two on non-functional requirements. Some may argue that improvisation could be an alternative approach (Ciborra 1999), but following the homo oeconomicus theory we believe the best way to tackle the increasingly volatile environment is reasoning on *cause and effect chains*. Thus, a series of indicators have to be collected in order to detect threats and opportunities to anticipate for proactive corporate management.

A *first finding* can be proposed as follows: *Take a 360-degree approach to support executives' "managing a company" task, but select just the most important scanning areas to keep focus.* When designing ESS, we recommend starting with the most popular and wide-spread conceptual design of Xu et al. (2003) and prioritize task-related environmental areas. Because executives have the task of managing a company, a "360 degree" radar is needed (Figure 4). It should reflect the organization's vision and strategic program (Yasai-Ardenaki et al. 1996) and then follow the value chain for their scanning areas of procurement, production and sales (Day et al. 2005). Following El Sawy (1985) and his non-functional perspective on requirements that just the most important scanning areas should be considered to keep focus, most important supporting areas are capital supply, research and development, and human resources. The more volatile the company's environment, the more the peripheral areas should be scanned. Following the PESTL scheme e.g. (Daft et al. 1988), such peripheral areas are legal and compliance or shifts in social or political behaviour. IS support for this first activity of setting up a Corporate Radar is not mandatory.

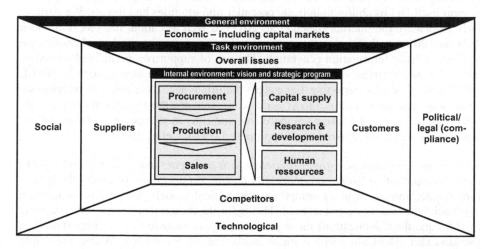

Fig. 4. Scanning areas for reworked environmental scanning systems

6.2 Models: Weak Signals Lack the "Grasp" to Apply in Practice

The most popular and widespread approach to find indicators giving executives the time for proactive decision making are *weak signals* (Figure 3). So we stick to that concept with the aim to improve their missing "grasp" which we identified in the literature systemization. What changes in organizations' environment are weak signals and so proactively show significant turbulences is unclear. Especially weak signals differentiation from day-to-day vibrations without consequences is difficult. With the following three findings we translate Ansoffs´ weak signals in a more pragmatic IT-based approach of indicators.

Second finding: Define concrete indicators and use IS to identify relevant cause-effective-chains. Based on our literature review, we see two levers to improve weak signals "grasp": first, distinguishing relevant indicators foreseeing changes from the mass of data available (Narchal et al. 1987) and give guidelines on how to identify patterns attaining their strategic advantages for the organization (Aguilar 1967). Following Davies (2006), we propose as evaluation criteria indicators' lead time, clarity, and their appropriate cost-/impact ratio. For example if sales is an important scanning area, the Baltic dry index, which measures the rates charged for dry-bulk vessels, could be used to indicate overall economic development.

Second, the barriers preventing people from identifying and processing weak signals can be circumvented with IS (Hand 2009). Structuring data, artificial neural networks, data mining, and semantic search should receive greater attention as ways to extract cause-effective-chains (Elofson et al. 1991). So, IS researchers should therefore focus on exploring techniques to extract non-trivial, implicit, previously unknown and potentially useful patterns.

Third finding: Leverage IT to automate day-to-day routines and to follow the variety of indicators' movements. In a third step, data sources and the frequency of data collection must be determined. A trade-off is necessary between the cost of data collection, such as license fees of data sources, costs of additional employees, the reporting system itself and its ability to indicate potential opportunities and threats. We particularly emphasize the Internet (Chen et al. 2011) as well as capital markets (Plambeck & Weber 2010) as data sources, because they have an inherent good cost/benefit ratio at least for basic information generation. The use of supportive, predefined and easy-to-handle user interfaces for data access or common IT languages, such as XBRL (eXtensible Business Reporting Language), facilitate accessing relevant information sources by automated routines to systematically monitor the movements of the most important indicators. To save even more cost and time to process information gathering data through computerized notes is proposed (Frolick et al. 1997).

Fourth finding: Leverage expert experience with an impact matrix and translate indicators' impact into a balanced opportunity-and-threat portfolio. To model the indicators' impact, instead of using complex mathematical models, we propose a heuristic approach based on the delphi method. This is for the reason that a basic understanding of risks and their implications on organizations' performance is more important than pseudo-exact calculations with difficult mathematical approaches. Within the delphi method for ESS, experts should be asked to qualify indicators' impact on threats and opportunities (Mayer and Wurl 2011). On the left hand side in Figure 5 the indicators, their scoring according to threats and opportunities (x-axis) and their estimated lead time (y-axis), are shown. The bundling is used to derive the associated opportunities and threats for the organization (right hand side): The balanced opportunity-and-threat portfolio draws on the results of an analysis quantifying the impact of each individual indicators on the most important threats and opportunities (Fontela 1976). We choose this visualization because it is comprehensive in terms of content, but in terms of presentation it represents a condensed overview about most important opportunities and threat for the organization.

6.3 Methods: Approaches Lack to Incorporate Results of Environmental Scanning Systems into Executives' Decision Making

Last, but not least, the third gap that becomes obvious is that environmental scanning is useless, as long as the results are not integrated in executives' decision-making processes. We derive another two findings for improving ESS towards more applicability from the method perspective.

Fifth finding: Incorporate scanning results more closely into executives' decision-making process by generating scenarios from a set of environment assumptions. To ensure that executives receive scanning findings in an amount and form that facilitates effective decision making, their reporting should cover critical opportunities and threats. For a periodical presentation, we propose linking the identified opportunities and threats with a companies' management control (Ansoff 1980; Frolick et al. 1997). We propose the form of an *economic value added at risk tree* (Chen et al. 2011, Figure 6). Once the indicators and the associated opportunities and threats have been identified, they should define three scenarios (Fontela 1976)

—optimistic, most probable and pessimistic—covering the set of opportunities and threats that the organization faces due to environmental changes (Narchal et al. 1987).

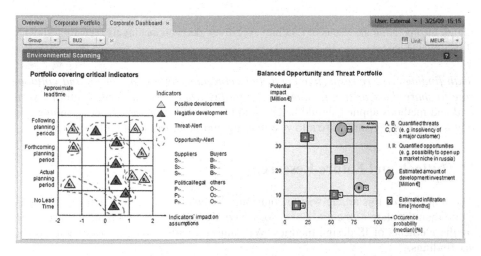

Fig. 5. Deriving and quantifying opportunities and threats in a balanced opportunity-and-threat portfolio

New business application and user-friendly interface ("frontend") should provide the scenario visualization that allows switching between the best, worst and most probable scenarios (Figure 6, right hand side). The best and worst case scenarios define the range of the most important value drivers such as net sales and costs. Because of the mathematical connections between them, also ranges for the financial performance indicators EBIT, ROCE and EVA (Figure 6, left hand side) are defined as well. The slider position shown here represents the most probable scenario. All drivers can be moved to the right or to the left to simulate changes no matter which scenario is selected. Furthermore, on an ad-hoc basis, "breaking news" and "turning points" that refute prior assumptions can be helpful.

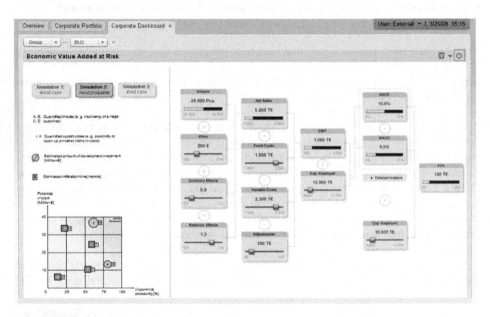

Fig. 6. Incorporating the results of ESS into executives' decision making by scenario technique (first instantiation)

Sixth finding: Use retrospective controls to continuously update the IS and collaborate to share the scanning findings in day-to-day work. Assumptions should be verified and methods applied should be checked for modifications due to new findings. In day-to-day work, group-ware allows e-mailing and other forms of collaboration.

7 Outlook and Future Research

The objective of this article was to contribute to developing ESS that are more applicable than the state of the art. To do so, we conducted a *literature analysis* structured by the elements of IS design theories. We came up with three gaps to overcome and six findings.

Comparing the findings with the state of the art reveals some points worthy of discussion. On the one hand, literature based findings offer greater rigor than action research does. Thus, they should be more sustainable. However, our research has been limited to a *restricted number* of publications. But, the fact that we covered the leading journals means major contributions should be included. We see the need to expand this coverage, especially by identifying practitioner publications that are not listed in the top IS and management literature we researched or publications that do not include any of our search terms. Another limitation is that the synthesis entails *subjectivity*. In short, the validity of the derived findings could have been increased if more researchers had been involved.

Regarding IS in environmental scanning, we expect *ongoing innovations*. Today's executives grew up with IT and have a more natural attitude toward IS. New technologies have been established in the field of corporate BI, such as EIS, which have evolved from a single-system approach to an integrated module in powerful data warehouse environments. More-over, new user interfaces and end-user devices, especially for mobile computing, should simplify IS handling. Hence, ESS should claim a position in the domain of MSS (Sec. 2) as it focusing on forward looking information for managers to plan and steer their organizations.

For future research it is important to specify the findings on hand with "build" and "evaluate" activities. Another contribution could be a *survey* to get a direct perspective on executives' requirements and to evaluate the findings in a broad sample. If someone may come to the conclusion that the body of knowledge from literature research is more wishful thinking than a sound basis for applicable design principles it would be interesting to define a set of evaluation criteria, take successful implementations from practice, evaluate them, ascertain what they have in common and compare these findings with the first design principles presented on hand. Our own research will use additional instantiations to determine the generalizability of the findings on hand and, hopefully, the forthcoming extensions.

References

Aguilar, F.J.: Scanning the Business Environment. Macmillan, New York (1967)

Albright, K.S.: Environmental scanning: radar for success. The Information Management Journal 38(3), 38–45 (2004)

Ansoff, H.I.: Managing Strategic Surprise by Response to Weak Signals. California Management Review 18(2), 21–32 (1975)

Ansoff, H.I.: Strategic Issue Management. Strategic Management Journal 1(2), 131–148 (1980)

Arnott, D., Pervan, G.: Eight key issues for the decision support systems discipline. Decision Support Systems 44(3), 657–672 (2008)

Choo, C.W.: Information Use and Early Warning Effectiveness: Perspectives and Prospects. Journal of the American Society for Information Science and Technology 60(5), 1071–1082 (2009)

Choudhury, V., Sampler, J.L.: Information Specificity and Environmental Scan-ning: An Economic Perspective. MIS Quarterly 21(1), 25–53 (1997)

Ciborra, C.: Notes in Improvisation and Time in Organizations. Accounting, Management and Information Technologies 9(2), 77–94 (1999)

Clark Jr., T.D., Jones, M.C., Armstrong Curtis, P.: The Dynamic Structure of Management Support Systems: Theory Development, Research Focus, and Direction. MIS Quarterly 31(3), 579–615 (2007)

Cohen, J.B., Zinsbarg, E.D.: Investment Analysis and Portfolio Management. Dow Jones-Irwing Inc., Homewood (1967)

Daft, R.L., Sormunen, J., Parks, D.: Chief Executive Scanning, Environmental Characteristics, and Company Performance: An Empirical Study. Strategic Management Journal 9(2), 123–139 (1988)

Dalkey, N.C.: The Delphi Method: An experimental study of group opinion. Rand, Santa Monica (1969)

Davies, J., Finlay, M., McLenaghen, T., Wilson, D.: Key Risk Indicators – Their Role in Operational Risk Management and Measurement. In: ARM and RiskBusiness International, Prague, pp. 1–32 (2006)

Day, G.S., Schoemaker, P.J.H.: Driving through the Fog: Managing at the Edge. Long Range Planning 37(2), 127–142 (2004)

Day, G.S., Schoemaker, P.J.H.: Scanning The Periphery. Harvard Business Review 83(11), 135–148 (2005)

Duncan, R.B.: Characteristics of Organizational Environments and Perceived Environmental Uncertainty. Administrative Science Quarterly 17(3), 313–327 (1972)

El Sawy, O.A.: Personal Information Systems for Strategic Scanning in Turbulent Environments: Can the CEO Go On-Line? MIS Quarterly 9(1), 53–60 (1985)

Elofson, G., Konsynski, B.: Delegation technologies: Environmental scanning with intelligent agents. Journal of Management Information Systems 8(1), 37–62 (1991)

Fahey, L., King, W.R.: Environmental Scanning for Corporate Planning. Business Horizons 20(4), 61 (1977)

Fontela, E.: Industrial Applications of Cross-Impact Analysis. Long Range Planning 9(4), 29–33 (1976)

Frolick, M.N., Parzinger, M.J., Rainer Jr., R.K., Ramarapu, N.K.: Using EISs for environmental scanning. Information Systems Management 14(1), 35–40 (1997)

Fuld, L.: Be Prepared. Harvard Business Review 81(11), 20–21 (2003)

Gregor, S.: The Nature of Theory in Information Systems. MIS Quarterly 30(3), 611–642 (2006)

Hand, D.J.: Mining the past to determine the future: Problems and possibilities. International Journal of Forecasting 25(5), 441–451 (2009)

Hopwood, A.G.: The economic crisis and accounting: Implications for the research community. Accounting, Organizations & Society 34(6/7), 797–802 (2009)

IEEE 1990. The Institute of Electrical and Electronics Engineers, Inc. - Standard Glossary of Software Engineering Terminology. IEEE Computer Society, New York (1990)

Kajüter, P.: Die Regulierung des Risikomanagements im internationalen Vergleich. Zeitschrift für Controlling und Management 47(Sonderheft 3), 12–25 (2004)

Kotonya, G., Sommerville, I.: Requirements Engineering Processes and Techniques. John Wiley & Sons Ltd., Hoboken (1998)

Krystek, U., Herzhoff, M.: Szenario-Technik und Frühaufklärung: Anwendungs-stand und Integrationspotential. Zeitschrift für Controlling und Management 50(5), 305–310 (2006)

Lenz, R.T., Engledow, J.L.: Environmental Analysis Units and Strategic Decision-making: a Field Study of Selected "Leading-edge" Corporations. Strategic Management Journal 7(1), 69–89 (1986)

Lesca, N., Caron-Fasan, M.-L.: Strategic scanning project failure and abandonment factors: Lessons learned. European Journal of Information Systems 17(4), 371–386 (2008)

Makridakis, S., Hogarth, R.M., Gaba, A.: Why Forecasts Fail. What to Do Instead. MIT Sloan Management Review 51(2), 83–90 (2010)

Mayer, J.H.: Managing the Future–Six Guidelines for Designing Environmental Scanning Systems. In: Jain, H., Sinha, A.P., Vitharana, P. (eds.) DESRIST 2011. LNCS, vol. 6629, pp. 276–290. Springer, Heidelberg (2011)

Mayer, J.H.: Organisatorische Veränderungen durch die aktuelle Wirtschaftskrise – Bestandsaufnahme und Implikationen für Unternehmenssteuerungssysteme. In: Proceedings des 25. Deutschen Controlling Congresses, Dortmund, Deutschland, pp. 209–228 (2010)

Mayer, J.H., Wurl, H.-J.: Strategische Früherkennung in internationalen Konzernen, pp. 1–28. University of St. Gallen, St. Gallen (2011)

MIS Journal Ranking (AIS 2007), http://ais.affiniscape.com/displaycommon.cfm?an=1&subarticlen br=432 (accessed January 17, 2011)

Narchal, R.M., Kittappa, K., Bhattacharya, P.: An Environmental Scanning System for Business Planning. Long Range Planning 20(6), 96–105 (1987)

Paech, B., Kerkow, D.: Non-Functional Requirements Engineering - Quality is Essential. In: 10th Anniversary International Workshio on Requirements Engineering: Foundation for Software Quality (REFSQ 2004), Riga, Latvia, pp. 27–40 (2004)

Power, D.J.: Decision Support Systems: A Historical Overview. Springer, Berlin (2008)

Rockfellow, J.D.: Wild Cards Preparing for "The Big One". The Futurist 28(1), 14–19 (1994)

Sherman, W.S., Chambers, V.: SOX as Safeguard and Signal: The Impact of The Sarbanes-Oxley Act of 2002 on US Corporations' Choice to List Abroad. The Multinational Business Review 17(3), 163–179 (2009)

Taleb, N.N., Goldstein, D.G., Spitznagel, M.W.: The Six Mistakes Executives Make in Risk Management. Harvard Business Review 87(10), 78–81 (2009)

Urbach, N., Smolnik, S., Riempp, G.: The State of Research on Information Systems Success – A Review of Existing Multidimensional Approaches. Business & Information Systems Engineering (BISE) 1(4), 315–325 (2009)

Vom Brocke, J., Simons, A., Niehaves, B., Riemer, K., Plattfaut, R., Cleven, A.: Reconstructing the Giant: On the Importance of Rigour in Documenting the Literature Search Process. In: 17th European Conference on Information Systems (ECIS), Verona, Italy, pp. 2206–2217 (2009)

Walls, J.G., Widmeyer, G.R., El Sawy, O.A.: Building an Information System Design Theory for Vigilant EIS. Information Systems Research 3(1), 36–59 (1992)

Webster, J., Watson, R.T.: Analyzing the Past to Prepare for the Future: Writing a Literature Review. MIS Quarterly 26(2), xiii-xxiii (2002)

Wixom, B.H., Watson, H.J.: The BI-based organization. International Journal of Business Intelligence 1(1), 13–28 (2010)

WKWI. WI-Liste der Konferenzen. Wirtschaftsinformatik 50(2), 155–163 (2008)

Xu, X.M., Kaye, G.R., Duan, Y.: UK executives vision on business environment for information scanning A cross industry study. Information & Management 40(5), 381–389 (2003)

Yasai-Ardenaki, M., Nystrom, P.C.: Designs for Environmental Scanning Systems: Tests of a Contingency Theory. Management Science 42(2), 187–204 (1996)

Table A1. Full list of researched articles

No	Author(s)	Year	Title	Publication	Elements of IS design	Research approach
1	Aguilar, F.	1967	Scanning the Business Environment	Macmilian	Information gathering	Survey
2	Ahituv, N. et al.	1998	Environmental Scanning and Information Systems in relation to success in introducing new products	Information & Management	Information gathering	Survey
3	Albright, K.	2004	Environmental Scanning: Radar for Success	The Information Management Journal	Information gathering	Single/list approaches
4	Anderson, M.H. & Nichols, M.L.	2007	Information Gathering And Changes in Threat and Opportunity Perceptions	Journal of Management Studies	Information gathering	Experiment
5	Ansoff, H.I.	1975	Managing Strategic Surprise by Response to Weak Signals	California Management Review	3rd generation IS	Framework
6	Ansoff, H.I.	1980	Strategic Issue Management	Strategic Management Journal	3rd generation IS	Framework
7	Arnott, D. & Pervan, G.	2008	Eight key issues for the decision support systems discipline	Decision Support Systems	Information gathering	Single/list approaches
8	Boyd, B. & Fulk, J.	1996	Executive Scanning and perceived Uncertainty: A multidimensional Model	Journal of Management	Information gathering	Survey
9	Chen, H. et al.	2011	Enterprise risk and security management: Data, text and Web mining	Decision Support Systems	Information gathering	Single/list approaches
10	Cho, T.	2006	The effects of executive turnover on top management teams: environmental scanning behaviour after an environmental change	Journal of Business Research	Information gathering	Survey
11	Choo, C.W.	1999	The Art of Scanning the Environment	Bulletin of the American Society for Information Science	Information gathering	Framework
12	Choo, C.W.	2001	The knowing organization as learning organization	Education + Training	3rd generation IS	Framework
13	Cohen, J.B. & Zinsbarg, E.D.	1967	Investment Analysis and Portfolio Management	Homewood	1st generation IS	Single/list approaches
14	Daft, R. & Weick, K.	1984	Toward a Model of Organizations as Interpretation Systems	Academy of Management Review	Information gathering	Framework
15	Daft, R.L. et al.	1988	Chief Executive Scanning, Environmental Characteristics and Company performance: An Empirical Study	Strategic Management Journal	Functional requirements	Survey
16	Daheim, C. & Uerz, G.	2008	Corporate Foresight in Europe: From trend based logics to open foresight	Technology Analysis & Strategic Management	3rd generation IS	Survey
17	Davies, J. et al.	2006	Key Risk Indicators - Their Role in Operational Risk Management	RiskBusiness International Limited	2nd generation IS	Framework
18	Day, G.S. & Schoemaker, P.J.H.	2004	Driving through the Fog: Managing at the Edge	Long Range Planning	Information gathering	Single/list approaches
19	Day, G.S. & Schoemaker, P.J.H.	2005	Scanning the Periphery	Harvard Business Review	Functional requirements	Single/list approaches
20	El Sawy, O.	1985	Personal Information Systems for Strategic Scanning in Turbulent Environments: Can the CEO go online?	MIS Quarterly	Nonfunctional requirements	Survey
21	Elofson, G. & Konsynski, B.	1991	Delegation Technologies: Environmental Scanning with intelligent agents	Journal of Management Information Systems	Information gathering	Case study
22	Elofson, G. & Konsynski, B.	1993	Performing organizational learning with machine apprentices	Decision Support Systems	3rd generation IS	Framework
23	Fontela, E.	1976	Industrial Applications of Cross-Impact Analysis	Long Range Planning	Analytical techniques	Single/list approaches
24	Frolick, M. et al.	1997	Using EISs for Environmental Scanning	Information Systems Management	3rd generation IS	Framework
25	Fuld, L.	2003	Be Prepared	Harvard Business Review	3rd generation IS	Survey
26	Garg, V. et al.	2000	Chief executives scanning emphasis, environmental dynamism and manufacturing firm performance	Strategic Management Journal	Information gathering	Survey
27	Glassey, O.	2008	Exploring the weak signals of start-ups as a folksonomic system	Technology Analysis & Strategic Management	3rd generation IS	Framework
28	Gleißner, W. & Füser, K.	2000	Moderne Frühwarn- und Prognosesysteme für Unternehmensplanung und Risikomanagement	Der Betrieb	Analytical techniques	Single/list approaches
29	Gomez, P.	1983	Frühwarnung in der Unternehmung	Haupt	3rd generation IS	Framework
30	Goul, M. & Corral, K.	2007	Enterprise model management and next generation decision support	Decision Support Systems	Information gathering	Single/list approaches
31	Gray, P.	2008	From Hindsight to Foresight: Applying Futures Research Techniques in Information Systems	Communications of the Association for Information Systems	Analytical techniques	Single/list approaches
32	Hahn, D. & Krystek, U.	1979	Betriebliche und überbetriebliche Frühwarnsysteme für die Industrie	Zeitschrift für betriebswirtschaftliche Forschung	2nd generation IS	Framework
33	Hambrick, D.C.	1981	Specialization of Environmental Scanning Activities Among Upper Level Executives	Journal of Management Studies	Information gathering	Survey
34	Hand, D.	2009	Mining the Past to determin the future	International Journal of Forecasting	Analytical techniques	Single/list approaches
35	Hough, J. & White, M.	2004	Scanning actions and environmental dynamism	Management Decision	Information gathering	Survey
36	Jain, S.C.	1984	Environmental Scanning in US Corporations	Long Range Planning	Information gathering	Survey
37	Jourdan, Z. et al.	2008	Business Intelligence: An Analysis of the Literature	Information Systems Management	Information gathering	Single/list approaches
38	Krystek, U.	1993	Frühaufklärung für Unternehmen: Identifikation und Handhabung zukünftiger Chancen und Bedrohungen	Schäfer-Poeschel	3rd generation IS	Framework
39	Kuvaas, B.	2002	An Exploration of two competing perspectives on informational contexts in top management strategic issue interpretation	Journal of Management Studies	Executive decision making	Survey
40	Lauzen, M.	1995	Toward a Model of Environmental Scanning	Journal of public Relations Research	3rd generation IS	Survey

Table A1. (*Continued*)

No	Author(s)	Year	Title	Publication	Elements of IS design	Research approach
41	Lenz, R. & Engledow, J.	1986	Environmental Analysis Units and Strategic Decision-Making: A field study of selected leading edge companies	Strategic Management Journal	3rd generation IS	Survey
42	Lenz, R. & Engledow, J.	1986	Environmental Analysis: The Applicability of current Theory	Strategic Management Journal	3rd generation IS	Framework
43	Lesca, N. & Caron-Fason, M.-L.	2008	Strategic Scanning Project Failure and abandonment factors: Lessons learned	European Journal of Information Systems	Information gathering	Survey
44	Liu, S.	1998	Data Warehousing Agent: In seeking of improved support for environmental scanning and strategic management	ECIS-Proceedings	Information gathering	Case study
45	Liu, S.	2000	Agent Based Environmental Scanning System: Impacts on Managers and Their Strategic Scanning Activities	AMCIS-Proceedings	Information gathering	Case study
46	Lönnqvist, A. & Pirttimäki, V.	2006	The Measurement of Business Intelligence	Information Systems Management	Functional requirements	Single/list approaches
47	Makridakis, S.	2010	Why Forecasts fail. What to Do Instead.	MIT Sloan Management Review	1st generation IS	Single/list approaches
48	McMullen, J. et al.	2009	Managerial (In)attention to Competitive Threats	Journal of Management Studies	Executive decision making	Survey
49	Menon, A. & Tomkins, A.	2004	Learning About The Markets Periphery: IBM´s WebFountain	Long Range Planning	Information gathering	Case study
50	Müller, R.M.	2010	Business Intelligence and Service-oriented Architecture: A Delphi Study	Information Systems Management	Information gathering	Survey
51	Nanus, B.	1982	QUEST - Quick Environmental Scanning Technique	Long Range Planning	Executive decision making	Framework
52	Narchal, R. M. et al.	1987	An Environmental Scanning System for Business Planning	Long Range Planning	3rd generation IS	Framework
53	Nastanski, M.	2003	The value of active Scanning to senior executives	Journal of Management Development	Information gathering	Survey
54	Nemati, H. et al.	2000	A Multi-Agent Framework for Web Based Information Retrieval and Filtering	AMCIS-Proceedings	Analytical techniques	Single/list approaches
55	Ngai, E.W.T. et al.	2011	The application of data mining techniques in financial fraud detection: A classification framework and an academic review of literature	Decision Support Systems	Information gathering	Framework
56	Nick, A.	2009	Wirksamkeit strategischer Früherkennung	Gabler	3rd generation IS	Case study
57	Plambeck, N. & Weber, K.	2010	When the glass is half empty and half full: Ceo interpretation	Strategic Management Journal	Executive decision making	Survey
58	Prahalad, C. K.	2004	The Blinders of dominant Logic	Long Range Planning	Information gathering	Single/list approaches
59	Qiu, T.	2007	Scanning for competitve intelligence: A managerial perspective	European Journal of Marketing	Information gathering	Survey
60	Reichmann, T. & Lachnit, L.	1979	Unternehmensführung mit Hilfe eines absatzorientierten Frühwarnsystems	Zeitschrift für Betriebswirtschaft	1st generation IS	Framework
61	Reinhardt, W. A.	1984	An Early Warning System for Strategic Planning	Long Range Planning	3rd generation IS	Framework
62	Romeike, F.	2005	Frühaufklärungssysteme als wesentliche Komponente eines proaktiven Risikomanagements	Controlling	3rd generation IS	Single/list approaches
63	Rossel, P.	2009	Weak Signals as a flexible framing space for enhanced management and decision-making	Technology Analysis & Strategic Management	3rd generation IS	Framework
64	Schoemaker, P.J.H. & Day, G.S.	2009	Gathering Information: How to make sense of weak signals	MIT Sloan Management Review	Information gathering	Single/list approaches
65	Simon, H.	1959	Theories of Decision-Making in Economics and Behavioral Science	The Economic Review	Executive decision making	Framework
66	Smallman, C. & Smith, D.	2003	Patterns of Managerial Risk Perceptions: Exploring the Dimensions of Managers Accepted Risks	Risk Management	Executive decision making	Survey
67	Sonnenschein, O.	2005	DV-gestützte Früherkennung	Controlling	3rd generation IS	Framework
68	Suh, W. et al.	2004	Scanning behaviour and strategic uncertainty	Management Decision	Executive decision making	Survey
69	Taleb, N. et al.	2009	The Six Mistakes Executives Make in Risk Management	Harvard Business Review	Executive decision making	Single/list approaches
70	Tan, S. et al.	1998	Environmental Scanning on the Internet	ICIS-Proceedings	Nonfunctional requirements	Survey
71	Thomas, J.B. et al.	1993	Strategic Sensemaking and organizational performance: Linkages among scanning, interpretation, action and outcomes	Academy of Management Journal	Executive decision making	Survey
72	Tseng, F.S.C. & Chou, A.Y.H.	2006	The concept of document warehousing for multi-dimensional modeling of textual-based business intelligence	Decision Support Systems	Analytical techniques	Framework
73	Vandenbosch, B. & Huff, S.L.	1997	Searching and Scanning: How Executives Obtain Information from Executive Information Systems	MIS Quarterly	Executive decision making	Survey
74	Walters, B. et al.	2003	Strategic Information and Strategic decision making: the EIS-CEO interface in smaller manufacturing companies	Information & Management	Functional requirements	Survey
75	Wei, C.-P. & Lee, Y.-H.	2004	Event detection from online news documents for supporting environmental scanning	Decision Support Systems	Analytical techniques	Single Item
76	Wheelwright, S. & Clarke, D.	1976	Probing Opinions	Harvard Business Review	1st generation IS	Single/list approaches
77	Wixom, B.H. et al.	2008	Continental Airlines Continues to Soar with Business Intelligence	Information Systems Management	Information gathering	Case study
78	Xu, K. et al.	2011	Mining comparative opinions from customer reviews for Competitive Intelligence	Decision Support Systems	Analytical techniques	Framework
79	Xu, X. et al.	2003	UK executives Vision on business environment for information scanning. A cross industry study	Information & Management	Functional requirements	Survey
80	Yasai-Ardenaki, M. & Nystrom, P.	1996	Designs for Environmental Scanning Systems: Tests of a contingency theory	Management Science	Functional requirements	Survey

Progress of Commitment in Co-operative Software Acquisition

Torsti Rantapuska and Sariseelia Sore

Lahti University of Applied Sciences,
Ståhlberginkatu 10, 15150 Lahti, Finland
Tel.: +358 50 5265867, +358 44 708 0174
{torsti.rantapuska,sariseelia.sore}@lamk.fi

Abstract. This paper reports on the results of a test on a Co-operative Software Acquisition (COSA) model in which the users carry out the ICT investment by themselves. The existing models meant to help in the ICT investments process are too heavy and technical to be used in SMEs. A successful ICT investment is an organisational change process in which people have a critical role. The COSA model applies user participation and team-working in the acquisition of Commercial Off-The-Shelf (COTS) software products. The model is designed bearing three objectives in mind: 1) business orientation, 2) agility, and 3) practicality. The model can be applied to ICT investments in SMEs which have a professional team leader with basic business and IT knowledge. The results show that people are willing to commit to the COSA process, but problems exist related to systems thinking, decision making and risk taking.

Keywords: ICT investment, decision making, ICT adoption, software acquisition, organisational learning, user participation.

1 Introduction

The work of job the enrichment school (Herzberg 1966) already realized that people seek cognitive and motivational growth in their work. Actually, people seek a work which has the typical characteristics of knowledge work such as "knowing more, acquiring relationships in knowledge and creativity". The further we go towards the information society, the more important it is to enrich the work in order to make people satisfied with their job. According to Herzberg the work can be enriched by: "removing controls, increasing accountability, creating natural work units, granting additional authority, providing direct feedback, introducing new tasks, and allocating special assignments". The characteristics of knowledge work are shown to increase satisfaction, motivation and commitment (Abrahamsson 2002). These factors increase, even if the relationship may be more complicated (Fisher C. D, 2003), job performance too (Wright T., Russel C., Bonett D. G., 2007; Ferris G. R., Hochwarter W. A., Buckley M. R., Harrell-Cook G., Frink D. D., 1999; Regoa and Cunha 2008; Wasti, 2005; Angle and Lawson 1993).

M. Nüttgens et al. (Eds.): Governance and Sustainability in IS, IFIP AICT 366, pp. 224–235, 2011.

Acquiring COTS software has become a critical management issue in SMEs. It is widely acknowledged that more than half of all systems fail (Goulielmos and Paraskevi, 2003). Besides the shortage of resources like finances, time (Richie and Brindley, 2005), knowledge (Proudlock M., Phelps B. and Gamble P., 1999) and skills (Comella-Dorda S., Dean, J., Morris E. and Oberndorf P., 2002), the actual nature of software adoption is not understood in the right way (Marchand and Hykes 2006). The acquisition of a software product cannot be taken as a traditional investment with its initial costs and repayment period. More likely, investing in ICT is an organisational change process in nature and therefore an issue managing the change in work. The success of an ICT investment is highly dependent on how effectively people accept the change and learn to work with the new system (Caldeira and Ward, 2002: Garcia, 2003; Lyytinen and Robey, 1999).

In spite of wide acknowledgement of the importance of user participation in ICT-projects (Hunton and Beeler, 1997; Winston and Benjamin, 2000) the models designed to help the acquisition and adoption of information systems stress mainly the technical and procedural features of the project. Social factors such as user acceptance, resistance, user satisfaction, user commitment, peer influence, peer support, external pressure, etc, are not addressed that much in the existing models, moreover to which extent the users themselves are capable of running ICT projects. Organisational learning (OL) approach (e.g. Nonaka, 1994; Brown and Duguid, 2001; Drucker, 1999) is an excellent method to accommodate social factors into organisational change initiatives. The human actors and the interplay between tacit and explicit knowledge between the actors are central to OL.

In this paper we apply the ideas of OL to software acquisition. As the practical case, we test the Co-Operative Software Acquisition (COSA) Model (Rantapuska and Ihanainen, 2008) which uses the ideas of organisational learning in software acquisition projects. The core idea of the COSA model is to take the users along the project already from the start. This is supposed to commit the people to the new system and finally, will also bring along business value in the future. The paper concentrates to the development of commitment and problems raised during the project.

2 Research Approach

The aim of the paper is to test how organisational learning approach should be applied in the context of COTS software acquisition. The COSA model is an application of OL approach which brings the software acquisition as close to the users as possible. In order to do the work properly, the users have to commit themselves to the COSA project, know their requirements, be capable to make the selection and finally use the software as well. The paper is a single case study which analyses the co-operation and interaction of the team members in COSA project.

The research questions are stated as follows:

1. How does the commitment to COSA project develop during the project lifetime?
2. How well does the COSA model work in relations to problems raised?

2.1 Case Company

The case company is a small company with 12 employees importing machinery, accessories and raw materials to the food industry. Their original intention is to acquire new COTS software to manage their customer relationships (CRM). According to COSA model, the employees formed a working team to analyse their needs and select a software that meets their requirements. The team represented all user groups as salespeople (SP, 2 persons, SP1 and SP2), sales assistants (SA, 1), service and installation (SI, 1) and administration assistant (AA, 1). The management view was represented by an outsider business advisor (BA). He was supposed not to lead or guide the selection as such, but help with the process itself. The researcher took part in the sessions and also helped with the COSA process. The project had seven sessions, which filled three of the five phases of COSA model. One session was for the socialisation and externalisation, four for the externalisation and two for the combination phase. The internalisation in which stage the system is finally adopted was not included in this study. One student participated in the meetings as a silent observer and brought her own suggestion about the system.

2.2 Data Collection and Analysis

The data is collected by recording the team sessions, collecting documents and interviewing participants. The team had seven team sessions each of which taking about four hours. The documents produced between the sessions were collected and analysed. The participants were interviewed twice, at the beginning and at the end of the project. The data was coded by looking for the expression related to commitment. The form of the commitment expression was evaluated in relation to the actions required by the informants. For instance, a general statement about the software in the case does not show so much commitment compared to an expressed claim for a feature which the informant needs in his/her job.

In our analysis, we first categorized the statements in each session. After that, we interpret how much commitment and capability were involved in each session. Based on the analysis we wrote a short summary of each session. Confidential interviews were used to help the interpretation of the statements in team sessions.

2.3 Key Concepts

Organisational learning is a widely used framework also in IS literature. According to Nonaka's (1994) theory of organisational learning, there are two dimensions of knowledge, tacit and explicit. New knowledge is generated in the process of knowledge conversion in which the two forms of knowledge are in a continuous interaction in human actions. Tacit knowledge is the practical working knowledge. Explicit knowledge is usually technical in nature which resides in written documents or somewhere else in a transferable form. An information system is typically a collection of explicit knowledge. The interplay between these two forms of knowledge goes through four phases of knowledge conversation. 1) In the socialization process, for instance in personal conversations, the knowledge is transferred from tacit to tacit knowledge. 2) In the externalization process, the people try to express their tacit understanding into an explicit form. 3) The analysis and document evaluation is a typical work of combination process in which explicit knowledge is converted into another explicit knowledge. Finally 4), the explicit knowledge, for instance an information system, will be converted into tacit knowledge in the internalization process when the users learn to use the system.

Co-operative Software Acquisition (COSA) Model (Rantapuska and Ihanainen, 2008) applies organisational learning (Nonaka I 1994; Nonaka I. and H. Takeuchi 1995) in software acquisition and adoption. The model is also designed as a business-oriented, easy-to-use and is practical enough to be used in small and medium sized (SME) companies. An ideal COSA project is a project affecting a limited number of users (<30) working in business processes linked together through a vertically functional (Morisio and Torchiano 2002) domain specific system (e.g. financial applications, accounting, ERP, CRM, etc.). The project should be more likely a process innovation (Agarwal et al. 1997) concentrating on the change in the working processes than just a product innovation requiring putting focus on learning to use the new software tool. As a change project, "the IT is used as a driver, but the users are prominently involved in that change" (Lynne, 2004).

In COSA projects, both the decision to adopt the system and the diffusion followed by that decision take place at the organisational level ("Organisational adoption and organisational diffusion", Agarwal et al. 1997). The organisation recognizes the potential benefits and is also committed to diffuse the system to the target audience. Still, the diffusion may take time and needs careful planning. By using COSA, the company can accelerate the diffusion process by embedding the two levels of adoption and diffusion in one co-operative team which is responsible both adoption decision making and using the system.

The COSA model interprets the four stages of organisational learning into for tasks. The building of team can be regarded as the fifth stage (Phase 0).

In the 0) *initiation phase*, the organisation prepares to ensure communication, motivation and commitment of the participating people. The team must have knowledge officers as well as practioners. The middle managers act in an intermediate "middle-up-down" role by organizing the "chaotic flow of ideas" from "bottom" and trying to put the top managers' visions into the daily work. In the 1) *externalisation* phase the team members identify problems, share experiences and express the domain-specific tacit knowledge in explicit form. When doing so, the shared understanding about the work content and software requirements will be specified. When the requirements are known, the team turns to the 2) *combination* phase. In this phase the team members search the candidate software products and evaluate their functionalities in order to select the promising ones into further testing. The 3) *internalization* phase serves as the final aptitude test of the candidate solutions. The 4) *socialization* phase is a diffusion process in which the skilled and active staff members support the spread of software usage throughout the organization.

A successful pass-through of the COSA project requires commitment of participating people. The concept of commitment refers to a relationship, which binds an actor to a course of actions. Although, a mere action does not necessarily mean commitment, the perception of commitment is transferred to others through action (Abrahamsson, 2002). The form of commitment defines the reason why an individual

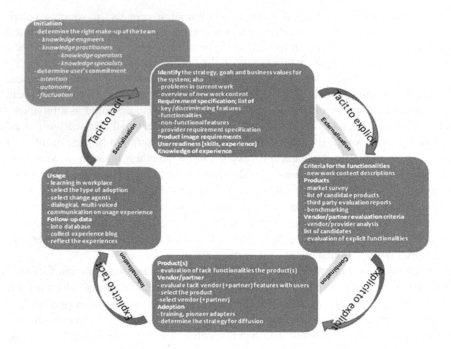

Fig. 1. Organizational Learning Based Model for ICT Acquisition (Rantapuska and Ihanainen 2008)

decision maker chooses to continue a specific action. The form can be divided into three categories (Allan and Mayer, 1997). 1) Affective commitment refers to the emotional orientation toward the target and its values for its own sake. This kind of commitment is related to intrinsic motivation, which keeps the actor to continue working because the work is enjoyable per sé. The affective commitment is suggested for the most desirable in software projects (Abrahamsson, 2002). 2) Continuance commitment refers to the profits and punishments related to the course of action when continuing or abandoning it. This type of commitment is based on extrinsic motivation, because the action is taken as an instrument for another target. The 3) Normative commitment refers to the internalised social pressure to act as to what is socially accepted. This type of commitment is based on the motivation to act in a way the individual considers is morally right. The three types of commitment are mutually inter-related. At least affective and normative commitments (Meyer J. P., Stanley D. J., Herscovitch L. and Topolnytsky L, 2001), are shown to correlate with each other.

3   Data Analysis

3.1   Project Summary

The sessions took place in the meeting room of the team members' working place. The team was quite busy with their daily work and did not have the time required for the project work between the sessions even if they worked in the same office. However, the team members participated very actively in the team sessions.

Session1 (socialization and externalization)

In the first session the BA presented himself as a support person for SME enterprises and the researcher as a participant observer. The researcher gave a short presentation about COSA. The general atmosphere was co-operative and the participants expressed a course of shared goals for the system. The issues of conversation stayed on the problems of the work and the future needs of the new system.

The sales people (SP1) talked the most. The sales are based on trust and personal visits. Many of the sales issues are not written down on paper. About 20-30 (10%) of the customers constitutes 80% of the total sales. However, the sales process is not a problem, but the order from the contractors. They use their own systems and the information is too often based on people who remember the exact needs of our customers. The whole customer process should be managed from our contractor to the delivery of the order to the customer. The company needs a CRM system solving the primary needs as: customer database, co-operation with sales and service and tasks management.

After some time of a diverse conversation the BA took a more active role by raising requests and wrapping up the conversation into a picture of the system as a whole. The project group made a list of needs concentrated mainly on the customer project management.

Session 2 (externalization)

The conversation in the next session brought up already raised, but also new requirements. The discussion took up issues in detailed and concrete terms. The BA's request about the needs went easily into a discussion about the existing problems related to the current system in use. The SP1 and SI talked more about the needs of the system whereas the SA and AA stressed the insufficient use of the existing system. The SA blamed the SPs for not entering their sales data into the existing system. For example, when the sales people discussed the importance of delivering sales information to administration, the SA noticed ironically "You don't do that".

After taking a more supervising role, the BA could draw a view about the system as a whole. The existing system was considered to be good, but insufficiently used.

Session 3 (externalization)

In the next session, the BA guided the conversation to wrap up requirements in a specification of the system. The sales process and project management were the main subjects of the discussion. The process should be managed from the customer's request to the expiration of the maintenance contract. The role of the existing system was pointed out as a hindrance by the SI. The discussion used concrete terms and dealt a lot with the insufficient use of existing systems.

Session 4 (externalization)

The focus was on the customer management and the future of their business in the coming few years. Concerning the state of the existing system, there are still major cancers waiting to be solved. The SI's department does not use the existing system. Before the team can go further the SI has to take up his position regarding the existing system, but he was not present. A concern was in the air that the SI is avoiding the sessions because he might think that the new system is a tool just for the sales people.

The further discussion dealt with the problems of the existing system and how the new CRM could be integrated into it. All the customer sales data should be in one place to which all others have access. The team members were quite confused and needed further knowledge about what to do next. One wish was to consult somebody in another company about how he uses the system in his work. The team had also got to know three candidate systems after the previous session. Still, they did not use the list of the requirements made in the previous session and therefore couldn't compare the candidates. However, the specification of the requirements was not yet ready and the discussion continued anyway. The task flow chart was also not completely understood and the service was missing in the chart. The researcher advised them to make a more concrete model about the desirable system by using more concrete elements like post-IT notes and pictures.

Session 5 (externalization)

The SI attended the session and the team could now discuss the state of the existing system and the role of service in it. The participants weighted the advantages and disadvantaged related to the existing system and a new one. There are big problems with the existing system, but replacing the system is risky and would cause a huge amount of extra work. The BA tried to lead the discussion to a decision, but without any success. More knowledge about the alternatives is also needed and the team does not "sit on coffers".

At the request of the BA, the researcher gave some advice about how to describe the system. The team restudied the requirements at the lead of the BA and researcher. The team was also instructed about how to use a weighted mean to compare the candidates according those requirements.

Session 6 (combination)

For this session both the project team and the student had prepared suggestion for the desired system. The team had two candidates: the first one extends the existing system with an integration of CRM and the second one replaces the existing system with the suggested system. The team preferred the first one. Still, the team did not use any explicit criteria and facts to substantiate the choice and they also didn't defend their choice with determination. The student also gave a short presentation about her investigation. Based on her observations in team sessions, she weighted the project management function in her choice. She came to a reasoned suggestion for a new system which was a different one than suggested by the team. The suggestion caused a long, but matter-of-fact discussion about the candidates. The team decided to choose two candidates for a use test. They also re-fixed the selection criteria.

Session 7 (combination)

For the final day, the team investigated three software candidates and prepared a suggestion. Two of the candidates had CRM functions, but not project management. The third one suggested by the student had project management, but not a good CRM. They used the list of requirements, which was also sent to the vendors one week before their company visit. The team was impressed on one easy-to-use CRM Software. They suggested that CRM Software, which can be extended with project management function later. The BA pointed out the importance of project management as it was stated in the earlier session. However, the team was inclined to recommend the selected software. The discussion moved on to weigh the importance and existence of the functionalities of the existing and candidate systems. Finally, the team, with the help of the BA came to the conclusion that the candidates should be tested once again. They can also use an independent IT adviser. The company concluded on acquiring the system suggested by the team.

3.2 Case Project Analysis

The initiation phase of the project was organized quite weakly. The project did not prepare itself for the change very much. The team members knew each other and they had already "experience about a project of this kind". At the start, the team did not show affective commitment towards the project. They did not talk very much about the importance of the project and nor did show any voluntary initiative of picking up the baton of new challenges. The only person (SP1) not present was chosen to be the project leader. Additionally, he was a new employee in the company.

The team members showed different attitudes and focuses towards the project depending on their job. The sales people (SP1) took a leading role in the requirement analysis and brought ideas for a better system. On the contrary, the SA and AA acted more as a practical voice against the SPs belief for the "definitive power of the new system" by focussing on the current problems. They felt excluded from customer projects, because of the lack of knowledge share and neglected use of existing systems. The SPs don't even enter the required data into the current system. However, the SA and AA had contradictory motives and commitments towards the project: On the one hand, acquisition of a new system directs attention from the real problems; on the other hand, participation in the project provides a chance to contribute to the new system as an equal participant. The first one shows continuance commitment to try to do the job whereas the latter indicates affective commitment. The user participation is regarded as important by the SP and SI as well. All informants also revealed normative commitment towards the project work. They see the importance of carrying the project through because "at least at this point, we have to believe in the project".

The conversation was business-oriented and avoided technical terms and software product names in this stage. The role and use of the existing system caused various statements and attitudes. It was quite difficult to see if the new system should replace the existing system in use. During the process of requirements analysis in the externalisation phase, the utterances showed mostly continuance commitment. This came up as practical and problem-oriented expressions linked to the requirements of the new system. This was true particularly among the SPs. The SA and AA were not that enthusiastic about the power of the new system. The discussion about current problems filled almost all the sessions from the start up to the final session.

It was also difficult for the participants to view the problems from a holistic viewpoint. This came up in the interviews and in practise when the team was expected to draw a total picture about the current and desired system. The participants were restricted to view the system from their own working context. They raised problems about their own information needs. Because the SPs were more talkative the issues of sales process were addressed more than the ones of administration. The issues in service were also addressed quite often by other members, but mostly in a form of criticism. The restricted view expressed itself also as reluctance to leave the existing system. The change is risky and there was not enough knowledge about the alternatives.

The team seemed to be reluctant to make decisions. When the discussion was calling for a decision to be made, the problem was usually postponed to the next session, even if the BA called for "reasoned and strong" decisions from the team. The team did not see themselves to have the power to make the selection. They saw the CEO as being in the background and making the final decision anyway. The BA was also seen as the representative of the CEO.

The team also had problems in the combination phase when the system candidates were expected to be evaluated. The team did not follow the earlier emphasises and evaluate the explicit functionalities of the candidate systems as was expected in COSA. The methods were used loosely and the evaluation was made more on impressions than rational reasoning.

4 Conclusions and Implications

The goal of the paper was to investigate how commitment develops when the users carry out the acquisition process of a new system by themselves. Another goal was to test how well COSA model works in that process.

The commitment developed during the COSA process and varied among team members. The team members were divided into two groups of commitment: The sales and service people saw the new system as a tool to make the work more efficient. The other group, the sales and administrative assistants stressed the importance of using the existing system more efficiently. Both groups showed continuance commitment for improving the working methods and saving costs. All the participants also showed normative commitment by attending meetings and believing in the project which was already started. However, the continuance commitment did not develop very fully during the project.

Problems rose regarding to skills and group interaction. In the working sessions, the team could do the externalisation phase professionally, but were engaged on the current work which also tied them to the existing system as well. The team could not create a general view about the system. This prolonged the externalisation phase and hampered objective conversation and decision making. The combination phase, in which the functionalities of the candidate software products were evaluated, caused problems as well. The team did not apply systematic methods and evaluation criteria in the selection. The final decision making was also a big challenge to the team.

This may originate from the above-mentioned factors but also from the key role of the owner-manager in decision making in SMEs (Reid 1981). The final phase of COSA model, the internalisation is not tested in the study because of the slower progression than expected in the study.

This study shows that users will have enough commitment towards selecting software for their own use. They are also capable of specifying their requirements in their work but the construction of requirements into a holistic system description needs an advisor. However, the advisor should be considered neutral and equal colleague in the eyes of the users. Based on the results the COSA model needs following modifications:

— The initiation and team building needs more time and attention. The team must get to know each other in a relaxed situation. The team must be motivated and empowered to take the responsibility about the system
— The COSA tasks should be modified focussing more on requirements speciation and less on tasks requiring systems thinking or general view about the system. When selecting a COTS software, the user requirements specification by business and user-oriented terms should be enough
— The COSA tasks should be defined clear and cleaned from references to the theoretical foundation of COSA

Despite the problems, the project was considered interesting, educational and challenging. They also felt ready to take the challenge, understand their responsibility and, when making the selection by themselves, also believed in using the system.

References

Abrahamsson, P., Iivari, N.: Commitment in Software Process Improvement – In Seach of the Process. In: Proceedings of the 35th Hawaii International Conference on Systems Sciences, HICSS-35 (2002)

Agarwal, R., Tanniru, M., Wilemon: Assimilating Information Technology Innovations: Strategies and Moderating Influences. IEEE Transactions on Engineering Management 44(4), 347–358 (1997)

Allen, N.J., Meyer, J.P.: The measurement and antecedents of affective, continuance and normative commitment to the organization. Journal of Occupational Psychology 63(1), 1–18 (1990)

Angle, H.L., Lawson, M.B.: Changes in affective and continuance commitment in times of relocation. Journal of Business Research 26(1), 3–15 (1993)

Brass, D.J.: Technology and the structuring of jobs: Employee satisfaction, performance, and influence. Organizational Behavior and Human Decision Processes 35(2), 216–240 (1985)

Brown, S.I., Duguid, P.: Knowledge and Organization: A Social Practice Perspective. Organization Science 12(2), 198–213 (2001)

Caldeira, M.M., Ward, J.M.: Using resource-based theory to interpret the successful adoption and use of information systems and technology in manufacturing small and medium-sized enterprises. European Journal of Information Systems Archive 12(2), 127–141 (2002)

Comella-Dorda, S., Dean, J., Morris, E., Oberndorf, P.: A Process for COTS Software Product Evaluation. In: Proceedings of the 1st International Conference on COTS-Based Software System, Orlando, FL, February 4-6, pp. 86–96 (2002)

Drucker, P.F.: Knowledge-Worker Productivity: The Biggest Challenge. California Management Review 41(2), 79–94 (1999)

Ferris, G.R., Hochwarter, W.A., Buckley, M.R., Harrell-Cook, G., Frink, D.D.: Human Resources Management: Some New Directions. Journal of Management 25(3), 385–415 (1999)

Fisher, C.D.: Why Do Lay People Believe That Satisfaction and Performance Are Correlated? Possible Sources of a Commonsense Theory. Journal of Organizational Behavior 24(6), 753–777 (2003)

Garcia, V.H.: Global Financial Services IT Spending in 2003: It Was the Best of Times, It Was the Worst of Times, Tower Group Research Notes, The TowerGroup, Inc. (February 2003)

Goulielmos, M., Paraskevi, A.: Outlining organisational failure in information systems development. Disaster Prevention and Management 12(4), 319–327 (2003)

Greene, C.N.: The Satisfaction-Performance Controversy. Engineering Management Review 7(3), 29–39 (1979)

Herzberg, F.: Work and the nature of man. World, Oxford, pp. xiv, 203 (1966)

Hochwarter, W.A., Perrewéb, P.L., Ferrisc, G.R., Brymer, R.A.: Job Satisfaction and Performance: The Moderating Effects of Value Attainment and Affective Disposition. Journal of Vocational Behavior 54(2), 296–313 (1999)

Lynne, M.: Technochange Management: Using IT to Drive Organizational Change. Journal of Information Technology 19, 4–20 (2004)

Lyytinen, K., Robey, D.: Learning failure in information systems development. Information Systems Journal 9(2), 85–101 (1999)

Marchand, D.A., Hykes, A.: Designed to fail: Why IT-enabled Business Projects Underachieve. IMD Perspectives for Managers 138 (2006)

Meyer, J.P., Allen, N.J.: Affective, Continuance, and Normative Commitment to the Organization: An Examination of Construct Validity. Journal of Vocational Behavior 49(3), 252–276 (1996)

Morisio, M., Torchiano, M.: Definition and Classification of COTS: A Proposal. In: Palazzi, B., Gravel, A. (eds.) ICCBSS 2002. LNCS, vol. 2255, pp. 165–175. Springer, Heidelberg (2002), doi:10.1007/3-540-45588-4_16

Meyer, J.P., Allen, N.J.: Commitment in the Workplace: Theory, Research and Applications. Sage Publications, California (1997)

Meyer, J.P., Stanley, D.J., Herscovitch, L., Topolnytsky, L.: Affective, Continuance, and Normative Commitment to the Organization: A Meta-analysis of Antecedents, Correlates, and Consequences. Journal of Vocational Behavior 61, 20–52 (2002), doi:10.1006/jvbe.2001.1842

Nonaka, I.: A Dynamic Theory of Organisational Knowledge Creation. Organisational Science 5(2), 14–37 (1994)

Nonaka, I., Takeuchi, H.: The knowledge-creating company - how Japanese companies create the dynamics of innovation. Oxford University Press, Oxford (1995)

Nonaka, I., Toyama, R., Konno, N.: SECI, Ba and leadership: a unified model of dynamic knowledge creation. Long Range Planning 33, 5–34 (2000)

Proudlock, M., Phelps, B., Gamble, P.: IT adoption strategies: Best practice guidelines for professional SMEs. Journal of Small Business and Enterprise Development 6(3) (1999)

Rantapuska, T., Ihanainen, O.: Acquiring Information Systems through Organisational Learning. In: Proceedings of the European Conference on Information Management and Evaluation (ECIME 2008), London, UK (2008)

Rantapuska, T., Ihanainen, O.: Use of Knowledge in ICT Investment Decision Making of SMEs. Journal of Enterprise Information Management 21(6), 585–596 (2008) ISSN: 1741-0398

Regoa, A., Cunha, M.P.: Authentizotic climates and employee happiness: Pathways to individual performance? Journal of Business Research 61(7), 739–752 (2008)

Reid, S.D.: The Decision-Maker and Export Entry and Expansion. Journal of International Business Studies 12(2), 101–112 (1981)

Richie, B., Brindley, C.: ICT adoption by SMEs: implications for relationships and management. New Technology, Work and Employment 20(3), 205–217 (2005)

Wasti, S.A.: Commitment profiles: Combinations of organizational commitment forms and job outcomes. Journal of Vocational Behavior 67(2), 290–308 (2005)

Williams, M.D., Williams, J.: A change management approach to evaluating ICT investment initiatives. Journal of Enterprise Information Management 20(1), 32–50 (2007)

Wright, T., Russel, C., Bonett, D.G.: The Moderating Role of Employee Positive Well Being on the Relation Between Job Satisfaction and Job Performance. Journal of Occupational Health Psychology 12(2), 93–104 (2007)

Part VI
Research in Progress and Practice

IT Governance Framework Adoption: Establishing Success Factors

Chadi Aoun[1], Savanid Vatanasakdakul[2], and Yang Chen[2]

[1] University of Technology Sydney, Australia
Chadi.Aoun@uts.edu.au
[2] Macquarie University, Australia
{Savanid.vatanasakdakul,yang.chen}@mq.edu.au

Abstract. The spectacular corporate collapses over the past decade, along with the introduction of the Sarbanes-Oxley Act and similar legislations across the world, have promoted significant awareness of IT governance. However, the causes of success and failure in IT governance framework adoption are yet to be adequately studied. This study aims to address this deficiency by proposing a research model to investigate factors influencing the success of IT governance adoption. The research model draws upon the information systems success model by Delone and McLean (2003) and the Technology-Organisation-Environment framework by Tomatzky and Fleisher (1990), to provide an integrated conceptual perspective for examining IT governance adoption and success.

Keywords: Australia, IS success model, IT governance, Organizational performance, Technology-Organisation-Environment framework, User satisfaction.

1 Introduction

Pressure from the Sarbanes-Oxley Act and similar legislations across the globe, along with the increase in business Information Technology (IT) investment, are pressuring top management to implement effective IT governance frameworks in order to comply with corporate governance goals and regulations (Brown et al. 2005; De Haes and Van Grembergen 2009). IT governance frameworks, such as the IT Infrastructure Library (ITIL), Control Objectives for Information and related Technologies (COBIT), and Information Technology-Code of Practice for Information Security Management (ISO 17799), are common frameworks adopted by organisations to ensure operational efficiency, decreased costs, and increased control of IT infrastructure, thereby achieving organisational goals through aligning IT and business (Iden and Langeland 2010; Wessels and Loggerenberg 2006). While there are various definitions to the term 'IT governance', this study adopts the definition suggested by the Information Technology Governance Institute, stating that "IT governance is the responsibility of the Board of Directors and executive management. It is an integral

M. Nüttgens et al. (Eds.): Governance and Sustainability in IS, IFIP AICT 366, pp. 239–248, 2011.

part of enterprise governance and consists of the leadership and organisational structures and processes to ensure that the organisation sustains and extends its strategy and objectives" (De Haes and Van Grembergen 2005, p.1).

However, despite the heralded benefits of IT governance to organisations, previous studies demonstrate that many firms are still struggling to implement and apply frameworks to their work environment (Pollard and Cater-Steel 2009). Approximately 80 percent of organisations in North America have not yet fully implemented IT governance frameworks and are yet to reap any benefits (Iden and Langeland 2010; Pollard and Cater-Steel 2009). Nevertheless, this is to attract significant IS research attention. Studies on IT governance are rare, with only a handful of papers investigating the ITIL adoption (Cater-Steel and Tan 2005; Hochstein et al. 2005). Such studies often identify various factors effecting IT governance, however, the relationships between these factors and user satisfaction or perceived organisational performance still require through consideration as they form crucial aspects of innovation adoption success (Delone and McLean 2003). This study aims to address these limitations by proposing a integrated research model to investigate factors influencing the success of IT governance framework adoption. The success factors influencing IT governance adoption are proposed via the established theoretical lens of Delone and McLean's Information Systems (IS) success model (2003) along with the Technology-Organisation-Environment (TOE) framework (Tomatzky and Fleisher 1990). The integration of these two frameworks will provide for a rich theoretical consideration of a wide range of contextual factors, and their potential influences on IT governance framework adoption success.

This paper is organised as follows: first, the development of the research model and hypotheses are presented and discussed; then, the paper concludes with direction for future research.

2   Theoretical Background

2.1   Delone and McLean: Information Systems Success Model

An assessment of IS success is critical to an organisation's understanding of the value and effectiveness of IS investment and management. Delone and McLean (1992, 2002, 2003) propose an influential framework for studying innovation adoption success. Their model is widely accepted among IS researchers (Bharati and Chaudhury 2004; Wang 2008). It was first presented in 1992 and updated in 2002 and 2003. The most recent iteration of the model consists of six dimensions, namely: information quality, system quality, service quality, use, user satisfaction and net benefits. Delone and McLean suggest that system quality, information quality, and service quality affect use and user satisfaction. In turn, both use and user satisfaction are direct antecedents of net benefits, which can be evaluated from individual and organisational impact.

This research model was used and validated by many IS researchers in various context. For example, the model was adopted to evaluate e-commerce and website success at an organisational level (Molla and Licker 2001; Wang 2008), and at an individual level (Liu and Arnett, 2000; Palmer 2002). Halawi et al. (2008) and

Kulkarni et al. (2006) adopted the model to investigate the success of knowledge management systems. However, the main limitation of the model is its consideration of a limited set of independent variables, which could be enriched and complemented by integrating it with the TOE framework.

2.2 Technology-Organisation-Environment Framework

Tomatzky and Fleischer (1990) developed the TOE framework to consider three aspects of innovation adoption, namely: technology, organisation and environment. The technological context refers to both internal and external technologies adopted by firms. The organisational context generally covers various aspects of characteristics and resources within firms, such as a firm's size, degree of centralisation, degree of formalisation, managerial structure and human resources. On the other hand, the environmental context refers to external pressures including size and structure of the industry, competition, macroeconomic milieu, dealings with government, and regulatory environment (Tornatzky and Fleisher 1990).

The TOE framework has also been adopted and examined by a number of IS researchers in various contexts of innovation adoption. The literature suggests that specific factors identified within its three dimensions can be varied across different contexts of study (e.g. Chang et al. 2007; Lee and Shum 2007; Zhu et al. 2006). Nonetheless, the framework has been proven as a sound theoretical basis and consistent empirical mechanism for IS research (Zhu et al. 2002). The next section presents the integrated research model as well as the development of hypotheses.

3 The Development of Research Model and Hypotheses

In addressing the research deficiencies identified above, we propose an integrated conceptual model for IT governance adoption success based on theoretical foundation of the IS success model by Delone and McLean (2003) and the TOE framework by Tomatzky and Fleisher (1990). The TOE framework is adopted because it comprehensively represents aspects that align with factors identified by previous research on ITIL adoption (Cater-Steel and Tan 2005; Hochstein et al. 2005; Iden and Langelan 2010). On the other hand, the IS success model of Delone and McLean allows the researchers to investigate the relationship between these identified factors and the perceptions of user satisfaction and organisational performance, in the context of IT governance framework adoption, which could be considered here as a type of innovation.

The proposed research model is presented in Figure 1. It is partially based on the IS success model, specifically user satisfaction and perceived net benefits to investigate IT governance adoption success at organisational level. The model posits eight predictors for IT governance adoption within the TOE framework. The identified factors in the technological context are ease of use and innovation compatibility. The organisational context includes top management support, availability of internal IT expertise and training; while competitive pressure, support from external vendors and consultants, and external pressures from government and industry are outlined in the environmental context. These factors are posited with user satisfaction and perceived benefits for hypotheses testing. The research model and research hypotheses are presented and discussed in the following sub-sections.

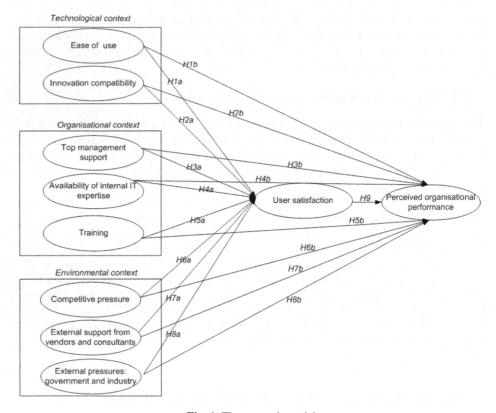

Fig. 1. The research model

3.1 Technological Context

Ease of Use

An innovation that is perceived as easy to use is more likely to be accepted by users (Davis 1989). Davis defines ease of use as the degree to which a particular system is perceived to be relatively free from operational effort (Davis 1989). Rogers (1983) asserts that a lack of perceived ease of use leads to resistance towards innovation adoption. This resistance in turn, may lead to lower user satisfaction. Such complex innovation may prevent employees from completing their tasks and this may lead to a reduction in benefits (or indeed a loss) due to innovation adoption (Bradford and Florin 2003). Here, the term users could refer to employees of a company adopting an IT governance framework. The following hypotheses are deduced:

H1a: Firms that perceive an IT governance framework as easy to use are likely to have high user satisfaction.
H1b: Firms that perceive an IT governance framework as easy to use are likely to have high perceived organisational performance.

Innovation Compatibility

Innovations introduced to a firm often require some degree of change or customisation to align with existing work environments and procedures. Implementing innovations that have a high degree of compatibility with a firm's environment are more likely to succeed (Fichman 2001; Kishore and McLean 2007). Innovation compatibility can therefore be viewed as "the degree to which an innovation is perceived as being consistent with the existing values, past experiences, and needs of the potential adopter" (Moore and Benbasat 1991, p.195). Similarly, if the firm perceives a good fit between an IT governance framework and its work environment, this may lead to success in IT governance framework adoption. The following hypotheses are therefore inferred:

H2a: Firms that perceive a good fit between an IT governance framework and their work environment are likely to have high user satisfaction.
H2b: Firms that perceive a good fit between an IT governance framework and their work environment are likely to have a high perception of organisational performance.

3.2 Organisational Context

Top Management Support

Support from top management is critical for successful information technology implementation. It is an essential factor contributing to employee satisfaction in innovation adoption (Bradford and Florin 2003; Purvis et al. 2001). Previous research indicate that that it is an important factor in successful ITIL adoption in the Australian context (Cater-Steel and Tan 2005; Pollard and Cater-Steel 2009). Thus, we hypothesise that:

H3a: IT governance framework adoption that has strong support from top management is likely to have high user satisfaction.
H3b: IT governance framework adoption that has strong support from top management is likely to have high perceived organisational performance.

Availability of Internal IT Expertise

Availability of internal IT expertise refers to the availability of a firm's personnel with relevant skills and experience to implement a selected technological innovation (Li et al. 2005), namely an IT governance framework in the context of this study. Previous studies point out that a higher availability of IT expertise correlate with a positive attitude and satisfaction in technology adoption (Bradford and Florin 2003; Chau and Tam 1997). Firms with in-house IT expertise tend to have greater control over the implementation and operation of systems, which may lead to relatively higher organisational performance. Thus, we hypothesise that:

H4a: Firms with internal expertise to support IT governance framework adoption are likely to have positive user satisfaction.

H4b: Firms with internal expertise to support IT governance framework adoption are likely to have positive perceived organisational performance.

Training

Training has been proven as an effective means to enhance employee productivity, which in turn contributes to higher organisational performance (Huselid 1995; Black and Lynch 1996). Igbaria et al. (1995) point out that having an adequate training program is likely to increase users' confidence and ability to use an innovation successfully and reduce resistance. Research conducted by Pollard and Cater-Steel (2009) found that training and staff awareness are important to ITIL adoption. Consequently, the following hypotheses are proposed:

H5a: IT governance framework adoption training will lead to a positive impact on user satisfaction.

H5b: IT governance framework adoption training will lead to a positive impact on perceived organisational performance.

3.3 Environmental Context

Competitive Pressure

Competitive pressure is recognised as an external driving force for technological innovation adoption (Bradford and Florin 2003). Zhu et al. (2002, p.340) refer to competitive pressure as "the degree of pressure from competitors, which is an external power pressing a firm to adopt new technology in order to avoid competitive decline". Firms that are under competitive pressure may find a need to match or outperform their competitors in innovation adoption in order to maintain their viability. Such innovation may be viewed by employees as essential. Based on this, the following hypotheses are posited:

H6a: Firms whose competitors adopted an IT governance framework are likely to have positive user satisfaction in IT governance framework adoption.

H6b: Firms whose competitors adopted an IT governance framework are likely to have positive perceived organisational performance due to IT governance framework adoption.

External Support from Vendors and Consultants

The availability of external expertise to expedite the implementation process and help organisations recognise industry best practice is deemed critical to innovation implementation success (Tasi et al. 2011). External support refers to the availability of expert support from vendors and consultants. Such support can contribute to implementation and post-implementation success by providing continuous assistance, such as system maintenance and system updates, to maintain system efficiency and effectiveness, and thus sustain the benefits of innovation adoption (Li et al. 2005). Consequently, this study hypothesises:

H7a: Firms with accessible external support from vendors and consultants are likely to have positive user satisfaction in their IT governance framework adoption.

H7b: Firms with accessible external support from vendors and consultants are likely to have positive perceived organisational performance due to their IT governance framework adoption.

External Pressures from Government and Industry

Firms may face pressures from government (in the form of legislation) and industry (in the form of standards and benchmarks) to adopt IT governance frameworks. A study conducted by Cater-Steel et al. (2009) found that coercive pressure from legislation could influence the adoption of ITIL among Australia firms. Employees may feel eager to meet such stipulated benchmarks or legal obligations meant to improve performance. Therefore, this study hypothesises:

H8a: Firms facing external pressure from Government and Industry to adopt IT governance frameworks are likely to have positive user satisfaction.

H8b: Firms facing external pressure from Government and Industry to adopt IT governance frameworks are likely to have positive perceived organisation performance.

User Satisfaction and Organisational Performance

As proposed by Delone and McLean (2003), user satisfaction in technology adoption may have a direct influence on perceived organisational performance. Similarly, we posit that:

H9: Firms with overall user satisfaction due to IT governance framework adoption are likely to have positive perceived organisational performance.

4 Conclusion and Future Research

This paper proposes an integrated research model to investigate factors influencing the success of IT governance framework adoption. In addressing the research objective, the research model proposed integrates Delone and McLean's IS success model and the TOE framework. Consequently, the model provides researchers with the means to broadly assess IT governance adoption through the lens of user satisfaction and perceived organisational performance.

Empirical data for our study was collected through survey questionnaires with Australian companies that have implemented IT governance frameworks. This is worthwhile noting, as Australia is considered a leading nation in regulating IT governance standards (Cater-Steel and Tan 2005). While the findings from our study will be reported in future publications, we encourage IS researchers to consider IT governance in their research, given its significance to industry and its global implications.

References

Bharati, P., Chaudhury, A.: An Empirical Investigation of Decision-Making Satisfaction in Web-Based Decision Support Systems. Decision Support Systems 37(2), 187–197 (2004)

Bradford, M., Florin, J.: Examining the Role of Innovation Diffusion Factors on the Implementation Success of Enterprise Resource Planning Systems. International Journal of Accounting Information Systems 4, 205–225 (2003)

Brown, A.E., Grant, G.G.: Framing the Frameworks: A Review of IT Governance Research. Communications of the Association for Information Systems 15, 696–712 (2005)

Cater-Steel, A., Tan, W.-G.: Implementation of IT Infrastructure library (ITIL) in Australia: Progress and Success Factors, paper presented to IT Governance International Conference Auckland, New Zealand (2005)

Cater-Steel, A., Tan, W.-G., Toleman, M.: Using Institutionalism as a Lens to Examine ITIL Adoption and Diffusion. In: 20th Australasian Conference on Information Systems, Melbourne, Australia (2009)

Chang, I.-C., Hwang, H.-G., Hung, M.-C., Lin, M.-H., Yen, D.C.: Factors Affecting the Adoption of Electronic Signature: Executives Perspective of Hospital Information Department. Decision Support Systems 44(1), 350–359 (2007)

Chau, P.Y.K., Tam, K.Y.: 'Factors Affecting the Adoption of Open Systems: An Exploratory Study'. MIS Quarterly 21(1), 1–24 (1997)

Chin, W.W.: Issues and Opinion on Structural Equation Modeling. Management Information Systems Quarterly 22(1) (1998)

Davis, F.D.: Perceived Usefulness, Perceived Ease of Use, and User Acceptance of Information Technology. MIS Quarterly 13(3), 319–340 (1989)

De Haes, S., Van Grembergen, W.: IT Governance Structures, Processes and Relational Mechanisms: Achieving IT/Business Alignment in a Major Belgian Financial Group. In: Proceedings of the 38th Hawaii International Conference on System Sciences, Big Island, Hawaii, USA (2005)

De Haes, S., Van Grembergen, W.: An Exploratory Study into IT Governance Implementations and its Impact on Business/IT Alignment. Information Systems Management 26, 123–137 (2009)

Delone, W.H., McLean, E.R.: Information Systems Success: The Quest for the Dependent Variable. Information Systems Reserach 3(1), 60–95 (1992)

Delone, W.H., McLean, E.R.: Information Systems Success Revisited. In: Proceedings of the 35th Hawaii International Conference on System Sciences, Big Island, Hawaii, USA (2002)

Delone, W.H., McLean, E.R.: The Delone and Mclean Model of Information Systems Success: A Ten-Year Update. Journal of Management Information Systems 19(4), 9–30 (2003)

Fichman, R.G.: The Role of Aggregation in the Measurement of IT-Related Organizational Innovation. MIS Quarterly 25(4), 427–455 (2001)

Halawi, L.A., McCarthy, R.V., Aronson, J.E.: An Empirical Investigation of Knowledge Management Systems Success. Journal of Computer Information Systems (JCIS), 121–135 (2008)

Hochstein, A., Tamm, G., Brenner, W.: Service-Oriented IT Management: Benefit, Cost and Success Factors. In: European Conference on Information Systems, Regensburg, Germany (2005)

Huselid, M.A.: The Impact of Human Resource Management Practices on Turnover, Productivity, and Corporate Financial Performance. Academy of Management Journal 38(3), 635–672 (1995)

Iden, J.: Implementing IT Service Management: Lessons Learned From a University IT Department. In: Cater-Steel, A. (ed.) Information Technology Governance and Service Management: Frameworks and Adaptations, Hershey, pp. 333–349 (2009)

Iden, J., Langeland, L.: Setting the Stage for a Successful ITIL Adoption: A Delphi Study of IT Experts in the Norwegian Armed Forces. Information Systems Management 27(2), 103–112 (2010)

Igbaria, M., Guimaraes, T., Davis, G.B.: Testing the Determinants of Microcomputer Usage via a Structural Equation Model. Journal of Management Information Systems 11(4), 87–114 (1995)

Kishore, R., McLean, E.R.: Reconceptualizing Innovation Compatibility as Organisaitonal Alignment in Secondary IT Adoption Contexts: An Investigation of Software Reuse Infusion. IEEE Transactions on Engineering Management 54(4) (2007)

Kraatz, M.S., Zajac, E.J.: Exploring the Limits of the New Institutionalism: the Causes and Consequences of Illegitimate Organisational Change. American Sociological Review 61, 812–836 (1996)

Kulkarni, U.R., Ravindran, S., Freeze, R.: A Knowledge Management Success Model:Theoretical Development and Empirical Validation. Journal of Management Information Systems 23(3), 309–347 (2006)

Lee, C.-P., Shim, J.P.: An Exploratory Study of Radio Frequency Identification (RFID) Adoption in the Healthcare Industry. European Journal of Information Systems 16, 712–724 (2007)

Li, Y., Tan, C.-H., Teo, H.-H., Siow, A.: A Human Capital Perspective of Organizational Intention to Adopt Open Source Software. In: Proceedings of International Conference on Information Systems 2005, pp. 11–14 (2005)

Lipovatz, D., Stenos, F., Vaka, A.: Implementation of ISO 9000 Quality Systems in Greek Enterprises. International Journal of Quality & Reliability Management 16(6), 534–551 (1999)

Liu, C., Arnett, K.P.: Eploring the Factors Associated with Web Site Success in the Context of Electronic Commerce. Information and Management 38, 23–33 (2000)

Molla, A., Licker, P.S.: E-Commerce Systems Success: An Attempt to Extend and Respecify the Delone and Maclean Model of IS Success. Journal Electronic Commerce Research 2(4), 131–141 (2001)

Moore, G.C., Benbasat, I.: Development of an Instrument to Measure the Perception of Adoption an Information Technology Innovation. Information Systems Research 2(3) (1991)

Palmer, J.W.: Web Site Usability, Design, and Performance Metrics. Information Systems Research 13(2), 151 (2002)

Pollard, C., Cater-Steel, A.: Justifications, Strategies, and Critical Success Factors in Successful ITIL Implementations in U.S. and Australian Companies: An Exploratory Study. Information Systems Management 26(2), 164–175 (2009)

Purvis, R.L., Sambamurthy, V., Zmud, R.W.: The Assimilation of Knowledge Platforms in Organisations: An Empirical Investigation. Organisation Science 12(2), 117–135 (2001)

Rogers, E.M.: Diffusion of Innovations, 3rd edn. Free Press, New York (1983)

Tornatzky, L.G., Fleischer, M.: The Process of Technological Innovation. Lexington Books, New York (1990)

Tsai, W.-H., Shaw, M.J., Fan, Y.-W., Liu, J.-Y., Lee, K.-C., Chen, H.-C.: An Empirical Investigation of the Impacts of Internal/External Facilitators on the Project Success of ERP: A Structural Equation Model. Decision Support Systems 50(2), 480–490 (2011)

Wang, Y.-S.: Assessing E-Commerce Systems Success: A Respecification and Validation of the DeLone and McLean Model of IS Success. Information Systems Journal 18, 529–557 (2008)

Wessels, E., Loggerenberg, J.V.: IT Governance: Theory and Practice. In: Proceedings of the Conference on Information Technology in Tertiary Education, Pretoria, South Africa (2006)

Zhu, K., Kraemer, K.L., Xu, S.: A Cross-Country Study of Electronic Business Adoption Using the Technology-Organisation-Environment Framework. In: Proceedings of International Conference on Information Systems 2002, Barcelona (2002)

Zhu, K., Kraemer, K.L., Xu, S.: The Process of Innovation Assimilation by Firms in Different Countries: A Technology Diffusion Perspective on E-Business. Management Science 52(10), 1557–1576 (2006)

Zhu, Q., Sarkis, J.: The Moderating Effects of Institutional Pressures on Emergent Green Supply Chain Practices and Performance. International Journal of Production Research 45(18-19), 4333–4355 (2007)

A Service Oriented Method for Health Care Network Governance

Hannes Schlieter[1], Stephan Bögel[2], and Werner Esswein[1]

[1] TU Dresden, Münchener Platz, Schumann-Bau, 01062 Dresden, Germany
Tel.: +49 (0)351 463-32173, +49 351 463-37671
{Hannes.Schlieter,Werner.Esswein}@tu-dresden.de
[2] Virtimo AG, Schlesische Str. 29-30, 10997 Berlin, Germany
Tel.: +49 (0) 30 609 225 56
Boegel@virtimo.de

Abstract. Governance and compliance of health care networks gain more and more attention in the IS research. The configuration of medical care workflow systems and the compliance check of care processes according to national and international guidelines is the motivation for this paper. We are following a process model based approach for the management of health care networks. We present a service-based method for the compliance check of process models and enable a configuration of information systems with process models. The application of the method as well as the discussion of the practical benefits is illustrated by a real world case.

Keywords: Conceptual Models, Vertical Integration, Conflict Management, Health Care Network, Service-oriented method, Care process compliance.

1 Introduction

1.1 Situation

A major problem in the health care sector is to improve the medical care and at the same time reduce costs. To improve the medical care Clinical Practice Guidelines (CPGs) and Clinical Pathways (CPs) are used to communicate best practices and to establish a standard care quality. CPGs provide decision guidance for health care provider that is based on evident practice for specific indications (diseases). CPs describe clinical processes for a specific diagnosis that is adapted to the local situation, e.g. in a specific hospital. CPGs are typically released by national or international medical associations like the European Stroke Association. CPs are created by the medical care provider according to their local processes.

1.2 Conceptual Models in the Health-Care Sector

Conceptual modeling is used in CPGs and CPs to standardize and communicate clinical processes (Schlieter & Esswein 2010; Wollersheim et al. 2005). A conceptual modeling language is the combination of a technical language with a modeling

M. Nüttgens et al. (Eds.): Governance and Sustainability in IS, IFIP AICT 366, pp. 249–258, 2011.

grammar, and results in the creation of conceptual models. Hence, the conceptual model comprises formal-structural representation and non-formal content (Frank 1999). Conceptual models are an accepted instrument to describe organizations in its various aspects such as structures and behavior.

In health care domain different models are constructed simultaneously for same indication by different groups of interests. These models are complementary and in relation but are not totally equal. We call this set of models "model landscape" and their implicit relation "hidden relation". The integration of CPGs and CPs is demanded in the literature but has not been completely realized (Wollersheim et al. 2005). Process compliance in clinical context becomes more and more important in a competitive health care market. Firstly, compliant CP can be used as an instrument to implement evident medical knowledge in organization. Secondly, they build a basis for continuous process improvement and measurement. CPGs could thus be used to govern the right implementation of CPs in practice. The CPGs are the regulatory element for the governance of clinical processes. To the extent of our knowledge there are no holistic approaches that provide the alignment or integration between CPG and CP models.

To illustrate the context of the present situation in a "big picture", we want to introduce the life cycle of the medical care processes (see figure 1). The life cycle can be divided into three phases or layers. Starting point is the model landscape in the first phase where models are isolated and inconsistent. With the help of the proposed method, the models are vertically integrated. The integration on the model layer is the prerequisite for the next two phases. On the organizational layer in phase 2 the result of the model integration is used to guide the compliance implementation. To be compliant with the guidelines operational procedures and organizational structures have to be adjusted. On the technical layer the hospital information systems is configured using the integrated models to support the execution of the medical care processes.

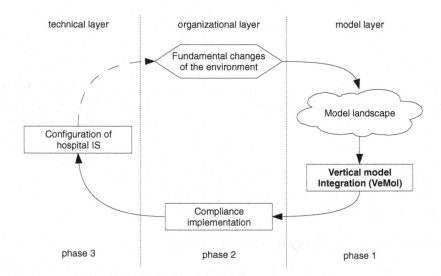

Fig. 1. The Life Cycle of Medical Care Processes

The life cycle starts, if the environment fundamentally changes, e.g. due to new laws. Because of the exceptional relevance of the model layer for the organizational and technical layer this research in progress paper focuses on the first step, i.e. the integration of these models. In this paper we aim to present the research goal and a proposal for a way to achieve the vertical model integration. Our research should build the linking element between those studies which demand a consideration of the CPGs while CPs development (Lelgemann & Ollenschläger 2006; Schnabel et al. 2003) and are dealing with discussion to transfer the CPG content in the formal – machine-readable – syntax (Seyfang & Miksch 2007; Peleg et al. 2003).

1.3 Research Method and Outline

The research can be assigned to the field of design science (Hevner et al. 2004; Peffers et al. 2007). Knowledge is gained hereby the creation and evaluation of artifacts in the form of languages, models, methods or systems. The investigation aims for the usefulness of the constructing artifact in the sense of a problem solution. We use a case scenario to make the requirements analysis and evaluate our artifact. In a descriptive case study (Yin 2003) we examine the situation of Stroke Network Saxony (SOS-NET).

In the first part of the paper, the theoretical foundations of integration conflicts are discussed shortly. Afterwards we examine the situation of the case scenario and derive requirements for a vertical model integration method. The paper finishes with the proposal for a vertical model integration method (VeMoI) and an outlook on further research.

2   Theoretical Foundations

2.1 Vertical vs. Horizontal Model Integration

In the context of model integration vertical and horizontal integration of model layers needs to be distinguished (Bögel and Esswein 2010). We speak of vertical integration if the integrated model layers concern the same part of the universe of discourse, but differ in the viewpoint. If we look on CPGs, the universe of discourse is a specific disease, while the viewpoint is the evident guideline viewpoint on this specific disease. For a corresponding CP, the universe of discourse is the same disease, but the viewpoint is that of a specific process in a certain hospital.

In contrast, the horizontal integration of two models on the same layer, differ in the universe of discourse but have the same viewpoint. Heterogeneity in vertical integration is therefore a result of different viewpoints.

2.2 Integration Conflicts

The heterogeneity of models leads to integration conflicts between those models. Diverse classifications of integration conflicts can be found in the literature. A common classification distinguishes type, structural and name conflicts (Pfeiffer and Gehlert 2005; Pfeiffer and Becker 2008; Rosemann 2002; Hars 1994). If a part of the real world is modeled semantically different in two models this is denominated as structural or semantic conflict (Pfeiffer and Gehlert 2005). These can further be distinguished as dependency conflicts, abstraction conflicts and level of detail (Kashyap and Sheth 1996).

Dijkman (2008) considers the horizontal integration of similar process models. He differentiates authorization, activity and control-flow conflicts. Weidlich et al. (2009) extend the list by process and data conflicts. Those conflicts relate to constructs of a modeling language. Others like (Pfeiffer and Becker 2008) are differentiating homonym, abstraction, separation, type, synonym, annotation and control-flow conflicts.

Table 1. Overview of Integration Conflicts

	Domain language	Modeling Language	Solutions
Syntax	Name conflict (homonym conflict, synonym conflict)	Type conflict	Ontologies, syntactical model comparison
Semantics	-	Authorization conflict, Activity conflict, Process conflict, Data conflict, Dependency conflict, Abstraction conflict, Level of detail conflict, Annotation conflict, Control-flow conflict, Order conflict, Separation conflict	VeMoI
Pragmatics	-	-	-

We consolidate these classifications according to table 1. The previously mentioned conflicts relate either to symbols of the domain languages or to concepts of modeling languages.

In the dimension of semiotics, the conflicts can be classified by looking at their occurrence. Name and type conflicts can be identified at the level of the syntax (for example, through the comparison of strings or two type identifiers). All the other conflicts mentioned (Dijkman 2008; Pfeiffer and Becker 2008) can only be detected by looking at the semantic layer. No conflicts could be found on the pragmatic layer. The mapping between syntax and semantics is an on-going process executed by human beings. Humans use symbols corresponding to his or her intentions and therefore constitute semantics (Holenstein 1982; Wittgenstein 1922). As a consequence, for the solution of these conflicts, the next semiotic level has to be considered.

3   Case Study

In industrialized countries, the stroke is the third major cause of death and the most frequent reason of lasting physical handicaps (Kolominsky-Rabas et al. 2006). In acute stroke care, the capabilities of therapy worsen with each minute the stroke is not diagnosed and treated accordingly. An immediate medical intervention is necessary to avoid consequential damage.

This is especially important for radiological findings. Further characteristics for an acute stroke are short delay for decision-making, limited local transfer possibility and symptoms that are difficulty diagnosed. In 2007, the SOS-NET was founded to build a telemedical infrastructure for regional stroke care. The goal of the network is to treat all stroke patients consitently and independently from distance to next stroke expert over the whole region. Within two years the SOS-NET is growing to an important stroke care network in Saxony (Germany).

Presently, there are fourteen hospitals participating in the network. 580 telemedical consultations were carried out in 2009. The suspicion of stroke was confirmed in 79% of the telemedical presented patients. 89 lyses-therapies were indicated. If the indication can be done at early stage, this therapy allows an almost complete rehabilitation of special stroke cases.

The different suspension of employees and the differences of the technical infrastructure necessitate a defined responsibilities and process within the network. The stroke center as the core of network allocates CPGs for the partners of the network (stroke units) to assure a network-wide high standard clinical care.

In figure 2, the situation is depicted in which the models interrelate. The framework shows three different and initially independent model layers. On the topmost layer professional associations and local experts create (CPG). CPs are located on the middle layer and are used by the hospital staff. The hospital information system (HIS) is shown on the bottom layer. Typically, on the technical layer, the HIS could be configured by workflow models via a XML-Transformation. The care process life cycle (see figure 1) is referenced through the different phases. In phase 1 the clinical pathways are checked against the appropriate CPG. The compliant models are than used to implement the organizational structures and in phase 3 to configure the hospital information system.

The integration of the layers delivers great potential to improve the recommendations themselves and thus the quality of clinical care. The following cases reflect the main goals of integration in the SOS-NET:

Case 1: Compliance check: The vertical integration makes a check of models concerning superordinate layer possible. The models are compliant, if all necessary advises are considered in the underling layer. Compliance should guarantee that the goals of care are reached as it is defined in the subordinate layer. Compliance is no structural or syntactical conformity. It depends largely on the content wise correspondence.

Case 2: Context sensitive help: If a link between the different layers exists, user can track where information come from. They can also get further information for special steps of the treatment or clinical decisions.

Case 3: Support of business-process-reengineering (BPR): In BPR it is necessary to know the current situation of the processes and the limits of BPR. The integration model could help to determine the flexibility for the restructure. On the other, the integration could help to identify weak parts in the processes.

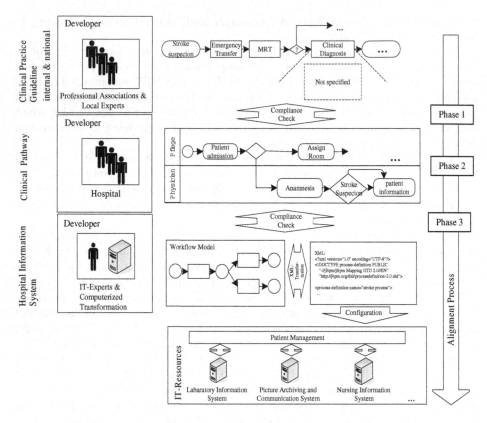

Fig. 2. Framework for medical care processes

4 Requirement Analysis

In this section, we want to present the results of our requirements analysis (figure 3). The analysis was done with the i*- (i-star)-framework. It provides a method to structure relations of actors and their influence to goals, to describe decompositions as well as means-ends-relation between tasks and resources which are necessary to achieve the (soft)goal(s) (Yu 2009). The starting point of the analysis is the goal to treat patient with the "Best Clinical Care". From this main goal, the goal of the evidence-based utilization of CP depends. This means integration between CPGs and CPs is needed.

Kaveh et al. showed that CPG are permanent under revision (Kaveh et al. 2007). Since CP guide evident clinical care, they need to be up-to-date against the CPG which was supported by the integration. Further the integration would encourage a context sensitive help in business-workflow as well as business-process-reengineering projects. To achieve these goals, a method would help to reconstruct the inherent relationships between the models. This can only be done with the knowledge about the conflicts ("conflict identification"). To allow a successful application of the method, a procedure model should document the main steps of the method.

Supporting techniques and heuristics are necessary for the automated and non-automated parts of the method. The case study shows that various modeling languages are used to describe clinical recommendations. Thus the method should be applied to various modeling languages.

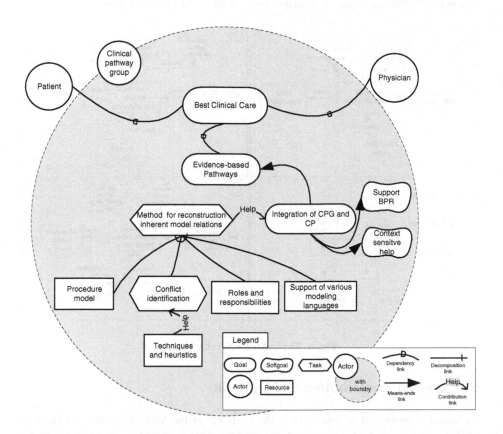

Fig. 3. Summary of the requirements (i*-model)

5 Intermediary Results – VEMOI

We want to introduce a service-oriented method based on the following considerations. First the health care network requires a distributed architecture. Second we gain flexibility in the orchestration of the services so we can integrate preliminary work, e.g. the integration of ontologies for the resolving of name conflicts. We can also change non-automated steps with automated steps, if such a service is available. A hospital or care network may also decide to outsource certain services like the classification step. In summary, our procedure model is described by orchestrating services and not by modeling a process diagram. Following this approach a method fragment is represented by a service. In Figure 4 three services: "classification", "anchor identification" and "domain conflict identification" and their orchestration are depicted. These step lead to the reconstruction of the inherent model relations. The central element of our approach "VeMoI" is the anchor model, which allows to represent inter-model relations as well as possible conflict situations. It guides also the participators of integration project to find and to eliminate conflict situations.

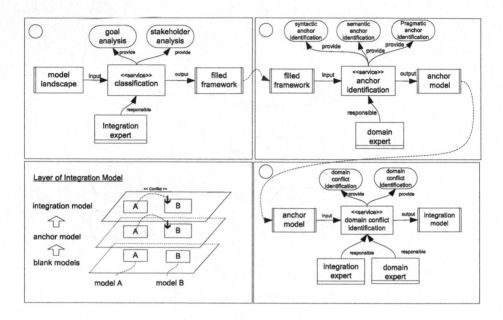

Fig. 4. The VeMoI – Service Model

6   Expected Contribution and Outlook

Expected contribution of this work is the proposal of the VeMoI method for the vertical integration of medical care process models. This is an important prerequisite for the organizational compliance implementation and the model-based configuration of the hospital information system. With this method we want to design a domain language based approach for conflict handling in heterogeneous model landscapes.

The identified domain conflicts should allow compliance checks against the CPG. The process of identifying conflicts also should shows relations between two models that hopefully can be used for context sensitive enrichment of the medical care process models. As a third use case the relations and domain conflicts might be used for business process reengineering. The enriched process models probably allow the identification of reengineering potential.

Next steps our research are the finalization of the integration method and its evaluation in the context of a greater case study inside the stroke and a cancer network.

References

Batini, C., Lenzerini, M., Navathe, S.B.: A comparative analysis of methodologies for database schema integration. ACM Computing Surveys (CSUR) 18(4), 364 (1986)

Beimborn, D., et al.: Die Bedeutung des Alignment von IT und Fachressourcen in Finanzprozessen Eine empirische Untersuchung. Wirtschaftsinformatik 48(5), 331–339 (2006)

Pfeiffer, D., Becker, J.: Solving the conflicts of distributed process modelling - towards an integrated approach. In: Proceedings of the 16th European Conference on Information Systems (ECIS 2008), Galway, Ireland (2008)

Dijkman, R.: Diagnosing differences between business process models. In: Dumas, M., Reichert, M., Shan, M.-C. (eds.) BPM 2008. LNCS, vol. 5240, pp. 261–277. Springer, Heidelberg (2008)

Frank, U.: Conceptual modelling as the core of the information systems discipline-perspectives and epistemological challenges. In: Proceedings of the Fifth Americas Conference on Information Systems (AMCIS 1999), pp. 13–15 (August 1999)

Hars, A.: Referenzdatenmodelle. Gabler, Wiesbaden (1994)

Hevner, A.R., et al.: Design science in information systems research. Management Information Systems Quarterly 28(1), 75–106 (2004)

Holenstein, E.: On the cognitive underpinnings of language. Semiotica 41(1-4), 107–134 (1982)

Kashyap, V., Sheth, A.: Semantic and schematic similarities between database objects: a context-based approach. The VLDB Journal 5(4), 276–304 (1996)

Katona, G.: Psychologie der Relationserfassung und des Vergleichens, Johann Ambrosius Barth (1924)

Kaveh, D., et al.: How quickly do systematic reviews go out of date? A Survival Analysis. Anal. of Internal Medicine 147(4), 224–233 (2007)

Kolominsky-Rabas, P.L., et al.: Lifetime Cost of Ischemic Stroke in Germany: Results and National Projections From a Population-Based Stroke Registry: The Erlangen Stroke Project. Stroke 37(5), 1179–1183 (2006)

Lelgemann, M., Ollenschläger, G.: Evidenzbasierte Leitlinien und Behandlungspfade. Der Internist 47(7), 690–698 (2006)

Mertens, P.: Die zwischenbetriebliche Kooperation und Integration bei der automatisierten Datenverarbeitung. Hain, Meisenheim am Glan (1966)

Peffers, K., et al.: A Design Science Research Methodology for Information Systems Research. Journal of Management Information Systems 24(3), 45–77 (2007)

Peleg, M., et al.: Comparing Computer-interpretable Guideline Models: A Case-study Approach. Journal of the American Medical Informatics Association 10(1), 52–68 (2003)

Pfeiffer, D., Becker, J.: Semantic business process analysis: building block-based construction of automatically analyzable business process models, Westfälische Wilhelms-Universität (2008)

Pfeiffer, D., Gehlert, A.: A framework for comparing conceptual models. In: Proceedings of the Workshop on Enterprise Modelling and Information Systems Architectures (EMISA 2005), pp. 108–122 (2005)

Rosemann, M.: Komplexitätsmanagement in Prozeßmodellen. Gabler, Wiesbaden (2002)

Rotter, T., et al.: A systematic review and meta-analysis of the effects of clinical pathways on length of stay, hospital costs and patient outcomes. BMC Health Services Research 8(1), 265 (2008)

Schlieter, H., Esswein, W.: From Clinical Practice Guideline to Clinical Pathway - Issues of Reference Model-Based Approach. In: Camarinha-Matos, L.M., Boucher, X., Afsarmanesh, H. (eds.) PRO-VE 2010. IFIP AICT, vol. 336, pp. 251–258. Springer, Heidelberg (2010)

Schnabel, M., et al.: Von der Leitlinie zum Behandlungspfad. Der Chirurg 74(12), 1156–1166 (2003)

Seyfang, A., Miksch, S.: Modelling Diagnosis and Treatment. International Journal of Clinical Monitoring and Computing 1 (2007)

Sinz, E.J.: Architektur von Informationssystemen. In: Rechenberg, P., Pomberger, G. (eds.) Informatik-Handbuch, pp. 1035–1046. Hanser, München (1999)

Wittgenstein, L.: Tractatus logico-philosophicus: philosophische Untersuchungen. Reclam-Verlag, Leipzig (1922)

Wollersheim, H., Burgers, J., Grol, R.: Clinical guidelines to improve patient care. The Netherlands Journal of Medicine 63(6), 188–192 (2005)

Yin, R.K.: Applications of case study research. SAGE, London (2003)

Yu, E.: i* an agent oriented modeling framework, Toronto (2011),
    http://www.cs.toronto.edu/km/istar/ (download: 16.04.2011)

Modeling and Analysis of Business Process Compliance

Jörg Becker[1], Christoph Ahrendt[1], André Coners[2],
Burkhard Weiß[1], and Axel Winkelmann[1]

[1] University of Muenster, ERCIS – European Research Center for Information Systems,
Leonardo-Campus 3, 48149 Muenster, Germany
Tel.: +49 (0) 251 83 38100, +49 (0) 251 83 38100,
+49 (0) 251 83 38089, +49 (0) 251 83 38086
{joerg.becker,burkhard.weiss,axel.
winkelmann}@ercis.uni-muenster.de, chris.a@uni-muenster.de
[2] Fachhochschule Südwestfalen, Haldener Str. 182, 58095 Hagen
Tel.: +49 (0) 2331 9330 717
coners@fh-swf.de

Abstract. Managing business process compliance is a highly important topic in the financial sector. Various scandals and last but not least the financial crisis have caused many new constraints and legal regulations that banks and financial institutions need to face. Based on a domain-specific semantic business process modeling notation, we propose a new approach to modeling and analysis of business process compliance through the use of compliance building block patterns and business rules. These business process compliance patterns and rules serve as a necessary basis for the automatic identification of compliance issues in existing processes (process models) and hence for managing business process compliance in the financial sector.

Keywords: Compliance, Business Process Modeling, Business Process Management, Governance, Finance.

1 Introduction

Although no general understanding of "compliance" exists, it can be understood as conforming to a rule such as a specification, a policy or a standardized procedure. In this context, "Business Process Compliance" (BPC) management is a new research field that addresses the coordination of business process management (BPM) and compliance (Rinderle et al. 2008). Regulations and laws force service companies to ensure compliant business processes (Basel Committee on Banking Supervision 2004). We therefore address business compliance rules for banks in this article because the automatic identification and analysis of financial sector processes, with regard to their alignment, with new compliance requirements, is still an unsolved problem.

Huge efforts are being spent on the actual modeling of business processes, but justified benefits in the analysis and usage of process models are rare (Becker et al. 2010d). It turns out that automated analysis of process models is hardly possible with

M. Nüttgens et al. (Eds.): Governance and Sustainability in IS, IFIP AICT 366, pp. 259–269, 2011.

standard business process modeling languages. Nevertheless, this is especially desirable, since many regulations have to be considered and new regulations require an ongoing analysis of business processes.

Hence, this paper aims at formalizing compliance-related business rules in a semantic way that is easily understood by compliance experts, while at the same time enabling banks to automatically check for these business rules in semantic business process models. We do this by proposing a business rule-based extension of SBPML, a semantic business process modeling notation that was developed specifically for the financial sector and represents an intuitive modeling approach for non-BPM experts (Becker et al. 2009; Becker et al. 2010b; Becker et al. 2010c; Becker et al. 2010e).

2   State of the Art in Modeling and Analysis of Business Process Compliance

In Information Systems Research, business rules are considered as self-contained scientific objects (Herbst and Knolmayer 1995). The core elements of the business rules approach have been determined by the BRG in their business rules manifesto (Business Rules Group 2003), which was later enhanced by OMG (Object Management Group 2006). According to Scheer and Werth (2006) they are „[…] guidelines or business practices […], that affect or guide the behavior of companies. Behavior means […], with which processes (how) and with which resources (whereby), which goods are produced." They can be of internal and external origin (e.g. laws). In this context, business rules shall be regarded as normative instructional statements that are distinguished by their specifying character, related to their process execution (Hay and Healy 2000). The fundamental purpose of business rules lies in securing conformity of business processes within legal and other guidelines, as well as verification of conformity.

By means of this specification, business rules can be created and transferred to business rules management systems (BRMS) (Hoheseil 2000). Rule editors support the creation, validation and simulation of business rules by providing an appropriate development environment. These rules can subsequently be stored in a repository, which is available to form the basis for process management. These rules are particularly effective with regard to controlling processes, if they are combined with operational systems, like ERP or workflow management systems, for example, via web services that access the BRMS during execution, using the output of rule analysis, to determine the follow-up actions (Grob et al. 2008).

With the help of business rules, process execution logic, stored in operative systems, can be transferred into BRMS and can be stored independently from its type and place of future application (Endl 2004). This allows advantages in flexibility, so that modifications of business rules in the operating departments are possible, for example, in order to adapt to changing conditions, like legal formalities. Furthermore, a centralized storage of control logic avoids the problem of a variety of different implementations of the same business rules in different application systems. Business processes have to provide valid and consistent control logic, in order to enable purposeful execution of processes and to avoid process anomalies on an instance level. The supervision and enforcement of these defined business rules, using BRMS, immediately intends to enforce existing (internal or external) guidelines of process instances.

Different language constructs can be used to design business rules (Scheer and Werth 2006). One possibility is to use simple IF-THEN-rules or their derived extensions of ECA-rules (event-condition-action) or ECAA-rules (event-condition-action-alternative) (Hanson 1992). Another possibility is the Business Process Compliance Language (BPCL) (Wörzberger et al 2008), which defines inclusion, precedence and existence conditions for business rules. However, all of these constructs can only partially be applied to very different types of business rules (not just regarding process control flows, but also business objects used in a process, as well as resources), not all of them are easily understood by business process compliance officers (e.g. BPCL) and all of these only support semantic interpretation on a very abstract level, since a predefined ontology for a domain-specific vocabulary is missing.

According to El Kharbili et al. (2008a) and El Kharbili et al. (2008b), successful BPC implementation:

- requires an integrated approach, reflecting the entire BPM lifecycle,
- should support compliance verification beyond simple control flow aspects,
- needs an intuitive graphical notation for compliance requirements that is also comprehend¬ible for non-experts and
- should support the application of semantic technologies for the definition, implementation and execution of automated compliance verification.

Hence, for the purpose of BPC management, we propose to develop a semantic approach to BRM that allows for intuitive modeling and analysis of business process compliance. Since especially the last two aspects target at an easy to use semantic modeling and analysis language and our focus is on the financial sector, we will build upon the Semantic Business Process Modeling Language (SBPML) notation (Becker et al. 2009; Becker et al. 2010d; Becker et al. 2010e), which we will describe briefly next.

3   SBPML as an Approach to Semantic Business Process Modeling and Analysis

SBPML was originally developed since researchers identified an inefficiency of generic process modeling languages in terms of modeling and analysis of business processes in the financial sector (Becker et al. 2010d). As a result, it focuses on an economic, domain-specific and thus semantic modeling approach, based on reusable process building blocks that are designed specifically for modeling and analysis of activities and processes in banks (Becker et al. 2009, Weiß and Winkelmann 2011).

The process modeling notation consists of four views, comprising a process view ("how is a service delivered?"), a business object view ("what is processed or produced?"), an organizational view ("who is involved in the process?") and a resource view ("what resources are used?") (cf. Figure 1). The core constructs of this language are domain-specific process building blocks (PBB), which have an integrating role by connecting all views (cf. Figure 1). A PBB represents a certain set of activities (e.g. "Enter Data into IT" or "Archive Document / Information") within an administrative process and applies a domain-specific vocabulary. PBBs are atomic, have a well-defined level of abstraction and are semantically specified by a domain concept. PBBs belong to the process view and represent the lowest abstraction level of a process

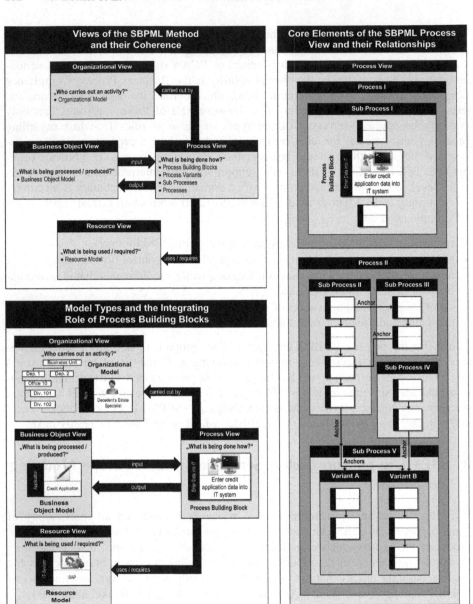

Fig. 1. SBPML Views, Model Types and Levels of Abstraction of the Process View

model. Processes are represented as a sequential flow of PBBs. PBBs are contained within different variants of sub processes. The sub processes, representing the activities of just one organizational unit, are in turn part of a larger process, which usually involves multiple organizational units and thus multiple sub processes (cf. Figure 1). Additional facts about the processes can be collected with the help of attributes (e.g. "Duration" for the PBB "Enter Data into IT"), assigned to each PBB. They establish a connection to the business object, organizational and resource view.

4 Developing Artifacts for Modeling Compliance-Related Business Rules in SBPML

Through a literature review we identified business rule types that are used in the context of BPC in banks. According to Sadiq et al. (2007) they include:

- flow tags, which represent rules regarding the business process control flow and thus the execution of certain activities in a process (e.g. order of activities, existence of certain activities etc.),
- time tags, which represent rules that depict temporal conditions or restraints within process flows (e.g. maximum time that may be needed to respond to a customer request),
- resource tags, which represent rules regarding the used resources, when executing a certain activity (e.g. authorization rules for IT systems or restrictions separations of duties within a process flow) and
- data tags, which represent rules regarding the (business object) data, used throughout a process (e.g. data like the name of the credit applicant that must be contained in a credit application).

Concerning the SBPML notation, there are business rules that refer to the process view solely (flow tags and time tags), the business object view, possibly in conjunction with the process view (data tags) and the resource view, as well as the organizational view, possibly in conjunction with the process view (resource tags). Since time tags can only be evaluated during run-time and not on the level of process models, they will not be considered further. Regarding different flow tags, we follow Awad and Weske (2009), who have concentrated on identifying and describing process control flow business rules for BPMN (Business Process Modeling Notation).

According to Awad and Weske (2009), control flow business rules define the sequence, in which activities can or should be performed. Generally, predecessor relations (Activity A "leads to" Activity B) and successor relations (Activity A "precedes" Activity B) are established, but also existence (inclusion) or non-existence constraints should be depicted. In addition, depending upon an activity's position within a process or sequence of activities, different scopes can be defined. The sequence, as well as the existence or non-existence of activities, is defined within a certain "scope" of an entire process. The scope of a constraint can either be "global", or with respect to another activity "before" or "after" that activity, or with respect to two other activities between those two activities.

In Figure 2 (a) Activity A must be part of a process; in (b) Activity A may not be part of the entire process. (c) describes the classical successor constraint, (e) the predecessor constraint. In (d) Activity A may not be executed before Activity B is finished; in (f) Activity B may not be executed after Activity A is finished. (g) and (h) describe the non-existence constraint of Activity B between Activity A and Activity C, with the difference that Activity A and Activity C in (g) are in a successor relationship, whereas they are in a predecessor relationship in (h) (cf. Becker et al. 2010a).

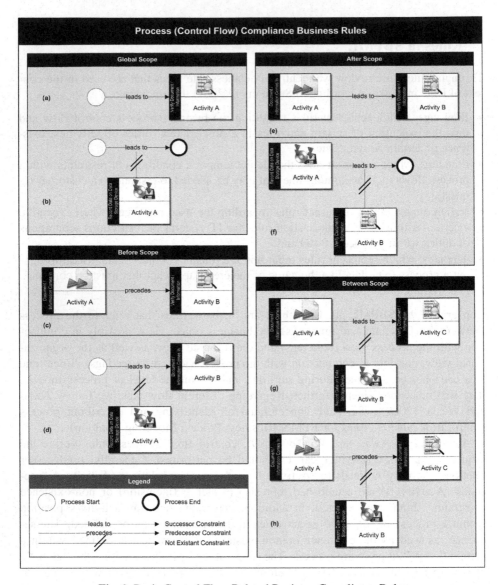

Fig. 2. Basic Control Flow-Related Business Compliance Rules

Figure 3 depicts further, more complex standard business rule patterns. In (k), in contrast to (d), Activity B must not be part of a process in all cases. However, if Activity B is used in a process, Activity A may not be executed before Activity B is finished. In (i) and (j) we suggest the use of a "'Variable Activity" PBB to define direct sequences. In (j) Activity A must be a direct predecessor of Activity B or vice versa Activity B must be a direct successor of Activity A. In (i), through the use of the global scope, we are able to define that Activity A must be the first activity within an entire process. Similarly, one could also predefine the last activity that must be at the

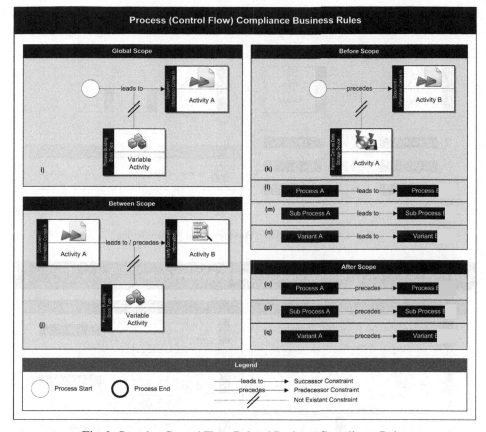

Fig. 3. Complex Control Flow-Related Business Compliance Rules

end of a process. In addition, these rules may not only be applied to activities in the SBPML notation, but also to processes, sub processes and sub process variants ((l), (m), (n), (o), (p), (q)). Through the combination of these simple patterns, more complex patterns can also be derived.

From a resource tag based view with its corresponding organizational view and resource view in the SBPML terminology, further rules can be specified. For resources in terms of the SBPML resource view in general, IT compliance of an IT system, as a resource used during a business process, can be modeled and analyzed, although we will not focus on IT compliance within this article. Focusing on the organizational view of the SBPML terminology, there are two further very common compliance requirements, which need to be captured by business rules. These are the application of a four-eyes-principle (cf. Figure 4 (w)), where one person executes Activity A as a "maker" and a second person as the "checker" verifies, if Activity A was done correctly and the aspect of separation of duties for certain activity sequences (cf. Figure 4 (s), (t), (u), (v)).

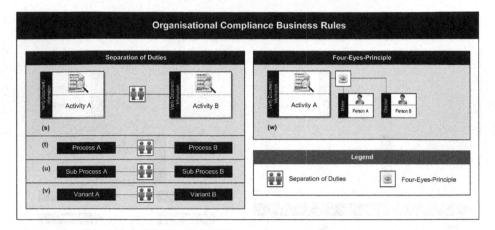

Fig. 4. Resource-Related Business Compliance Rules

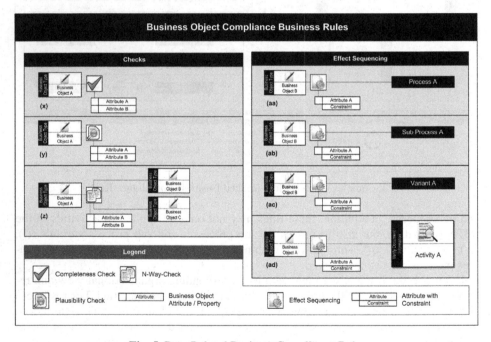

Fig. 5. Data-Related Business Compliance-Rules

Finally, the data tag view with its corresponding business object view in the SBPML terminology requires further types of compliance business rules to be modeled (cf. Figure 5). According to Namiri and Stojanovic (2007), the following data tag rules are important (cf. Figure 6):

a "completeness check" (x) is important to verify, if all mandatory fields or attributes of a data or business object have been completed (e.g. check if all necessary information is provided in a credit application), a "plausibility check" (y) is important to verify, if fields or attributes of a data or business object are plausible (e.g. valid address information),

a "n-way-check" (z) is important to verify, if fields or attributes of data or business objects are the same (e.g. if the birth date is the same on the personal identification card as well as on the credit application).

Besides these business rules, related to certain types of business objects, Zoet et al. (2009) also define "effect sequencing" ((aa), (ab), (ac), (ad)). Effect sequencing describes that business objects, which have certain characteristics, imply further activities to be executed (e.g. credit requests for more than 75,000 € must receive an additional vote inside a bank).

These specified business rules can all be applied to SBPML process models, since the rules only use predefined patterns of activities that are also the basis of the SBPML specification.

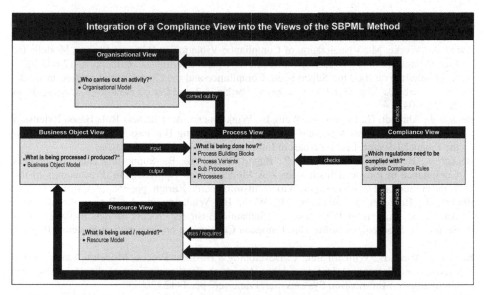

Fig. 6. SBPML Compliance View

Since all these business rules will usually be maintained by a compliance officer, with expertise in the area of compliance management on an enterprise level, as opposed to a process modeler, with expertise in business process management and especially process modeling, we propose to add a compliance view to the SBPML views. This should be linked to all existing views and should give the compliance officer the ability to model, maintain and analyze the compliance business rules with respect to the available elements, used in all other existing views (cf. Figure 6).

5 Conclusion

Undoubtedly, the automatic enforcement of compliance and compliant business processes is a very important topic in the financial sector. This is especially due to the different scandals, financial crisis and the ongoing regulation debate that will lead to new rules and laws on national and international levels. Therefore, an automated analysis of existing process models is a prerequisite for ensuring BPC. In identifying relevant business rule design patterns, we provide a basis for instantiations, based on the SBPML notation for banks, but also for other notations. The instantiation of the generic rules will allow for an automatic identification of design patterns in process models in banks (cf. Becker et al. 2011) and hence for the discovery of critical compliance issues. At this stage of research, we believe these results to be valid for most purposes in banks. However, in a next step, we are going to further evaluate our findings with the help of various SBPML process models from different banks. Furthermore, by testing the theoretical concepts in practical depth, we may also add new process compliance business rules to our business process compliance pattern library.

References

Awad, A., Weske, M.: Visualization of Compliance Violation in Business Process Models. In: Proceedings of the 5th Workshop on Business Process Intelligence, Ulm, pp. 1–12 (2009)

Basel Committee on Banking Supervision. Compliance and the Compliance Function in Banks (2004), http://www.bis.org/publ/bcbs113.pdf?noframes=1 (accessed on 2010-03-04)

Becker, J., Ahrendt, C., Coners, A., Weiß, B., Winkelmann, A.: Business Rule Based Extension of a Semantic Process Modeling Language for Managing Business Process Compliance in the Financial Sector. Lecture Notes in Informatics 175(1), 201–206 (2010a)

Becker, J., Bergener, P., Delfmann, P., Eggert, M., Weiß, B.: Supporting Business Process Compliance in Financial Institutions – A Model-Driven Approach. In: Proceedings of the 10th International Conference on Wirtschaftsinformatik, Zürich, pp. 355–364 (2011)

Becker, J., Bergener, P., Räckers, M., Weiß, B., Winkelmann, A.: Pattern-Based Semi-Automatic Analysis of Weaknesses in Semantic Business Process Models in the Banking Sector. In: Proceedings of the 18th European Conference on Information Systems, Pretoria (2010b)

Becker, J., Weiß, B., Winkelmann, A.: Developing a Business Process Modeling Language for the Banking Sector – A Design Science Approach. In: Proceedings of the 15th Americas Conference on Information Systems, San Francisco, pp. 1–12 (2009)

Becker, J., Weiß, B., Winkelmann, A.: Transferring a Domain-Specific Semantic Process Modeling Language – Findings from Action Research in the Banking Sector. In: Proceedings of the 18th European Conference on Information Systems, Pretoria (2010c)

Becker, J., Weiß, B., Winkelmann, A.: Utility vs. Efforts of Business Process Modeling – An Exploratory Survey in the Financial Sector. In: Proceedings of the Multikonferenz Wirtschaftsinformatik, Göttingen, pp. 41–54 (2010d)

Becker, J., Thome, I., Weiß, B., Winkelmann, A.: Constructing a Semantic Business Process Modelling Language for the Banking Sector – An Evolutionary Dyadic Design Science Approach. Enterprise Modelling and Information Systems Architectures 5(1), 4–25 (2010e)

Business Rules Group. Business Rules Manifesto – The Principles of Rule Independence (2003), http://www.businessrulesgroup.org/brmanifesto/BRManifestB.pdf (accessed on 2010-05-02)

El Kharbili, M., Alwes de Medeiros, A.K., Stein, S., van der Aalst, W.M.P.: Business Process Compliance Checking: Current State and Future Challenges. In: Proceedings of the Modellierung betrieblicher Informationssysteme, Saarbrücken, pp. 107–113 (2008a)

El Kharbili, M., Stein, S., Markovic, I., Pulvermüller, E.: Towards a Framework for Semantic Business Process Compliance Management. In: Proceedings of the 1st International Workshop on Governance, Risk and Compliance – Applications in Information Systems, Montpellier, pp. 1–15 (2008b)

Endl, R.: Regelbasierte Entwicklung betrieblicher Informationssysteme: Gestaltung flexibler Informationssysteme durch explizite Modellierung der Geschäftslogik," Doctoral Thesis, University of Bern, Bern (2004)

Grob, L., Bensberg, F., Coners, A.: Rule-Based Control of Business Processes – A Process Mining Approach. Wirtschaftsinformatik 50(4), 268–281 (2008)

Hanson, E.N.: Rule Condition Testing and Action Execution in Ariel. In: Proceedings of the ACM-SIGMOD International Conference on Management of Data (1992)

Hay, D., Healy, K.: Defining Business Rules – What are They Really? (2000), http://www.businessrulesgroup.org/first_paper/BRG-whatisBR_3ed.pdf (2010-05-02)

Herbst, H., Knolmayer, G.: Ansätze zur Klassifikation von Geschäftsregeln. Wirtschaftsinformatik 37(2), 149–159 (1995)

Hoheseil, H.: Temporale Geschäftsprozessmodellierung, Doctoral Thesis, University of Bern, Bern (2000)

Namiri, K., Stojanovic, N.: Pattern-based Design and Validation of Business Process Compliance. In: On the Move to Meaningful Internet Systems 2007, CoopIS, DOA, ODBASE, GADA, and IS, pp. 59–76 (2007)

Object Management Group, Semantics of Business Vocabulary and Business Rules (SBVR), v1.0 (2006), http://www.omg.org/spec/SBVR/1.0/PDF (accessed on 2010-05-02)

Rinderle-Ma, S., Ly, L.T., Dadam, P.: Business Process Compliance. EMISA Forum, 24–29 (2008)

Sadiq, S., Governatori, G., Namiri, K.: Modeling Control Objectives for Business Process Compliance. In: Alonso, G., Dadam, P., Rosemann, M. (eds.) BPM 2007. LNCS, vol. 4714, pp. 149–164. Springer, Heidelberg (2007)

Scheer, A.-W., Werth, D.: Geschäftsprozessmanagement für das Unternehmen von morgen. In: Karagiannis, D., Rieger, B. (eds.) Herausforderungen in der Wirtschaftsinformatik – Festschrift für Hermann Krallmann, Berlin, pp. 49–64 (2006)

Weiß, B., Winkelmann, A.: A Metamodel Based Perspective on the Adaptation of a Process Modeling Language to the Financial Sector. In: Proceedings of the 44th Hawaii International Conference on System Sciences, Koloa (2011)

Wörzberger, R., Kurpick, T., Heer, T.: Checking Correctness and Compliance of Integrated Process Models. In: Proceedings of the 10th International Symposium on Symbolic and Numeric Algorithms for Scientific Computing, Timisoara, pp. 576–583 (2008)

Zoet, M., Welke, R., Versendaal, J., Ravesteyn, P.: Aligning Risk Management and Compliance Considerations with Business Process Development. In: Di Noia, T., Buccafurri, F. (eds.) EC-Web 2009. LNCS, vol. 5692, pp. 157–168. Springer, Heidelberg (2009)

Assessing Cloud Readiness: Introducing the Magic Matrices Method Used by Continental AG

Claudia Loebbecke[1], Bernhard Thomas[2], and Thomas Ullrich[2]

[1] Dept. of Business, Media and Technology Management, University of Cologne,
Pohligstr. 1, 50969 Cologne, Germany
Tel.: +49 (0) 221 470 5364
Claudia.Loebbecke@uni-koeln.de
[2] Continental AG, Vahrenwalder St. 9, 30165 Hannover, Germany
Tel.: +49 (0)511 938 1038, +49 (0)511 938 11048
{Bernhard.Thomas,Thomas.Ullrich}@conti.de

Abstract. Whereas recently cloud computing has gained enormous interest in research and practice, the deployment of cloud computing in larger companies and multi-nationals is still in its infancy. Practice often lacks a sufficiently specific, yet applicable method to determine a company's cloud readiness and to identify and assess IT services to be taken to the cloud. This paper introduces such a field-tested method for assessing a multi-national's cloud readiness. Beginning with Continental's expectations towards cloud computing, the paper presents the Magic Matrices Method applied by Continental. The paper discusses the suitability of the method for research and practice. It concludes that the trend towards cloud computing may lead to easing assessment regarding the most critical stumbling blocks along the lines of compliance, security, and hence user control.

Keywords: Cloud Computing, Cloud Readiness, Assessment Method, Practitioner Experience, Compliance Risks.

1 Introduction

Cloud computing recently has gained enormous interest in research and practice (e.g., Armbrust et al. 2010, Erdgomus 2009; European Commission 2010; Ramireddy et al. 2010; Weinhardt et al. 2009). Even the lack of a generally agreed upon definition and at the best imprecise delineations from related concepts such as off-shoring and internal sourcing have not slowed down the growth of companies such as salesforce.com, who very successfully ride the cloud computing wave. However, the deployment of cloud computing among larger companies and even multi-nationals is still in its infancy. For this to change, companies look for clear assessments methods concerning the appropriateness of cloud computing for their IT services.

Any significant cloud computing diffusion into the corporate world requires potential user companies to evaluate the value and opportunities as well as the challenges and threats of cloud computing. User companies need a method to assess

M. Nüttgens et al. (Eds.): Governance and Sustainability in IS, IFIP AICT 366, pp. 270–281, 2011.

cloud-readiness. The method needs to be simple enough to make its application feasible in parallel to ongoing business activities. It also needs to be sufficiently complex in order to take into account the multitude of a company's IT services and the various types of cloud computing.

Here this paper aims to make a contribution. It offers a practitioner experience report of a large cloud user company, who has developed a method for assessing a multi-national's readiness for cloud computing, or – in brief – it offers *a method for assessing a multi-national's cloud readiness* helping to answer "what company specific conditions have to be created for which form of cloud computing fulfilling the expectations for which precisely defined application field?" (Thomas, Ullrich 2011).

After outlining the concept of cloud computing, the paper introduces the Magic Matrices Method for assessing a company's cloud readiness as it has been applied by Continental AG, one of the world's leading automotive suppliers. The paper concludes with a short discussion of the applicability of the method and closes with an outlook to further research at the edge between scientific rigor and practitioners' relevance.

2 Company Overview: Continental AG

Continental AG, founded in 1871 in Hanover, Germany, is a leading global automotive supplier and the second largest in Europe. In 2010, Continental counted approximately 149,000 employees at nearly 190 locations in 46 countries for research and development as well as production. The company achieved sales of about € 25.5 Billion with an adjusted Earnings Before Interest and Taxes (EBIT) margin of about 9.5 %.

With its six divisions – Chassis & Safety, Powertrain, Interior, Passenger and Light Truck Tires, Commercial Vehicle Tires, and ContiTech – Continental is a driving force for future mobility concepts, in the automotive industry and beyond. Most of its business units hold leading competitive positions. For example, they are number one worldwide for hydraulic brake systems, driver assistance systems, sensor technology, airbag control units, air suspension systems, telematics, vehicle instrumentation, and fuel supply systems; and they are number two for electronic brake systems and brake boosters. In the tire sector, Continental ranks fourth worldwide and is the market leader in Europe in passenger and light truck tires and industrial tires. With the acquisition of Motorola's automotive-electronics unit in 2006, Continental added telematics to its portfolio and strengthened its position. In 2007, the acquisition of 'Siemens VDO Automotive AG' led the company into the global top five of automotive suppliers.

The Chief Technical Officer (CTO) and the Chief Security Officer (CSO) leading the cloud readiness project are responsible across divisions and located on corporate-level, from where they reach into all business units and govern company-wide IT decisions.

In the past, about 40,000 IT users coming from the Siemens VDO acquisition had to be integrated among others into a common e-mail system. They were familiar with Outlook Exchange whereas Continental has been using Lotus Notes Domino. Would mailbox services 'from the cloud' have allowed for smooth and cost-efficient integrated mailbox services, as cloud service providers promise?

3   Cloud Computing: Continental's Definition and Understanding

According to Wikipedia (Feb. 2011), cloud computing refers to "location-independent computing, whereby shared servers provide resources, software, and data to computers and other devices on demand, as with the electricity grid. Details are abstracted from consumers, who no longer have need for expertise in, or control over, the technology infrastructure 'in the cloud' that supports them." Whereas this definition is rather vague and certainly only one of many[1], it serves first communication needs of practice. Continental uses a similarly broad approach and conceptualizes cloud computing by what it demands from 'the cloud', that is, Continental requires services coming from the cloud *as highly standardized, automatically provisioned, and on-demand available IT services in a clearly defined and measurable quality, with any options for up- and downscaling and usage dependent charging from more than one provider.* Continental stresses the two-sided phenomenon 'on demand'. It understands 'on demand' as 'pay per use', which also implies no payment if not used or in more system oriented terms, the option to scale down service use on short term notice.

While such broad definition helps to motivate further discussions on the pros and cons of cloud computing, assessing a company's cloud readiness requires a more precise understanding of the kind of cloud services under consideration. To that end, Figure 1 shows three relevant dimensions of cloud computing that Continental feeds into its cloud readiness assessment. Almost any combination of Location Model, Deployment Model, and Service Model is possible and likely leads to different assessments regarding the cloud readiness of specific Continental IT services.

In Figure 1, the dimension *'Location Model'* should be self-explanatory; obviously, some locations are bound to the deployment model chosen.

On the dimension *'Deployment Model'* (Figure 1), the Economies of Scale (EoS) increase from a Private Cloud via a Hybrid Cloud to a Public Cloud, whereas the adaptation options and the controllability decrease.

— *A Private Cloud* relates standardized, virtualized, and effective manageable IT environment based on cloud design criteria which offers services for defined user groups, typically within an organization or organizational unit, under customer control.

---

[1] Gartner Group (e.g., www.gartner.com/technology/initiatives/cloud-computing.jsp) defines cloud computing as a style of computing in which scalable and elastic IT-enabled capabilities are delivered as a service to external customers using Internet technologies. Forrester Research (e.g., Staten 2009) defines cloud computing as a standardized IT capability (services, software, or infrastructure) delivered via the Internet in a pay-per-use and self-service way.

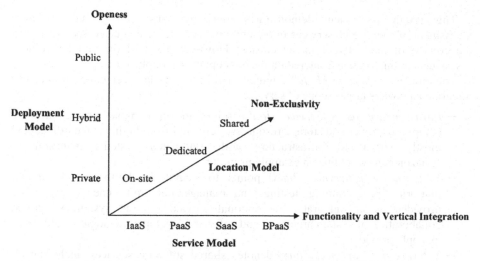

Fig. 1. Dimensions of Cloud Computing (Source: Thomas; Ullrich 2011)

— *A Hybrid Cloud* points to the interconnections between on-premise IT, private deployments models, and public ones. The overall responsibility stays with the customer; the responsibility for the operations is typically shared.

— *A Public Cloud* denotes the offering of highly standardized and scaleable services on a pay-per-use model. The same infrastructure, accessed via Internet technology, is used in parallel by users from different organizations. Exclusive or dedicated delivery models are typically organized using logical segmentation methods like multi-tenancy. Owner and operator are external service providers.

Table 1 depicts Continental's comparison of the three different cloud deployment models – private, hybrid, and public – according to nine criteria, namely security (archiving and privacy), degree of integration, cost-benefit analysis, risk transparency, financial / investment needs, transparency (data storage and access), control over data, scalability, and flexibility.

Table 1. Exemplary Assessment of Deployment Options per IT Service(Source: Thomas; Ullrich 2011)

	Private Cloud	Hybrid Cloud	Public Cloud
Security (Archiving, Privacy)	++	+	O
Degree of Integration	++	+	O
Cost-Benefit Analysis	O	+	++
Risk Transparency	++	+	O
Financial / Investment Needs	O	O	++
Transparency (Data Storage, Data Access)	++	+	O
Control Over Data	++	+	O
Scalability	O	+	++
Flexibility	O	+	++

This rough assessment demonstrates that any subsequent 'cloud readiness assessment of specific IT services in the end also need to be evaluated specifically in the context of the delivery model chosen. However, most of the cloud readiness assessment at this stage is centered on the concept of the 'public cloud'.

The dimension *'Service Model'* (Figure 1 and Figure 2) has been conceptualized to integrate an always larger scope of service.

— *Infrastructure as a Service (IaaS)* refers to on demand provisioning of computing power and storage resources, delivered from highly standardized and mostly virtualized infrastructure with automated systems management. Amazon.com would be an example provider.

— *Platform as a Service (PaaS)* points to shared development and runtime platforms, programming, testing, and management environments, which are provided as an integrated or optional service for the system integrated collaboration of system architects and software developers. Google would be an example provider.

— *Software as a Service (SaaS)* denotes shared software services, including all necessary IT resources (e.g., infrastructure, systems management, application management and maintenance), accessible by Internet technology and network connection, and accounted for billing unit. A prominent provider would be salesforce.com.

— *Business Processes as a Service (BPaaS)* relates to business process operations as a combination of software services and functional services - prevailing for HR processes.

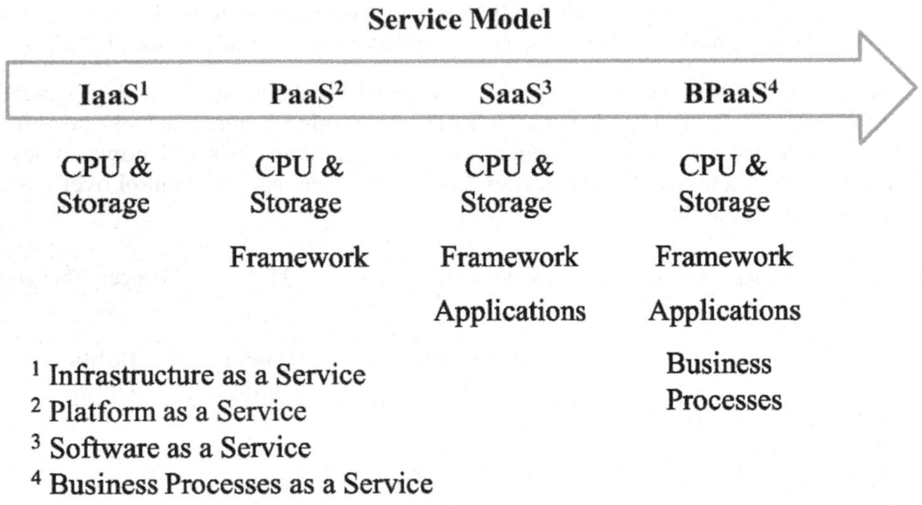

Service Model

IaaS[1]	PaaS[2]	SaaS[3]	BPaaS[4]
CPU & Storage	CPU & Storage	CPU & Storage	CPU & Storage
	Framework	Framework	Framework
		Applications	Applications
			Business Processes

[1] Infrastructure as a Service
[2] Platform as a Service
[3] Software as a Service
[4] Business Processes as a Service

Fig. 2. The Service Model Dimension of Cloud Computing

This conceptualization of cloud computing serves Continental's needs. Alternatively one could also assess cloud readiness for individual services, i.e., exclude CPU and applications when taking business processes from the cloud. Continental's understanding of cloud computing, which stresses the need for IT services and applications to be available in a flexible and on-demand manner and in a clearly defined and measurable quality, requires comparing cloud computing with other delivery models. Continental lists commonly – and often similarly – named delivery characteristics of cloud computing and grouped those characteristics according to their perceived importance to Continental (Table 1, column 2).

It then checked whether other traditional delivery modes would promise similar performance characteristics (Table 1, columns 3, 4, and 5). It made the case for further pursuing cloud computing and specifying a method for assessing its IT services regarding cloud readiness. Being aware that such brief analysis can only provide rough estimates rather than detailed comparisons, which would require detailed definitions, service requirements, and contracts, it serves Continental's upfront need to gain insights into the potential of cloud computing.

Table 2. Comparison of Cloud Computing to other Delivery Modes and Attractivity Profile (Source: Continental AG)

Cloud Delivery Characteristics	Importance of Characteristics for Continental	Cloud Delivery Characteristics Shown by Other Traditional Delivery Models		
		Out-Tasking Models	Off-Shoring	Internal Sourcing
Service Level Quality	++	x		
On-Demand	++	(x)		
Pay per Use	++	(x)		
Always-on Availability	+	x	(x)	(x)
Scalable w/ Growth and Reduction	+	(x)	x	
Supplier Market	+	x		
Easy to Obtain	+			x
Fast Availability	+			(x)
Standardized	+			
Dynamic	O	x	(x)	x
Customer Market	O			
Flexible	O			

Legend: ++ = very important, + = important, O = neutral
x = shows characteristic; (x) = barely shows characteristic

4 The Magic Matrices Method for Assessing Cloud Rediness

In December 2010, Continental started its 'Cloud Readiness Project' in order to develop and apply a customized assessment method for investigating selected, but rather specific IT services, applications, and processes (in the following just 'IT services') with respect to their cloud readiness. The resulting Magic Matrices Method is based on the persuasion that the IT landscape in no larger company will be completely 'cloud ready'.

The method consists of three main steps, Identification, Screening, and Categorization. The novelty lies in the approaches to screening and categorization. In the following, we will briefly outline the main steps.

Identification. Continental organized several workshops with management, employees, technology providers, and an external service provider in order to increase the internal motivation for cloud computing and to subsequently identify some IT services for further investigation. It has become obvious that mainly commodity like IT services and applications would be at the core of early cloud computing initiatives. The first Identification phase ended with 29 IT services to be investigated in the light of cloud promises.

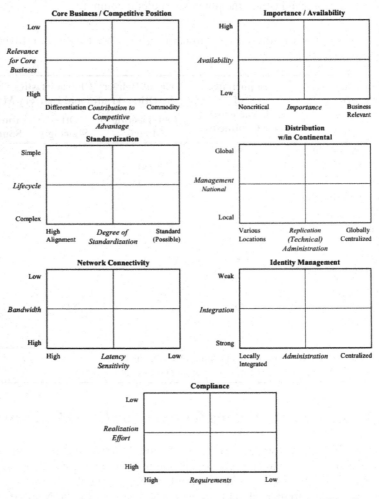

Fig. 3. Cloud Computing Assessment Criteria - Magic Matrices Details

---

Core Business / Competitive Position

Relevance for the Core Business (high – low). Relevance of an IT service is high if the service (significantly) contributes turnover and rents.

Contribution to the Competitive Position (differentiation – commodity). Contribution is high if an IT service helps differentiating in terms of innovations, business process speed, and agility.

Tendency for Cloud Readiness. An IT service with low relevance for the core business and a low contribution to the competitive position (differentiation) is likely to be cloud ready.

Importance / Availability

Importance (non-critical – critical). Importance is critical if core processes cannot run if the IT service is not available.

Availability (low – high). Availability is high if the IT service can be used 365/24 without interruptions.

Tendency for Cloud Readiness. An IT service that requires high availability and is of critical importance for core business processes is likely to be cloud ready.

Standardization

Lifecycle (complex – simple). An IT service with strong integration into other systems and many dependencies to other processes is complex. Its actualization requires intense planning and coordination.

Standardization (high alignment – standard). Standardized IT services are not adapted to the company needs.

Tendency for Cloud Readiness. A standardized IT service with simple lifecycle is likely to be cloud ready.

Degree of Distribution within Continental

Management (local – global). Locally organized management tasks related to an IT service have no central administrative structures. Roles and rights differ among locations.

Replication (Technical) Administration (various locations – globally centralized). Hard- and software are centrally provided and configured.

Tendency for Cloud Readiness. An IT service with global management and global technical administration is likely to be cloud ready.

Network Connectivity

Bandwidth (high – low).

Latency / Sensitivity (high – low).

Tendency for Cloud Readiness. An IT service with low bandwidth requirements and low latency / sensitivity is likely to be cloud ready.

Identity Management

Integration (strong – weak). Integration is low if an IT service has its own identity management and is independent of the identity directory of the company / enterprise.

Administration (locally integrated – centralized). Administration is centralized if the provisioning and de-provisioning of users follows central guidelines including conventions for naming and security.

Tendency for Cloud Readiness. An IT service with weakly integrated and centrally administrated identity management is likely to be cloud ready.

Compliance

Realization Effort (high – low). Realization efforts are high if extensive organizational and technical provisioning is to be fulfilled.

Requirements (high – low). Requirements are high if the processed data need to match strict legal and regulatory standards. Company-specific standards also increase requirements.

Tendency for Cloud Readiness. An IT service with low realization efforts and low compliance requirements is likely to be cloud ready.

Fig. 4. Assessment Criteria: Two parameters and General Tendency for Cloud Readiness (After: Thomas, Ullrich 2011)

Screening. Continental has identified seven overall criteria to assess the cloud readiness of an IT service. The seven criteria are (1) Core Business / Competitive Position, (2) Importance / Availability, (3) Standardization, (4) Degree of Distribution within Continental, (5) Network Connectivity, (6) Identity Management, and (7) Compliance. For each criterion, Continental has developed a 'Magic Matrix' (Figure 3), which allows digging deeper into two major parameters of any criterion (Figure 4). All seven Magic Matrices are designed so that the upper right area within a matrix is the most cloud promising one.

Having designed the seven Magic Matrices, all IT services under consideration are placed in each of the Magic Matrices. Figure 5 provides an idea of ten IT services in the Magic Matrix of Standardization.

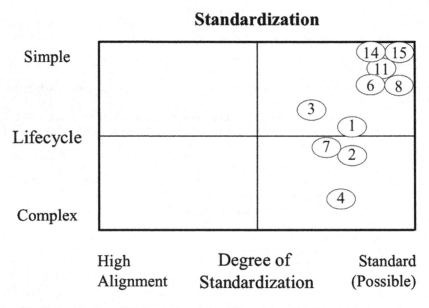

Fig. 5. Positioning of IT Services and Applications in a Magic Matrix (Example)

Continental then aggregates the assessment for each of the seven assessment criteria (Magic Matrices) in the resulting Criteria Assessment Framework (Figure 6). To enhance readability, the diagram of the Criteria Assessment Framework shows a rather general labelling of the two axes. Each criterion is assessed across all IT services based on its specific parameters shown in Figure 3 in order to the adequate position in the Criteria Assessment Framework.

Starting with one criterion, for instance Standardization (C), Continental adds up the assessments of the Magic Matrix of Standardization in Figure 3 across all services and applications. Thus it determines the positioning of Standardization (C) in Figure 6. It then repeats the procedure for the other six criteria, and positions all of them together in one Criteria Assessment Framework.

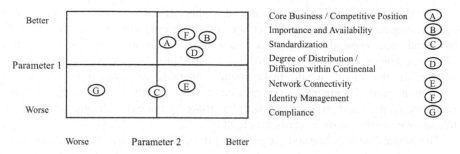

Fig. 6. Cloud Computing: Criteria Assessment Framework

At the end of the Screening phase, Continental found the criteria 'Compliance' and 'Distribution within Continental' to be most frequently (i.e., for 9 and 8 services respectively of 29 services screened) in the critical area of the matrices. 'Standardization' and 'Network Connectivity' ended up in the critical areas for six and five services respectively, and finally 'Importance / Availability', 'Identity Management' and 'Core Business / Competitive Position' for four or three of 29 services.

Categorization. Refocusing on the cloud readiness of Continental's IT services, Continental builds on the Screening Phase, i.e., on the assessed criteria for cloud readiness. It investigates all 29 identified IT services according to the seven criteria. It takes into account the relative importance of the criteria as determined in the Screening phase and categorizes the 29 IT services into A (likely could ready), B (not yet cloud ready), and C (unlikely to be assessed as cloud ready in the next years).

Fifteen of 29 IT services resulted as 'likely cloud ready' (Thomas, Ullrich 2011). These IT services are (1) Intranet (CMS), (2), Internet (CMS), (3) Messaging, (4) Online Collaboration, (5) Office, File Viewer, (6) Internet Access Gateway, (7) DMZ[2] Service, (8) Internet Mail Gateway, (9) Managed Server, (10) Archiving, (11) Managed User Workstation, (12) Patch Management, (13) Virus Protection Management, (14) Vulnerability Management, (15) IT Service Manager Tool

5 Discussion and Outlook

As a large multi-national, Continental acts in global, competitive markets where IT services have been the backbone for most distributed business processes. Many IT services have reached commodity status; hence, they should be assessed in light of a 'cloud movement' gaining speed across business sectors and countries. Just pointing to the commonly accepted trade-off between resource allocation and cost-benefit advantages on the one hand and still open compliance and security issues on the other hand does not contribute to moving in any direction.

---

[2] A DMZ, or demilitarized zone, is the physical or logical sub-network that exposes Continental's external services to the Internet.. It adds an additional security layer to Continental's internal network.

The Magic Matrices Method introduced in this paper has served as effective eye-opener, especially as numerous IT services under investigation have come out in the 'no-cloud' area. Typically, compliance issues drive such positioning. The CIO and the IT department as well as division managers fear that hosting crucial data or key IT services in the 'cloud' would make them vulnerable to external threats or data corruption. For Continental, compliance issues complemented with concerns regarding security and process control and availability issues are the greatest obstacles to a more extensive move towards the cloud.

The Magic Matrices Method for assessing the cloud readiness of a user company's IT services certainly has conceptual weaknesses and open ends. Assessment criteria partially overlap and there are no ex-ante assigned weights to the different criteria. However, those shortcomings foster the application of the method in the real world towards properly assessing cloud readiness and then selectively adopting cloud computing. Thus the proposed method may trigger company-wide discussions and change initiatives on the path to cloud readiness.

At first sight, the Magic Matrices method may resemble Gartner's Magic Quadrants (Blechar 2008; Elliot, Blood 2009, Smulders 2011, www.gartner.com/it/products/ mq/mq_ms.jsp). The design of the figures and graphs may seem familiar. However, Gartner's Magic Quadrants are typically applied for evaluating providers (vendors) to deliver a specific service to a specific company. With the proposed Magic Matrices Method instead, we assess IT services – potentially to be 'procured' from cloud vendors.[3] Selecting the most suitable provider or providers for 'likely cloud ready' IT services follows the application of the Magic Matrices Method. To that end, a company may use a version of Gartner's Magic Quadrants. The purpose, the criteria, and the parameters would be different, though.

In the first half of 2011, ongoing work at Continental covers exactly that issue. For each or all of the selected IT services, Continental needs to find a 'cloud service provider' that is 'ready for Continental' – this could be where Gartner's Magic Quadrants may come into play, adding another x matrices or quadrants to the picture.

The future will show whether current rather 'cloud critical' assessments in the real user world will remain dominant and whether the diffusion of cloud computing will remain limited. Alternatively, laws and regulations as well as a company's perception of compliance requirements may change. Perhaps, rather sooner than later, procuring IT services from the cloud will be as 'normal' as it is for energy and communication services. We hope that the presented method and any subsequent debate will stimulate further research into the problem.

---

[3] In addition to consultancy white papers and reports, one also finds quadrants and matrices in the scientific IS literature. Two-by-two matrices are far from rare. For instance, Farbey et al. (1992) suggest a method for evaluating IT investments, which contains several 'matrices' (pp. 117-119). Further, the phenomenon of the wide-spread use of Gartner's Magic Quadrants has entered the IS literature. Pollock and Williams (2009) investigate the role that industry analysts like Gartner, with such widely used tools such as the Magic Quadrants, have on developing and mobilizing technology procurement markets.

References

Armbrust, M., Fox, A., Griffith, R., Joseph, A., Katz, R., Konwinski, A., Lee, G., Patterson, D., Rabkin, A., Stoica, I., Zaharia, M.: A View of Cloud Computing. Communications of the ACM 53(4), 50–58 (2010)

Blechar, M.: Magic Quadrant for Business Process Analysis Tools, Gartner Report, ID G00161090 (2008)

Erdogmus, H.: Cloud Computing – Does Nirvana Hide behind the Nebula? IEEE Software 26(2), 4–6 (2009)

Elliot, B., Blood, S.: Magic Quadrant for Unified Communications, Gartner Report, ID G00169996 (2009)

Jeffery, K., Neidecker-Lutz, B. (eds.): European Commission 2010. The Future of Cloud Computing: Opportunities for European Cloud Computing Beyond 2010, Expert Group Report (2010)

Farbey, B., Land, F., Targett, D.: Evaluating Investments in IT. Journal of Information Technology 7, 109–122 (1992)

Pollock, N., Williams, B.: The Sociology of a Market Analysis Tool: How Industry Analysts Sort Vendors and Organize Markets. Information and Organization 19(2), 129–151 (2009)

Smulders, C.: Magic Quadrants and Market Scopes: How Gartner Evaluates Vendors within a Market, Gartner Report (2011), http://www.gartner.com/DisplayDocument?doc_cd=154752 (accessed on May 05, 2011)

Ramireddy, S., Chakraborthy, R., Raghu, T.: Privacy and Security Practices in the Arena of Cloud Computing. In: Proceedings of the 16th Americas Conference on Information Systems (AMCIS 2010), Lima, Peru (August 12-15, 2010)

Staten, J.: Cloud Computing for the Enterprise, Forrester Research Presentation (2009), http://www.forrester.com/imagesV2/uplmisc/CloudComputingWebinarSlideDeck.pdf (accessed on May 05, 2011)

Thomas, B., Ullrich, T.: Cloud-Readiness – Continental IT Corporate Infrastructure & Security Strategy (based on Cloud Readiness at Continental AG Presentation developed by Krings, K., Dalbert, U., Workshop 'eco – Verband der deutschen Internetwirtschaft e.V.', Cologne, Germany (February 2011)

Weinhardt, C., Anandasivam, A., Blau, B., Borissov, N., Meinl, T., Michalk, W., Stoesser, J.: Cloud Computing – A Classification, Business Models, and Research Directions. Business & Information Systems Engineering 1(5), 391–399 (2009)

An Efficient Business Process Compliance Checking Approach

Jörg Becker, Philipp Bergener, Dominic Breuker, Patrick Delfmann,
and Mathias Eggert

University of Muenster, ERCIS – European Research Center for Information Systems,
Leonardo-Campus 3, 48149 Münster, Germany
Tel.: +49 (0) 251 8338 100
{becker,bergener,breuker,delfmann,eggert}@ercis.uni-muenster.de

Abstract. Assuring compliant business processes is an important task of business process management, which is commonly supported by the use of business process models. As every compliance rule corresponds with a typical structure, the detection of those corresponds to a pattern matching problem. More specifically, we encounter the problem of subgraph isomorphism. In this paper we propose an automatic business process compliance checking approach that relies on a subgraph isomorphism algorithm and that is suitable for process models in general. As common subgraph isomorphism is a problem that can only be solved in exponential time, we use an algorithm that simplifies the problem through pre-processing. This makes the isomorphism solvable in polynomial time. With the approach, we aim at supporting decision makers in business process compliance management.

Keywords: Compliance, Business Process Management, Pattern Matching, Subgraph Isomorphism, Efficiency.

1 Introduction

The financial crisis has demonstrated impressively how difficult it is to adhere to legal regulations and internal as well as external compliance requirements concerning business processes. The financial crisis even aggravates the complexity by introducing more and tighter regulations for financial institutions (Caldwell 2009; Caldwell, Bace and Lotto 2009; Opromolla 2009). This trend towards more regulation has also had an impact on IS research. Throughout the last years, an increasing number of approaches to solve compliance issues were published in this research area (Abdullah, Indulska and Sadiq 2009).

In this paper, we introduce a flexible model-driven business process compliance checking approach. It allows for specifying (nearly) any type of compliance rule, whose instances can be searched in any type of conceptual model. For this purpose, we make use of an efficient subgraph isomorphism (Ullmann 1976) approach. Its general applicability distinguishes our approach from existing ones. As the general subgraph isomorphism problem is only solvable in exponential processing time (Garey and Johnson 1979), according algorithms are inefficient and not suitable for

M. Nüttgens et al. (Eds.): Governance and Sustainability in IS, IFIP AICT 366, pp. 282–287, 2011.

large process models. Therefore, we propose reusing a subgraph isomorphism algorithm that makes use of pre-processing, making the isomorphism itself solvable in polynomial time. A precondition for consistent pattern matching results is that the process models are semantically unambiguous. Therefore, we restrict our approach to business process models that are semantically standardized.

2 Related Work

2.1 Business Process Compliance Checking

The concept of business process compliance denotes that the execution of certain processes complies with a set of regulations (Sadiq, Governatori and Namiri 2007). Kharbili et al. (2008) classify the implementation of control mechanisms in three time-dependent phases "Design-Time Compliance Checking", "Runtime Compliance Checking" and "Backward Compliance Checking". In this paper, we focus on Design-Time Compliance Checking.

It is related to modeling compliance rules and process models. Notable research in this field has been done by Governatori et al. (2008), Governatori et al. (2010), Stijin et al. (2006), Wörzberger et al. (2008), Sadiq et al. (2007), Liu et al. (2007). The approaches in this phase mainly focus on the extension or creation of modeling languages that are able to represent compliance rules or might be used for (semi-)automated compliance checking. One example is the Formal Contract Language (FCL) (Sadiq et al. 2007). Within this approach, the identified controls are transformed into control rules and classified with particular control tags. These control tags combine control rules with process models. This allows for (automatic) assignment to corresponding process elements (Sadiq et al. 2007).

Our approach differs from existing ones inasmuch it is generic and thus it abstracts from specific modeling languages. It is applicable to any modeling language that can be formalized as a graph (Harary 1969). This means that both the models and the compliance rules are regarded as graphs, where the compliance rule graph is searched in the model graph. Searching for (small) graphs in (large) graphs corresponds with the problem of subgraph isomorphism known from algorithmic graph theory (Ullmann 1976). Regarding compliance checking as a subgraph isomorphism problem allows for representing compliance rules of arbitrary structure. This aspect constitutes another difference to existing approaches.

2.2 Subgraph Isomorphism

One of the most widely known matching algorithms is Nauty, developed by Mckay (1981). This algorithm is based on group theory and computes the automorphism group of both the search graph and the subgraph which is then used to create a canonical labeling defining a node ordering. Subgraph isomorphism can be found by finding identical adjacency matrices of the two graphs in canonical form. This last verification step can be computed in $O(n2)$ time. The construction of the canonical labeling, however, is a preprocessing step requiring exponential time in the worst case.

Messmer et al. (2000) extend this approach by proposing an algorithm for finding isomorphisms in a library of graphs. Their approach is based on a recursive decomposition of each graph into smaller subgraphs until the decomposed graphs consist of single nodes. The matching algorithm then exploits the fact that some decomposed graphs are identical and avoids redundant comparisons. In another work, the same authors include a decision tree into their algorithm that allows for matching an input graph against an entire library of graphs in O(n2) time with n being the size of the input graph (Messmer and Bunke 1999). This algorithm exploits both the facts that the underlying graphs are labeled and directed and accomplishes the subgraph search with impressive speed. While the construction of a decision tree is rather costly, the effort can be justified assuming that the processes in which patterns shall be searched do not change very often. Given this assumption, the decision tree has to be recomputed infrequently. This is why we chose this algorithm as a basis for our compliance checking approach (cf. Conte el al. (2004) for a detailed description of related algorithms).

3 Pattern Matching

3.1 Definition of Compliance Rules

In general, there are an infinite number of compliance rules depending on the actual domain and subjective perception. As such, we are not able to explain and pro¬vide an exhaustive list of identification heuristics for all of the rules. Instead, we show an exemplary excerpt which is based on the German money laundry law (ger. Geldwäschegesetz, GWG) (cf. Becker et al. (2010) for a comprehensive list of compliance rules).

Two sample compliance rules are depicted as subgraphs in Figure 1. A sequence requires a specific activity (here: "B") to be placed between two other subsequent activities (here: "A" and "C"). The corresponding subgraph is defined as GS=(VS,ES) with VS={A,B,C} and ES={(A,B),(B,C)}. Separation of duties requires two subsequent activities (here: "A" and "B") to be performed by two different people

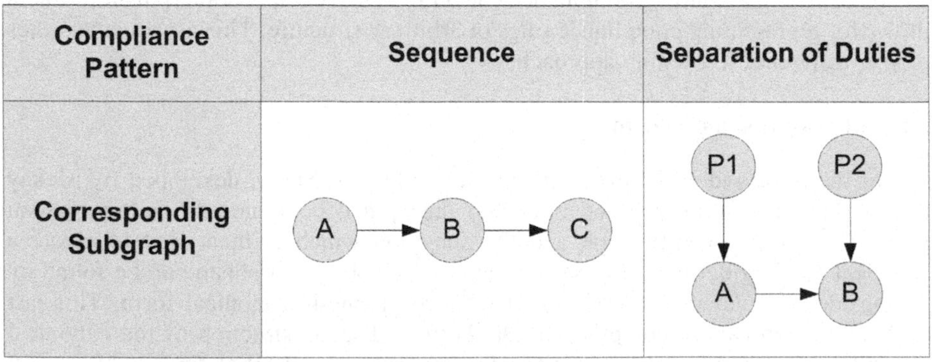

Compliance Pattern	Sequence	Separation of Duties
Corresponding Subgraph	A → B → C	P1 → A, P2 → B, A → B

Fig. 1. Examples of Compliance Rules and Corresponding Subgraphs

(here: "P1" and "P2"). The corresponding subgraph is defined as GS=(VS,ES) with VS={A,B,P1,P2} and ES={(A,B),(P1,A),(P2,A)}. Different types or names of the subgraph's vertices are realized by using a labeled graph. Unique names stored in the graph's labels are realized through semantic standardization (cf. previous section).

3.2 The Messmer-Bunke-Algorithm for Sub-graph Isomorphism

To detect such compliance rule patterns in a library of process models we propose using an adapted version of the algorithm for subgraph isomorphism presented by MESSMER AND BUNKE in (Messmer et al. 1999). The algorithm operates on a number of a priori known model graphs (in our case the process models) and an input graph (the pattern). The basic idea of the algorithm is to compute all possible permutations of the adjacency matrices of the model graphs, with the vertex labels on the main diago¬nals of the adjacency matrices, and to arrange them in a decision tree during a pre-processing step. At runtime the adjacency matrix of the input graph is used to find identical matrices in the decision tree. The corresponding permutation matrices repre¬sent the searched subgraph isomorphism. The exact algorithm is given in (Messmer et al. 1999).

3.3 Algorithm Adaptation

There are a few modifications neces¬sary to account for particularities of our patterns. First, due to the possibility to incor¬porate wildcard elements standing for a number of arbitrary activities and prohibited activities into a pattern, we do not solve the traditional subgraph iso-morphism problem but rather a modified one in which two nodes of a pattern may be connected by a path of length k instead of being directly connected via a single edge.

To cope with this challenge we compute, for each of the model graphs, a distance matrix containing a vector of distances of all paths with maximum length k between any combinations of nodes. For each of these paths, we also associate a list of labels encountered on that path. During the creation of the decision tree, the distance matrix is treated analogously to the adjacency matrix. Thereby, for each row column element of the adjacency matrix that is associated to a node of the search graph, we also associate an appropriately permuted row column el¬ement of the distance matrix. If we now encounter a wildcard while searching the tree for a subgraph occurrence, we look up the entry of the distance matrix instead of the adjacency matrix and check if there exists a path being short enough. If the wildcard prohibits the occurrence of certain labels on the path, we additionally check if the candidate path is free of such labels.

Another problem of the original algorithm is that it solves the induced subgraph problem. That is, it requires for each edge between nodes in the model graph the presence of an edge between the associated nodes in the pattern. However, we are interested in any match of our pattern regardless of additional edges between nodes of the model graph. To adapt the algorithm in such a way that it finds every pattern, we again need to extend the decision tree. The original tree has, on each level k, a node for each permutation of an adjacency matrix of all the subgraphs of size k. Our modification is that we do want to include not only all these subgraphs but, for each of the subgraphs GS, additional subgraphs being equal to GS except that an arbitrary set of edges has been removed. When searching a pattern we can then not only find an occurrence with nodes being connected exactly as it is specified in the pattern graph but we also find any occurrence having additional edges in the model graph by matching it to one of the newly incorporated tree nodes for which exactly these edges have been removed.

A third issue with the algorithm is that we interpret the building block type assigned to a vertex as its label. However, it might be that there are certain attributes of vertices that might be of relevance when defining a pattern. Consequently, a pattern should only be returned if, besides the labels of the vertices, the corresponding attributes of the vertices also match each other. A straightforward solution to this problem would be to interpret the combination of building block type and attribute as the label of a vertex. Unfortunately, this demands that, when creating a compliance rule pattern, a value has to be assigned to all available attributes of vertices. Thus, this solution is not an option, since many patterns will leave certain attribute values unspecified. The only other option left is to apply the algorithm with labels being building block types and to subsequently check each identified occurrence of the pattern for correctness of attributes. During this post-processing step, each identified subgraph whose attributes do not match the pattern is discarded.

4 Outlook

In the short term, research will continue along two consecutive lines. We first in¬tend to implement the algorithm in order to test it on a large library of business processes. In a second step we aim at defining a large set of compliance rule patterns. With these two librar¬ies of both input graphs as well as process models we intend to conduct an empirical analysis of the algorithm's practical runtime behavior, since the algorithm has to prove its efficiency not only theoretically but also in practice. Results will point to further optimiza¬tion potential of the extended algorithm.

Although the relevance of our approach was confirmed in preliminary discussions with compliance experts in the financial sector, the support of compliance management experts through the introduced approach must be shown in detail through qualitative and quantitative studies. First evidence from accompanying research to this paper in conjunction with compliance experts suggests that the complexity of compliance management will be better handled and thus the effort for compliance checking will be lower by using the presented approach.

References

Abdullah, S.N., Indulska, M., Sadiq, S.: A Study of Compliance Management in Information Systems Research. In: ECIS, Scholar One, Verona (2009)

Becker, J., Ahrendt, C., Coners, A., Weiss, B., Winkelmann, A.: Business Rule Based Extension of a Semantic Process Modeling Language for Managing Business Process Compliance in the Financial Sector. Lecture Notes in Informatics: Modellierung betrieblicher Informationssysteme (MobIs) 175(1), 201–206 (2010)

Caldwell, F.: The Worldwide Economic Crisis will Bring Real-Time Reporting for Risk Management Gartner Research. Gartner, Inc. (2009)

Caldwell, F., Bace, J., Lotto, R.J.D.: U.S. Financial System Regulatory Overhaul Brings More Scrutiny Gartner Research. Gartner, Inc. (2009)

Conte, D., Foggia, P., Sansone, C., Vento, M.: Thirty Years of Graph Matching in Pattern Recognition. International Journal of Pattern Recognition and Artificial Intelligence 18(3), 265–298 (2004)

Garey, M.R., Johnson, D.S.: Computers and Intractability: A Guide to the Theory of NP-Completeness. W.H. Freeman, New York (1979)

Governatori, G., Hoffmann, J., Sadiq, S., Weber, I.: Detecting regulatory compliance for business process models through semantic annotations. In: Workshop on Business Process Design, Milan (2008)

Governatori, G., Rotolo, A.: A Conceptually Rich Model of Business Process Compliance. APCCM, Brisbane (2010)

Harary, F.: Graph Theory Reading (1969)

Kharbili, M.E., de Medeiros, A., Stein, S., van Der Aalst, W.M.P.: Business Process Compliance Checking: Current State and Future Challenges. Lecture Notes in Informatics: Modellierung betrieblicher Informationssysteme (MobIs) 141, 107–113 (2008)

Liu, X., Müller, S., Xu, K.: A static compliance-checking framework for business process models. IBM Systems Journal 46(2), 335–361 (2007)

McKay, B.D.: Practical Graph Isomorphism. Congressus Numerantium: 30), 45–87 (1981)

Messmer, B.T., Bunke, H.: A Decision Tree Approach to Graph and Subgraph Isomorphism Detection. Journal of Pattern Recognition 32(12), 1979–1980 (1999)

Messmer, B.T., Bunke, H.: Efficient Subgraph Isomorphism Detection: A Decomposition Approach. IEEE Transactions on Knowledge and Data Engineering 12(2), 307–323 (2000)

Opromolla, G.: Facing the Financial Crisis: Bank of Italy's Implementing Regulation on Hedge Funds. Journal of Investment Compliance 10(2), 41–44 (2009)

Sadiq, S., Governatori, G., Namiri, K.: Modeling control objectives for business process compliance. In: Alonso, G., Dadam, P., Rosemann, M. (eds.) BPM 2007. LNCS, vol. 4714, pp. 149–164. Springer, Heidelberg (2007)

Stijin, G., Vanthienen, J.: Designing Compliant Business Processes with Obligations and Permissions. In: Eder, J., Dustdar, S. (eds.) BPM Workshops 2006. LNCS, vol. 4103, pp. 5–14. Springer, Heidelberg (2006)

Ullmann, J.R.: An Algorithm for Subgraph Isomorphism. Journal of the Association for Computing Machinery 23(1), 31–42 (1976)

Wörzberger, R., Kurpick, T., Heer, T.: Checking Correctness and Compliance of Integrated Process Models. In: 10th International Symposium on Symbolic and Numeric Algorithms for Scientific Computing, pp. 576–583 (2008)

A Maturity Model for Segregation of Duties in Standard Business Software

Jan Omland[1], Nick Gehrke[2], and Niels Müller-Wickop[3]

[1] Benrather Schlossallee 99, 40597 Düsseldorf, Germany
jan.omland@bfcs.de
[2] Köllner Chaussee 11, 25337 Elmshorn, Germany
nick.gehrke@nordakademie.de
[3] Max-Brauer-Allee 60, 22765 Hamburg, Germany
niels.mueller-wickop@wiso.uni-hamburg.de

Abstract. Maturity models are widespread used in several domains ranging from business processes to complete management frameworks like CMMI, ITIL or Cobit. In the paper on hand we develop a detailed maturity model for the management of segregation of duties in ERP systems. Our model includes several aspects starting with simple access rights management of individual systems and leading to comprehensive organizational aspects of multiple systems environments. Applying this model, organizations are enabled to improve compliance regarding access rights using a step by step approach. The approach described can also be used to assess existing segregation of duties processes of an organization in order to reveal further improvement opportunities.

Keywords: Maturity Model, Segregation of Duties, SoD, Authorization Process, Authorization/Access Controls, Rule Set.

1 Introduction

When it comes to business process implementation and integration of business data throughout all value chain activities, a lot of companies rely on standard business software (for definition cf. Staud 2006, p.33). This is only justified, if the software is sufficiently secured. (Hendrawirawan et al. 2007, p.46). It seems necessary to provide an authorization concept for system security, which incorporates thoroughly implemented segregation of duties (SoD). Many Companies have problems implementing segregation of duties accurately (Krell 2007, p.18). One significant reason is the inherent complexity of ERP systems. Due to the comprehensive application range and the high grade of process integration it is not only necessary to have business process skills, but to have technical knowledge as well. The high complexity of SoD, the growing quality awareness and the claim for an efficient approach underline the need for SoD standards and maturity models (Chandra und Beard 2007, p.2). The application of maturity models facilitates the quality measurement of SoD.

M. Nüttgens et al. (Eds.): Governance and Sustainability in IS, IFIP AICT 366, pp. 288–294, 2011.

2 Conceptual Design of the Maturity Model

In general, maturity models range from three to six maturity degrees (Fraser et al. 2002, p.246). We decided to use five maturity levels. In a second step rating criteria were developed, these are used to determine maturity levels. The number of complexity level ranges from two to five. Altogether 31 questions have been developed to determine maturity level for SoD in standard business software. For the purpose of giving a structured overview to the developed maturity model, rating criteria are assigned to the following 4 categories: *rule set, control processing, SoD reporting and organizational framework* (COSO 2004, pp.3-4). For our maturity model we use the staged representation (In this context "staged" means that every maturity level fulfills all criteria of maturity levels below (Fraser et al. 2002, p.246)) Following the four categories and their assigned rating criteria are specified in more detail.

Category *"rule set"*: A rule set is the foundation of every SoD analysis. All relevant SoDs are defined here (Little und Best 2003, p.421). First of all, the quality of SoD in standard business software depends on the applied rule set. Thereby certain rule set characteristics are relevant which are usable as rating criteria for the maturity model (Hendrawirawan et al. 2007, p.3). When analyzing SoD it is only possible to detect those conflicts that have been defined in advance. Apart from completeness, being up-to-date is another important criterion. Based on the risk identification the rule set has to be updated continuously to achieve a high quality SoD process (Chandra und Beard 2007, p.11). For the category "rule set" altogether four questions are posed to determine the maturity level (cp. figure 1 in appendix). Existence resp. complexity level (cl) is used as unit of measurement (um) (cp. figure 2 in appendix).

Category *"control procedure"*: This category summarizes those criteria which deal with guidelines and procedures to mitigate relevant risks. Following the stages of the SoD process (Wolf und Gehrke 2009, p.3) it is possible by means of these criteria to control the before defined compliance of rule sets (COSO 2004, p.4). Basically three different criteria are pointed out which can be used for control procedure maturity level assessment: point of time, character of control and frequency (Debreceny 2006, p.4). Regarding the time of control procedure preventive and detective controls can be classified. Thus by means of a control risk occurrence can be avoided (ex ante) or retrospectively discovered (ex post).

Another criterion is the type of control execution. A differentiation is made between manual and automatically executed controls. Especially SoD controls provide a strong link to automated approaches. It is crucial for the sustainable implementation of SoD that the control activities are carried out regularly (Taiariol 2009, p.23). Before mentioned questions of control activity assessments are presented in the appendix (see Figure 1).

Category *"SoD Reporting"*: This category includes SoD reporting criteria describing the preparation of the analysis results as well as criteria that address the clean-up of identified SoD conflicts. Hence the sustainable implementation of the defined rules is also subject to this category. For example, the comparison of the last SoD analysis results reveals the success or failure of the SOD activities over time (also taking the timely removal of identified conflicts into account) (Taiariol 2009, p.25). Thus indicators of possible process improvements can be identified. A structured approach to eliminate the weak points we pointed out is also useful to prioritize the individual SoD conflicts. This can ideally be done by a risk assessment of the different SoD conflicts (Krell 2007, p.19). Thereby it is important to question risks according to the risk management process to challenge the rule set and adjust it if necessary. In accordance with the determined risks, escalation mechanisms should be implemented for the purpose of eliminating assessed conflicts. A differentiation of escalation mechanisms, considering the calculated risks and temporal evolution, is worth taking into account.

Category *"Organizational Environment"*: Criteria grouped under this category are primarily concerned with the assessment of process safety consciousness within the company. This category is essential for the quality of SoD processes executions. Although so-called Computer Assisted Audit Techniques (CAAT) are used to support the automation of SoD activities, the employment of employees in many areas is still essential (Hendrawirawan et al. 2007, p.3).

From an organizational perspective a criterion for assessing the maturity level is the definition of responsibilities (Herbsleb et al. 1997, p.38). Usually, the IT department is responsible for ERP security-related issues. The business departments employees - as business process owners - typically lack the technical knowledge for the maintenance, allocation and testing of permissions. Therefore, the separation of duties within standard business software should be an inter-divisional anchored task (Taiariol 2009, p.23). The integrative character is also reflected in properly implemented authorization assignment processes (Chandra and Beard 2007, p.14). Because of the far-reaching consequences approval by the line manager is not sufficient, a so-called "role owner" must be defined.

Further criteria include the involvement of senior management and the definition of target values. Assuming the management is informed regularly about the development of SoD conflicts a high priority of the issue within the company can be assumed (Herbsleb et al. 1997, p.38).

Maturity Level 0: The maturity level 0 is present if a company carries out its authorization management for business standard software, but does not consider SoD issues. The perception of SoD issues within the company does not exist. The purpose of the authorization management is only to allow employees access the ERP system.

Maturity Level 1 - Initial: Similar to known maturity models such as CMMI and BPMM SoD projects in standard business software have the degree of "initial" if they are assigned to the lowest possible maturity. In this stage, processes are executed in an unplanned and unstructured way, thus the quality of SoD analysis is difficult to assess (OMG 2008, p.20). This is mainly due to the lack of formalization of the rule sets, which complicates the traceability of activities regarding completeness and correctness. Rules are defined on an ad hoc basis by the participating employees, creating a company-wide heterogeneous landscape. In addition, the definition of rules is not based on risk assessments within the meaning of the risk management process. Therefore a full consideration of all high-risk business processes is not given. This also implies a lack of dynamism of rules. Adjustments based on risk assessments are not made.

Maturity Level 2 - Repeatable: In comparison to the maturity level "Initial " a formalized rule set - defining SoD conflicts - is existent. This increases the transparency of SOD activities within the company and facilitates the formalization of a re-implementation of SoD analysis. From an organizational perspective on this level of maturity the department is more involved in the SoD process. On the one hand, this increases the quality of the rule set. On the other hand, departments as recipients of reports are enabled to identify and evaluate SoD conflicts as well as assisting with their removal. The successful elimination of SoD conflicts is reflected in passed follow up audits. The results are documented and reported.

Maturity Level 3 - Defined: At this maturity level rules for multiple risk prone business processes and supporting application systems are existent. Rule sets are updated as soon as relevant changes are made to the business processes. To increase the effectiveness of the control system the rule set includes both - detective and preventive - controls. In the case of inapplicable rules, decentralized local controls are executed in order to minimize potential risks. To support a company-wide process improvement, conflicts are tagged with "risk values" in the regular reporting. Based on the risk values managers can derive a prioritization of follow-up activities to ensure effective use of their resources. The communication of conflicts is integrated in the escalation management to ensure timely processing. Overall, the SoD approach at this level is structured. Responsibility for SoD processes lies with the departments. Departments develop rule sets in cooperation with IT staff and remove identified conflicts. The increased awareness of SoD is also reflected in the further development of the authorization management.

Maturity Level 4 - Managed: At this maturity level a generic rule set is used. Based on the risk assessment SoD are defined for all relevant business processes. These SoD are defined independently of the (IT-) system. Before deriving controls from the rule sets transactions are mapped to relevant application systems. In this way it is easier to maintain a company-wide uniform rule set. In case of process changes only one rule set needs to be adapted. Vice versa the rule set is still usable if IT systems are replaced. Only system-specific transformations need to be adapted. All control activities are automatically carried out on a regular basis. This enables responsible personal to make a statement about compliance regarding SoD aspects in the short term. The sustainable elimination of conflicts is supported by an automatic escalation management. Furnished with a priority conflicts are communicated to corresponding departments depending on age and risk assessment. Reports also include figures about process improvements.

Maturity level 5 - Optimizing: The maturity level "Optimizing" describes the highest level of SoD projects in standard business software. At this level SoD processes are constantly being developed and improved. A process to update the rule set in the case of relevant processes changes is in place. Also included is the systems specific rule set transformation, linked control activities, the risk assessment and the reporting as well as the escalation management. At this maturity level the company-wide uniform rule set is characterized by its completeness. It includes not only all high risk classified processes and the linked application systems, but also SoD aspects across different systems. To ensure uniform implementation of all control activities compensating controls are defined and rolled out centrally. An autonomous approach by departments is precluded. Compared to maturity level 4 there are not only set targets for the elimination of SoD conflicts, but the management also designs an incentive system. Thereby incremental and innovative process and technology improvements are encouraged.

3 Conclusion

In this paper a maturity model for segregation of duties in standard business software is presented. Both the complexity of the issue and the lack of research in this area illustrate the need of such a model. In the categories rule set, control activities, reporting and organizational environment we developed 31 questions that can help assess the current state of SOD activities. Furthermore, based on the results improvement opportunities can possibly be identified and prioritized accordingly. In comparison to other maturity models the relatively simple structure should provide high user friendliness. In order to aggregate important information a future graphical presentation of results is possible (Carbonel, 2008, p.4).

References

Carbonel, J.: Case Study: Assessing IT Security Governance Through a Maturity Model and the Definition of a Governance Profile. Information Systems Control Journal 2, 29–32 (2008)

Chandra, A., Beard, M.: Towards a Framework for Achieving Effective Segregation of Duties (2007),
http://artsms.uwaterloo.ca/accounting/UWCISA-new/symposiums/symposium_2007/Chandra-SOD.pdf
(retrieved August 25, 2009)

COSO Committee of Sponsoring Organizations of the Treadway Commission, Enterprise Risk Management - Integrated Framework - Executive Summmary 2004 (2004)
http://www.coso.org/Publications/ERM/COSO_ERM_ExecutiveSummary.pdf (retrieved September 15, 2009)

Debreceny, R.S.: Re-Engineering IT Internal Controls: Applying Capability Maturity Models to the Evaluation of IT Controls. In: Proceedings of the 39th Annual Hawaii International Conference on System Sciences, HICSS 2006, vol. 8, p. 196c (2006)

Fraser, P., Moultrie, J., Gregory, M.: The use of maturity models/grids as a tool in assessing product development capability. In: Proceedings of Managing Technology for the New Economy, St John's College, Cambridge, UK, August 18-20, pp. 244–249. IEEE Service Center, Piscataway (2002)

Gehrke, N., Wolf, P.: Continuous Compliance Monitoring in ERP-Systems – A Method for Identifying Segregation of Duties Conflicts. Wirtschaftsinformatik 2009, 347–356 (2009)

Hendrawirawan, D., Tanriverdi, H., Zetterlund, C., Hakam, H., Kim, H.H., Paik, H., Yoon, Y.: ERP Security and Segregation of Duties Audit: A Framework for Building an Automated Solution. Information Systems Control Journal 2, 46–50 (2007)

OMG (2008), Business Process Maturity Model (BPMM), Object Management Group (OMG),
http://www.omg.org/spec/BPMM/1.0/PDF/ Abgerufen am (08.02.2011)

Herbsleb, J., Zubrow, D., Goldenson, D., Hayes, W., Paulk, M.: Software Quality and the Capability Maturity Model. Communications of the ACM 6(40), 30–40 (1997)

International Federation of Accountants (IFAC). Handbook of international quality control, auditing, review, other assurance and related services pronouncements, 2010 edition, New York (2008) ISBN: 978-1-60815-052-6

Krell, E.: ERP System Controls. Business Finance 4(13), 18–22 (2007)

Little, A., Best, P.J.: A framework for separation of duties in an SAP R/3 environment. Managerial Auditing Journal 5(18), 419–430 (2003)

OMG Object Management Group. Business Process Maturity Model (BPMM) (2008), http://www.omg.org/spec/BPMM/1.0/PDF/ (Retrieved September 9, 2009)

Staud, J.L.: Geschäftsprozessanalyse. Ereignisgesteuerte Prozessketten und objektorientierte Geschäftsprozessmodellierung für Betriebswirtschaftliche Standardsoftware. Dritte Auflage. Springer (Springer-11775 /Dig. Serial), Heidelberg (2006)

Taiariol, R.: Segregated Duties in Fashion. Internal Auditor 1(66), 23–25 (2009)

Appendix A. Definition of maturity level with associated questioner

Category	Criterion	1	2	3	4	5	Question	
Risk Set	1	0	1	1	1	1	Is there a formalized rule set that defines the individual SoD conflicts, for example a SoD-Matrix?	Yes/No
	2	1	1	2	3	4	Does the rule set include all processes classified as "risky" and the relevant associated application systems?	DoC
	3	0	0	0	1	1	Is it a company-wide or group-wide uniform rule set?	Yes/No
	4	1	1	2	2	3	Is a review of the rule set carried out, if changes of underlying processes take place?	DoC
Controls	5	1	1	1	1	1	Are there enough detective SoD controls implemented?	Yes/No
	6	0	1	1	1	1	Is the regular execution of detective SoD controls adequate?	Yes/No
	7	0	0	1	1	1	Is the execution of detective SoD controls as far as possible automated?	Yes/No
	8	0	0	0	1	1	Are there enough detective controls to review transaction- and master data in order to detect fraud as well as error or abuse of individual authorizations?	Yes/No
	9	0	0	1	1	1	Are there enough preventive SoD controls implemented?	Yes/No
	10	0	0	0	1	1	Is the regular execution of preventive SoD controls adequate?	Yes/No
	11	0	0	0	1	1	Is the execution of preventive SoD controls as far as possible automated?	Yes/No
	12	0	0	1	1	1	Are there enough compensating SoD controls implemented?	Yes/No
	13	0	0	1	2	3	How are compensating controls defined and executed?	DoC
	14	0	0	0	1	1	Is the regular execution of compensating SoD controls adequate?	Yes/No
	15	0	0	0	0	1	Is the execution of compensating SoD controls as far as possible automated?	Yes/No
	16	1	1	2	2	3	Is there a process in place that ensures the adaption of control activities as a result of a rule set changes?	DoC
SoD-Reporting	17	0	1	1	1	1	Is a SoD-Reporting existent?	Yes/No
	18	0	0	1	1	1	Is the regular reporting adequate?	Yes/No
	19	0	0	0	1	1	Does the reporting take the chronological sequence of the identified SoD conflicts removal into account?	Yes/No
	20	0	0	1	1	1	Are there risk values calculated for each SoD conflict?	Yes/No
	21	0	0	0	1	1	Is the risk value calculation review regularly?	Yes/No
	22	1	1	2	2	3	Are there escalation mechanisms existent that are used to eliminate SoD conflicts?	DoC
	23	0	0	0	1	1	Are escalation mechanisms initiated automatically depending on the reporting results?	Yes/No
	24	1	1	1	2	3	Are there target reviews (e.g. KPIs) included in the reporting?	DoC
	25	0	0	0	1	1	Are there metrics for process improvement included in the reporting (e.g. optimizing the role concept and user administration)?	Yes/No
Organization	26	1	2	3	3	3	Is only the IT-department involved in SoD issues? Are other departments only informed about SoD-analysis results?	DoC
	27	0	1	1	1	1	Is every department responsible for granting authorization (is this document in specific work instructions)?	Yes/No
	28	0	0	1	1	1	Is there separate process for special user rights like "Super-User/SOS-User"?	Yes/No
	29	1	2	3	4	5	Is a monitoring process for special users like "Super-User/SOS-User" in place (e.g. review of system logs)?	DoC
	30	0	0	0	0	1	Are there incentives for reaching set SoD aims?	Yes/No
	31	0	0	0	1	1	Is the management regularly informed about the development of SoD conflicts?	Yes/No

Appendix B. Degree of complexity for different questions

Degree of Complexity - Question 2

DoC	Characteristic
1	The rule sets are existent per "risk process" and an application system. It is defined system-specific.
2	The rule set is existent for a number of "risk processes" and an application systems. It is system independent (generic) defined.
3	A generic rule set exists for all "risk processes" and was transformed for some application systems.
4	A generic rule set exists for all "risk processes" and was transformed for all application systems. It also includes cross-system SoD.

Degree of Complexity - Question 4

DoC	Characteristic
1	No. The rule set is static.
2	In some cases, the rule set is reviewed. However, there is no systematic review.
3	A process is in place for updating the rule set as soon as relevant process changes occur.

Degree of Complexity - Question 13

DoC	Characteristic
1	Compensating controls are decentrally defined and executed.
2	An approval is centrally given for decentral defined controls.
3	Compensating controls are centrally defined and executed.

Degree of Complexity - Question 16

DoC	Characteristic
1	No. Controls are not reviewed.
2	In some cases a control review is carried out. However, there is no systematic review.
3	There is a process that ensures that controls are checked at each rule set change.

Degree of Complexity - Question 22

DoC	Characteristic
1	No. There are no procedures for the elimination of identified SoD conflicts.
2	Yes. Once SoD conflicts were identified, the department manager is prompted to resolve these conflicts.
3	Yes. Depending on the calculated risk value different levels of hierarchy are notified.

Degree of Complexity - Question 24

DoC	Characteristic
1	No. There are no target Values.
2	Yes. There are rudimentary targets, for example the elimination of all conflicts by the end of the year.
3	Yes. There are dedicated targets. These values are determined on risk basis.

Degree of Complexity - Question 26

DoC	Characteristic
1	No involvement of the departments.
2	The department is informed of SoD analysis results.
3	The departments are responsible for the SoD process.

Degree of Complexity - Question 29

DoC	Characteristic
1	There is no review Process
2	Activation/Configuration of system log files
3	Random review of system logs
4	Regular manual review of logs
5	Automatic control of system logs

Investigating the Influence of Information Management Practices on IS Governance

Ioanna Constantiou[1], Sabine Madsen[2], and Anastasia Papazafeiropoulou[3]

[1] Department of IT Management, Copenhagen Business School Howitzvej 60,
5.12, DK 2000 Frederiksberg, Denmark
Tel.: +45 3815 2353
ic@inf.cbs.dk
[2] Roskilde University, Universitetsvej 1, 43.2, DK-4000, Roskilde, Denmark
sabinem@ruc.dk
[3] Department of Information Systems and computing, Brunel University, Uxbridge,
UB8 3PH, United Kingdom
Tel.: +44 (0)1895 266035
Anastasia.papazafeiropoulou@brunel.ac.uk

Abstract. Information technology especially through Internet applications provides tremendous possibilities to knowledge workers, in any domain, to get access to vast amounts of data. This is a development with great benefits but also some challenging implications. In other words, as the information available increases, the knowledge workers' needs to make sense of information, i.e. for, prioritizing, organizing, and interpreting information intensify. Yet, the information management practices, which are based on the user's characteristics, have not been studied extensively. In this paper we suggest the examination and explication of the information management practices used by knowledge workers today in order to provide useful insights to managers involved in IS governance in the organisation. We also introduce specific theories which can be used as a lens to analyse the knowledge workers' practices and offer useful theoretical insights into the domain. We contend that such research could provide a set of guidelines that can be adopted by organisations in order to offer their employees a structured way to deal with information management which is supported by the information technologies and systems available. We argue that our results could be useful to knowledge workers looking to exploit available information while overcoming information overload.

Keywords: Information management practices, IS governance, knowledge workers.

1 Introduction

Internet and social networking systems emerge every day and Internet-based communication tools such as skype, facebook, twitter and on-line meeting spaces are part of every knowledge worker's life. Thus, finding a productive way to manage information coming from all those sources becomes paramount for preserving their productivity. As new communication software systems become available every day,

M. Nüttgens et al. (Eds.): Governance and Sustainability in IS, IFIP AICT 366, pp. 295–299, 2011.

knowledge workers are struggling to find ways to cope with information overload and survive the overwhelming amount of information that is available to them. This vast amount of data available to knowledge workers has been reported to create 'pathologies of information' which are hard to overcome (Bawden and Robinson, 2009). It has been reported that as knowledge workers are exposed to an increasing amount of information, they lose their ability to concentrate, solve problems and handle every-day tasks. Consequences of the information overload may involve shrinking of creativity or even lead to a melt down of knowledge workers because of stress (Hallowell, 2005). Multi-tasking and breaking down of attention to a number of different sources of information is a typical experience of people working in an office environment. Although it has been suggested that knowledge workers need easy access to information through a single interface (Feldman, 2004) as well as the use of software tools for filtering information, little has been done by organisations to tackle a problem as big as information overload (IEEE Spectrum, 2009).

The question raised is about how we can support knowledge workers information management practices through IS governance. We emphasise the importance of studying information management practices in relation to IS governance, a topic which has only been investigated by a limited amount of researchers. We contend that there is a need for introducing formal methods and practices, supported by information systems, to be used by knowledge workers in order to cope with information overload. This could enable the knowledge workers to use information provided by the information systems more efficiently and add quality rather than confusion to the workplace. In turn, this may increase the productivity and efficiency in the organisation.

2   Proposed Theoreatical Approach

We conceptualize information management as double-edged in the sense that it encompasses practices (a) for coping with information overload as well as (b) for benefitting from the use of information (information empowerment). Moreover, we draw on different theoretical approaches to address information management from different perspectives. We propose the use of three theoretical dimensions for the study of the knowledge worker information management practices and of how they are supported by the information technologies and systems available in the organisation.

1. **How the knowledge worker creates meaning from online information (Sense-making).** Intention shapes attention (Weick, 1995). It is to a large extent the way the person defines her motivations, goals, priorities, and tasks at a given point in time that makes her notice and act in accordance with certain cues while ignoring other cues completely (See e.g., Choo, 1996; Solomon, 1997; Weick, 1995; Weick et al., 2005). In other words, intention strongly influences what kind of information the knowledge worker pays attention to and creates meaning from. The created meaning in turn affects the knowledge worker's decisions.

2. **How the knowledge worker interacts with, and manage information available via Internet technologies, so as to make decisions (Decision-making).** Humans are subject to bounded rationality which in turn affects their information

processing abilities (Simon 1955). In the process of decision making people have to cope with the information available in a specific situation (March 1978). Internet technologies increase information availability, which in turn may empower or impede the knowledge worker. The information management strategy is shaped by the knowledge worker's cognitive processes or intuitive approaches based on heuristics (Kahneman 2003). The knowledge worker uses heuristics to reduce the cognitive effort required to deal with all the available information in the situation at hand (Bazerman 2008). However, the use of heuristics may create bounded awareness (Chugh & Bazerman 2007) which in turn makes the knowledge worker ignore relevant, and available information (e.g., information in one's email inbox).

3. **How the knowledge worker maintains a balance between a focused mind and openness to emerging and contextual information (Mindfulness).** Mindfulness is a state of mind where the individual shows openness to new information and different points of view while remaining aware of the context and in control of the situation at hand (Langer, 1989). Being mindful as a knowledge worker demands a great deal of self-observation and development of decision-making strategies which are ad-hoc and always relevant to the context of work. Maintaining a mindful state of mind gives people the possibility to avoid a situation where information is either ignored or misinterpreted with adverse effects for decision-making (Langer, 1989). Being mindful means being aware of the diversity of tasks coming your way but also being open to experiences which have not been planned or organised. Mindfulness is also about keeping a focused attention to the task at hand and performing one-thing-at-a-time in order to keep the consecration going while welcoming new inputs if they arrive.

We use a simple case of information management, where the knowledge worker only has one task, in order to explain how the three theoretical perspectives interrelate. A knowledge worker always has a state of mind while performing a specific task. Mindfulness enables her to keep overview of all the relevant information, thus reducing the cognitive bias in accessing the necessary information for the task (i.e., be able see more information). Then, mindfulness enables her to focus on creating meaning from information relevant to the task. The next step is to evaluate the information and make a decision about the task, based on the created meaning. Here, mindfulness reduces the cognitive burden for the decision-maker because she focuses on the respective activity. It is clear that in practice, knowledge workers experience more complicated situations and multi-tasking is often required and this can be the context of our proposed study.

3 Future Research Plan

Our suggested research method involves a longitudinal study to investigate the proposed research problem. We have divided the research work in three phases:

In the **first phase** we will conduct a pilot study for understanding the knowledge worker's information management practices when using Internet-based applications. We will conduct interviews with knowledge workers from organisations in different domains. Moreover, we will conduct interviews at the top management level to identify the link between information management and organisational goals. The outcome of this phase will be the formation of the knowledge base about the empirical context.

In the **second phase** we will collect data about the knowledge workers' information management practices in the workspace. We will capture the knowledge workers' perceptions and behaviours using a triangulation of data collection techniques, such as observation, interviews and log files. Data collected over a period of time and via different techniques will allow us to understand information processing behaviour in context and to alleviate the discrepancy between intentions/perceptions and actual behaviours. Data analysis will be performed with a focus on the use of information in different processes (e.g., during project prioritisation) and the organisational implications. The outcome of the phase is a set of information management practices as well as a set of "new" heuristics that can be adopted in the organisation and used by knowledge workers.

In the **third phase** we assess the impact of the identified information management practices. We will invite a group of employees from the participant organisations and ask them to use the information management practices, identified in the research for a period of time. During this period we will use observations and interviews to follow-up on the knowledge workers' use of these practices. The observations and interviews will be structured around the information use as described in the first phase. The outcome of the phase will be a set of information management practices that are better aligned with individual and organisational goals and provide useful insights to managers involved in IS governance in the participating organisations.

References

Bawden, D., Robinson, L.: The dark side of information: overload, anxiety and other paradoxes and pathologies. Journal of Information Science 35, 180–191 (2009)

Bazerman, M.H.: Judgment in managerial decision making, 7th edn. John Wiley & Sons, Chichester (2008)

Choo, C.W.: The Knowing Organization: How Organizations Use Information to Construct Meaning, Create Knowledge and Make Decisions. International Journal of Information Management 16(5), 329–340 (1996)

Chugh, D., Bazerman, M.H.: Bounded awareness: what you fail to see can hurt you. Mind & Society 6, 1–18 (2007)

Feldman, S.: The high cost of not finding information (2004),
http://www.kmworld.com/articles/readarticle.aspx?articleid=95
34 (accessed on February 26, 2010)

Hallowell, E.M.: Overloaded circuits: Why Smart People Underperform. Harvard Business Review, 1–10 (2005)

IEEE Spectrum. How to beat information overload (2009),
http://spectrum.ieee.org/computing/it/how-to-beat-
information-overload/0 (accessed on February 26, 2010)

Kahneman, D.: Maps of bounded rationality: Psychology for behavioral economics. American Economic Review 93(5), 1449–1475 (2003)

Langer, E.J.: Mindfulness. Da Capo, Cambridge (1989)

March, J.G.: Bounded rationality, ambiguity, and the engineering of choice. The Bell Journal of Economics 9(2), 587–608 (1978)

Simon, H.: A behavioral model of rational choice. The Quarterly Journal of Economics 69(1), 99–118 (1955)

Solomon, P.: Discovering Information Behavior in Sensemaking, Time and Timing. Journal of American Society of Information Science 48(12), 1097–1108 (1997)

Weick, K.E.: Sensemaking in Organizations. Sage Publications, Thousand Oaks (1995)

Weick, K.E., Sutcliffe, K.M., Obstfeld, D.: Organizing and the Process of Sensemaking. Organization Science 16(4), 409–421 (2005)

The Green Vistas of Sustainable Innovation in the IT Domain

Wietske van Osch and Michel Avital

University of Amsterdam, 1018WB Amsterdam, Netherlands
Tel.: +31(0) 20 525 7584, +31 (0) 20 525 5059
{W.vanOsch,Avital}@uva.nl

Abstract. Sustainable innovation is about creating social, environmental, and economic value for all stakeholders involved. The sustainable innovation lens offers an extension of the prevailing discourse on Green IT/IS and renders a three-fold approach that encompasses social, environmental and economic dimensions of sustainability. Moreover, sustainable innovation entails a proactive approach that focuses on developing creative solutions to environmental and social challenges rather than merely on reducing the IT footprint by waste management and regulation compliance. Building on a longitudinal analysis of sustainable innovation in the automotive industry, we gained a number of relevant insights that can be applied to the information technology domain. First, our results illustrate that a sustainable innovation approach can serve as a source of creativity and innovation that enables firms to aim for generating bigger wins for businesses, the environment, and society overall. Second, our results suggest that sustainable innovation requires a concerted effort of all stakeholders to reshape existing norms and values, formulate new standards, and reconfigure work systems vis-à-vis the social and environmental vistas of sustainable value. Building on our study, we provide further recommendations for IT research and practice.

Keywords: Green IT, Green IS, Sustainability, Innovation.

1 Introduction

With the centrality of information technology and charges that it is responsible for 2% of the world's total CO_2 emissions (Gartner, 2007), it is not surprising that in recent years the issue of Green IT/IS has gained momentum. Overall, so far we can identify two primary approaches to sustainability—one focuses on how to reduce the negative ecological impact of information technologies, Green IT, and the other focuses on how to leverage information technologies for solving our environmental problems, Green IS. The former approach treats information technologies as part of the problem and addresses the question of how to reduce their ecological footprint by cutting CO_2 emissions, energy consumption, and waste throughout their lifecycle. The latter approach considers information technologies or information systems as part of the solution and analyzes their potential role in helping organizations to manage their environmental footprint.

M. Nüttgens et al. (Eds.): Governance and Sustainability in IS, IFIP AICT 366, pp. 300–305, 2011.

Notwithstanding the valuable insights that the Green IT/IS[1] movements have contributed, we posit that they have largely overlooked two important issues. First, both approaches have been focused on the ecological (i.e. environmental) facet of sustainability, while falling short of noticing the significance of its social aspect. Second, Green IT/IS has been driven largely by regulation and the desire to reduce costs, while virtually disregarding the potential generative and value added capacity of sustainable innovation with respect to the prevailing technologies. Compliance with regulation and cost reduction have steered the discussion and subsequent efforts toward mitigating and managing technology's negative environmental effects through primarily reactive approaches, which have in turn led to downplaying the potential of IT/IS in fostering sustainable innovation as a source of social, environmental, and economic value for all stakeholders involved.

To that end, we propose approaching the underlying topic through the sustainable innovation lens (Cooperrider, 2008), which builds on, yet extends, the prevailing conceptions of Green IT/IS. Overall, sustainable innovation refers to designing and implementing sustainable organizational processes and practices that generate social, environmental, and economic worth for all stakeholders involved (Thatchenkery et al. 2010). Applying the sustainable innovation lens to the discourse on Green IT/IS has two appealing promises. First, it offers reframing the underlying issues with an extended approach to sustainability that addresses a range of environmental, social, and economic values in the context of information technology. Second, it redirects our attention to the importance of innovation and multi-stakeholder collaboration in proactively addressing challenges and opportunities of sustainability.

Building on analysis of sustainable innovation in the automotive industry, we draw two insights with respect to the information technology domain. First, a sustainable innovation approach can serve as a source of creativity and innovation that enables firms to generate bigger wins for the business, the environment, and society overall. Second, the study suggests that sustainable innovation requires a concerted effort by all stakeholders to reshape existing norms and values, to formulate new standards, and to reconfigure work systems for diffusing sustainable technologies.

In what follows, we first describe the prevailing IT-related context of sustainability. Then, we present the findings through a brief synopsis of sustainable innovation in the automotive industry. Finally, we apply the generated findings regarding sustainable innovation to information technology and discuss its implications for research and practice.

2 Three Perspectives on Sustainable Information Technology

Sustainability in the context of IT is often addressed through the narrative of Green IT (i.e. greening IT) or Green IS (i.e. greening by IT), and we offer an alternative, namely Sustainable Innovation. In this section we briefly describe the three different approaches to sustainability and juxtapose them in Table 1.

---

[1] The abbreviated term "Green IT/IS" throughout this paper denotes Green IT and Green IS. It does not imply that Green IT and Green IS are similar or interchangeable. Rather, we view Green IT and Green IS as two unique approaches and relate them separately as well as jointly to sustainable innovation.

Table 1. Summarizing Approaches to Green and Sustainable IT/IS

	Green IT	Green IS	Sustainable Innovation
Focal Point:	IT artifact	Environment	Society
Description:	Reducing IT footprint	Managing environmental footprint	Generating overall sustainable value for all stakeholders
Driver of Change:	Regulation	Costs and regulatory compliance reporting	Technical and social innovation
Nature of Change:	Reactive	Reactive/Proactive	Proactive
Dimensions of Sustainability:	Environmental sustainability	Environmental sustainability	Social and environmental sustainability

2.1 Green IT

The bulk of the nascent literature on Green IT to date is concerned with greening IT, that is, with mitigating the negative impact of IT on energy consumption and CO_2 emissions (Murugesan, 2008; Gartner 2007; Pernici et al., 2008). The most prominent drivers of Green IT are regulation (Mingay, 2008) and the increased concerns about the impact of IT on a company's energy spending. The research and business practice in this area aimed at eliminating waste, increasing efficiency, and lowering energy costs. Thereby, it is primarily reactive and focused on the environmental facet of sustainability.

2.2 Green IS

A smaller set of studies has addressed the potential role of information technology in helping organizations to manage their environmental footprint, i.e. greening by IT. This approach has been referred to as Green IS (Boudreau et al., 2008) stressing the greater potential of information systems rather than information technology in dealing with environmental management. The most prominent driver of Green IS is regulatory compliance reporting as well as the desire to reduce costs of energy and carbon emissions (Mingay, 2008). Thereby, it is also primarily reactive and focused on the environmental facet of sustainability.

2.3 Sustainable Innovation

Taking an affirmative holistic stance, sustainability can be seen as "a business approach to creating long-term shareholder and stakeholder value by embracing opportunities and risks derived from economic, environmental and social developments" (Dow Jones Sustainability Group). Hence, generating environmental, social, and economic sustainability is not perceived as a burden for businesses, but rather as an innovation challenge, a strong differentiator, and a potential source of competitive advantage (Cooperrider, 2008, Laszlo, 2008). Sustainable innovation draws on the intrinsic motivation of companies to take responsibility for all stakeholders, future generations, and the environment itself. It stresses the crucial role businesses can play in creating a sustainable world when acting as a source of innovation and creativity to address sustainability-related challenges in a holistic manner. Additionally, sustainable innovation highlights the importance of multi-stakeholder innovation—e.g., of collective engagements among businesses, governments, educational institutions, and the community—for generating sustainability. In short, the sustainable innovation approach provides a wider and inclusive boundary-spanning outlook on the underlying subject matter (see Table 1).

3 Findings

In what follows, we briefly explore some general findings regarding sustainable innovation in the automotive industry over the past two decades. Building on our generalized observations regarding the potential benefits of adopting the sustainable innovation approach in the context of information technology, the subsequent section provides insights for both IT research and IT practice. Sustainable innovation holds that companies can take a proactive role in solving sustainability-related challenges only if they look beyond regulation compliance and cost reduction, and subsequently search for opportunities to shape legislation, to create value for the community and all stakeholders, and to rethink and redesign unsustainable products, processes, and entire systems.

The generated findings clearly reflect this proactive and collaborative nature of sustainable innovation in the automotive industry. First, the study shows that the development and successful diffusion of technologies is highly dependent on a sequence of contingencies including technical, economic, regulatory, social, and environmental junctures. Second, the successful diffusion of new technological innovation depends on how well a company links the innovation to the expectations and demands in the broader social environment. Hence, sustainable innovation could succeed only when important players in the automotive industry were able to understand and rethink the unsustainable nature of existing processes and systems and to proactively search for sustainable alternatives that appeal to their respective markets.

For example, the great success of hybrid vehicles, in particular Toyota's Prius, and at the same time, the failure of electric and fuel cell vehicles have not been solely based on technological considerations or performance, but also on social circumstances. The successful hybrid technology, did not require a significant disruption of existing technologies, norms, and standards, rather was it designed to use the existing technology base, such as refueling infrastructure, functional requirements, and institutional frameworks, that was already in place for traditional cars. In contrast, electric and fuel cell cars, entailed a radical discontinuity from the internal combustion engine, and called for fundamental reframing of preferences and expectations, values and norms, standards and regulations. Although electric vehicles and fuel cell cars can create *environmental* value and *social* value simultaneously, the diffusion of such sustainable alternatives has been impossible without the proper multiple complementary social and institutional measures. Therefore, sustainable innovation requires the concerted efforts of all stakeholders to change related norms, formulate new standards, alter prevailing preferences, and reshape dominant practices for opening up paths to sustainable innovation.

4 Discussion and Conclusion

Sustainable innovation requires a broad and inclusive view of the underlying issues with a long-range perspective that is rooted in historical depth. Just as management is an instance of governance, green IT can be seen as an instance of sustainable innovation. In spite of the limitations to generalizing from a different industry, we propose the sustainable innovation approach as an extension of the current Green IT/IS frameworks. Sustainable innovation redirects our efforts to the creation of sustainable environmental, social, and economic value, and does not limit our actions to environmental concerns. Moreover, it offers an augmented perspective by focusing on *creating* positive solutions to environmental and social challenges through multi-stakeholder collaboration rather than on *reducing* and *managing* the IT footprint.

In what follows, we apply the accumulated insights regarding sustainable innovation in the car industry to information technology, and discuss how it can shed light on the challenges and opportunities ahead.

4.1 Implications and Recommendations for IT Research

Sustainable innovation, as introduced in this paper, can serve as a rhetorical device that can extend the Green IT/IS discourse far beyond ecological considerations. Adopting the sustainable innovation lens would provide researchers with the leverage necessary to elevate their research beyond environmental sustainability into a wider context relating to innovation and society; for instance, by studying how companies, through their IT innovation efforts, can contribute to sustainability, diversity, human rights, employee relations, safe and clean products, as well as good governance structures. Furthermore, by relying on sustainable innovation, researchers can look for ways in which contemporary social and global challenges can be turned into business opportunities and how innovation can be used for generating a sustainable world. This implies not only adopting a broader perspective on sustainability—by incorporating its three pillars—but also a wider approach to innovation—by acknowledging the need for collaborative engagements between businesses and society.

4.2 Implications and Recommendations for IT Practice

Our observations can also provide insights into the practice of sustainable use and application of IT, which seems to leave much room for improvement according to watchdog groups who monitor the situation. For instance, *Greenpeace's 2009 Guide to Greener Electronics* indicates that only a few companies in the IT industry have made an effort to become greener and that most companies perform unsatisfactorily[2]. Overall, new information technologies and systems will be able to generate more environmental and social value for stakeholders only if the current efforts that focus on incremental and reactive innovation programs (such as the reduction of energy consumption and waste disposal) will be reinforced with more radical technological innovations that reshape current practices and reconfigure existing work systems.

---

[2] http://www.greenpeace.org/international/campaigns/toxics/electronics/how-the-companies-line-up

Moreover, our findings show that creating sustainable information technology is likely to require multi-stakeholder involvement. The IT industry, let alone a single organization, is unlikely to drive successfully a significant change or manage the sustainable challenge single-handedly, using the leverage of technological innovation. Instead, leading companies and the IT industry as a whole should seek involvement of the public, interest groups, universities, non-profit organizations, and government agencies.

Finally, our results indicate that merely responding to social and economic factors that trigger needs for more sustainable technologies is unlikely to be sufficient for reshaping the extraordinary potential of information technology in creating significant sustainable value. Rather, applying the sustainable innovation approach, companies need to adopt a leading role in shaping radical new technologies that provide environmental, social and economic value for all stakeholders involved and in reshaping the respective societal and institutional frameworks.

References

Boudreau, M., Watson, R.T., Chen, A.: From Green IT to Green IS. Cutter Benchmark Review 8(5), 5–11 (2008)

Cooperrider, D.: Sustainable Innovation. BizEd, 32–37 (2008)

Gartner Research, Gartner Symposium/ITxpo 2007: Emerging Trends, Gartner Inc. (2007)

Laszlo, C.: Sustainable Value. In: How the World's Leading Companies Are Doing Well by Doing Good. Greenleaf Publishing, Sheffield (2008)

Mingay, S.: Green IT: The New Industry Shock Wave. In: Gartner, Green IT Grand Conference, vol. 7 (2008)

Murugesan, S.: Harnessing Green IT: Principles and Practices. IT Professional 10(1), 24–33 (2008)

Pernici, B., Ardagna, D., Cappiello, C.: Business Process Design: Towards Service-based Green Information Systems. In: SSME Cross Session in IFIP World Computer Congress, vol. 280, pp. 195–203 (2008)

Thatchenkery, T., Cooperrider, D., Avital, M.: Positive Design and Appreciative Construction: From Sustainable Development to Sustainable Value. Advances in Appreciative Inquiry Series, vol. 4. Emerald Publishing, Bingley (2010)

Position Statement: Sustainable Information and Information Systems (SIIS)

Duane Truex, Leif Olsson, Katarina Lindblad-Gidlund, Johanna Sefyrin,
Aron Larsson, Olof Nilsson, Karen Anderson, Erik Borglund, and Viveca Asproth

Department of Information Technology and Media, Mid Sweden University
Tel.: +46 (0) 771-975000
katarina.lindblad-gidlund@miun.se

Abstract. In this position statement we provide our understanding of the relation between the IS field and the notion of sustainability, and present our focus through a characterization of the "sustainability research" construct. By doing so, we hope to contribute to the discourse on a clarification of the construct itself in our research community.

Keywords: information, information systems, sustainability, economical, ecological and social dimensions.

1 Introduction

The three-fold purpose of this position statement is to first provide a space within which we conceptualize the relation between the IS field and the notion of sustainability. Second, the statement aims at presenting the focus of a community of scholars at a mid-sized Scandinavian university; our current work is collectively characterized as falling under the umbrella notion of "sustainable information and information systems" (SIIS). Thirdly, through the description of this group's characterization of the "sustainability research" construct, to contribute to a clarification of the construct itself in the IS research community.

We are well aware of the definitional disputes around the meaning of "sustainability" and, as Poet Mark vanTiblurg reminds, "In naming meaning begins", that a robust debate about the meaning(s) of the term is essential in developing standards, metrics and acceptable approaches to researching the topic. There exist a wealth of literature reviews and other articles that elaborate the definition of sustainability and describe a range of projects falling in the domain of sustainability research. We do not aim to replicate that work but rather summarize key threads that have helped establish the boundaries of our own definition, one that guides our inter and multi disciplinary inquiries currently in the early stages of development. We share that definition below.

1.1 Sketching the Field of Sustainability

In the Brundtland report (Our Common Future, 1987) sustainable development is defined as: "Sustainable development is development that meets the needs of the

M. Nüttgens et al. (Eds.): Governance and Sustainability in IS, IFIP AICT 366, pp. 306–309, 2011.

present without compromising the ability of future generations to meet their own needs". However, sustainability is usually divided into three interdependent dimensions: 1) economic, 2) environmental and 3) social sustainability (e.g. McKenzie, 2004). In the realm of *economic sustainability* we concur with Daly (1990, 1991) who discusses growth versus development, and underscores that while ""growth" refers to expansion in the scale of the physical dimensions of the economic system ... "development" refers to qualitative change of a physically nongrowing system in a state of dynamic equilibrium maintained by its environment" (1990, p. 33). Daly's conclusion is that sustainable economic development is a better term than sustainable economic growth. With regards to *environmental sustainability* we find Williams' and Millington's (2004, p. 101) distinction between weak and strong sustainability helpful in anchoring ends of a continuum; i.e., strong- as the expansion of the stock of resources in order to meet the increasing demands, vs. weak-a focus on revision of these demands. The basic problem with this continuum is the so-called 'environmental paradox', referring to the "mismatch between what is demanded of the Earth, and what the Earth is capable of supplying" (Williams & Millington, 2004). Finally, in relation to social sustainability McKenzie (2004, p. 18) writes that: "Social sustainability occurs when the formal and informal processes, systems, structures and relationships actively support the capacity of current and future generations to create healthy and livable communities. Socially sustainable communities are equitable, diverse, connected and democratic and provide a good quality of life". Based on McKenzie (2004) we view social sustainability as a locally situated condition and a process.

1.2 Sustainability in Relation to Information and Information Technologies Systems

It is hardly possible to address the concept of sustainability and avoid the notion of technologies since technologies often are either expected to solve many of the problems and tensions linked with a sustainable future or are viewed as part of the source that creates them (Daly, 1990, 1991; Williams & Millington, 2004; McDermott & Hagemann, 2010). Irrespective of perspective, reflections on the intersection of sustainability and technologies demand theoretically well-founded analyses and close empirical studies in order to create valuable knowledge on how they interact. On a general level, analyses of how technologies and societal development interrelate are to be found in several reference disciplines of IS such as Sociology of Technology (Berg, 1998), Science and Technology Studies (1998), and Philosophy of Technology (Feenberg, 1999). Sustainability in specific is however a more scarcely treated concept even though it has gained in attention lately (see for example Mihelcic et al, 2003 for engineering and Mitrea et al, 2010 for ICT construction). An exception is though the linkage between information systems and sustainable competitive advantage (Clemens, 1986) and economic growth (Avgerou, 2003) that has played a more prominent part. Thus, as indicated by the choice of definitions above we would like to propose a slightly different pathway.

2 Our Points of Departure

As a starting point in our work we interpret sustainability to refer to a complex and multidimensional ontological space addressing economic, ecological and social / societal concerns. Situated in a Swedish context that presumes democratic participation and commitment to social justice and societal equality, our preliminary conception of sustainability pays attention to unequal power relations and injustices, prefers development rather than growth, and the reuse of existing resources rather than finding or exploiting new extractive resources. In our view a robust concept of sustainability is defined locally and is not scalable from the local, regional or global domains. Finally, we concur with McKenzie's argument that sustainability is not only a condition but also a process in which participation and democracy are central.

2.1 Our Approaches to the Field

In the Mittuniversitetet SIIS group three different research approaches to Information and Information systems are united:

- The ValIT (Value creation with IT) group focuses on how value is translated, enacted and performed in IT-related processes.
- The CEDIF group brings together professional and research expertise in: a) Recordkeeping (archives and records management) b) Business process analysis c) Systems design d) Information architecture e) Long-term digital preservation.
- The CRIINFO group focuses on design of systems for accessibility of critical information which is carried out through applied research in close cooperation with stakeholders in order to create benefit.

Within the SIIS solutions-oriented approaches to sustainable information and information technologies coexist with approaches that focus on problematizing the issues related to sustainability and definitions thereof. These approaches are not necessarily based on the same worldviews, definitions of sustainability or the same science theoretical points of departure, and this sometimes causes tensions. However, we view of these tensions and differences as productive in that they give rise to new questions and understandings of the issues at hand.

2.2 Preliminary Research Questions

A general aim is to explore how IT is used in efforts to develop a more sustainable society. We have four preliminary research questions:

- How are information technologies present / involved / active in the doing of transition processes to a more sustainable society; how do they hold unforeseen potential, and how may they make visible activities outside of the established?

We also examine how investments in infrastructure and new technologies can be evaluated regarding uncertain profitability as well as how their contribution to the three dimensions of sustainable development can be aided by computer based decision support. Of particular interest is the employment of societal decision analysis together with methods for valuation of investment decisions under uncertainty. This drive two further research questions are:

- How is it possible to use information technologies in order to promote infrastructure investments, for instance, investments in renewable energy as part of the transition towards sustainability?
- How are information technologies involved in various solutions believed to lead to a more sustainable development?
- Finally we investigate the design and develop IT solutions in support of an effective management of the transition process by asking:
- How may information technologies be utilized when developing towards a more sustainable development, in terms of IT-design solutions?

3 Conclusions

In conclusion, by first providing our understanding of the relation between the IS field and the notion of sustainability, and second presenting our focus through a characterization of the 'sustainability research' construct, we hope to contribute to a clarification of the construct itself in our research community.

References

Agyeman, J.: Where justice and sustainability meet. Environment 47(6), 10–23 (2005)

Avgerou, C.: The link between ICT and economic growth in the discourse of development. In: Korpela, M., Montealegre, R., Poulymenakou, A. (eds.) Organizational Information Systems in the Context of Globalization. Kluwer Academic Publishers, Boston (2003)

Berg, M.: The Politics of Technology: On Bringing Social Theory into Technological Design. Science, Technology, & Human Values 23(4), 456–490 (1998)

Daly, H.E.: Sustainable development: from concept and theory to operational principles. Population and Development Review 16, 25–43 (1990)

Daly, H.E.: Operational principles for sustainable development. Earth Ethics (1991)

Feenberg, A.: Questioning Technology. Routledge, New York (1999)

McDermott, B., Snabe, J.H.: 2010 Sustainability Report 4 (2010),
    http://www.sapsustainabilityreport.com

Sustainability and IS Research – An Interaction Design Perspective

Gitte Skou Petersen

Department of Informatics, Copenhagen Business School
Howitzvej 60, 5. sal. 2000 Frederiksberg, Denmark
Tel.: (+45) 24676744
gsp.inf@cbs.dk

Abstract. The intention of this paper is to propose interaction design as a venue for IS research into sustainability and in that connection also propose a new theoretical psychological approach to interaction design. This new theoretical psychological framework is based on ecological psychology and activity theory. The paper will outline the scientific demands for the framework as well as the frameworks focus areas that are: 1) Intentional-motivational aspects of interaction 2) Sensory-motor aspects of interaction 3) Behavior-context aspects of interaction. Furthermore the paper will briefly present a design science research project applying the framework to interaction design for a climate management ICT system in greenhouses.

Keywords: Sustainability, Interaction design, IS research, Activity theory, Ecological psychology, HWID.

1 Introduction

Sustainability has the attention of the public eye and the debate typically centers on topics like global warming, sustainable agriculture and renewable energy sources. The role of information systems and IS research in dealing with the challenges of sustainability could be important, but as researchers point out then sustainability within IS research is presently only an emerging focus (Melville, 2010; Watson et al., 2010). This paper suggests interaction design as an IS research approach to sustainability. As an example saving energy, and avoiding to waste energy, has been investigated in relation with interaction design of domestic technology. In an experiment well-designed feedback in domestic central heating systems have been found to support users in achieving both efficient energy use as well as energy waste level reduction (Wastell et al., 2009). Likewise an interaction design experiment resulted in savings when the users were supported in setting goals for the energy usage of a washing machine (McCalley & Midden, 2002). These experimental results suggest that interaction design actively supporting user intentions in regard with energy usage can be one viable approach to sustainability for IS research.

The first point promoted by this paper is therefore that interaction design can contribute to attaining efficiency in energy consumption both in domestic and professional settings. A second point that will be presented is that a development of

M. Nüttgens et al. (Eds.): Governance and Sustainability in IS, IFIP AICT 366, pp. 310–316, 2011.

the theoretical approach to interaction design is necessary to allow for a further scientific development of the field. Currently the interaction design field suffers from two problems 1) Commonsensical guidelines often guides interaction design e.g. Normans guidelines of visibility or feedback (Norman, 1998). Scientifically it is presently necessary to mature the field further and analyze what the guidelines mean in term of human behavior. 2) Research on interaction design has followed the technological development and is organized by technologies instead of by human behavioral characteristics.

Both of these problems can be addressed by introducing a unified theoretical approach to human-artefact interaction. This will provide both a structured scientific approach to interaction design and allow for the generalization and transfer of knowledge of human behavioral characteristics across technological niches. The concept of 'artefact' is used as an umbrella term and refers to man-made objects including both material and abstract objects. This will be elaborated upon in the next part of the paper.

This paper will first outline the scientific demands for a new theoretical approach to interaction design grounded in psychological theory and then the outline will be followed by a presentation of the contents of such a new theoretical psychological framework. As a conclusion the research project, where the framework will be applied, is briefly described.

2 The Scientific Demands for a New Theoretical Approach to Interaction Design

Since human (hominid) tool-use has been around for literally millions of years it means that human-artefact interaction is as much a product of our evolutionary development as are our perceptual systems and our social and cognitive abilities (Leontyev, 2009). From an activity theoretical standpoint: "The development of activity brings us into closer and closer contact with still greater parts of, and still more layers of the world - it makes increasingly more of the world into objects for us" (Mammen, 1989, p.86) meaning that during evolutionary development of animals the animal-environment interaction has become increasingly complex - so far culminating in the human-artefact interaction. Buchanan (1995) provides an illustrative example of the diversity of material and abstract objects we interact with. From the field of design thinking he makes a broad outline of 4 areas where design affects contemporary life 1) Symbolic and visual communications, e.g. graphic design, books, magazines, scientific illustration 2) Material objects, e.g. tools, instruments, clothing, machinery 3) Activities and organized services, e.g. logistics, logical decision making, strategic planning 4) Complex systems or environments for living, working, playing and learning, e.g. systems engineering, architecture, urban planning. An artefact today is therefore not only a physical, material thing, it can also be an abstract object (Gregor & Jones, 2007) as information systems are an excellent example of. A theoretical psychological framework of human-artefact interaction can therefore not limit itself to addressing only material objects, but must also include abstract objects.

Presently knowledge of interaction design is organized according to technological niche which is reasonable seen from the technological R&D point of view. The argument put forward here is that in order to further the research on interaction design then it is necessary to organize research around human behavioral characteristics instead. Even though there is great diversity in artefacts as illustrated by Buchanan (1995) then we, as human beings who interact with the technology, share common characteristics of perception, cognition and action that prevails regardless of technological niche. This line of argumentation is not new. Carroll (2003) concludes that the "golden age" of HCI was characterized by a unified theoretical approach – cognitive science. Even though cognitive science has failed to fulfil the expectations and the field of HCI today is multidisciplinary and fragmented then there still is a need for a "comprehensive and coherent methodological framework" (p.7). The theoretical psychological framework put forward in this paper is an attempt to provide a coherent theoretical approach to human-artefact interaction and thereby interaction design. Dealing theoretically with the behavioral characteristics of human-artefact interaction, however, place certain demands on the framework:

Following the above mentioned arguments then a theoretical psychological framework firstly needs to concern itself with human-artefact interaction (in psychological terminology: the subject-object relationship) of both material and abstract objects across technological niches.

Secondly the framework has to be able to describe and analyze real world human behavior meaning human behavior as it occurs outside of the psychological laboratory. Cognitive psychology has long dominated psychology and "...presented us with a world not just devoid of things but also agents" (Costall & Dreier, 2006, p.1). This does of course not mean that the full breath of psychological methodology including lab experiments will be rejected. It just means that the focus is on producing theory and models that accommodates the need for a field of applied psychology dealing with the nature of the human-artefact relationship as it unfolds in real-world settings.

Thirdly the framework has to encompass theoretical interdisciplinarity both within HCI but also with regard to psychological subdisciplines. Currently relevant knowledge is spread across research fields like IS, anthropology, HCI, design thinking, etc. but also across psychological subdisciplines like perception, cognition, and social psychology.

A theoretical psychological framework centered on three analytical focus areas is now constructed and it will address the above mentioned scientific demands.

3 The Theoretical Psychological Framework

The three analytical focus areas of the framework are based on the theoretical approaches to human-artefact interaction described by Bærentsen (2000) and Petersen (2005). This thereby allows for the theoretical stretch across different technological niches as well as it includes both material and abstract objects and the interactional differences they cause.

To ensure that the theoretical psychological framework allows for the description of real world user behavior it is based on activity theory and ecological psychology

(Gibson, 1986; Leontyev, 2009; Schoggen, 1989) as these approaches focus on human behavior as it unfolds outside of the psychological laboratory. The laboratory as a main working area has been one of the main points of criticism directed at cognitive psychology along with the problems brought on by the paradigm of representationalism as interceding between the subject and the surrounding world (Carrol, 2003; Costall, 2007).

As this addresses two of the above mentioned scientific demands then the third demand for interdisciplinarity will be invoked within the individual focus areas thereby informing the framework of activity theory and ecological psychology with relevant knowledge from other theoretical perspectives.

The three focus areas are now briefly outlined. The framework will be further elaborated upon and tested during the course of the research project that is described in the last section of this paper.

1. **Motivational-intentional aspects of human-artefact interaction**
   The motivational-intentional area concerns the part of the interaction that is purposeful and task-oriented on the user's behalf (Bærentsen, 2000). In short terms, this aspect of interaction addresses the work/task level of a given system. The functionalities have to be relevant to the user and also the user has to have a conceptual understanding of the system's functions in order to be able to use it. Key theoretical perspectives will be activity theory (Bærentsen, 2000; Leontyev, 2009), the HWID framework (Orngreen et al., 2008) as well as cognitive work analysis (Fidel & Pejtersen, 2004; Vicente, 1999).

2. **Sensory-motor aspects of human-artefact interaction**
   The sensory-motor aspects concerns the part of the interaction that are outside the user's conscious attentional focus e.g. object behavior in digital user interfaces such as changing the position of channels in a TV channel list (Bærentsen, 2000) or physical aspects of interaction such as tactile feedback in buttons (Wensveen et al., 2004). The importance of sensory-motor aspects for interaction is hereby stressed by making it an independent analytical focus area. Key theoretical perspectives will be activity theory (Bærentsen, 2000; Leontyev, 2009), ecological psychology (Gibson, 1986), embodied interaction (Dourish, 2001), human factors (Rasmussen, 1986; Rasmussen & Vicente, 1987) and infant cognition research into core cognition (Kintzler & Spelke, 2007) as well as application of core cognition theory to interaction design (Nørager, 2009)

3. **Behavior-context aspects of human-artefact interaction**
   The behavior-context aspects of human-artefact interaction is introduced in order to enable an analysis of how behavior and context interacts as well as to define context in terms of human behavior. The behavior settings theory (Barker, 1968; Schoggen, 1989) - a little known theoretical contribution within the field of ecological social psychology - has through extensive empirical studies of children's behavior in their daily environment concluded that real world behavior has both structure and patterns. These structures and patterns interact with a given context making up what Roger G. Barker termed a behavior setting (Barker, 1968). Behavior settings theory will be a key theoretical perspective as it offers an understanding of context involving both objects and behavior (Petersen, 2005).

The last section will briefly outline how the scientific demands and the framework are applied in an interaction design research project targeting climate control and efficient management of energy in green houses.

4 The Research Project

The project outlined here is a research project on interaction design that is a part of a Human Work Interaction Design (HWID) research project developing an internet- and sensor-based ICT system for climate management in greenhouses (Clemmensen & Pedersen, 2010; HWID webpage, 2011). Greenhouse growers use information systems for climate management in plant and vegetable production in greenhouses. Efficient management of energy consumption in this type of setting both concerns economic considerations as greenhouses are dependent on light, water and warmth, but also concerns optimization of growth without introducing stress conditions for the plants. This research project is a design science research projects methodology allows for a focus on the production of practically-oriented knowledge and therefore makes it possible to research an interaction design development process (Hevner et al., 2004; Wastell et al., 2009). Furthermore it also allows for research into real world user behavior and the project is therefore a design science research project where the artefact created is the interaction design for climate management software (Hevner et al., 2004).

The structure of the research design for this project is inspired by a design science research study where kernel theory, in the form of design principles, was first applied to interaction design and then evaluated and revised (Åkesson et al., 2010). In the same manner this project will apply a kernel theory to create interaction design for climate control software. As justificatory knowledge (kernel theory) to guide the interaction design the theoretical psychological framework will be developed, applied and evaluated (Gregor & Jones, 2007).

The research project will consist of two main empirical components. One will be a work observation field study collecting knowledge of greenhouse growers work routines with regard to climate control as well as a mapping of the knowledge and technology involved in climate management. The knowledge gathered here will be channeled in to the second component that is the interaction design proposals for the new climate management ICT system.

Greenhouses are heavy consumers of energy resources and the climate management software and the associated technology that is used to control the energy consumption is becoming increasingly complex. This research project is itself a symptom, so to speak, of that tendency. The aim of this project – to develop an interaction design actively supporting user intentions to attain efficient energy usage - will therefore address if interaction design is a viable IS research approach to sustainability.

References

Barker, R.G.: Ecological Psychology. Stanford University Press, CA (1968)
Buchanan, R.: Wicked problems in design thinking. In: Margolin, V., Buchanan, R. (eds.) The Idea of Design, pp. 3–20. The MIT Press, Cambridge (1995)

Bærentsen, K.B.: Intuitive user interfaces. Scandinavian Journal of Information Systems 12, 29–60 (2000)

Carroll, J.M.: Introduction: Toward a multidisciplinary science of human-computer interaction. In: Carroll, J.M. (ed.) HCI Models, Theories and Frameworks, pp. 1–9. Morgan Kaufmann Publishers, USA (2003)

Clemmensen, T., Pedersen, R.: A Human Work Interaction Design (HWID) perspective on Internet- and sensor based ICT system for climate management. In: NordiCHI 2010, Reykjavik, Iceland (October 16-20, 2010)

Costall, A.: How cognitive psychology highjacked thinking. Anthropological Psychology 18, 21–23 (2007)

Costall, A., Dreier, O.: Introduction. In: Costall, A., Dreier, O. (eds.) Doing Things with Things, pp. 1–12. Ashgate, UK (2006)

Dourish, P.: Where the action is. Bradford Book (2001)

Fidel, R., Pejtersen, A.M.: From information behaviour research to the design of information systems: the Cognitive Work Analysis framework. Information Research 10(1), paper 210 (2004), http://InformationR.net/ir/10-1/paper210.html (February 22, 2011)

Gibson, J.J.: The ecological approach to visual perception. Psychology Press, San Diego (1986)

Gregor, S., Jones, D.: The anatomy of a design theory. Journal of the Association for Information Systems 8(5), article 2, 312–335 (2007)

Hevner, A.R., March, S.T., Park, J., Ram, S.: Design science in information systems research. MIS Quarterly 28(1), 75–105 (2004)

HWID webpage (2011), http://hwid.cbs.dk/ (February 22, 2011)

Kintzler, K.D., Spelke, E.S.: Core systems in human cognition. In: von Hofsten, C., Rosander, K. (eds.) Progress in Brain Research, vol. 164, pp. 257–264 (2007)

Leontyev, A.N.: Activity and consciousness. Marxists Internet Archive (2009), http://www.marxists.org/archive/leontev/works/activity-consciousness.pdf (February 22, 2011)

Mammen, J.: The relationship between subject and object from the perspective of activity theory. In: Engelsted, N., Hem, L., Mammen, J. (eds.) Essays in General Psychology, Seven Danish Contributions, pp. 71–94. Århus University Press, Århus (1989)

McCalley, L.T., Midden, C.J.H.: Energy conservation through product-intergrated feedback: The roles of goal-setting and social orientation. Journal of Economic Psychology 23, 589–603 (2002)

Melville, N.P.: Information systems innovation for environmental sustainability. MIS Quarterly 34(1), 1–21 (2010)

Norman, D.A.: The design of everyday things. The MIT Press, Cambridge (1998)

Nørager, R.: Low level cognition in user interfaces. PhD-dissertation, University of Aarhus, Department of Psychology, Denmark (2009)

Orngreen, R., Mark Pejtersen, A., Clemmensen, T.: Themes in Human Work Interaction Design. In: Clemmensen, T. (ed.) Cultural Usability and Human Work Interaction Design - Techniques that Connects: Proceedings from NordiCHI 2008 Workshop, CBS, Department of Informatics, Working paper no. 01-2008 (October 19, 2008)

Petersen, G.S.: Dealing with reality – in theory. In: Clemmensen, T., Nielsen, L. (eds.) Proceedings of the 5th Danish Human-Computer Interaction Research Symposium 2005, Copenhagen, November 8, pp. 74–79 (2005)

Rasmussen, J.: Information processing and Human-Machine Interaction. North Holland Series in Systems Science and Engineering, vol. 12. Elsevier Science Publishing Co., NY (1986)

Rasmussen, J., Vicente, K.J.: Cognitive control of human activities and errors: Implications for ecological interface design, Risø-M-2660. Risø National Laboratory, DK 4000 Roskilde, Denmark (1987)

Schoggen, P.: Behavior Settings. Stanford University Press, CA (1989)

Vicente, K.J.: Cognitive work analysis. Lawrence Erlbaum Associate Publishers, New Jersey (1999)

Wastell, D., Sauer, J., Schmeink, C.: Time for a "design turn" in IS innovation research? A practice report from the home front. Information Technology & People 22(4), 335–350 (2009)

Watson, R.T., Boudreau, M., Chen, A.J.: Information systems and environmentally sustainable development: Energy informatics and new directions for the IS community. MIS Quarterly 34(1), 23–38 (2010)

Wensveen, S.A.G., Djajadiningrat, J.P., Overbeeke, C.J.: Interaction Frogger: A design Framework to couple action and function through Feedback and Feedforward. In: DIS 2004, Cambridge, MA, USA (August 2004)

Åkesson, M., Kautz, K., Ihlström, C.: Engaged design science: Developing design visions for future E-newspaper. In: Thirty First International Conference on Information Systems, St. Louis (2010)

Sustaining Data Quality – Creating and Sustaining Data Quality within Diverse Enterprise Resource Planning and Information Systems

Markus Helfert[1] and Tony O'Brien[2]

[1] Dublin City University
Dublin 9, Ireland
Tel.: +353 1 700 8727
`markus.helfert@computing.dcu.ie`
[2] Manor Mill Lane
Leeds, West Yorkshire
Tel.: +44 79 67477336
`tony.obrien@hotmail.com`

Abstract. Many studies have confirmed the challenges relating to data quality in enterprises. This practice oriented research confirms the premise that data quality is of paramount importance to the efficiency and effectiveness of all organizations and that data quality management needs to be embedded within the organizational routines, practices and processes. In this paper we present a study on how to incorporate data quality management principles into organisations. The overriding measure for 'real' success is the sustainability of quality data, thus improving the quality of data over time, to engender long term success. The proposed principles and concepts were applied within a case study. The conclusions drawn from this study contends that this research has unearthed new knowledge as to the means by which data quality improvements may be sustained within diverse enterprise planning and information systems.

Keywords: Data Quality, Data Governance, Enterprise Resource Planning, Key Performance Assessments.

1 Introduction

Over the last two decades data quality has been identified as a major concern for many enterprises Redman (1995); English (1998); Redman (1998); English (1999); Loshin (2001); Redman (2001); Eckerson (2002); Redman (2002); Redman (2004); English (2009), none more so than those operating enterprise resource planning and information systems (Deloitte 1999). For this reason this study, allied to a practical data quality improvement initiative, attempted to discover 'How can an organisation create an environment where data quality improvements can be sustained'. Any attempt to determine the means by which the quality of data can be improved will produce only temporal ameliorations, unless such improvements become embedded. Without the latter, any gains emanating from the former will be merely marginal or short term at best.

M. Nüttgens et al. (Eds.): Governance and Sustainability in IS, IFIP AICT 366, pp. 317–324, 2011.

In this paper we use a dual research approach employing both qualitative and quantitative research strategies focussed within the researcher's own organisation. Section 2 places this study within the confines of an actual ongoing data quality improvement initiative, within which the research process described within Section 3 is undertaken. In Section 4 we summarize the practical benefits of this study and present our research findings. Finally in Section 5 we conclude that the outcomes of this research have important implications for both theory and practice

2   Case Study

2.1   Case Background and Description

The basis of the detailed research undertaken as part of this entire study was carried out within the researcher's own organisation Remploy. Remploy is the largest provider of employment opportunities for disabled persons in the UK, currently employing over three thousand disabled people in over sixty individual factories and offices across the entire country, whilst placing over 10,000 others into external open employment each year. A Baan/Infor ERP system was implemented over ten years ago and whilst there have been many benefits overall it was identified that there was still scope for further improvements especially within the areas of data quality and system complexity.

2.2   Initial Progress

This research study coincided with the commencement of a data quality improvement initiative within Remploy during 2005. An initial approach was made across a number of fronts to attempt to promote education and training; documentation of procedures; the acceptance of responsibility, ownership and accountability at all levels for processes and data; together with better management of master data with the identification and implementation of 'quick wins'.

2.3   Development of Data Accuracy Key Performance Indicators

As part of this initiative seven key performance indicators (KPIs) were established around the order fulfilment process, historically the sources of many of the data quality issues. The KPIs were chosen specifically to reflect the salient elements of these essential commercial operations relating to servicing customer needs. The KPIs were designed to reflect the view of the world as seen through the lens of the ERP system, compared with an *actual* view which could be obtained by direct observation of the actual physical order process. In other words how closely the 'system' (*data within the ERP system*) reflects reality (the real world) in the manner described by Wand and Wang (1997: 94), whilst also providing a measure of the quality of the actual *data* and the related *processes*. From the individual KPIs an aggregated *Index* was developed weighted to take account of the aging of the various transactions and this was then used as the definitive measurement of the ongoing quality of the data within the KPIs.

3 The Research Process, Results and Discussion

3.1 Qualitative Study

The qualitative element of the research took the format of a series of discussion-type focus group meetings sharing experiences, ideas, issues, problems and successes, around a basic flexible agenda, employing an action research approach. This approach attempted to generate discussion and interaction to discover peoples' real feelings and attitudes towards *their* data. In all, forty eight of the fifty four factories and seven business operations and sales teams were covered.

The use of action research in this environment provided the study with a considerable degree of richness in that the researcher had been a member of the organisation for almost twenty years. During this time this 'insider researcher' had worked directly with the majority of the participants and was known to virtually all. This unique approach generated loyalty and trust amongst all parties and not only provided rich material for this study, but also enabled the researcher's colleagues to gain a greater understanding of the significance of quality data and to appreciate the importance of taking ownership of 'their' data. These latter consequences are seen as key to the subsequent improvements that were achieved.

From the outset certain important notions and impressions emerged from the discussions and the analysis and these were subsequently developed as key findings. It was felt that these fell in three broad categories relating to: *lessons learnt* that should be put in practice at all sites, involving basic quality management principles, ownership, responsibility and support, together with measurement and reporting; positive personal *motivational factors* which help to engender commitment from individuals, relating to internal competition and targets, an acceptance of best practices and how these relate to one's ideas and principles; together with organizational and cultural *environmental elements* essentially involving leadership and management issues.

3.2 Measurement and Reporting Process

The importance of measurement, analysis, reporting and feedback was emphasised continually throughout the entire research. Figure 1 below traces the progress of the improvement programme by tracking the Index over the initial three years, highlighting a real trend of improvement over this period, albeit with various explainable fluctuations.

A summary of the progress indicates:

- 29% improvement in the first six months to March 2007
- 33% improvement in the first year to September 2007
- 16% improvement in the year to March 2008
- 40% improvement in the first eighteen months to March 2008
- 27% decline in the eight months to November 2008- which coincided with the Company's Modernisation Programme
- 37% improvement in the year to November 2009
- 52% improvement between September 2006 and November 2009

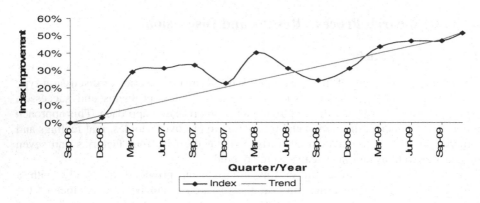

Fig. 1. Data Accuracy KPI Index Improvement tracker

Table 1 below relates the movements in the KPI Index with progression of the site meetings qualitative study both during and following the programme.

Table 1. Data Accuracy KPI Monthly Performance

Month	11	12	01	02	03	04	05	06	07	08	09	10	11
Year	08							09					
No of Meetings	0	13	18	3	15	8	0	0	0	0	1	0	0
Index Impr. % Month	0%	9%	7%	-4%	16%	1%	1%	5%	0%	2%	-3%	7%	2%
Index Impr. % Cum	0%	9%	15%	12%	26%	27%	27%	31%	31%	32%	30%	35%	37%

From analyzing the Table 1, it is evident that there was a significant improvement in the Index (27%), following the commencement of the factory and business meeting programme from December to April, in line with the number of meetings carried out. In addition it may be seen that this level of improvement was maintained immediately following the study and then further improved as the concept of data quality became more established within the organisation.

3.3 Summary of the Findings of the Study

There is considerable evidence to suggest that the progress and improvement described above have real significance leading one to believe that there is potential for real cultural change to take place if improvement initiatives are managed correctly.

This has implications for the wider context of this research as seen by the evolution of the measurement, reporting and overall improvement process, which may best be summarised below in Table 2.

Table 2. Evolution of the improvement process

"What gets measured gets done"	A good start, but by whom?
moving to:	
"What gets measured by the Exec gets done quicker"	A further improvement, but too top-down
leading finally to:	
What is measured, communicated, discussed and agreed at all levels has a very good chance of becoming embedded"	Bottom-up supported by top-down A potential key to sustaining any kind of change?

This highlights the way the improvement process progressed from a traditional top-down management approach to an all encompassing company-wide programme embracing all areas of the business, in line with the development and progression of this entire study.

There is considerable evidence to claim that any improvement initiative cannot be undertaken in isolation and that everyone needs to become involved. There is also however a caveat, in that at this stage it appears that the level of progress achieved appears to be commensurate with the levels of activity of the internal champions or change leaders, suggesting a climate of 'controlled sustainability' rather than 'self sustainability'. This may be a reflection of the relevant infancy of the overall initiative.

3.4 Quantitative Survey

To build upon the progress made within the Data Quality Improvement Programme and the qualitative study, a web-based survey was carried out during the summer of 2009 amongst fellow Remploy colleagues as a means of determining their views, attitudes, thoughts, feelings and opinions with regard to data quality. The overall response to the survey was extremely constructive and encouraging and it identified a significant positive attitude towards data quality in critical areas. One significant result identifies a disparity between peoples' perception of the quality of the data they receive and their own perceived ability to influence and pass on data of sufficient quality to satisfy their own information customers' needs.

3.5 Summary of the Findings of the Survey

Table 3 below summarises the organisational-specific findings into a more 'general' format that will enable them to be applied within a wider environment.

Table 3. Summary of the survey findings

Generic Data Quality	Remploy Data Quality
• There is a high appreciation of the influence that People, Processes and Data have on the quality of data • There is a realisation of the importance of having the data right first time • The level of positive responses compares very favourably with the previous survey held amongst the data quality community	• The overall attitude towards measurement, reporting and feedback was very positive • There was an appreciation of the importance of education and training • Almost 60% felt that 'everyone' has a responsibility to improve the quality of their own and the organisation's data • There was a huge disparity between the respondents' perception of the quality of the data they influence (82%) and that which they receive (26%) • 90% of respondents identified measurement and reporting, problem resolution and process improvement as key elements for improving data quality

4 Analysis of Findings

The direct operational benefits to Remploy of this study as highlighted by the improved Data Accuracy Index have been referred to in depth, but there is also evidence to suggest that there have also been considerable improvements of a cultural and strategic nature. Further operational and strategic advantages have been derived from enhanced reporting, budgeting and forecasting. The myriad of small meaningful ameliorations, both technical and procedural, which have been applied by passionate people during the period since the original Baan implementation, are now gaining greater maturity alongside higher quality data to generate both operational and informational benefits. Finally the recognition of the importance of data in relation to overall governance, risk and compliance has provided enhanced levels of authority and control.

The analysis of the *key findings* from this research and the subsequent detailed discussion enabled certain principle findings to emerge and these are seen as the main outcomes for knowledge and learning for both practice and theory that have emanated from this study to bring about change not only to improve the quality of data but also impart some degree of permanency.

The *role of the champion* is seen as key to promoting and embedding change and innovation. Local champions have emerged at various levels and from various functions within the organisation embracing the essential cultural and motivational philosophies to make improvements within their spheres of influence. The concept of *measurement, reporting and feedback* is a prerequisite for any successful change programme. Within this study this element is not viewed as a mere 'central' monitoring and control mechanism, but has been developed into a reporting process to provide sites and businesses with the information to manage their operations on a day to day basis. The necessity of *time and maturity* is seen as vitally important in embedding change. This element of 'organisational patience' is important to allow new 'processes', changes and improvements to become accepted and embedded as well as to enable 'people' to accept change, develop themselves, gain experience and learn new skills. In discussing the concept of *sustainability*, emphasis has been placed upon maintaining the momentum of improvement particularly within the process of measuring the quality of data. One has to be aware however that there may be occasions where the 'costs' of making further improvements within a particular field may outweigh the benefits that may accrue with the risk of sub-optimization. The quantitative survey and subsequent related detailed discussions have highlighted the huge disparity in peoples' *perceptions of data quality* between the data they influence (82%) and that which they receive (26%). This raises concerns in general as to the quality of communication and the way people view their roles and their own performance and the performances of others.

5 Conclusions and Implications

The conclusions drawn from this study contend that this research has unearthed new knowledge as to the means by which data quality improvements may be sustained within diverse enterprise planning and information systems. Further evidence of some form of real sustainability becomes apparent when one examines the overall performance of the KPI Index in subsequent years. During the year to 31st Match 2011 a further 7% improvement was achieved making an aggregate 59% improvement overall in the four and a half years. This substantiates the belief that the data quality improvement processes described are becoming truly embedded in many area of the organisation.

References

Deloitte Consulting LLP. ERP's Second Wave-Maximizing the Value of Enterprise Applications and Processes, Deloitte Consulting (1999)

Eckerson, W.: Data Quality and the Bottom Line: Achieving Business Success through a Commitment to High Quality Data, The Data Warehouse Institute (2002)

English, L.P.: The High Cost of Low-Quality Data. Information Management Magazine (January: 1-5, 1998)

English, L.P.: Improving Data Warehouse and Business Information Quality- Methods for Reducing Costs and Increasing Profits. Wiley Computer Publishing, New York (1999)

English, L.P.: Information Quality Applied. Wiley Publications Inc., Indianapolis (2009)

Loshin, D.: The Cost of Poor Data Quality. DM Review Magazine (June 2001)

Redman, T.C.: Improve Data Quality for Competitive Advantage. Sloan Management Review, 99–107 (Winter 1995)

Redman, T.C.: The Impact of Poor Data Quality on the Typical Enterprise. Communications of the ACM 41(2), 79–82 (1998)

Redman, T.C.: Data Quality: The Field Guide. Butterworth-Heinemann, Woburn. MA (2001)

Redman, T.C.: Data: An Unfolding Quality Disaster," DM Review Magazine, 1–7 (August 2004)

Wand, Y., Wang, R.Y.: Anchoring Data Quality Dimensions in Ontological Foundations. Communications of the ACM 39(11), 86–95 (1996)

Sustainability in IS: The Case for an Open Systems Approach

Peter M. Bednar[1] and Christine Welch[2]

[1] School of Computing, University of Portsmouth, UK
[2] Dept. Strategy & Business Systems, University of Portsmouth, UK
{peter.bednar,christine.welch}@port.ac.uk

Abstract. Common sense tells us that cost cutting leads to saving, and spending should therefore be minimized. However, a little reflection tells us that this sometimes leads to false economies. In an organizational context, these can lead on to a downward spiral of organizational 'suicide'. Examples of false economies may include: saving on maintenance; saving on research and development expenditure; saving on margins (waste or just-in-time management); and saving on 'how' we do things, as opposed to 'what' we do. Common sense cost cutting makes 'how' invisible, and only recognizes 'what'. It is vital that we also remember to consider 'why' activities are undertaken. Professional competence implies not only skill/knowledge in a particular field, but also desire to apply that knowledge in accordance with certain values, and engagement with the context of application so that learning through reflection may take place. Professional work therefore includes scope for extra-role behaviour, such as suggesting innovative methods or identifying and developing new opportunities (Bednar and Welch, 2010). We suggest that a naïve pursuit of 'efficiency' is likely to constrict and curtail possibilities for extra-role behaviour, with disastrous consequences for the development and growth of the business. Creation of systems experienced as sustainable therefore requires us to focus attention on perceived usefulness, rather than efficiency.

Keywords: Contextual Analysis, Open Systems Approach, Contextual Dependency, Socio-Technical Design, Complex Information Systems.

1 Background

It is possible to conceive of an organization as a particular instance of a purposeful human activity system (Checkland, 1981). A precise agreement about the nature of that system would be difficult to achieve since individual experiences of the same phenomenon vary widely. Boundaries drawn by a person in conceiving of a human activity system will depend upon her changing perspectives over time, which are unlikely to concur precisely with those of others. Organisations subsist as complex, open systems that are continually co-created and recreated through the interactions between their individual members. Open systems that we experience as useful involve a certain ambiguity – a tolerance for variations and imperfections. Maintenance of a perfect equilibrium at all times would be both impossible, in the light of individual,

M. Nüttgens et al. (Eds.): Governance and Sustainability in IS, IFIP AICT 366, pp. 325–329, 2011.

contextually-dependent interpretations of system boundaries. This is, in essence, the reason why Vickers (1972), for instance, preferred a model of relationship maintaining to one of goal seeking when he reflected upon the nature of organizational management. ICTs are deployed in a purposive, contextually-dependent way, i.e. relevant to some particular members of the organization who expect to engage with them in their work. The information needs of those individuals will be recreated continuously over time in the context of activity. Use of the data system will therefore need to be adaptive to these needs. Attempts to design perfect equilibria in such systems would be likely therefore to have an adverse effect on usefulness in practice.

Recently an insurance company perceived a problem in their order processing system, resulting in a significant decline in customer satisfaction. In response, a new IT system was developed early in 2010 intended to improve productivity by enabling each operator to answer four calls simultaneously, together with on-line ordering and a facility for customers to look up product information for themselves. Statistics covering the following year showed an increase in customer inquiries answered. However, the number of actual orders placed remained remarkably constant throughout the period of the project. The impact of the new system was marginal on productivity, but customer satisfaction continued to decline drastically throughout the period measured. However, the exponents of the new system continued to assert its vaunted benefits – these were, they implied, still hidden in undiscovered and unspecified 'qualitative' data. This appears to be an instance of a solution looking for a problem – an assumption that whatever difficulties the order processing system was experiencing, the answer must surely be a new piece of software. The lack of any evidence of progress was then disqualified by the evaluators themselves with the suggestion that they simply had not looked for it in the right place. This case reminds us of work by Williams (2007) reporting research by the IT Governance Institute into 1600 projects in UK businesses. More than half of these projects in organizations were seen to deliver only marginal benefits, but in approximately one third of cases projects actually destroyed organizational value. He also puts forward evidence to suggest that managers continue to support these projects beyond the point where they already know that this will happen.

Why this apparent paradox? We suggest that it is the undue focus on the 'what' (e.g. "functional requirements") of system developments, as opposed to the 'how' (e.g. "non-functional requirements"). Managers simply say to themselves that the initiative must deliver value (according to common sense logic). We suggest that this phenomenon is caused by a fragmented view of the development process, brought about by a lack of a sound and holistic socio-technical approach to systems analysis. Although analysts may recognise the importance of a socio-technical stance, taking into account context, this is frequently limited to local context. Analysis is then restricted by a closed systems perspective (focusing on 'what' a system is intended to do) but sustainability in IS depends upon an open systems perspective (including 'how' and why a system may be experienced as useful by someone). Managing effective transfer and diffusion of technologies requires consideration of the wider environment within which a company is operating and not just its own, internal technical systems.

2 Problem Space

Langefors (1966) pointed out that those engaged in managing an organization need to know about the behaviour and condition of all its component elements, and the wider environment in which it operates at any given time. It is possible to develop a data system to support managers in their tasks, which becomes an information system for any given individual through direct and interpretive participation. Langefors originally considered that the purpose of an information system was to promote attainment of organizational goals. However, he soon realised that expression of any such goals was itself a problematic task, itself requiring a supporting information system. A reflexive relationship can therefore be seen between these defined purposes of IS: promoting the attainment of organizational goals and also support for goal setting. Viewed as a human activity system, the elements of an organization are all interrelated – operational units, sub-systems to monitor their operations and a managing sub-system interpreting data from them, in order to support operations with appropriate resources and directions. Since these interrelated elements are co-ordinated through interconnected information-generating units, it may be preferable to view the organization and its information system as different views of the same phenomenon (Langefors, 1995, p53).

Consideration of sustainability in information systems requires us to pay further attention to the nature of organisations. A system may be described as autopoietic (self re-creating) if its component parts interact with each other so as to continually [re] produce and maintain that set of components and the relationships between them (Maturana and Varela (1980, pp. 78-79). There must be sub-systems perceived to be allopoietic, i.e. that have a purpose other than continuation of their own integrity. Luhmann (1990 in Midgley, 2003 p.67)) has suggested by analogy that social systems, such as organisations, can be seen as autopoietic within a given boundary, i.e .a homeostatic, self-referential system whose critical variable is its own existence - not, of course, living, conscious beings. It is not 'life' that is continually [re]produced but 'meaning'. Such a system constantly creates and recreates itself within its autopoietic space in the context of interactions with its environment. Any structural element of the system may change radically over time, but the existence of the system is maintained. Within the context of an organisation, the elements of which it is comprised may be observed as allopoietic sub-systems, i.e. their interactions make up inputs and outputs to organisational processes and are therefore purposeful in that organisational context. An organisation is part of the wider environment with which the individual system must interact in maintaining its ontological integrity – the sole ultimate goal of an autopoietic system. It is interesting to reflect upon this in comparison with Vickers' idea of organisational management systems as relationship maintaining, rather than goal seeking. If the theory of Autopoiesis is accepted, then the goals of the disparate elements cannot be identical, or congruent with the expressed goals of the wider organizational system, at any given time.

There have been examples of companies which thrive in the initial stages of marketing a new product, while the market is expanding. However, once the market nears saturation point, the initial success is not sustained because the company is too product-oriented (and confuses usability with usefulness). Customers do not necessarily choose products on their technical specifications alone, but on a whole range of 'qualities' influenced by convenience, fashion and availability. An example can be found in the experience of Nokia during 2010 leading to total restructuring of its mobile business 2011 (Orlowski, 2011). The need for an ecological approach is illustrated by Capra (1996) who discusses the example of a bicycle perceived as a system. An ecological awareness goes beyond perceptions of the cycle as personal transport, to consider its natural/social environments. This incorporates awareness of the materials from which it is made; the sources of those materials and the processes by which they were derived; how and where the bicycle was designed, manufactured and marketed; what potential riders are seeking for in their use of the bicycle; its impact on the environment in which it is ridden and the society in which the riders live, and so on.

When a business wishes to deal with losses or to increase profits, there are two alternatives: reduce costs or increase revenue streams. The first alternative is clearly a good idea if there is a lot of wasteful inefficiency in the firm, e.g. a lot of wastage in the production process or poor management of administrative functions. However, great care is necessary because cuts to essential services can be counter-productive. For example, suppose the Board of a company look around for areas to cut costs and see the R&D as a drain on resources. They may choose to cut the research budget, with the result that the firm does not develop or apply relevant technology, notice a new development in technologies, or a change in customer tastes. The rival firm in the next town, which still has its R&D department fully functioning, may well notice these trends and respond to them effectively, thus taking away some of the cost cutters' market share. This will lead to a fall in that firm's existing revenue streams – i.e. reduction in profit. In effect, the business is shrinking. It is possible to view this in systemic terms as an instance of a positive feedback loop having a destructive effect on system behaviour. The action taken in the firm to bring output in line with expectations has actually had the opposite effect and the discrepancy between planned and actual output increases (See Schoderbek, et al 1990, pp112-113). In the 1970's and 1980's, when 'new technologies' were first given serious consideration in business organizations, much emphasis was on cost savings. This is quite logical: one word processor operator could achieve the same work output as several typists. Similarly, if a production line can be 'manned' by software controlled robots, there are savings in wage costs – particularly as robots do not take sick leave or need holidays. Thus, a dominant idea grew that ICTs are a means of saving on costs. Of course, considerable investment in new systems was needed in order to attain these desirable savings. The difference between costs and investment is an important one and must always be borne in mind by those spending organizational budgets. The Law of Diminishing Returns in classical economics tells us that, as investment in capital increases, so the marginal increase in revenue diminishes (Samuelson and Nordhaus, 2009). In a similar way, the extent to which investment in ICTs can deliver efficiency gains will be limited. Especially if the necessary investment in the organisational development, behaviour and change-process is ignored, underestimated or not understood. The emphasis on efficiency gains also ignores the important role of ICT investment in improving effectiveness. Often, these systems are enablers of progress (or sometimes just keeping up with the on-going needs of users for enhanced utility).

3 Conclusion

Developments in ICTs have not focused just upon efficiency. We have faster machines and smarter software systems than those of the 1980's. No bricks-and-mortar bookshop of the 1980's could have carried out the kind of analytics on customer purchasing behaviour that Amazon.com is able to do today. Profits can be increased not through efficiencies but through change of organizational behaviour and thus generation of enhanced and new revenue streams. However sustainable effectiveness is a sociotechnical phenomenon requiring a focus not on technology dissemination, usability and potential use - but on contextually relevant application and usefulness. Traditional socio-technical approaches (e.g. Mumford, 1983) do not go far enough in promoting systems experienced as useable in context. Methods are required that are based in phenomenology, to address complex open systems by providing support for inquiry into multiple levels of contextual dependencies (e.g. Bednar, 2000). Sustainability in business requires understanding of the (complex) relationship between investment, cost control and profitability. Leaders and "visionaries" often engage in rhetoric suggesting that their policies will simultaneously achieve cost savings and improvements in quality. It is necessary to be sceptical about such claims however and challenge paradoxical thinking which leads to creation of IS that are not only not perceived as useful by organizational actors, but which can actually destroy value for the business.

References

Bednar, P.: A Contextual Integration of Individual and Organizational Learning Perspectives as Part of IS Analysis. Informing Science 3(3), 145–156 (2000)

Bednar, P., Welch, C.: Professional desire, competence and engagement in IS context. In: D'Atri, A., de Marco, M. (eds.) Management in the Interconnected World: Exploring the Connection between Organizations and Technology, pp. 359–366. Springer, Heidelberg (2010)

Capra, F.: The Web of Life: A new scientific understanding of living systems. Anchor Books, NY (1996)

Grant, I.: India deal clears Skandia's app maintenance backlog. Computer Weekly, 4 (November 6, 2007)

Langefors, B.: Theoretical Analysis of Information Systems, Studentlitterature (1966)

Langefors, B., Dahlbom, B. (ed.) Essays on Infology, Studentlitteratur, Lund (1995)

Maturana, H.R., Varela, F.J.: Autopoiesis and cognition. D. Reidel Publishing Company, Dordrecht (1980)

Midgeley, G.: Systems Thinking. Sage, Thousand Oaks (2003)

Mumford, E.: The story of socio-technical design. Information Systems Journal 16(4), 317 (2006)

Orlowski, A.: Why Nokia failed: Wasted 2000 man years' on UIs that didn't work. The Register, Mobile (March 10, 2011)

Samuelson, P.A., Nordhaus, W.D.: Economics, 19th edn. McGraw-Hill, New York (2009)

Schoderbek, P.P., Schoderbek, C.G., Kefalas, A.G.: Management Systems: conceptual Considerations, 4th edn (1990), Richard D. Irwin

Williams, P.: Make sure you get a positive return. Computer Weekly (November 13, 2007)

Potentials of Living Labs for the Diffusion of Information Technology: A Conceptual Analysis

Dorothée Zerwas[1] and Harald F.O. von Kortzfleisch[2]

[1] Mainzer Str. 117, 56068 Koblenz, Germany
Tel.: +49(0)17661621046
Dorothee.Zerwas@uni-koblenz.de
[2] Sertürnerstr. 41, 53127 Bonn, Germany
Tel.: +49(0)1775533221
harald.von.kortzfleisch@uni-koblenz.de

Abstract. In the past, the development of information systems (IS) for companies was mostly driven by experts from the information technology (IT) department. Up to today, the users' experiences, valuation of usability and suggestions for improvements have become important components in the research and development (R&D) process in order to ensure efficiency, usability and sustainability of the IS. Many newly developed IS components do not fail in terms of usability and effectiveness due to a lack of advanced technology, but because of failure to understand the users' needs. Living Labs - open innovation environments - offer a unique opportunity for IT departments to involve users at each stage of the R&D process.

The objective of this paper is to provide a conceptual framework for discussing the question to what extent the Living Lab methodology is able to overcome problems concerning the diffusion of IT. Therefore, major challenges will be deduced from factors that influence IT adoption: characteristics of the technological innovation, communication channels and social context. Afterwards, potentials of Living Labs for the diffusion of IT, i.e. to what extent this methodology is able to meet the major challenges, will be analyzed.

Keywords: Living Lab, information technology, diffusion, open innovation, user orientation.

1 Challenges for the Diffusion of Information Technology

Nowadays, IT is the backbone of almost all distributed business processes in a company's daily business. Efficiency, usability, capacity and sustainability of an IS are the result of interaction between the requirements of a company and the design of technology that is supposed to meet them. Since IT is implemented in order to improve productivity, it must be accepted and used by the employees: IT needs to be diffused.

For many decades, researchers repeatedly reviewed the diffusion of IT and developed frameworks to guide future research, e.g. Fichman (1992) in his seminal paper on "Information Technology Diffusion: A Review of Empirical Research". We

M. Nüttgens et al. (Eds.): Governance and Sustainability in IS, IFIP AICT 366, pp. 330–339, 2011.

rely on the more recent work of Peansupap et al. (2005) who used theories of innovation diffusion, change management and learning and sharing knowledge to develop a framework for influencing users' diffusion of IT within a company. He claimed that the success of diffusion is determined by three factors that influence IT adoption: characteristics of the technological innovation, communication channels and social context.

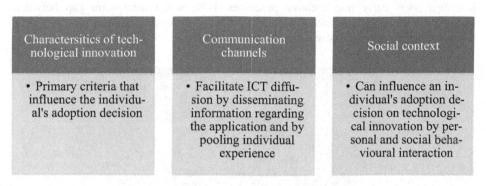

Fig. 1. Factors of innovation diffusion (Peansupap et al. 2005)

In the following, certain major challenges for the diffusion of IT will be deduced from these three factors.

1.1 Challenges Regarding Characteristics of Technological Innovation

There is no general solution for the diffusion of IT that can be applied to all companies, because the procedures, employees etc. are different. A special selection of software and subsequent adaption to the company needs is necessary. Therefore, the relevant parameters in the selection of systems need to be examined, e.g. what is processed, are special wizards needed etc? To ascertain these parameters, real and virtual concepts that support user-centred and innovation-oriented R&D have to be created.

1.2 Challenges Regarding Communication Channels

New IS should not replace existing systems without user tests and validation. This requires a specific research infrastructure, which grants IT departments access to user-centred research: a user experience prototyping environment. Therefore, to ascertain data and to increase the user experience and observation, new models are necessary.

1.3 Challenges Regarding Social Context

User problems with the IS have to be detected and suggestions for improvements confirmed. More influence and room has to be granted for providing expertise and participation in the conceptualizing of the IS. Therefore, the users have to be involved as "co-creators" and the IT professionals have to be sufficiently trained to mentor the users. Teamwork has to be fostered.

2 Living Labs

The Living Lab approach originates from the Massachusetts Institute of Technology in Boston and owes its existence to the work of William Mitchell. Living Labs are certain environments or methodologies created with the aim of involving users in innovation and R&D. The task of a Living Lab can be summarized as shown in figure 2: it brings users early into creative processes, bridges the innovation gap between technology development and the uptake of new products, and allows for early economic implications of new technological solutions.

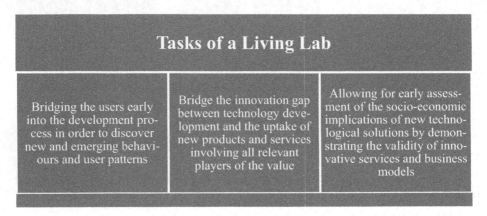

Fig. 2. Tasks of a Living Lab (Mulder et al. 2009)

In order to come up with a comprehensive overview of Living Labs and to analyze their respective characteristics, secondary literature was analyzed with regard to Living Lab definitions. Only the most commonly used and most frequently cited definitions will be compared. The characteristics user-centered, real testing environment, regionality, ICT, public-private partnership (PPP) and open innovation are the key words of single definitions, and allow to clearly work out differences and similarities of the definitions.

The number of ticks shows that "real testing environment" and "user- centered" are the lowest common denominator. These two characteristics influence the definition for this paper:

Living Labs are open innovation and real testing environments in real life context, in which user-driven innovation is fully integrated into the co-creation process of new services and products.

The Living Lab methodology is based on the theory of Open Innovation, which was defined by Chesbrough (2006) as "a paradigm that assumes that firms can and should use external ideas as well as internal ideas, and internal and external paths to market, as the firms look to advance their technology" (Chesbrough 2006, p. xxiv). In this case, companies acknowledge the potential of users as co-creators.

Table 1. Analysis of the Living Lab definitions

Definition	User- centred	Real testing environment	Regionality	ICT	PP	Open innovation
"Living Labs represent a user-centric research methodology for sensing, prototyping, validating and refining complex solutions in multiple and evolving real life contexts" (Livinglabs 2010).	x	x				
"A Living Lab is a city area which operates a full-scale urban laboratory and proving ground for inventing, prototyping and marketing new mobile technology applications" (Living Labs Europe 2010, p. 2).		x	x	x		
"Living Labs are open innovation environments in real-life settings, in which user-driven innovation is fully integrated within the co-creation process of new services, products and societal infrastructures in a regional harmonized context (the "Open Innovation Functional Region") catalyzing the synergy of SMEs Collaborative Networks and Virtual Professional Communities in a Public, Private, People Partnership" (Santoro 2009, p. 1).	x	x	x		x	x
"Living Labs are open innovation environments in real-life settings, in which user-driven innovation is fully integrated within the co-creation process of new services, products, and societal infrastructures" (Mulder et al. 2009, p. 1).						
"Living Labs represents a research methodology for sensing, validating and refining complex solutions in multiple and evolving real life contexts. Here, innovations, such as new services, products or application enhancements, are validated in empirical environments within specific regional contexts" (Schumacher et al. 2007, p. 1).	x	x				
"Living Labs are environments for involving users in innovation and development, and are regarded as a way of meeting the innovation challenges faced by information and communication technology (ICT) service providers" (Følstad 2008, p. 99).	x	x		x		
"The living lab concept creates innovation ecosystems that bring policy stakeholders and players of the value network including SMEs and end-users (citizens) early into the innovation process to discover new and emerging user patterns and allow for early experimenting and validating new products and services" (Schaffers et al. 2010, p. 3).	x	x			x	
Total	5	6	2	2	2	1

3 Potentials of Living Labs for the Diffusion of Information Technology

The potentials of Living Labs are conceptually analyzed to meet the challenges of the diffusion of IT by referring to the Living Lab characteristics "real testing environment" and "user-centred design".

3.1 Real Testing Environments

There is a need for a specific infrastructure granting IT professionals access to the users. The infrastructure should support the involvement of users within the R&D process of the IS "in order to better understand the relationship between new innovative concepts and related users' behaviour within specific situations as well as potential cognitive workload in interpreting received signals" (Pallot et al. 2010, p. 16).

Technological Innovation Challenge: Implementation of Rooms
IT departments attempt to enhance their innovation capacity through opening the R&D process. The users' feedback is taken into consideration in order to better understand the several needs of the different departments and to customize the IS. A basic metaphor for openness is the space-metaphor that manifests itself in a virtual or real way. Examples are "enterprise 2.0", "virtual communities" and the "entrepreneurial design thinking" approach. Such physically real and digital-virtual space concepts support innovation-oriented R&D. Living Labs as open spaces realistically depict the situation of users in particular, thus make it tangible for the IT department.

Communication Channels Challenge: Development of New Models and Tools
Companies have to deal with the management of large, complex and heterogeneous socio-technical systems that integrate human, technological and environmental elements. For that purpose, the models incorporate socio-cognitive, cognitive ergonomic, socio-emotional and economic aspects to increase the quality of user experience and observation.

Scenario and session models
- Context- and user-centred sessions
- Defining interaction steps between users and their experience environment

User models
- Collecting usage data/experience
- Pre-processing data for collective usage data
- Clustering users and concepts, individual and collective behavioural aspects, user or session profiling

Cooperation models
- Networks forms of cooperation

Fig. 3. New models (Pallot et al. 2010)

All models entail growing data sets. As a consequence, data acquisition, data mining and user experience research techniques have to be improved.

Data acquisition techniques
- Synchronizing heterogeneous data
- Ascertainment of structured data inside collective dynamic situations

Data mining techniques
- Some ICT research could be very relevant for user experience context an should be validated in this context
- Example: Usage data is a kind of very large data sets and could be a good context of validating algorithms in mining data streams

User experience research techniques
- Constituting a catalogue of research methods that could be combined for being able to understand and interpret phenomenon from different perspectives
- It should go beyond the current socio-cognitive and related methods such as cognitive task analysis, structured, semi-structured and unstructured interviews, group interviews, formal usability studies and ergonomics checklists

Fig. 4. New techniques (Pallot et al. 2010)

The models and techniques can be implemented in Living Lab as standard from an external consultant. This kind of tool box can be used in every context.

3.2 User-Centred Design

Living Labs are characterized by the "users as innovators" approach, meaning that "the basic idea is not about using the users as 'guinea pigs' for experiments, it's about getting access to their ideas and knowledge" (Gonçalves et al. 2007, p. 283).

Technological Innovation Challenge: Usage of Internal Resources
IT professionals are often not aware of the potential of integrating their own employees, because they underestimate the users' understanding of IT etc. Furthermore, it is often time-consuming and expensive to obtain information about user behavior or emerging problems. However, to solve a problem the needed information (user) and problem-solving capabilities (IT departments) must be brought together (von Hippel 1994). A Living Lab solves this problem by providing rooms and methods to involve the employees in the R&D process.

Communication Channels Challenge: Methodologies for User Integration
To facilitate co-creation, each stage of the innovation process has to be supported by traditional and collaborative working environment (CWE) methods.
"Traditional methods, of course, have their value in ethnographic research, however, they might not exploit Living Labs as an infrastructure that comes close to the user as well as make use of the potential of Living Labs as a methodology to get richer insights in what drives people" (Mulder 2009 et al., p. 4).

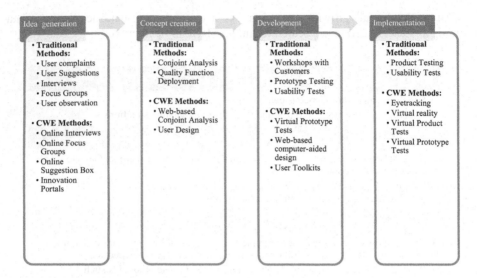

Fig. 5. User integration methods (Reichart 2002; Mulder et al. 2009; Schumacher et al. 2007)

Social Context Challenges: User as "Co-creator" and the Role of IT Professionals

Holtzblatt (2001) wrote that "great product ideas come from a marriage of the detailed understanding of a customer need with the in-depth understanding of technology. The best product designs happen when the product's designers are involved in collecting and interpreting customer data and appreciate what real people need" (Holtzblatt 2001, p. 19). A Living Lab allows the integration of the users in the R&D and supports innovations that are "validated in collaborative, multi-contextual, empirical real-world environments" (Kusiak 2007, p. 867).

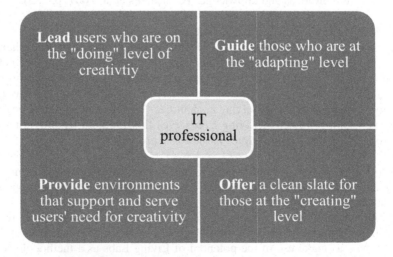

Fig. 6. Tasks of an IT professional (Sanders et al. 2008)

IT professionals usually serve as translators for users and programmers. Within Living Labs, they change between being translators and facilitators for new tasks.

To offer relevant experiences to facilitate user expressions of creativity, leading, guiding and providing a corresponding environment to encourage users is necessary.

4   Conclusion, Limitation and Further Research Needs

In response to the challenges of the realization of employees' internal potential and for the purpose of improving the effectiveness of policy instruments to support the development of sustainable IS, a stronger orientation towards interactive learning within companies is necessary (Nauwelaers et al. 2006). This analysis is just conceptual: Propositions have to be deduced and hypotheses have to be proven in the future.

The static factors (characteristics of technological innovation, communication channels and social context) can be used to determine the primary individual's adoption decision (Peansupap 2005). Nevertheless, these factors do not explain the dynamic nature of the diffusion processes that drives innovation. Peansupap (2005) identified two dynamic factors: "change management" and "learning and sharing of knowledge". They compliment the static factors and involve supportive change mechanisms that facilitate the diffusion of IT.

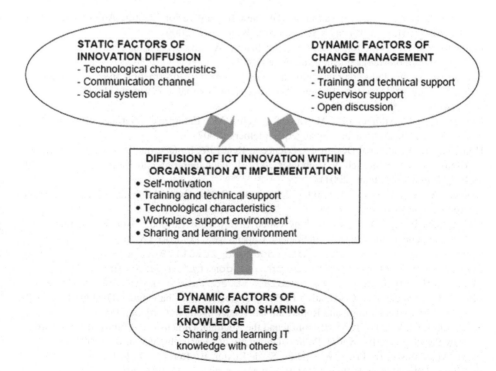

Fig. 7. Integration of factors related to IT diffusion (Peansupap et al. 2006)

Living Labs can build the basis for the static as well as the dynamic factors, because they bring all stakeholders early into the R&D process

— to discover new and emerging user patterns,
— to allow early experimentation and validation of components of the IS and
— to customize or improve existing components.

Nevertheless, the implementation of a Living Lab is a expenditure, because the rooms have to be implemented and users have to be trained to use the tools. It has to be checked whether the gains in efficiency, the cost savings and the improvements are at an appropriate rate compared to the efforts. Also, it needs to be determined whether the company can operate the IS on its own or whether this results in further costs for consulting and administration, because hiring external companies or further employees gets necessary.

However, a Living Lab facilitates the development of a user-friendly IS that is adjusted to the sustainable fulfillment of tasks.

This paper was confined to a specific context, and other topics have to be explored. Research, for example, needs to be conducted in order to learn in greater detail how and why individuals adopt new information technologies.

References

Chesbrough, H.W.: Open Innovation. In: The New Imperative for Creating And Profiting from Technology. Harvard Business School Press, Watertown (2006)

Fichman, R.G.: Information Technology Diffusion: A Review of Empirical Research. MIT Sloan School of Management, Cambridge (1992)

Følstad, A.: Living Labs for Innovation and Development of Information and Communication Technology: A Literature Review. The Electronic Journal for Virtual Organizations and Networks 10, 99–131 (2008)

Gonçalves, R.J., Müller, J.P., Mertins, K., Zelm, M.: Enterprise Interoperability II: New Challenges and Approaches. Springer, Heidelberg (2007)

Holtzblatt, K.: Contextual Design: Experience in Real Life. In: Oberquelle, H., Oppermann, R., Krause, J. (eds.) Mensch & Computer 2001: 1. Fachübergreifende Konferenz, pp. 71–89. B.G. Teubner, Stuttgart (2001)

Kusiak, A.: Innovation: The Living Laboratory Perspective. Computer-Aided Design & Applications 4(6), 863–876 (2007)

Living Labs Europe. What's this thing called Living Labs Europe? User-Driven Innovation Environments in the Information Society, Copenhagen, Denmark (2010),
http://www.gencat.cat/diue/doc/doc_29961179_1.pdf

Livinglabs (2010), http://www.livinglabs.com.tw/En/index.html

Media.mit II. (2010), http://www.media.mit.edu/about/mission-history

Mulder, I., Stappers, P.J.: Co-creating in Practice: Results and Challenges. ID-StudioLab, Delft University of Technology and Rotterdam University, Delft/Rotterdam (2009)

Nauwelaers, C., Wintjes, R.: SME policy and the Regional Dimension of Innovation Towards a New Paradigm for Innovation Policy? University of Maastricht, Maastricht (2006)

Pallot, M., Trousse, B., Prinz, W., Richir, S., de Ruyter, B., Rerolle, O., Katzy, B., Senach, B.: Living Labs Research. ECOSPACE Newsletter no. 5, AMI@Work Communities Wiki (2010),
http://www.ami-communities.eu/wiki/ECOSPACE_Newsletter_No_5

Peansupap, V., Walker, D.H.T.: Factors enabling information and communication technology diffusion and actual implementation in construction orgaisations. ITcon 10, 193 (2005)

Reichart, S.V.: Kundenorientierung im Innovationsprozess. Gabler, Wiesbaden (2002)

Sanders, E.B.-N., Stappers, P.J.: Co-creation and the new landscapes of design (2008), http://www.informaworld.com/

Santoro, R.: Living Labs in Open Innovation Functional Regions. ESoCE-Net, Rome (2009)

Schumacher, J., Feurstein, K.: Living Labs – the user as co-creator. Research Centre for Process- and Product-Engineering, University of Applied Sciences, Vorarlberg (2007)

von Hippel, E.: Sticky Information and the Locus of Problem Solving: Implications for Innovation. Management Science 40(4), 429–439 (1994)

A Media Discourse of Broadband Policy
in a Developing Country Context

Johannes Vergeer, Wallace Chigona, and Andile Simphiwe Metfula

Department of Information Systems, University of Cape Town, Cape Town, South Africa
{Johannes.Vergeer,Wallace.Chigona,Andile.Metfula}@uct.ac.za

Abstract. Abstract: The formation of bodies like the World Summit on the Information Society (WSIS) and the incorporation of Information and Communication Technologies (ICTs) in the Millennium Development Goals (MDGs) have given birth to the importance of connectivity, thus putting the Internet on the national agenda of every nation in the world. Countries (especially developing nations) have started drafting their own broadband policies so as to be able to 'quickly' provide Internet access to 'all' their citizens and to be able to 'immediately' start 'reaping' the fruits provided by broadband. This paper, therefore, looks at this process in the Republic of South Africa – that is, the discourses around the formulation of the National Broadband Policy – in order to uncover possible distortions and misconceptions. Moreover, it also looks at the interactions that existed amongst the actors that were involved or were supposed to be involved in the policy-formulation process. This is done by using Habermas' Critical Discourse Analysis (CDA).

Keywords: Broadband Policy.

1 Introduction

1.1 Background

Nowadays the importance of the Internet, especially Broadband Internet, cannot be over-emphasised. Governments see it as a catalyst to speed up service delivery; capitalists see it as a dynamic business tool; educators see it as a new knowledge provider; youngsters see it as a new form of expressing dissent and entertainment. In his budget speech to Parliament on the 20th of April 2010, the then Minister of Communications, Siphiwe Nyanda made a statement that by 2019 South Africans would enjoy universal access to broadband. This was a bold statement considering the current ICT penetration rate in the country. Benefits of the access, Nyanda stated, would include the provision of multimedia, e-governance and economic growth (Nyanda, 2010). The Broadband Policy – which would in turn bring all these benefits into fruition – was finalised on the 13th of July 2010 after parliamentary deliberations and, most importantly, supposed public consultations. Considering the importance of the policy and the dismal outcomes of other ICT policies in the developing countries, it is of academic interest to investigate the likelihood of the policy succeeding.

M. Nüttgens et al. (Eds.): Governance and Sustainability in IS, IFIP AICT 366, pp. 340–356, 2011.
© IFIP International Federation for Information Processing 2011

As the formulation of a Broadband Policy was highly topical at this time, both locally and internationally, it is important to note concerns raised about the generally poor policy outcomes of Information and Communication Technology (ICT) in Africa. Gillwald (2010) attributes the poor outcomes to the paucity of critical research that recognises the political dimensions of policy reform and economic regulation.

1.2 Media Discourse and the Public Sphere

To contribute towards this understanding, this study traces the South African media reporting (both print and electronic) and the response of civil society (often via dedicated web-based environments) on the rhetoric of 'Broadband' and, in particular, focuses on its role during the South African Broadband Policy formulation process. Consequently, the theoretical foundation used in this paper is Habermas' Theory of Communicative Action (Habermas, 1984), which focuses on the impact and implications of a discourse.

Habermas posits that the conceptual category of the public sphere is essential to the evolution and maintenance of a democratic society. This public sphere, he asserts, consists of politicians and their political parties, lobbyists, non-governmental organisations (NGOs) and other pressure groups, as well as mass media professionals with their networks of electronic and print media. The public sphere actors often compete to set the agenda on crucial public issues like policy formulation (Mills, 2009). Norton-Griffiths (2010) noted that this competition culminates in the adoption of minority views of the powerful, thus defeating the whole purpose of a democratic society and process. The media, as part of the public sphere, plays a central role in shaping public discourses (Cukier, Ngwenyama, Bauer & Middleton, 2009b). It provides a primary source of information (Melody, 2006). It is also a vehicle by which civil society obtains information and becomes involved in the political process. The media are not only consumed by the public, but also by politicians who use the media to learn of the needs of the people and to influence public opinion. Thus, in many ways, the media affects the political and more importantly, the policy process (Cooper & Johnson, 2007). Figure 1 further illustrates this.

Fig. 1. The Media und the Policy Process (Coopers & Johnson, 2007)

Therefore, as they (the media) have an influence on what we think about and how we think about it, it is important to highlight distortions in these discourses (Chigona & Chigona, 2008). The identification of distorted media discourses, especially those dealing with policy formulation, is important, as the possibility exists for political elites and privileged groups to deflect citizens' individual and collective interests (Guardino, 2009).

1.3 Research Aims, Claims, Questions and Approach

This paper, therefore, seeks to understand the workings of the public discourse surrounding the South African Broadband Policy debate, thus facilitating a better understanding of the factors influencing the debate about the availability and adoption of broadband technologies and services in the South African context. Its main intention is to answer the call made by Gillwald (2010) to contribute towards indigenous research that engages in the ICT policy space. This research aims specifically at understanding the interplay between various institutions and the roles they play, particularly in the telecommunications arena. Thompson & Walsham (2010) once called upon researchers in Information Systems to critically look at national and international policies, so as to be able to make sound and meaningful contributions to individual national ICT policies. In the same vein, Delano (2009) noted that there was a need for more research so that more rational ICT policies and strategies are realised and are efficiently put to use to end the existing digital divides in the world. The synchronisation of regional and international ICT policies with local ones is imperative; local initiatives and policies should not be affected by foreign ones, but should be the other way around (McBride & Stahl, 2009). The research question answered by this paper is:

What distortions and misconceptions does media discourse have about the South African Broadband Policy?

It answers this question by using Habermas' Theory of Communicative Action (TCA) to analyse the discourse that surrounded the formulation of the Broadband Policy in South Africa.

1.4 Structure of the Paper

The structure of this paper is as follows:

- The following section talks about the background of broadband.
- Section three looks at the broadband environment in South Africa.
- Section four is the theoretical framework.
- Section five is the research methodology.
- Section six looks at the findings.
- Section seven is the discussion of the findings.
- Section eight makes some conclusions and recommendations.

2   Broadband Background

The term 'broadband' has no universally accepted definition, but generally refers to high bandwidth Internet access (Van den Broeck & Lievens, 2007). The Broadband Commission for Digital Development defines it as a cluster of concepts ranging from instantaneous updates to simultaneous provision of services (The Broadband Commission, 2010a).

2.1   Overview of Broadband

The discussion around broadband should however move beyond the merely technical aspects of access and speed. Attention also has to be directed to the social dimensions of having broadband connectivity, considering the potential benefits to users and society as a whole. In many respects the technology is not as important as what can be accomplished by using it (Van den Broeck & Lievens, 2007). Kim, Kelly & Raja (2010) see broadband as an ecosystem (see Figure 2), consisting of networks, services carried on these networks, the applications they deliver and the users making use of these.

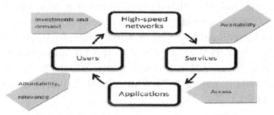

Figure 2: The Broadband Ecosystem (Kim et al., 2010)

Fig. 2. The Broadband Ecosystem (Kim et al., 2010)

It is important to point out that to facilitate an end-to-end communication service, different network elements, processes and business services need to be present, as illustrated by William (2008) in his layered broadband supply chain model (see Figure 3). At the top of his supply chain are the international connectivity links, usually provided via submarine fibre-optic or satellite links. The second level is the regional and domestic backbone, allowing traffic to flow both domestically and between the international links. The third level represents the routing and switching or the so-called 'intelligence' in the network. Below this is the typical customer network access. Finally, there is the layer of 'soft' retail services such as customer acquisition, customer care and billing.

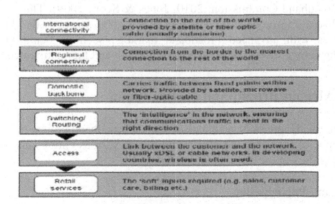

Fig. 3. The Broadband Commuications Supply Chain (Williams, 2008)

2.2 Socio-economic Impact of Broadband

Pickot & Wernick (2007) stress that the economic relevance and societal importance of broadband is becoming more important, due to the diffusion of broadband Internet infrastructure reshaping the traditional ICT landscape. According to Kim et al (2010), broadband is a technological innovation that will immensely change people's lives and day-to-day activities, thus enabling economic development and national competitiveness.

There are various positive socio-economic benefits that broadband can deliver, but it is important to note that 'broadband connectivity is a means and not an end in itself' (Jones & Scott, 2009). Substantial research has been done to show that broadband can play a crucial role in productivity, job creation, innovation, entrepreneurial activities, health, education, e-governance, political activities and personal relations (World Bank, 2009; Katz & Avila, 2010; Jones & Scott, 2009; The Broadband Commission, 2010; Willson, Marshall, Young & McCann, 2009; Srivastava, 2008; Firth & Mellor, 2005; Horrigan, 2009).

2.3 Broadband Policy

Katz & Avila (2010) found that the formulation of policy is determined by the overarching government vision, and as such impacts on the development of broadband. They note that institutional strength and platform-based competition, and not so much the independence of the regulator, appear to be the most important variables driving broadband innovation and development in a country. In order to implement broadband development strategies, a number of policies, regulations and programmes need to be implemented (Kim et al, 2010).

Policy leadership and political will in government are crucial for the deployment of broadband networks and, most importantly, for the enhancement of local content and skills. Developing countries, conscious of the widening digital divide and the risk that some groups may be missing the economic and social benefits that broadband access promises, are eager to stimulate and promote the uptake of broadband (Kim et al, 2010; The Broadband Commission, 2010; Jones & Scott, 2009). This, as outlined in Kim et al (2010), can be done by adhering to the good practices that have emerged from countries with advanced broadband markets, such as being visionary and flexible, using competition to promote market growth and facilitating demand.

3   South African Broadband Environment

To appreciate the dynamics of media discourse on broadband policy, it is important to take cognisance of the roles and responsibilities of various entities and the activities of various operators in the broadband domain.

3.1 Actors and Participation

The major players in the South African broadband arena include state agencies, state-owned enterprises, incumbent operators, Internet Service Providers (ISPs) and resellers. Disappointingly, the role of civil society organisations is limited and thus insignificant. Comninos, Esselaar, Gillwald, Moyo & Naidoo (2010) note that, in South Africa, the state is still a significant player in the communications sector with full ownership of some enterprises and direct shareholding in major operators like

Telkom (the incumbent telecommunication provider) and Vodacom (the leading mobile operator).

Communication-related state agencies – which include the Department of Communication (DoC), the Independent Communications Authority of South Africa (ICASA) and the Universal Service and Access Agency of South Africa (USAASA) – have a function of formulating policy, regulating the industry and playing an advisory role. Their main responsibility is to create a vibrant ICT sector that will enable all citizens to have access to affordable ICT services, so as achieve socio-economic development goals and to fight the scourge of poverty.

State-owned enterprises, with an interest in communications, are Infraco and Sentech. Infraco is a broadband infrastructure company that was created to intervene in the broadband market and bring down the cost of communicating. Prior to its inception, Telkom was the only company providing national and international broadband backbone access; it was charging Internet service providers and other telecommunications service providers rates far exceeding those seen in other countries. Sentech, a signal distributor and broadcasting network operator, was the first in South Africa to provide wireless broadband service (BMI-T, 2010).

The role played by the civil society was found to be of a less 'formal' nature. Other than minimal contributions from blogs and some civil organisations such as the South African National Broadband Forum (SANBF) and the Association for Progressive Communications (APC), there was no direct contribution from members of the public (see Table 1). The SANBF was the most active civic group, although it became dormant after the draft of the policy was released.

3.2 Access and Infrastructure

The commissioning of the SEACOM high capacity bandwidth undersea cable, linking Southern and East Africa to Europe and Asia, attracted considerable media interest. The added backhaul capacity is invaluable but, as in many other developing countries, the problem of the 'last mile' is the true issue at hand in the South African context. Goldstuck (2010) claims that current and future undersea cable projects (like SEACOM) will have a positive impact on accessibility.

Until recently, Telkom held the monopoly in providing urban fibre capacity. With the licensing of Neotel and with the backing of its parent company Tata, about ZAR 10 billion was committed to building a new fibre network. Also, during this time, another key infrastructure player, Dark Fibre Africa (DFK), entered the market (Goldstuck, 2010).

3.3 Policy Formulation Process, Events and Discourse

With issues surrounding accessibility and infrastructure arising, the South African Government engaged in sporadic exercises to formulate the National Broadband Policy (see Table 1 for the timelines). Reviewing government's early involvement with driving the Broadband Policy process, there is a noticeable 28-month gap in action. The earliest documents referring to a National Broadband Policy are in those of the Department of Communications Strategic Plan for 2005 to 2008. Following this are regular mentions of a Broadband Policy in Budget Vote speeches in 2005 and

2006. A final mention is made to it in a speech at the Government Technology Conference in November 2006. Only in March 2009 is mention made again of the Broadband Policy, this time in the 2009/2010 Budget Vote Speech for the Department of Communications.

During 2007, the academic community in South Africa brought broadband back on the agenda, through a special issue of the Southern African Journal of Information and Communication (SAJIC) dedicated to this theme (SAJIC, 2007).

The first mention of a South African Broadband Strategy was found in a blog by Willie Currie (Currie, 2008), although prior to this time mention was only made to Broadband Policy, not strategy. The formation of the South African National Broadband Forum (SANBF) during early 2009 was the next significant event that mobilised support to engage with government and get broadband back on the agenda. After the appointment of a new Minister of Communications in 2009, events moved swiftly towards the publishing of a Draft Broadband Policy in September of 2009.

Table 1. Time-line of Key South African Broadband Policy Events

Date	Initiative
5 Apr 2005	The first mention of a Broadband Policy in a Government document or statement: The Department of Communications Strategic Plan 2005 - 2008. http://www.info.gov.za/view/DownloadFileAction?id=82991
3 Nov 2006	The last mention of a Broadband Policy in a Government document or statement before the extended period of silence. http://www.info.gov.za/speeches/2006/06110712151002.htm
2007	Issue 8 of The Southern African Journal of Information and Communication focusing on broadband. http://link.wits.ac.za/journal/journal-08.html
26 Nov 2008	Willie Currie BLOGs: Towards a National Broadband Strategy. http://www.southafricaconnect.org.za/?p=157
26 Mar 2009	The first mention of the Broadband Policy in a Government document or statement after the extended period of close on 28 months of government silence. http://www.info.gov.za/speeches/2009/09032616151004.htm
24 Mar 2009	A forum is convened by The Association for Progressive Communications (APC), along with South Africa Connect, Sangonet and The Shuttleworth Foundation to formulate a national broadband strategy.
6 April 2009	Compilation of input from participants in the workshop convened by the SA National Broadband Forum (SANBF) on 24 March 2009 http://www.apc.org/en/system/files/Broadband+strategy+framework_compiled_input_06042009.pdf
15 Apr 2009	YouTube video providing an overview of discussions held at the March Forum: http://www.youtube.com/watch?v=xd36YFmc8LU
Apr 2009	The SANBF publishes a Framework for a Comprehensive National Broadband Strategy in South Africa. http://www.broadband4africa.org.za
May 2009	Retired General Siphiwe Nyanda is appointed as communications minister with as deputy minister Ms Dina Pule.
23 Jun 2009	Minister Nyanda delivers DoCs 2009/2010 Budget Vote speech.
23 Jul 2009	SEACOM, the 15,000 km undersea fibre-optic cable began operations, providing Djibouti, South Africa, Tanzania, Kenya, Uganda and Mozambique, with high speed Internet connections to Europe and Asia.
Aug 2009	The SANBF meets with the Department of Communication (DoC) signifying a change in the previous stance of the ministry.
Aug 2009	Ms Mamodupi Mohlala is appointed to the post of Director General (DG) in the DoC.
15 Sep 2009	The DoC's DG presents the International Peer Benchmarking Study on SA's ICT sector to the Parliamentary Portfolio Committee on Communications. http://www.pmg.org.za/files/docs/091020telecoms.pdf
18 Sep 2009	The DoC publishes the Draft Broadband Policy for South Africa in the Government Gazette. http://www.info.gov.za/view/DownloadFileAction?id=107663
18 Oct 2009	Deadline for written submissions to the DoC on the proposed Draft Broadband Policy.
18-19 Nov 2009	The DoC hosts a colloquium where government and telecommunications industry representatives debated the draft policy document. http://www.ellipsis.co.za/wp-content/uploads/2009/11/BB-Policy-Workshop-Agenda.pdf
11 Mar 2010	A government spokesperson announces that Cabinet has established an Inter-Ministerial Committee to finalise the Draft National Broadband Policy for South Africa. The committee will consist of the ministers of Science and Technology, Public Enterprises, Rural Development and Land Affairs, Economic Development and Public Service and Administration. (Vecchiatto, 2010)
20 Apr 2010	The minister of communications announces in his budget speech that the Broadband Policy has been finalized for implementation. (Nyanda, 2010)
13 Jul 2010	The DoC publishes the Broadband Policy for South Africa in the Government Gazette. http://www.info.gov.za/view/DownloadFileAction?id=127922
31 Oct 201	Retired General Siphiwe Nyanda is replaced by former deputy communications minister Roy Padayachie and the new deputy minister is Mr. Obed Bapela.

4   Theoretical Framework

This section highlights the theoretical framework used and motivates the choice of the critical epistemology and, in particular, the choice of CDA as the research strategy.

Habermas' Theory of Communicative Action (TCA) is introduced and a method of using it in practice is discussed.

4.1 Habermas' Discourses and Theory of Communicative Action

The use of critical research in Information Systems (IS) is recognised as the third research approach besides positivist and interpretivist research; it is defined by critical intention and critical topics (Stahl, 2008).

Habermas places discourse in the centre of his theoretical writing. Habermas' Theory of Communicative Action (TCA) argues that our ability to jointly coordinate our actions using language and communication is a fundamental feature of humans that distinguishes us from all other species (Mingers, 2009). This ability to communicate is grounded in our capacity to understand one another.

Habermas' TCA helps to explain rationality and is based on the anthropological assumption that, as human beings, we require social interaction to survive and thrive. As such, the role of communication is to facilitate cooperation. During the process of communication, each statement or expression is associated with certain validity claims. These validity claims are discussed below and are categorised by Chigona & Chigona (2008) in Table 2.

Table 2. Summary of Validity Claims (Chigona & Chigona, 2008)

Competence	World	Claim	Explanation
Linguistic		Comprehensibility	Utterance should be clear in terms of syntax and semantics.
Communication	Objective	Truth	Utterance should match what the case is in reality.
	Subjective	Sincerity	Checks the intentions of the speaker. Cannot be observed, can only be inferred.
	Social	Legitimisation	Utterance should be in accordance with socially accepted norms.

- **Comprehensibility (C)** addresses the technical, syntactical and semantic clarity of the communication. Essentially, it is a qualification that what is being communicated is intelligible, audible or legible.
- **Truth (T)** validity claim looks for falsehoods and bias interpretations in the texts. It requires that the corpus is examined in a contextualised situation and examines utterances against the Objective (real) World and, as such, requires a comprehensive understanding of the context in which the statements are presented (Chigona & Chigona, 2008).
- **Sincerity (S)** looks to see whether what is being communicated is consistent with what is meant and forms the basis of the claim. Sincerity can only be inferred; examining the actions of the speaker and how a message is communicated needs to be compared to what is being said (Chigona & Chigona, 2008).
- **Legitimacy (L)** covers the question as to whether the communication conforms to the social environment where it is being delivered. It considers who is silenced and who is considered an expert and evaluates if there is a balance in the communication (Chigona & Chigona, 2008).

4.2 Operationalising Habermasian CDA

Cukier, Hodson & Ryan (2009a) recommend a four-step approach for conducting analysis of the data associated with a discourse under review:

Step 1: *Defining the corpus to be analysed* - Multiple data sources should be used to facilitate being able to gather all relevant material that will explain the situation or artefact under consideration.

Step 2: *Analysing the content and doing the coding* - The analysis is done for each document within the corpus and also over the full set. This is done to find empirical evidence pertaining to the various validity claims that may be supported or validated.

Step 3: *Reading and interpreting the empirical evidence from Step 2* - The documents are now re-read to uncover and test both implied and explicit validity claims. The test involves searching for imperial observations that contradict the validity claims made in the texts.

Step 4: *Explaining the findings* – This explores and explains the findings in the context of the broader environment of the study area.

5 Methodology

The logical starting point to gather the information about the National Broadband Policy is to examine the original documents and statements from Government or political parties. Government statements or press releases related to the National Broadband Policy, as well as speeches by ministers or deputies that referred to the Broadband Policy, were retrieved. Both print and electronic media that had contributed to the broadband debate were included in the corpus. Moreover, a number of well-established web-based IT publications and focused news forums exist and their articles were also included in the corpus. In total, 112 media articles consisting of 24 items from the traditional print media domain and 88 from specialist or other web media sites were identified for analysis.

A number of specialist websites were also identified; these were either specifically dedicated to the National Broadband Strategy or were concerned with general ICT issues in South Africa. These sites are typically maintained by civil society organisations or interest groups and did not yield information that contributed directly to the formal corpus of media articles under review in this paper; however, their activity was deemed an important indicator to the health of public discourse on broadband policy in South Africa.

The various articles were printed and chronologically ordered and put in a binder to enable easy access and to facilitate the reading of all the material in a chronological order. The electronic versions of the articles were uploaded into the Computer Assisted Qualitative Data Analysis System, Nvivo 8. Then the validity claims were tested against the rest of the corpus.

6 Findings

6.1 Comprehensibility

As the corpus consisted of material from both the general press and more technically-focused publications, it was to be expected that a considerable amounts of industry-specific language or jargon would be present. However, these technical terms are well understood by the industry professionals that the publications are intended for and, as such, do not need further clarification.

6.2 Truths

The government, in a bid to frame the draft and the final Broadband Policy for the media, made assertions that broadband would provide multimedia, e-governance, e-commerce, e-health, e-education and many others. These positive claims were similar to the ones that were made in articles that dealt with the policy. Negative claims were also made regarding issues such as the lack of consultative process, lack of clear deliverables in broadband policy, financial constraints, lack of education and awareness.

The media discourse clearly points to the need for a broadband policy, by highlighting the failure of government's managed liberalisation in the telecommunications sector. The SANBF articulates that:

The NBF feels government's efforts have failed, as issues of limited competition and the high cost of services still remain. The solution, it says, lies in the creation of a comprehensive national broadband policy which will help it deal effectively with broadband extension. [ITWeb]

The SANBF further clarifies what it believes to be the main benefits to be derived from an effective broadband policy, placing emphasis on the educational possibilities offered by broadband:

... high-speed broadband access will in turn stimulate the creation of commerce and digital broadband content by content providers, such as educators, so that Government's mandate of affordable learning and teaching can be fully realised. [MyBB]

Quickly, it (the discourse) moves on to bring to the limelight the main benefits that can be derived from an effective Broadband Policy. However, the emphasis on the ability of broadband to facilitate the improvement of education is lost in the overriding e-government rhetoric framing the Broadband Policy view from government. While one of governments espoused benefits of broadband does include e-education, the focus of government's drive for broadband seems to be more on e-government and economic benefits to be derived from broadband availability.

One of the most glaring omissions from the Broadband Policy discourse by the Department of Communications is that of cost and actual information about implementation. Although it could be argued that such items are to be addressed outside of the policy document, for example in a detailed implementation strategy, this is never made clear, hence leaving many unanswered questions in the mind of the observer, which ultimately could lead to doubt in the policy as a whole. It led an IT publication, ITWeb, to conclude:

No financial strategy has yet been provided to meet the objective, but the policy does mention that government will use state-owned enterprises, such as Sentech and Infraco, for the provisioning of electronic communications network services. The biggest challenges will be that of actual implementation ... [ITWeb]

Furthermore, one assumption that is not adequately explored in the discourse is whether government departments are indeed ready for e-government. There are no questions raised about whether government IT departments have been integrated into an e-government environment, or whether departments are ready to offer e-services and e-transactions, or if government officials are ready to deliver and support e-government services to the public. One of the few statements in the discourse on this matter is by Minister Nyanda when he alludes to the probability that government departments are, indeed, not ready, as he urges the adoption of ICT:

Therefore, the development of a coherent framework for the deployment and utilisation of ICT in government is critical. It is urgent that the government adopts and uses ICT in order to modernise services, improve administration and efficiency. [ServPub]

6.3 Sincerity

There is some evidence of hyperbole, metaphor and connotative language to reinforce certain perspectives in the discourse and, most importantly, to elicit an emotive response. The most prominent of these are the use of terms like 'digital divide', 'bridging' of this divide, or 'being on the wrong side' of the divide. There are also examples where disappointment and frustration about certain aspects or aspirations come to the fore e.g. the feeling of mediocrity or the lack of ambition:

... aims to provide all citizens with a 256 Kbps connection by 2019. This lacklustre (sic) goal from Government is falling well behind other similar projects. [MyBB]

In addition, South Africa was at times compared with more economically advanced nations, in respect of broadband penetration or broadband access speeds. This has the potential to elicit an emotional response of inferiority and triggers the expectation that the Broadband Policy should be able to get South Africa on a par with these leaders. Most often, these links with advanced economies serve to illustrate how far behind South Africa is to the developed world and implies that having a Broadband Policy would facilitate a way for South Africa to close the gap. Generally, the discourse elicits a response of technological inferiority and the need to catch up.

6.4 Legitimacy

The overriding contributor to the discourse is the Department of Communications through statements by the minister, his deputy and director-general. The next dominant voice in the discourse is that of market analysts, most notable those of BMI-TechKnowledge Managing Director Denis Smit with 11 articles quoting him, while World Wide Worx Managing Director, Arthur Goldstuck and Steve Ambrose had seven articles reflecting their views. As 'experts' and 'neutral bystanders', their views often provided the only alternative non-governmental insights into the discourse.

The civil society in general is not at all well represented in the discourse, primarily because even news publications did not carry stories on the Broadband Policy.

The SANBF initially had a strong voice in the discourse with a total of 12 articles, but it fell silent after the Draft Broadband Policy was announced in September 2009. Although substantial press coverage was given to the SANBF's website and the partners responsible for its launch, it is surprising that, after the government's publication of the Draft and Final Broadband Policy, there was no ongoing dialogue via this website or any statements of endorsement or rejection. As a result the Broadband Policy was formulated through a closed and non-transparent process; public participation was only 'symbolic'. Public participation does not only ensure success and effectiveness of the policy formulation process, but it also creates ownership of the policy amongst the civil society (Kendall et al, 2006; Barnes, 2006; Mohamed, 2006).

State owned enterprises (SOEs) are also silent on the specifics of the policy. References are made to Sentech and Infraco, but no representation from these entities in the discourse ever touches on the actual Broadband Policy. Surprisingly, these are the institutions which are expected to play a crucial role in order for the policy to be successfully implemented. It is even more worrying that they are not represented in the debate. Nevertheless, it can be argued that the lack of leadership and clear direction at the state entities and state-owned enterprises are the reasons they are not engaged with the media on this matter. Lastly, there was also no input from any of the major broadband providers such as Telkom, Vodacom, MTN or Cell C.

7 Discussion

The general atmosphere of the broadband discourse under review is that of 'techno-optimism', the 'technology imperative' and 'technological determinism'. Roode et al. (2004) note how technological optimism relates to the belief that developmental problems can be resolved by the availability of, and access to, ICTs. According to Wilson (2002), the technology imperative or technological determinism discounts the fact that information or knowledge do not necessarily have to be associated with ICTs. While ICTs may provide a conduit to accessing certain types of information, or to gain certain knowledge, this is not necessarily the only way.

Generally, in the discourse, the Broadband Policy does not appear to feature prominently in the collective minds of the general public. The government ignored the fact that effective policies can only be achieved through outlining clear and possible goals that will be achieved by the policy improvements and, most importantly, by appealing to societal interests – no power can ever be exercised without consent and interest from the civil society (Boswell, 2009). Most policies in developing countries, even in developed nations, meet resistance due to the lack of instrumental participation on the part of civil society in the development of these policies (Hideg et al, 2011). Moreover, an inclusive policy formulation process which involves all actors, even latent ones, other than civil society, does not only create the effectiveness of the policy, but it goes to the extent of creating its ownership (Hicks & Buccus, 2007; Sack & Marope, 2007). The case in point in this research is the non-participation of the private sector which may have a negative impact on the policy outcomes.

It can be argued that the policy has the potential to significantly improve people's lives and wellbeing, but currently the development of a Broadband Policy is secondary to more pressing issues such as basic services provision. Issues that directly affect people's quality of life inevitably take precedence. One reason for this poor public engagement is perhaps related to the way that the non-ICT focused media reported on the Broadband Policy. These sources closely followed the press releases from government, but rarely added substantial commentary to the statements. This is in line with the findings of Quail & Larabie (2010) that the poor coverage of the topic 'does not lend itself to a critically informed and engaged public'. Moreover, the withdrawal of civil society groups such as the SANBF was also a cause for serious concern – lobbyists and pressure groups are members of the public sphere and are essential for maintaining and evolving a democratic society (Cukier et al, 2009b).

During the period under review, there was a notable change in the discourse from optimism to a less favourable, pessimistic outlook. The importance of following this mood change in the discourse is that the policy is inextricably linked to the DoC and its senior officials e.g. the Minister. As these entities are afforded the custodianship of the Broadband Policy, the observer's feelings about the policy become entangled with feelings about the custodian. A brief review of activities at the department and the general resultant turmoil, lead to the conclusion that the Broadband Policy gets affected by these events. Some events and signs of disarray are shown in Table 3. As Gillwald (2010) pointed out, it is necessary to recognise the political dimensions of policy reform and to examine the interaction of the state and the market if we are to understand the general failure of ICT policy outcomes in Africa.

Table 3. Time-line of key events at the DoC

Date	Event
May 2009	Retired General Siphiwe Nyanda is appointed as communications minister with as deputy minister Ms Dina Pule.
Aug 2009	Ms Mamodupi Mohlala is appointed to the post of Director General (DG) in the DoC.
Oct 2009	The DoC's head of Human Resources (HR), Ms Basani Baloyi is reinstated after an earlier suspension on disciplinary charges.
Nov 2009	Ms Basani Baloyi is suspended again.
Oct 2009	Deadline for written submissions to the DoC on the proposed Draft Broadband Policy.
July 2010	Minister Nyanda suspends the DG, Mamodupi Mohlala.
Aug 2010	Dr Harold Wesso is appointed acting DG.
Oct 2010	Ms Mohlala leaves the DoC
Oct 2010	Retired General Siphiwe Nyanda is replaced by former deputy communications minister Roy Padayachie and the new deputy minister is Mr. Obed Bapela.

One important question that emanates from these events is how an entity, with this level of instability and upheaval and with apparent lack of continuity in its leadership structure, can function. As the Broadband Policy is so closely linked and associated with the DoC, it is hard not to project the negative sentiments about the department onto the policy. To make matters worse, throughout the discourse there are repeated references to not only the DoC being in a state of crisis, but also to the unrest in associated and crucial state entities, like ICASA, USAASA, Sentech and Infraco – the very entities that are supposed to implement the policy. In the same way that one would associate the policy with the custodians, one would also associate the policy with the implementers.

Furthermore, the exclusion of large local corporate broadband providers raised concerns about the prevailing uncoordinated efforts. The ability of the SOE's to deliver on the Broadband Policy objective was questionable and therefore allowed private enterprises to continue to follow their own agendas. Finally, although international best practice seems to suggest that policy is needed, this clearly needs to be balanced by action. So far, the feeling created in the discourse is that the Broadband Policy is 'lip service' and that it 'ticks the boxes'. There is no optimism that it will make a real difference to the citizens of the country.

8 Conclusion

The analysis revealed that the association and disassociation of various role players in the South African broadband environment has created a negative perception around the Broadband Policy. Although the government's rhetoric on the Broadband Policy is of a positive nature, the constant linking of the policy to reporting on negative industrial and political aspects ultimately influences the perception about the policy and the ability for the policy to be implemented.

This study has contributed to the body of knowledge about the formulation of ICT Policy and Broadband Policy in the context of a developing country. Moreover, some contribution was made to unravelling the complexities of the political and regulatory aspects in the South African telecommunications environment, although this is an area where further ongoing research is needed.

Considering the generalizability of this research (Lee & Baskerville, 2003), the theoretical contributions of this paper to understanding media involvement in ICT and Broadband Policy formulation may be of value in other settings, or when considering other policy formulation processes. Most developing countries have similar, if not the same, institutions and, most importantly, they also have similar ways of doing things. Therefore, on a practical note, the results and lessons extracted from this study can be used to understand the 'noise' that surrounds policy formulation processes in developing countries and hence the failure of many policies. Furthermore, the contributions of this paper also bring to the limelight the importance of government institutions, in the sense that poor government institutions result in poor policies and outcomes. Weak institutions beget a state that fails to deliver on its promises and a sceptical private sector and civil society that lacks confidence in any government process or intervention.

The paper recommends that for governments of developing countries to have effective policies that will be owned by the masses, these governments need to start viewing civil society as a partner in policy-formulation exercises. Civil society can only be equipped to partake in such activities if there is a vibrant and an encouraged media that is willing to educate the population on emerging technologies and policies. Finally, governments should strengthen state institutions that are involved in the telecommunications sector so that benefits of broadband or any development-related technologies are clear and well appreciated.

References

Barnes, T.: Nation-Building without Mortar? Public Participation in Higher Education Policy-Making in South Africa. Research Article. Perspectives in Education 24(1), 1–14 (2006)

BMI-T. SA Wireless Access and Broadband Market. Business Monitor International – TechKnowledge Group (October 2010)

Boswell, C.: Knowledge, legitimation and the politics of risk: the functions of research in public debates on migration. Political Studies 57, 165–186 (2009)

Chigona, A., Chigona, W.: MXit up in the media: media discourse analysis on a mobile instant messaging system. The Southern African Journal of Information and Communication 9(0), 42–57 (2008)

Comninos, A., Esselaar, S., Alison Gillwald, A., Moyo, M., Naidoo, K.: South African ICT Sector Performance Review 2009/2010. Research ICT Africa (2010), http://www.researchictafrica.net/new/images/uploads/SPR20092010/SA_SPR-final-web_Master_13Oct.pdf (retrieved November 28, 2010)

Cooper, C.A., Johnson, M.: News Media and State Policy Process: Perspectives from Legislators and Political Professionals, State Politics and Policy Conference. University of Texas, Austin (February 22-24, 2007)

Cukier, W., Hodson, J., Ryan, P.M.: A Critical Discourse Analysis of Amazon.com's Rise in the Media 1995-2008. In: World Congress on Privacy, Security, Trust and the Management of e-Business, pp. 1–10, 25–27 (2009a)

Cukier, W., Ngwenyama, O., Bauer, R., Middleton, C.: A Critical Analysis of Media Discourse on Information Technology: preliminary results of a proposed method for critical discourse analysis. Information Systems Journal 18(2), 175–196 (2009b)

Currie, W.: Towards a National Broadband Strategy (2008), http://www.southafricaconnect.org.za/?p=157 (retrieved November 8, 2010)

Delano, R.: The globalisation of ICT. Black Business Quarterly 30(7), 40–41 (2009)

Department of Communications (DoC). (n.d.). About the DoC, http://www.doc.gov.za/index.php?option=com_content&view=article&id=428&Itemid=505 (retrieved November 28, 2010)

Department of Communications (DoC). Broadband Policy for South Africa (2010), http://www.info.gov.za/view/DownloadFileAction?id=127922 (retrieved November 19, 2010)

Firth, L., Mellor, D.: Broadband: benefits and problems. Telecommunications Policy 29, 223–236 (2005)

Gillwald, A.: The Poverty of ICT Policy, Research, and Practice in Africa (2010), http://itidjournal.org/itid/article/viewFile/628/268 (retrieved December 5, 2010)

Goldstuck, A.: Internet Access in South Africa 2010 – A Comprehensive Study of the Internet Access Market in South Africa. World Wide Worx (2010)

Guardino, M.: Media Discourse, Public Policy and Democracy: A Preliminary Case Study of the Reagan Tax and Budget Plans of 1981 (2009), http://jpm.syr.edu/pdf/fellowpdfs/31_a.pdf (retrieved December 11, 2010)

Habermas, J.: The Theory of Communicative Action. Beacon Press, Boston (1984)

Hideg, I., Michela, J.L., Ferris, D.L.: Overcoming negative reactions of nonbeneficiaries to employment equity: The effect of participation in policy formulation. Journal of Applied Psychology 96(2), 363–376 (2011)

Hicks, J., Buccus, I.: Crafting new democratic spaces: participatory policy-making in KwaZulu-Natal, South Africa. Transformation 23(65), 94–119 (2007)

Horrigan, J.: Home Broadband Adoption 2009. Pew Internet & American Life Project (2009), http://www.pewInternet.org/~/media//Files/Reports/2009/Home-Broadband-Adoption-2009.pdf (retrieved September 13, 2009)

Jones, D., Scott, M.: Creating successful broadband policies in developing countries. Research Report – Analysys Mason (2009)

Katz, R.L., Avila, J.G.: The impact of broadband policy on the economy. In: Proceedings of the 4th ACORN-REDECOM Conference, Brasilia (May 14-15, 2010)

Kendall, K.E., Kendall, J.E., Kah, M.M.O.: Formulating information and communication policy through discourse: how internet discussions shape policies on ICTs for developing countries. Information Technology for Development 12(1), 25–43 (2006)

Kim, Y., Kelly, T., Raja, S.: Building broadband: Strategies and policies for the developing world. Global Information and Communication Technologies (GICT) Department, World Bank (2010), http://www.infodev.org/en/Document.756.pdf (retrieved November 5, 2010)

Lee, A.S., Baskerville, R.L.: Generalizing generalizability in information systems research. Information Systems Research 14(3), 221–243 (2003)

McBride, N., Stahl, B.C.: Egypt's Information Society Strategy: A Critical Lexicography. Journal of International Technology and Information Management 18(1) (2009)

Melody, W.H.: Policy implications of the new information Economy (2006), http://lirne.net/resources/papers/ToolBook-NIE.pdf (retrieved December 11, 2010)

Mills, R.: The Effect of Legislative Professionalism on Agenda Setting at the State Level. Conference Papers – Midwestern Political Science Association, p. 1 (2009)

Mingers, J.: Discourse Ethics and Critical Realist Ethics: An Evaluation in the Context of Business. Journal of Critical Realism 8(2), 172–202 (2009)

Mohamed, S.E.: From ideas to practice: The involvement of informal settlement communities in policy-making at city level in South Africa. South African Review of Sociology 37(1), 35–47 (2006)

Norton-Griffiths, M.: The growing involvement of foreign NGOs in setting policy agendas and political decision-making in Africa. Economic Affairs 30(3), 29–34 (2010)

Nyanda, S.: Minister of Communications S. Nyanda Budget Vote speech - ICT for accelerated service delivery and empowerment! (April 20, 2010), http://www.info.gov.za/speech/DynamicAction?pageid=461&sid=9573&tid=9590 (retrieved August 8, 2010)

Pickot, A., Wernick, C.: The role of government in broadband access. Telecommunications Policy 31(10-11), 660–674 (2007)

Quail, C., Larabie, C.: Net Neutrality: Media Discourses and Public Perception. Global Media Journal – Canadian Edition 3(1), 31–50 (2010), http://www.gmj.uottawa.ca/1001/v3i1_quail%20and%20larabie.pdf (retrieved December 11, 2010)

Roode, D., Speight, H., Pollock, M., Webber, R.: It's Not The Digital Divide – It's The Socio-Techno Divide! Presentation to the 12th European Conference on Information Systems, Turku (June 14, 2004)

Sack, R., Marope, M.: The Pedagogy of Education Policy Formulation: Working from Policy Assets. Perspectives in Education 25(1), 11–30 (2007)

SAJIC. The Southern African Journal of Information and Communication. Issue 8 (2007), http://www.sajic.org.za/index.php/SAJIC/issue/view/32 (retrieved December 19, 2010)

Srivastava, A.: Broadband for Health in Developing Countries. Handbook of Research on Global Diffusion of Broadband Data Transmission (2008)

Stahl, B.C.: The ethical nature of critical research in information systems. Information Systems Journal, Special Issue on Exploring the Critical Agenda in IS Research, edited by Brooke, C., Cecez-Kecmanovic, D., Klein, H.K., 137–163 (2008)

The Broadband Commission. A 2010 Leadership Imperative: The future built on broadband (2010a), http://www.broadbandcommission.org/report1.pdf (retrieved November 19, 2010)

The Broadband Commission. Broadband: A platform for progress (2010b), http://www.broadbandcommission.org/report2.pdf (retrieved November 19, 2010)

The Broadband Forum (n.d.). Call for a Comprehensive National Broadband Strategy for South Africa, http://www.broadband4africa.org.za (retrieved May 2, 2010)

Thompson, M.P.A., Walsham, G.: ICT research in Africa: a need for a strategic developmental focus. Working Paper Series edn. Judge Business School, University of Cambridge (2010)

Van den Broeck, W., Lievens, B.: Why Broadband? The meaning of broadband for residential users. South African Journal of Information and Communication 8, 30–52 (2007)

Williams, M.: Broadband for Africa – Policy for promoting the development of backbone networks. infoDev, The World Bank (2008)

Willson, P., Marshall, P., Young, J., McCann, J.: Evaluating the Economic and Social Impact of the National Broadband Network. In: 20th Australasian Conference on Information Systems, Melbourne, Australia (December 2-4, 2009)

Wilson, M.: Understanding the International ICT and Development Discourse: Assumptions and implications. South African Journal of Information and Communication 3(0) (2002)

World Bank. Information and Communications for Development 2009: Extending Reach and Increasing Impact (2009), http://go.worldbank.org/55ZNQF16N0 (retrieved May 17, 2010)

ERP Implementation in an Indian Context: Examining Perceptions on Success Factors

Yogesh K. Dwivedi[1], Raghav Sukumar[2], Anastasia Papazafeiropoulou[3],
and Michael D. Williams[1]

[1] School of Business and Economics, Swansea University, Swansea, SA2 8PP, UK
Tel.: +44 (0) 1792 602340, +44 01792 295181
ykdwivedi@gmail.com,
m.d.williams@swansea.ac.uk
[2] Business & Decision, 8th Floor, 55 Old Broad Street, London, EC2M 1RX, UK
Tel.: +44 (0) 207 997 6060
sukumar.raghav@gmail.com
[3] Department of IS & Computing, Brunel University, Uxbridge, UB8 8PP, UK
Tel.: +44 (0) 1895 266035
Anastasia.Papazafeiropoulou@brunel.ac.uk

Abstract. This research aims to explore factors responsible for successful implementation of ERP systems in Indian organizations. The paper also aims to explore the similarities and differences in ERP system adoption between locally-owned and multinational companies in India. The data was collected from 56 project managers and business analysts with ERP expertise from both locally-owned Indian and multinational companies. The findings suggest that Business Plan and Vision, Project Management and Top Management Support were perceived as the three most important factors responsible for successful implementation. The result revealed no significant differences between Indian and multinational companies, hence indicating that both types of firms undertake the ERP implementations in the same manner.

Keywords: ERP, Implementation Factors, Locally-owned Indian Organizations, Multinational Organizations.

1 Introduction

ERP is widely implemented by organisations in developed countries and is considered as the backbone of E-business (Al-Mashari et al. 2001; Rajapakse and Seddon 2005). However, its implementation is less prevalent in the developing countries context. Although India is considered an important provider of IT services to other countries, its own organizations are comparatively slower in technology adoption. Considering India's position in IT development and the fact that it is a developing country, this study aims to examine the implementation of ERP systems in an Indian context. There have been numerous studies listing the critical success factors (CSF) for successful ERP system implementation for developed countries. However, very few

M. Nüttgens et al. (Eds.): Governance and Sustainability in IS, IFIP AICT 366, pp. 357–363, 2011.

studies have examined these factors from a developing country perspective and have compared the factors from locally-owned and multinational companies.

This paper therefore aims to explore factors responsible for successful implementation of ERP systems in an Indian context. The paper also aims to explore the similarities and differences in ERP system adoption between locally-owned and multinational companies in India.

The remaining paper is organized as follows: The next section will provide an overview of the research method utilized. The findings will then be presented and discussed in subsequent sections. The last section of this paper will outline the conclusions.

2 Research Method

To achieve the specified research aim, this research considered survey as an appropriate method to collect data on factors important for implementation of ERP in an Indian context. Considering the research context, it was decided to collect data from project managers and business analysts from Indian organisations that have experienced ERP implementation process. These are the two positions which play key roles in the ERP implementation process and generally are proficient in both business and technical knowledge. A total of 56 responses were received from contacted organisations.

2.1 Survey Questionnaire

Based on factors identified from a systematic literature review there were fourteen questions (representing 14 success factors listed in Table 5) in the questionnaire. The questions were Likert scale type and were designed to examine the respondents' perception of the importance of different factors (adapted from Arunthari and Hasan 2005; Ehie and Madsen 2005; Nah et al. 2003) that determines successful implementation of ERP in Indian organisations. The respondents were requested to rate each of the factors on a five-point scale: "1 = Neither critical nor important for success"; "2 = important but not critical/necessary for success"; "3 = somewhat critical and important for success"; "4 = critical and important for success"; "5 = extremely critical and important for success". The fourteen success factors included in the questionnaire are listed in Table 5. The first twelve factors are adapted from Nah et al. (2003), Cost/Budget from Ehie and Madsen (2005) and Vendor Selection from Arunthari and Hasan (2005).

3 Findings

3.1 Demography of Profile of Respondents

Considering the responses from an organization type perspective, as shown in Table 1, out of the total 56 responses, 41.1 percent (Count = 23) were locally-owned Indian companies and 58.9 percent (Count = 33) were from multinational companies in India.

Table 1. Organization Types: Locally-owned Indian vs. Multinational Companies

Organization Type	Frequency	Percent
Indian Companies	23	41.1
Multinational Companies	33	58.9
Total	56	100.0

Considering the responses from the perspective of type of position held (by the respondent), as shown in Table 2, the total of 56 responses have been split into almost equal halves with 51.8 percent (Count = 29) coming from project managers and 48.2 percent (Count = 27) coming from business analysts.

Table 2. Respondent Types: Project Managers vs. Business Analysts

Respondent Type	Frequency	Percent
Project Manager	29	51.8
Business Analyst	27	48.2
Total	56	100.0

Consolidating Table 1 and Table 2 gives a cross tabulation of both organization type and respondent type to better understand the break-up of the responses as shown in Table 3. The number of responses from project managers from locally-owned Indian companies and multinational companies are almost equal with 14 and 15 respectively. The number of responses from business analysts in multinational companies is 18, which is twice the number that came from Indian companies (see Table 4).

3.2 Descriptive Statistics: Importance of Examined Factors

Table 4 illustrates the number of responses, the mean score and the standard deviation for each of the identified success factors. It is evident from Table 5 that F2 (Business Plan and Vision), F10 (Project Management) and F12 (Top Management Support) are the three most important success factors as perceived by project managers and business analysts regarding the implementation of ERP systems (see Table 4).

The t – test for equality of means for organization type (see Table 5) indicates that there is no significant difference in the perceptions of the success factors between the two types of companies. Among the 14 success factors, there is not a single factor with s significance value less than or equal to 0.05. This indicates that locally-owned Indian companies are weighing ERP implementation projects in the same lines as multinational companies.

Table 3. Organization Type and Respondent Type: Cross Tabulation

Organization Type		Respondent Type		
		Project Manager	Business Analyst	Total
Locally-owned Indian Companies	Count	14	9	23
	% of Total	25.0%	16.1%	41.1%
Multinational Companies	Count	15	18	33
	% of Total	26.8%	32.1%	58.9%
Total	Count	29	27	56
	% of Total	51.8%	48.2%	100.0%

Table 4. Descriptive Statistics of the 14 Success Factors

Factors		N	Mean	S.D.
Business Plan and Vision	F2	56	4.52	.786
Project Management	F10	56	4.25	.769
Top Management Support	F12	56	4.21	.986
Software Development, Testing and Troubleshooting	F11	56	4.16	.804
Cost / Budget	F13	56	4.09	.959
Vendor Selection	F14	56	4.09	.996
Effective Communication	F6	56	3.98	.842
User Training and Education	F5	56	3.89	.947
Business Process Reengineering	F3	56	3.73	.842
ERP Teamwork and Composition	F7	56	3.66	.815
Appropriate Business and Information Technology (IT) Legacy Systems	F1	56	3.62	.983
Change Management Culture	F4	56	3.54	.972
Project Champion	F9	56	3.48	.972
Monitoring and Evaluation of Performance	F8	56	3.43	.912

Table 5. Group Statistics and t – test for Organization Type and Success Factors

FACTORS	Organization Type	N	Mean	Std. Deviation	t-test for Equality of Means for Organization Type		
					t	df	Sig. (2-tailed)
F1	IC	23	3.57	1.080	-.377	54	.708
	MN	33	3.67	.924			
F2	IC	23	4.70	.559	1.426	54	.160
	MN	33	4.39	.899			
F3	IC	23	3.83	.576	.694	54	.491
	MN	33	3.67	.990			
F4	IC	23	3.61	.988	.466	54	.643
	MN	33	3.48	.972			
F5	IC	23	4.04	.706	.993	54	.325
	MN	33	3.79	1.083			
F6	IC	23	3.96	.767	-.188	54	.851
	MN	33	4.00	.901			
F7	IC	23	3.52	.665	-1.066	54	.291
	MN	33	3.76	.902			
F8	IC	23	3.26	1.054	-1.153	54	.254
	MN	33	3.55	.794			
F9	IC	23	3.39	.783	-.580	54	.564
	MN	33	3.55	1.092			
F10	IC	23	4.48	.593	1.899	54	.063
	MN	33	4.09	.843			
F11	IC	23	4.17	.576	.102	54	.919
	MN	33	4.15	.939			
F12	IC	23	4.43	.788	1.410	54	.164
	MN	33	4.06	1.088			
F13	IC	23	4.09	.733	-.015	54	.988
	MN	33	4.09	1.100			
F14	IC	23	4.35	.832	1.647	54	.105
	MN	33	3.91	1.071			

4 Discussion

Many organizations in developing countries may not be able to invest the initial cost of ERP implementations (Rajapakse and Seddon 2005). Hence cost is a critical success factor which needs to be considered during the start or proposal of ERP projects. In terms of a project, the business case should reflect rigorous cost benefit analysis to clearly illustrate viability of the project and to convince and gain management support. Top management support in terms of resource remittance and making major decisions is very crucial during ERP implementations (Al-Mashari et al. 2001). Considering the low regulation levels and unconventional business processes, it may be a challenge to find an appropriate fit between the business process and the ERP system, hence the business process re-engineering becomes crucial (Rajapakse and Seddon 2005). Training and education is an important factor and it may need extra emphasis in developing countries where ERP knowledge is less for end users (Rajapakse and Seddon 2005). The best human resources when used effectively lead to a successful implementation of ERP projects. Hence the composition and teamwork of an ERP project must be given importance and it is recommended that managers do not compromise on technical expertise when assigned to the project. Vendor selection is another fundamental key to success because a wrong decision in choosing a vendor may lead to aligning issues of the business process and the ERP system (Arunthari and Hasan 2005). "Software development, testing and troubleshooting" and "Monitoring and evaluation of performance" should run parallel as they are closely associated. However, the finding from Table 5 reveals that the level of importance given to software development, testing and troubleshooting is much higher than monitoring and evaluation of performance. The reason may be because India is one of the largest outsourcing hubs for IT development and the importance of software development has become a part of the culture. According to the findings, a business plan and vision are considered the most critical and important ingredients for success (Table 5). This study recommends that managers must make sure that the business plan and vision are transparent to all the members of the team. A successful ERP implementation is possible only if all the contributing members have a common business vision and goal.

5 Conclusions

This study made an initial attempt to understand the adoption of Enterprise Resource Planning Systems in an Indian context. The success factors identified from the literature review were rated on the level of criticality and importance of success by project managers and business analysts from locally-owned Indian companies and multinational companies in India. The findings illustrate that Business Plan and Vision, Project Management, Top Management Support, Software Development, Cost/Budget and Vendor Selection are the factors that play the most important role in ERP implementation. The results also revealed that there was no significant difference in the perception towards the success factors between locally-owned Indian companies and multinational companies. This information may be considered useful when locally-owned Indian companies and firms outside decide to implement ERP systems. However, there existed a significant difference in the level of importance given to two of the fourteen success factors by project managers and business analysts.

References

Al-Mashari, M., Al-Mudimigh, A., Zairi, M.: ERP implementation: An integrative methodology. European Journal of Information Systems 10(4), 216 (2001)

Arunthari, S., Hasan, H.: ERP System Adoption and Vendor Selection by Locally-owned and Multinational Companies in Thailand. In: Proceeding of Pacific Asia Conference on Information Systems (2005), http://www.pacis-net.org/file/2005/241.pdf

Ehie, I.C., Madsen, M.: Identifying critical issues in enterprise resource planning (ERP) implementation. Computers in Industry 56(6), 545–557 (2005)

Nah, F.F.H., Zuckweiler, K.M., Lau, J.L.S.: ERP implementation: Chief Information Officers perceptions of critical success factors. International Journal of Human-Computer Interaction 16(1), 5–22 (2003)

Rajapakse, J., Seddon, P.B.: Why ERP may not be suitable for organizations in developing countries in Asia. In: Proceedings of PACIS, pp. 1382–1388 (2005)

The Adoption of Web 2.0 Platforms

Nikhil Srinivasan and Jan Damsgaard

Department of Information Technology Management, Howeitzvej 60,
Frederiksberg, Copenhagen, DK 2000
Tel.: +45 (21603788), +45 (24794309)
{Ns.caict,Jd.caict}@cbs.dk

Abstract. In this paper we study the adoption of Web 2.0 platforms. Existing theoretical approaches to understand the adoption of IT are critically re-examined for their applicability in the Web 2.0 domain. We find that the two basic assumptions of traditional approaches 1) the unit of analysis is a person and 2) the technology´s primary utility is personal, does not hold for Web 2.0 platforms. Instead, we argue, the appropriate unit of adoption is the social network and the utility stems mainly from collective use.

Keywords: web 2.0, adoption, social network, diffusion.

1 Introdution

Web 2.0 platforms have in very short time integrated into people´s lives both socially and professionally. A Web 2.0 platform is loosely defined as an aggregation of technologies such as blogs, wiki's, mash-ups, social bookmarking sites, and others that are build around social relations that individuals establish or confirms with each other for the purpose of communication, collaboration and coordination of information, knowledge and activities (O'Reilly 2005). A web 2.0 platform is inherently a participative environment where the consumers of information and knowledge are simultaneously the co-creators and consumers of information and knowledge (Parameswaran et al. 2007).

Web 2.0 has attracted the attention of researchers, practitioners and organizations alike. One reason is that the estimated value of a platform, for example Facebook is worth $11.5 Billion according to Bloomberg Business Week (March 3, 2010 edition) and the revenue made on ads is enormous, so the value of predicting and understanding which platform succeeds and why is substantial. However before we are overwhelmed by the success of a few platforms we must remember that most Web 2.0 platforms never gain much attention and become abandoned after the first colonists realize that too few are following to make the platform viable. Most settlers therefore move on leaving behind a "ghost town" platform of forgotten passwords, profiles that are never updated, and connection requests that are never granted.

Academic studies have examined the adoption of specific Web 2.0 technologies (Hester 2008) and employed popular and widely acknowledged models such as Diffusion of Innovation (DOI) (Rogers 1995), Technology Acceptance (TAM) or

M. Nüttgens et al. (Eds.): Governance and Sustainability in IS, IFIP AICT 366, pp. 364–370, 2011.

Unified Theory of Acceptance and Use of Technology (UTAUT) (Davis et al. 1989; Venkatesh et al. 2003) that have proven themselves in the past. However many extend DOI and TAM to cover Web 2.0 platforms without revisiting the basic assumptions of the models and their acclaimed validity domain (Sledgianowski et al. 2009). One profound difference is that Web 2.0 platforms only have value when many are using them, which is not paramount for many previous IT applications that were perfectly useful for an individual alone e.g. word processing. This weighty difference is often neglected. Therefore Web 2.0 represents a paradigm shift in IT and as such traditional models of adoption and diffusion may not readily apply. The central point of departure is thus the following research question.

How to understand the adoption of Web 2.0 platforms?

The remainder of this paper is organized the following way. In the next section we describe Web 2.0 platforms and review the classical diffusion literature and pinpoint some of the limitations of an extension of their validity domain. In the third section we propose the social network lens as a better explanatory vehicle for understanding and predicting the adoption and diffusion of Web 2.0 platforms. Finally we make some conclusions and discuss the potential implications of our work.

2   The Nature of Web 2.0 Platforms

In this section we first summarize and discuss the literature surrounding web 2.0 platforms and we then review the literature in adoption and diffusion literature.

2.1   Web 2.0 Platforms

Web 2.0 platforms refer to technological and social infrastructures that are used to support specific and generalized modes of communication and collaboration between distributed individuals that share a common interest. Web 2.0 platforms are often referred to as social media platforms. Social media have been described as having the unique feature of "active creation of content by their users or members"(Scott et al. 200,O'Reilly 2005) where the creation of content takes place through the building and maintaining of social   relations. Technologies such as wikis, blogs, podcasts, folksonomies, mash-ups, social networks, virtual-worlds and crowd-sourcing are also referred to as web 2.0 technologies (Andriole 2010).

2.2   Revisiting Classical Adoption and Diffusion Theory

The diffusion and adoption of technologies have been examined from two broad perspectives. The first perspective focuses on the personal adoption of a technology. The second perspective focuses on the spread of a technology among a group of people.

The individual adoption of a technology is based on two broad theories from social psychology i.e. the theory of reasoned action (Fishbein et al. 1975) and the theory of planned behavior (Ajzen 1985). The first work by Davis, Bagozzi and others (1989; 1989) was referred to as the technology acceptance model (TAM). TAM has been applied across cultures (Straub et al. 1997), gender (Gefen et al. 1997), extended with social influence (Malhotra et al. 2002), accounted for task-technology fit (Dishaw et al.

1999), and other extensions. A comprehensive review performed by Venkatesh et al. (2003) compared 8 different user acceptance models and synthesized them into a comprehensive model referred to as the Unified Theory of Acceptance and Use of Technology (UTAUT). Since an extensive review of the theory is beyond the scope of the paper please refer to Venkatesh (Venkatesh et al. 2007; Venkatesh et al. 2003) and the special issue of JAIS for a more extensive literature review. Broadly speaking within the individual technology acceptance literature characteristics such as habit, self-efficacy, experience, task relevance, and others are primary and important determinants of behavior regarding individual technology adoption and use (Davis et al. 1989; Venkatesh et al. 2003).

The second perspective on the spread technology exists at a broader level and examines the factors that contribute to and the manner in which technologies diffuse across a population of potential adopters similar to the spread of a virus. Rogers (1995) named adopter categories that characterize the nature of the adopters along a Sigmoid curve of innovation adoption and places them in four categories; innovators, early majority, late majority and laggards. Since the work of Rogers, DOI theory has been extensively applied in IS (Attewell 1991; Moore et al. 1991; Mustonen-Ollila et al. 2003). However despite its extensive application and popularity, DOI has also received some criticism (Lyytinen et al. 2001; Lyytinen et al. 2011) noting that DOI may not be sophisticated enough to address complex IT. DOI theory is especially effective at examining singular, monolithic technologies or well-defined systems with a apparent function such as TV sets or coffee makers (Lyytinen et al. 2001). Such technologies typically rely on economies of scale on the supply side and the use of the system on the demand side is fairly independent of others use of the same technology. For instance, the use of a coffee maker is pretty straight forward and your usage is fairly independent of other individuals' use of coffee makers. Furthermore, mass production on the supply side drives prices down leading to wider diffusion. As such, DOI theory is successful in examining the diffusion of simple technologies as an aggregated phenomenon across a population of would be adopters.

2.3   Revisiting the Assumptions of TAM and DOI

In the TAM and DOI approach to the adoption of innovations and technologies, individual characteristics are the primary determinant of individual adoption and use behavior. In examining the adopter population, individuals are treated as relatively isolated from the group thereby separating them from the social setting in which they are embedded. By treating individuals as independent in their adoption behavior, the TAM and DOI perspectives do not focus on the interplay between users and between user behaviors (Benbasat et al. 2007). Furthermore, TAM and associated theories of adoption do not explain why parts of the population are more likely to adopt the technology or service and the other parts of the population less so despite sharing similar individual characteristics (Lyytinen et al. 2011). While they do a good job of explaining why specific individuals adopt technologies and services, they do a relatively poor job of understanding and explaining why others do not adopt the technology or service despite being similar and belonging to the same pool of potential adopters (Lyytinen et al. 2011).

2.4 Differentiating Web 2.0 Platforms

Web 2.0 platforms as infrastructures bind social networks together through which existing and new social relations are established and maintained. Due to network effects inherent in web 2.0 platforms the social relationships and transactions are not mobile and individuals are relegated to adoption of web 2.0 platform based on similar adoptions by members of his or her social network. Consequently, the adoption of a web 2.0 platform by an individual is subordinated to the adoption of web 2.0 platforms by the social network. The superior predictor of the use of web 2.0 platforms by an individual is consequently the social network that a specific person belongs to and not some personal traits or fit with a specific platform as DOI and TAM models would assume.

Individuals may probe web 2.0 platforms in search of the most appropriate one but the social network can only adopt a single web 2.0 platform due to the network externalities associated with it. We therefore need to shift the unit of analysis from the singular person to the social network. The individual user may prefer a different platform but adoption would lead to online social exclusion and therefore the individual is obliged to adopt the same platform as the social network regardless of personal preferences and past experiences (analogously a goose may prefer to fly a different way but will lose its flock if it does so). Behavior in such platforms is not coordinated but rather based on informal rules and spontaneity that govern interactions and is similar to social norms. Similarly behavior and knowledge in web 2.0 platforms is conditional on the use of the system by others.

3 Insights from Social Network Research

Social network literature highlights the role of friends, family and coworkers in driving the adoption and the diffusion of technologies and services (Siam et al. 2008; Sykes et al. 2009; Vannoy et al. 2010; Vilpponen et al. 2006). Furthermore, it also highlights the manner in which the embeddedness of individuals in networks increases the likeliness of adoption. To do this it relies on characteristics, relationships between individuals, and the structure of the social network that people are embedded in. Individuals replicate their real-world social relationships in web 2.0 platforms (Wellman et al. 1996). However web 2.0 based social networks are often incompatible with each other as they both increase the visibility of social networks and makes the communication boundaries between them transparent.

As we have characterized adoption and diffusion process of social media services as a network phenomenon, we are agnostic about the boundaries of the network. Social networks on web 2.0 platforms are exceptionally large and the ease of forming and maintaining relationships makes a clear demarcation of network boundaries conceptually and practically impossible. As such, in the context of web 2.0 platforms, social media services and social networks, it is important to examine both a specific social network and the global network of social networks. Social networks are important in social media service since they are likely the first and major sources of influence in adoption decisions. Global networks of social networks unlike single social networks focus on all the relationships that might exist between all the social networks in a specific demarcated system that exist on a specific Web 2.0 platform. For instance, a social network around fridge door magnet collectors on Facebook would be a specific social network while the global network would be the all the social networks existing on Facebook and all the relationships between the active social networks. The local configuration of relationships and the social network's adoption of technology represents a "we-intention" (Bagozzi 2007) on part of the social network. The local configuration of relationships can be described in a variety of ways ranging from traditional social network analytic measures to more generalized measures of social structure.

4   Conclusions

In this research-in-progress we examined social networks´ adoption of Web 2.0 platforms. The social network is an emergent entity of many individuals and their relations, yet it cannot be reduced to its constituent parts. Individualistic model that focus on adoption of such services by the individual user are less suitable for such analysis since they ignore the emergent properties of the social network and privilege the "parts" instead of the "whole". A social network perspective drives us to examining groups of related individuals in examining adoption web 2.0 platforms. The social network lens drives us towards examining relations and relational structures that comprise groups and social networks. The primary question that emerges from the use of the network lens is; how do social network characteristics influence adoption of web 2.0 platforms? While previous research may have examined web 2.0 and social media service adoption through the individualistic lens, they have included certain social network components in their analysis. Our question privileges the social network perspective above the individual and consequently the social network characteristics are not merely mediators or moderators but rather the independent determinant in adoption of web 2.0 platforms.

This approach accommodates the puzzling fact that many people adopt several Web 2.0 platforms even though this is both ineffective and troublesome. An apparent anomaly that cannot be explained by the classical diffusion and adoption models but our approach provides a plausible explanation. Namely that the adopting unit for Web 2.0 platforms is the social network and since a person naturally belongs to multiple platforms she will have to adopt several platforms – in principle one for each social network that she feels part of and wishes to contribute to. Consequently a person may very well adopt several Web 2.0 platforms.

References

Adler, P.S., Kwon, S.-W.: Social Capital: Prospects for a New Concept. Academy of Management Review 27(1), 17–40 (2002)

Ajzen, I.: From intentions to actions: A theory of planned behavior. Action-control: From cognition to behavior (11), 39 (1985)

Andersen, P.B., Emmeche, C., Finnemann, N.O.: Downward Causation: Minds, bodies and matter. Aarhus University Press (2000)

Andriole, S.J.: Business Impact of Web 2.0 Technologies. Communications of the ACM 53(12), 67–79 (2010)

Attewell, P.: Technology diffusion and organizational learning: The case of business computing. Organization Science 3(1), 1–19 (1991)

Benbasat, I., Barki, H.: Quo vadis, TAM. Journal of the Association for Information Systems 8(4), 211–218 (2007)

Bovasso, G.: A Network Analysis of Social Contagion Processes in an Organizational Intervention. Human Relations 49(11), 1419 (1996)

Burt, R.S.: The Contingent Value of Social Capital. Administrative Science Quarterly 42(2), 339–365 (1997)

Burt, R.S.: Structural Holes versus Network Closure as Social Capital. In: Lin, N., Cook, K.S., Burt, R.S., Gruyter, A.D. (eds.) Social Capital: Theory and Research, p. 1 (2000)

Buskens, V., Yamaguchi, K.: A New Model for Information Diffusion in Heterogeneous Social Networks. Sociological Methodology (29), 281–325 (1999)

Chi, F., Yang, N.: Twitter Adoption in Congress. Social Science Research Network (2010)

Coleman, J.S.: Social Capital in the Creation of Human Capital. The American Journal of Sociology (94), S95-S120 (1988)

Davis, F.D.: Perceived usefulness, perceived ease of use, and user acceptance of information technology. MIS Quarterly 13(3), 319–340 (1989)

Davis, F.D., Bagozzi, R.P., Warshaw, P.R.: User acceptance of computer technology: A comparison of two theoretical models. Management Science 35(8), 982–1003 (1989)

Dishaw, M.T., Strong, D.M.: Extending the technology acceptance model with task-technology fit constructs. Information & Management 36(1), 9–21 (1999)

Fishbein, M., Ajzen, I.: Belief, attitude, intention, and behavior: An introduction to theory and research. Addison-Wesley, Reading (1975)

Galaskiewicz, J., Burt, R.: Interorganization Contagion in Corporate Philanthropy. Administrative Science Quarterly 36(1) (1991)

Gefen, D., Straub, D.W.: Gender differences in the perception and use of e-mail: An extension to the technology acceptance model. MIS Quarterly 21(4), 389–400 (1997)

Granovetter, M.S.: The Strength of Weak Ties. The American Journal of Sociology 78(6), 1360–1380 (1973)

Hester, A.: Innovating with organizational wikis: factors facilitating adoption and diffusion of an effective collaborative knowledge management system, pp. 161–163. ACM, New York (2008)

Lyytinen, K., Damsgaard, J.: What's wrong with the diffusion of innovation theory? Diffusing Software Products and Process Innovations, 173–190 (2001)

Lyytinen, K., Damsgaard, J.: Inter-organizational information systems adoption - a configuration analysis approach. European Journal of Information Systems 18(1) (2011)

Malhotra, Y., Galletta, D.F.: Extending the technology acceptance model to account for social influence: theoretical bases and empirical validation, p. 14. IEEE, Los Alamitos (2002)

Moore, G.C., Benhasat, I.: Development of an instrument to measure the perceptions of adopting an information technology innovation. Information Systems Research 2(3), 192–221 (1991)

Mustonen-Ollila, E., Lyytinen, K.: Why organizations adopt information system process innovations: a longitudinal study using Diffusion of Innovation theory. Information Systems Journal 13(3), 275–297 (2003)

O'Reilly, T.: What is web 2.0. Design Patterns and Business Models for the Next Generation of Software 30 (2005)

Parameswaran, M., Whinston, A.B.: Research issues in social computing. Journal of the Association for Information Systems 8(6), 336–350 (2007)

Rogers, E.M.: Diffusion of innovations. Free Pr., New York (1995)

Scott, S.V., Orlikowski, W.J.: Getting the truth': exploring the material grounds of institutional dynamics in social media (2009)

Siam, A., Esfahanipour, A.: Effect Of Network Relations On The Adoption Of Electronic Trading Systems. Journal of Management Information Systems 25(1) (2008)

Singh, J.: Collaborative networks as determinants of knowledge diffusion patterns. Management Science 51(5), 756–770 (2005)

Sledgianowski, D., Kulviwat, S.: Using Social Network Sites: The Effects of Playfulness, Critical Mass and Trusti in a Hedonic Context. Journal of Computer Information Systems 49(4), 74–83 (2009)

Straub, D., Keil, M., Brenner, W.: Testing the technology acceptance model across cultures: A three country study. Information & Management 33(1), 1–11 (1997)

Sykes, T.A., Venkatesh, V., Gosain, S.: Model of Acceptance with Peer Support: A Social Network Perspective to Understand Employees' System Use. MIS Quarterly 33(2), 371–393 (2009)

Vannoy, S.A., Palvia, P.: The social influence model of technology adoption. Communications of the ACM 53(6), 149–153 (2010)

Venkatesh, V., Davis, F.D., Morris, M.G.: Dead or alive? The development, trajectory and future of technology adoption research. Journal of the Association for Information Systems 8(4), 267–286 (2007)

Venkatesh, V., Morris, M.G., Davis, G.B., Davis, F.D., DeLone, W.H., McLean, E.R., Jarvis, C.B., MacKenzie, S.B., Podsakoff, P.M., Chin, W.W.: User acceptance of information technology: Toward a unified view. Inform Management 27(3), 425–478 (2003)

Vilpponen, A., Winter, S., Sundqvist, S.: Electronic Word-of-Mouth in Online Environments: Exploring Referral Network Structure and Adoption Behavior. Journal of Interactive Advertising 6(2), 71–86 (2006)

Author Index